D1732050

# AMERICAN INDIAN THOUGHT

# AMERICAN INDIAN THOUGHT

## Philosophical Essays

*Edited by*
Anne Waters

**Blackwell**
Publishing

*dWind*
OX 2006

© 2004 by Blackwell Publishing Ltd
except for editorial material and organization © 2004 by Anne Waters

350 Main Street, Malden, MA 02148-5020, USA
108 Cowley Road, Oxford OX4 1JF, UK
550 Swanston Street, Carlton, Victoria 3053, Australia

First published 2004 by Blackwell Publishing Ltd

*Library of Congress Cataloging-in-Publication Data*

American Indian thought : philosophical essays / edited by Anne Waters.
p. cm.
Includes bibliographical references and index.
ISBN 0-631-22303-7 (alk. paper) — ISBN 0-631-22304-5 (pbk. : alk. paper)
1. Indian philosophy—North America. 2. Indians of North America—Ethnoscience.
3. Indian cosmology—North America. I. Waters, Anne.

E98.P5.A44 2003
191′.089′97—dc21

2003044369

A catalogue record for this title is available from the British Library.

Set in 10.5 on 12.5 pt Bembo
by Kolam Information Services Pvt. Ltd, Pondicherry, India
Printed and bound in the United Kingdom
by TJ International, Padstow, Cornwall

For further information on
Blackwell Publishing, visit our website:
http://www.blackwellpublishing.com

*In the spring of 1992 two American Indian women, one Apache and one Seminole, received the first two PhDs in Philosophy to be granted to American Indians in the United States. We have shared many conversations over the years, and together we have both pushed to make this volume a reality, so that all who follow the path we choose would benefit from our having gone that way. As a Seminole woman, I dedicate this book to my Apache sister, Viola Cordova, and to those who would walk this path of philosophical contemplation with us.*

# CONTENTS

# NOTES ON CONTRIBUTORS

**Annette Arkeketa** (Otoe-Missouria/Muscogee Creek) holds a Master of Arts degree in Interdisciplinary Studies (English/TV/Film/Marketing). In addition to producing public-access TV, she has produced, written, directed, and narrated film and theater, including seven productions of her own plays. Having done over 20 poetry readings, 15 writing workshops, publishing plays in two anthologies, and poetry in 16 anthologies, in 1998 Annette received the Wordcraft for Native Writers and Storytellers Writer of the Year Award for playwriting, for her play *Hokti*. For further details see her web page at <http://www.hanksville.org/storyteller/annette>.
Email: <*arkeketa2001@yahoo.com*>

**Brian Yazzie Burkhart** (Cherokee) is a PhD candidate at Indiana University, Bloomington. He is completing a dissertation entitled "Relational wisdom: American Indian epistemology and philosophy of Science."
Email: <*baburkha@indiana.edu*>

**Gregory Cajete** (Tewa, Santa Clara Pueblo, New Mexico) is currently Director of Native American Studies and Associate Professor in the College of Education, University of New Mexico. His work is primarily in Native American science, art, and multicultural education. His publications include *Look to the Mountain* (Kivaki, 1994), *A People's Ecology* (Clearlight, 1999), *Igniting the Sparkle* (Kivaki, 1999), and *Native Science* (2000).
Email: <*gcajete@unm.edu*>

**V. F. Cordova** (Jicarilla Apache/Hispanic) received her PhD from the University of New Mexico in 1992, and was one of the first American Indians to receive a PhD in Philosophy in the United States. Dr Cordova taught courses in Native American and comparative philosophies at the University of Alaska at Fairbanks, Oregon State University, and Idaho State University. A Rockefeller Foundation Fellow at Lakehead University in Thunder Bay, Ontario, in 1996–97, she helped to found both the first university graduate program in Native American Philosophies, and *Ayaangwaami zin: The International Journal of Indigenous Philosophy*. She was also founding co-editor, and more recently editor, of the *American Philosophical Association Newsletter* on American Indians in Philosophy. Dr Cordova died on November 2, 2002.

**Vine Deloria, Jr.**, is an enrolled member of the Standing Rock Sioux Tribe, Fort Yates, North Dakota. He is a former Executive Director of NCAI, Professor of Political Science, University of Arizona, Professor of History Emeritus, University of Colorado. His publications include *Custer Died for Your Sins*, *God is Red*, *Red Earth, White Lies*, and *Documents of American Indian Diplomacy*.
Email: <vine@spot.colorado.edu>

**John DuFour** (Standing Rock L/Nakota) received his PhD in Philosophy from Yale University. He is a part-time instructor in Philosophy at Albuquerque TVI Community College and at the College of Santa Fe at Albuquerque. His research interests lie in ethics, epistemology, and philosophy of religion.
Email: <jddj@bwn.net>

**Thurman Lee Hester, Jr.**, is a citizen of the Choctaw Nation of Oklahoma. He is Director of American Indian Studies, and Director of the Pan-American Indian Humanities Center at the University of Science and Arts of Oklahoma at Chickasha. Lee is interested in Indian law and policy, and is co-founder of *Ayaangwaamizin: The International Journal of Indigenous Philosophy*.
Email: <fachester1@usao.edu>

**Ted Jojola** is Regents' Professor in the Community and Regional Planning Program, School of Architecture and Planning, University of New Mexico. Formerly, he was Director of Native American Studies at UNM, and is currently pursuing scholarship pertaining to an emerging field in tribal community development, Indigenous Planning. Dr Jojola is an enrolled member of the Pueblo of Isleta, where he currently resides, along with his wife.
Email: <tjojola@unm.edu>

**David Martínez** (Gila River Pima) is currently a Professor of American Indian Studies, American Studies, and Philosophy at the University of Minnesota. Dr Martínez teaches courses in American Indian Philosophies, Esthetics, and Intellectual History. His research is in the areas of American Indian esthetics and religious traditions. He is also the author of *Native American Legends and Lands*, which will be published jointly by Sterling

(New York) and Penn (Israel). Lastly, Dr Martínez is in the process of writing a book titled *Pulling Down the Clouds: The Pima and Papago Philosophies of the Sonora Desert*, which will be published by Rodopi Press as a part of their series "Indigenous Philosophies of the Americas."
Email: <*marti247@umn.edu*>

**Amy Miskowski** graduated from Alma College in 2002, and is currently a graduate student in the philosophy program at Washington University in St. Louis.

**Leslie Nawagesic**, faculty member of the Ayaangwaamizin Academy of Indigenous Learning, Thunder Bay, Ontario, Canada, is an Ojibwa from Gull Bay First Nation on Lake Nipigon, near Armstrong, Ontario. He received his BA and HBA in Political Studies, and his MA in Native and Canadian Philosophy from Lakehead University. He also completed the pre-law programme at the University of Saskatchewan, and developed and taught "Native People and the Law" at Confederation College, drawing on his studies at Saskatchewan and his experience as a Native courtworker. He worked as a Health Research Worker for DILICO Ojibwa Child and Family Services, Thunder Bay, and has served as Assistant Executive Director of the Thunder Bay Indian Friendship Centre. His graduate research in Native philosophy resulted in a phenomenological study of his experience as a young student at St. Joseph's Orphanage, Fort William, Ontario.
Email: <*dwawia@sky.lakeheadu.ca*>

**Thomas M. Norton-Smith**, an enrolled member of the Piqua Sept Shawnee Tribe, Associate Professor of Philosophy at Kent State University, earned his PhD from the University of Illinois at Urbana–Champaign. His professional interests include the philosophy of mathematics and American Indian philosophy. He is also a contributor to the ethical debate on the use of American Indian sports team mascots and nicknames. Dr Norton-Smith serves on the American Philosophical Association's Committee on the Status of American Indians in Philosophy and on the Executive Committee of the American Indian Philosophy Association. His publications include "An arithmetic of action kinds," *Philosophical Studies*, 63 (1991), and "A consideration of the use of Indian sports team mascots," *American Philosophical Association Newsletter of American Indians in Philosophy*, 1 (2001).
Email: <*TNORTON-SMITH@stark.kent.edu*>

**Steve Russell** is an enrolled Cherokee and retired Texas trial court judge. He is currently Associate Professor of Criminal Justice, Indiana University, Bloomington. His current research involves individual rights theory within Indian nations.
Email: <*swrussel@indiana.edu*>

**Maureen E. Smith** is an enrolled member of the Oneida Indians of Wisconsin, and Director of Native American Studies at the University of Maine since 1997. She received her PhD in educational psychology from the University of Maine.
Email: <*maureen.e.smith@umit.maine.edu*>

**Dale Turner** is a Teme-Augama Anishinabae from Bear Island, Ontario. He is also an Assistant Professor of Government and of Native American Studies at Dartmouth College in Hanover, NH.
Email: <Dale.A.Turner@Dartmouth.edu>

**Marilyn Notah Verney**, from Gallup, New Mexico, is a member of the Diné tribe, of the Tah'bah'hee clan, and born for Tai'chee'nee'. She received degrees in philosophy and psychology from the University of El Paso, Texas. An active member of the American Indian Philosophy Association, she is currently a scholar in the Religious Studies Graduate Program at the University of California, Santa Barbara.
Email: <marilyncoun@yahoo.com>

**Anne Waters** (Seminole) is a Research Associate at the State University of New York, Binghamton, and the founder and president of the American Indian Philosophy Association. She is Associate Editor of the Value Inquiry Book Series (VIBS) for Editions Rodopi, and Editor of Value Inquiry Book's Special Series, "Indigenous Philosophies of the Americas." She edits the American Philosophical Association (APA) *Newsletter on American Indian Philosophy* and is chair of the APA Committee on American Indians in Philosophy. Among other publications, she is co-editor of *American Philosophies: An Anthology* (Blackwell, 2001), and co-guest editor of *Hypatia: A Journal of Feminist Philosophy: Indigenist Women of the Americas* (2003)
Email: <BRENDAM234@aol.com>

**Laurie Anne Whitt**, of Choctaw descent, received her PhD in philosophy of science from the University of Western Ontario. Currently an Associate Professor of Philosophy at Michigan Technological University, her research deals primarily with issues that lie at the intersection of Indigenous studies, science studies, and legal studies.
Email: <lawhitt@mtu.edu>

# ACKNOWLEDGMENTS

This volume begins an ongoing process to develop the field of American Indian philosophy. It is a humble gift from many people who worked hard on manuscripts. Most important in the beginning were Milton Chee, John DuFour, and Viola Cordova. John and Milton were present early on when no one else believed in the project. Milton provided the basic categorization that he thought the book ought to have in order to use it at the Dineh College in Tsaile, New Mexico. John nourished our spirits when negotiations began. After Milton, John, Viola, and I reached consensus with our publisher, we knew the project would be done. In five years we worked with three different editors; each wanted the volume to be something different. During this time I talked with Nirit Simon on a regular basis, and it is to Nirit that I give thanks for the continuity of this book. Nirit was there when things seemed to be going too slowly, or when there was a breakdown of communication, always trying to bring forth the positives of the work, and inspiring me to continue.

Ongoing encouragement was gifted to me by Viola Cordova, Laurie Whitt, and Marilyn Notah Verney. I would engage in long conversations with Viola about what should be in the volume, why this paper and not that one, the overall purpose of the book, why it was so important, how it could be used, and why I, and not her, had to do it! Her patience with my ongoing questions guided my understanding, and her queries about the work helped to frame my own ideas. Laurie gave unconditional support through the web as our emails flew back and forth from summer to winter and spring to fall. Her faith in the importance of this project raised my spirits and gave me joy to know she was walking the path with me. Marilyn attended American Philosophical Association (APA) meetings with me, where she inspired authors to finish papers. I am thankful to the APA for providing a forum for us to get professional feedback on some of the papers.

Vine Deloria mentored all authors through his presence at our meetings, and via his responses to my continuous emails. I am indebted to Vine for sharing so much of himself, and guiding us to take on what he perceived to be important issues for philosophy in Indian country. Throughout the five years, I resided in Canada, Albuquerque, California, Texas, and back to Albuquerque, and Vine was a constant email companion, friend, and mentor. Attending (APA) meetings, he let us know that he believed in this work, and in what we were doing to build this field. He advised us to pay close attention to metaphysics and epistemology, in addition to ethical and legal issues. He challenged us to reach beyond where we thought we might go, and to count coup along the way! Ever present, and ever kind, I thank Vine for giving us the joy of having the first essay in this book be his contribution.

In Canada I am grateful to Delores Nawagesic for enabling me to maintain contact with Leslie Nawagesic as he finished his Masters Degree in Native Philosophy. Thanks to Leslie for believing in himself, to Steve Russell for telling me, "You need to get it done," and to David Martínez who believed Native Studies could benefit from interaction with academic philosophers. I am grateful to Amy Miskowski for assisting me with the bibliographies, to Thurman Lee Hester, Annette Arkeketa, Dale Turner, Ted Jojola, Gregory Cajete, Brian Yazzie Burkhart, Thomas M. Norton-Smith, and Maureen E. Smith, who, each in their own way, walked with me, and shared their lives during the making of this project.

Thanks are due to Nancy Tuana, Leonard Harris, and Lucius Outlaw, who inspired philosophers in this volume to maintain our presence at the APA meeting; and to Richard Simone, who wrote an article for *Indian Country Today* about our new organization, the American Indian Philosophy Association, about our new APA Committee on American Indians in Philosophy, and who came to Albuquerque to take a group picture, as well as individual pictures of many of these authors signing their contracts.

For not complaining about my working on this manuscript while unemployed, for tolerating me day to day when food cabinets were bare, for patience with my traveling and accepting teaching positions out of town, I am forever grateful to my extended family, Brenda McDuffie, Lea Shonnel McDuffie, Danesha Angelic McCloud, Michelle, Angela, and Darlyn McDuffie, to P. M. Dubhaigh Ingrassia, Barbara and Margaret Dowling, Coffey, and to all who inspired, and helped keep things going this past five years – Wa Do, O Si Yo.

A.W.

# INTRODUCTION

This is the first book to publish a collection of articles written by American Indians with a PhD in philosophy. When I started this collection there were only four such American Indians. At the publication of this book, there are now eight of us! The American Indian contributors to this volume who do not hold a PhD in philosophy have been carefully chosen based upon their interdisciplinary philosophical contributions to American Indian Studies. This collection is a testament to the ability of American Indians to successfully navigate two very different cultures in our academic careers, to break through academic doors previously unopened to us, and blend our future research with interdisciplinary studies.

The goal of this book is to present a different way of looking at and being in the world. American Indian philosophy is more than critique. As we move through the Reader, we come to understand that American Indian philosophy embodies epistemologies and metaphysics totally different from what has come to be known as "Western" thought, and perfectly commensurable with worlds of science and spirituality. Beginning with Deloria's articulation of a fundamental difference in American Indian and Western philosophical method, this book unfolds the thought of seventeen different American Indian philosophers and returns the reader to epistemic identity in the context of tribal nations culture. These philosophers are all educated, and live in two worlds, the Western and American Indigenous. Our struggles have led to excellence, working in at least two philosophical traditions, always playing one against the other, as a symphony of thought.

Vine Deloria, Jr., one of our most senior and distinguished American Indian academic philosophers, has been an inspiration and mentor for all of us. Because Deloria has been on the frontline, a leader in the work of building the American Indian Movement and the field of American Indian philosophy, it is appropriate that he present the lead essay in this book. As the leader that he is, he escorts us into the intellectual world of American Indians as professional philosophers, both in traditional indigenous, and contemporary academic senses of "philosopher." In "Philosophy and the Tribal Peoples" Deloria refers to philosophy as the capstone discipline of "the Western Academy." About this discipline he wants to know: "How do Indians fit in?"

This profound question is especially appropriate as a guiding tool throughout this book. Some of us philosophers have dedicated our lives to the study of American Indian thought. At the beginning of this volume Deloria turns an hermeneutical twist on us, attracting our attention to reflect back on the context of this work. In doing so, he adeptly captures a question that lies heavy on the hearts of American Indian philosophers: "Will the hegemony of professional philosophy allow assimilation without acculturation?" For if not, it is time to move on; but if so, what is the role of American Indian philosophers in circles of professional philosophy, Native American studies, other disciplines, and Indigenous communities?

Even assuming American Indian scholars can move past bias and institutional handicaps, Deloria wants to know what we can hope to accomplish in our professional fields. He warns us that the liberty from the "giants" to deconstruct unexamined beliefs can only be granted by white men, who carefully guard the definition of objectivity. Any contributions of Indians to philosophy not received favorably, and within the prevailing paradigms, will carry the burden of struggle to trade white male epistemic privilege. But rest assured, we have good traveling companions, for Deloria is in this struggle with us.

Deloria would not count these collected papers as "Indian philosophy" simply because they are written by Indians. An Indian philosophy would not simply interject Indian ideas into Western philosophy, but would interject Western ideas into an Indian philosophy to explain Indian philosophy. An Indian philosopher might critique Kantian ethics, Deloria tells us, in parity of kinship ethics. Such a critique might interject Kantian ethics into a discussion of a kinship ethics framework, in order to juxtapose a different type of moral universe.

Deloria queries whether the discipline of philosophy could keep the equality and respect of two parallel ethical systems, or whether Indian philosophy is too much of a threat to the status quo. He explains a difference in method between Indian philosophy and Western philosophy: "A Western concept wants to subsume the experiences, rough off the edges, and verify the general proposition. An Indian statement wants to be expansive and have applicability to many things which are distinguished by specific details. Both ways of thinking have the capability of devising subsets within their general statements to provide guidance. But Indian statements are not going to be useful to Western thinkers and Western classifications are going to be seen as too crude by Indians." The present volume talks to this schism.

A book of this nature ought to address what we can know about the world, and ourselves as part of that world. There is not yet an American Indian dissertation on epistemology, but perhaps the beginning of such an endeavor appears in Part II of this text, "Epistemology and Knowing," where articles by Brian Yazzie Burkhart,

V. F. Cordova, and John DuFour address the question of what constitutes knowing. Learning about both a Western and an American Indian approach to world descriptions expands our understanding of the diversity of human thought. Indian methods of knowing differ from Western methods. If we are to distinguish a boundary between Indian and Western thought, as Deloria tells us we must, then epistemology, or how we know things, is a good place to carve a difference. And one difference is that reflective memories of our Native elders have stories that explain human reality and confrontations in the world. Brian Yazzie Burkhart, beginning with epistemology, the smallest unit of measurement of what we can know about the world, shows us how both the content and method of an American Indian philosophy embrace a way of seeing and experiencing the broad circles of our everyday lives.

Brian Yazzie Burkhart, in "What Coyote and Thales Can Teach Us," claims that we participate in meaning-making in the world: the world itself, as well as our truth, meaning, and value, arise in our intersecting with the world. Our acts shape meanings, and these meanings create our acts. Burkhart articulates four fundamental principles of Indian knowing: the principle of relatedness; the principle of the limits of questioning, and two principles of action. The first principle, that of relatedness, is about how we, by our actions in the world, relate to all things; hence we must keep everyone (all our relations) in mind when we act. The second principle, of the limits of questioning, reminds us that, for example, if the earth sat on the back of a turtle in the beginning, then "there are turtles all the way down." The third principle is the first principle of action. This has two parts: (1) that we *should* not speak or act regarding some things, and (2) that we *cannot* speak or act regarding some things. The second part of this third principle reminds us of the fourth principle, sometimes referred to as the moral universe principle: what is true is what is right. Hence, Burkhart holds that all investigations are moral investigations in Indian knowing.

The only real philosophical quest, according to Burkhart, is the quest for knowing: "What is the right road for humans to walk?" Western philosophy cannot accept that there are some things that cannot or should not be known because Western philosophy operates by a fundamental belief that more knowledge is better, and all knowledge is of a propositional type. Indian philosophy, on the other hand, entertains a way of knowing by direct access, or awareness of experience, i.e. an integrated "how-to" knowing. The Indian philosopher can accept that the world is "turtles all the way down," i.e. that the foundation does not rest on anything else.

By contrast, the Western philosopher seeks a justification for claims to knowledge whose foundation itself is questioned. The Western philosopher must ask, "If the turtle holds the earth, what holds the turtle?" The Indian philosopher wants to know what the basis of this question is for the Western philosopher.

For Indians, the story conveys knowledge, knowledge does not convey the story, as it does for Western philosophy. In his explanation of the Seneca story of the three sisters (corn, beans, and squash), Burkhart provides us with an example of knowledge about how to live right or well. Moreover, if knowledge is knowing how, then animals and rivers, Burkhart claims, also have this knowledge. He gives us the example of a song: knowing a song does not require the knowing of the notes. (I would add that knowing the notes of a song is also not to know the song.) In the same way that water knows the way around the rock, so also we can know a song. The knowing is in the performance, or ceremony; it is in the living, or life of the ceremony. Indian knowing is not propositional knowledge that can be had about the ceremony.

Western thought holds knowledge to be an end in itself, and mistakes propositional information for knowledge. If propositional information constitutes knowledge, then adding more and more propositional information would amount to making progress toward the attainment of knowledge, or progressively knowing more! Burkhart points to what appears to him to be a fundamental confusion about knowing and collecting information. To know is to synthesize the information in living. Thus, from an Indian perspective, as Deloria has indicated, one must be very old and accumulate much information before wisdom, or the synthesis of that information, occurs.

One of the most astute claims that Burkhart makes, distinguishing an Indian knowing from a Western knowing, is the difference between the Western belief that philosophy and science hold knowledge, and the belief that literature and religion hold human expression. Indian philosophy fuses science and knowing with literature and religion. This dichotomy of Western thought disciplines can be juxtaposed with American Indian philosophy, which is multidisciplinary and multicultural. Our stories, ceremonies, and prayers at once speak and create a moral universe, or practical, lived knowledge. This claim is not to romanticize, but rather to articulate, a theory of knowing through synthetic processes.

Burkhart believes that there is a commonality with Indian thought in Husserl's recognition that all knowledge comes from the lifeworld and must return to it. Yet for Husserl, experiences in a natural attitude (daily concerns) are understood by reflection and description of how we are directed to the world (intentionality). We have the ability to refer to the natural attitude in order to understand the world and our place in it. Yet we can get lost when so engaged, and fall in a well or puddle of water, as Narcissus does while reflecting upon his own beauty.

American Indian philosophy, for Burkhart, would have us retain the natural attitude in all of our affairs. We would not dally in the phenomenological attitude, but maintain connectedness and relations, and find understanding of the world through them, not abstracted from them. Synthesizing all that is removes the possibility of contradictions because anomalies do not exist in an ever-open and ever-changing world. Without contradictions, Indian philosophy cannot be narrowly dogmatic, but embraces all that is. Because of this, Burkhart refers to Indian philosophy as a thinking philosophy. Yet it is not "I think, therefore I am," but rather "We are, therefore I am." An understanding of all that I and others see and experience is accounted for and passed down through generations in the art of story and ceremony.

For an Indian knowing, Burkhart tells us that the data of experience are in the form of We, not I. Hence, I cannot tell you your experiences are not valid. Burkhart claims that in Western philosophy it is possible to say: "My claims count for more than yours because I have them and not you!" But in Indian philosophy this would be like the hand of a body telling the body that the experience of the hand, and not the foot, is valid. Indian philosophy would retain the experience of the whole body, i.e. all of human experience would be synthesized in story. Burkhart reminds us about the ear of corn that Greg Cajete uses to present an understanding of our relations in the world. We are each a kernel, but the aggregate of the kernels is the ear of corn – to think only of each kernel is to take away the whole of the corn and forget how we are related.

Finally, Burkhart reminds us that the desire for an unchanging, eternal life, knowledge, or truth, takes us away into the clouds and, forgetting our feet on the earth, we follow Thales and Coyote into the deep well. American Indian philosophy teaches us that life and knowing are not permanent. Just so, corn remains itself only through change, through growing, living, and transforming itself through dying. Yet corn remains corn. To step out of this circle of life is to forget our relations, what our elders teach us in the stories of our ancestors. For Burkhart, it is to forget who we are.

The second epistemology paper is by V. F. Cordova, "Approaches to Native American Philosophy." Cordova reminds us that ideas are nothing if taken out of context – it is context that allows us to recognize and understand ideas. Meanings exist only in contexts of experience and environment. One of the problems of Western philosophy, for Cordova, is that Descartes removes context. Ethical systems are contextual, and they are tied to a concept of human nature. Cordova tells us that missionaries look to these ethical systems for self-affirmation, not for a ground of communication. In this way Cordova distinguishes theology from philosophy.

Cordova identifies three roadblocks of Western philosophy that prevent humans from seeing a different human worldview. The first roadblock is the search for a common theme, recognized in the type of statement that claims: "Ahh...this idea is just like ours!" The second is the denial of subjective knowing, or a belief that humans are not caught in cultural perspectives, that one's own culture can provide "objectivity." The third is the non-awareness of reification with respect to concepts such as deity, time, change, and motion. Cordova tells us that for Indian philosophy, there is no concept such as the Western reified notion of progress, for example, but rather an understanding that the world always embodies diversity, continuity, difference, and change.

John DuFour writes the third epistemological paper, "Ethics and Understanding." In turning to DuFour's claims, we turn to the question of what it means to be a responsible believer. DuFour holds that belief can be grounded in practice; practices such as the belief in the ritual of sundance expands knowledge. Foreshadowing Gregory Cajete's claims about philosophy of science, DuFour explains that ceremonies themselves become ways of coming to know and understand; for example, cultural practice gives individuals knowledge and understanding of personal identity.

For DuFour ceremonial ways of understanding are meritorious because they promote and ground values and community in a context of morality. To explain how ceremony promotes and grounds values in a moral context, DuFour develops a distinction between content merit and state merit. A belief has content merit (*epistemic* acceptability) if it is reasonable, relevant, or sufficient to a situation at hand. A belief has state merit (*ethical* acceptability) if how one came to the belief is associated with a social practice that embodies ethical concerns (cannot come to belief through prejudice).

DuFour holds that social practices that determine state merit (ethical acceptability, or entitlement to belief) are belief practices. He does not tell us if belief practices also determine social practices, but we may infer that belief practices are social practices "all the way down." Moreover, belief practices serve to meet the human ethical and epistemic needs of beliefs.

This position brings DuFour to a real philosophical concern about the voluntariness of belief formation. He tells us that if "ought implies can," then to say that "you ought to believe" only means you "ought to practice as though you did believe." This ethical mandate appears to be grounded in the influence our beliefs have on our communities, since beliefs are dispositions that emerge into actions that can harmonize or fragment a community. Thus, belief practices may embody a communal moral concern for the care of belief, beliefs are a matter of communal moral concern, and community members are entitled only to beliefs that promote a harmonious community.

DuFour further tells us that the acts of experienced practitioners of the belief practices give rise to normative belief practice. Thus claims to knowledge, or to the need for change, may be ethically objectionable or not admirable. Balanced belief systems would be the product of concern for the appropriate place of belief in a well-lived life. An interesting question arises here: whether the belief practices, as deriving from social practices, carry an epistemic or moral weight apart from their benefit (mandate) to maintain the harmony of a social group. Since DuFour does not explicitly explain how a social practice may be valuable in itself, we may assume that he means social practices to be valued for the benefit of the harmony and balance they bring about as a result of creating belief practices.

Two problems with this analysis can be detected. The first that DuFour alludes to is the non-voluntary nature of the belief practices. The second issues out of the concern for harmony as a bottom-line value in a native community. If a harmonious community is to embody injustice, then an unjust or unreasonable system, so long as it is harmonious, would earn state merit (ethical acceptability, or entitlement status).

DuFour's claims seem to agree with other Native writers in that in an Indian epistemology, there is no knowledge that is an end-in-itself. Greg Cajete, for example, claims that the notion that knowledge exists for its own sake lies outside of a moral framework of Native understanding. DuFour says that the moral framework itself is the context of determining what constitutes morally acceptable beliefs by reference to an appropriately relevant belief practice. Further, because deep knowledge brings with it responsibility in its application and sharing, communal guides are necessary in order to acceptably implement belief practice; when beliefs are properly balanced, they reflect belief practice. Thus the context for implementing a belief practice determines the standard of ethically acceptable beliefs. So, for DuFour, an American Indigenous theory of epistemology would be contextualist, that is, justification for belief is grounded in the context of belief practice, whose aim is harmony of the community.

One problem Western philosophers may have with this essay is that it does not tell us why the ultimate epistemic justification is in the value of communal balance, or harmony. So also, as a contextualist theory of knowledge, without the context there can be no knowledge, or knowing, and hence knowledge exists only when belief practices develop, and are in harmony with communal well-being.

Part III, "Science, Math, Logic," begins with a chapter by Gregory Cajete, "Philosophy of Native Science." Cajete holds that Native science is based upon a perceptual phenomenology; science is supported by lived subjective experience that operates as a basis for objective explanation of the world. Lifeworld experience undergirds cultural mediation and is the foundation of Native science. The human species shares experience and knowledge of nature with all living things. Different experiences are a function of unique biological difference. Cultural concepts of space, time relationship, and linguistic form are "rooted in a precultural biological awareness."

Cajete tells us that Native American philosophy is ecological philosophy because it incorporates information gained from "interaction of body, mind, soul, and spirit with all aspects of nature"; with roots in cosmology, speculative explanations of the universe, its origins, characteristics and essential nature. Metaphysics roots cosmology because the method of research has a cultural orientation of some tradition.

To understand cycles of nature is to recognize interdependencies of all things in nature; it is to have a physical, cognitive, and emotional orientation like a map in the head. We are of nature, having an organic basis of thought, and we interpenetrate nature as we breathe. Native science includes philosophy, art, agriculture, ritual, ceremony, technology, astronomy, farming, plant domestication, plant medicine, hunting, fishing, metallurgy, and geology. Cajete would place philosophy in the context of science.

Cajete contrasts Native science with Western science. Western science views nature as a static collection of objects. Native science views nature as a "dynamic, ever-flowing river of creation, inseparable from our own perceptions, the creative center from which we and everything else have come and to which we always return." Cajete tells us that chaos, for example, from a Native view, "is both movement and evolution, the process through which everything in the universe becomes manifest and then returns. Flux is the evolving universe in self-creation. Everything comes into being from chaos and its "offspring," creativity. These two forces of life, chaos and creativity, guide the universe. If we ask whether these ideas constitute philosophy or poetry, Cajete would likely tell us that they are both, that life is like a poem, the manifestation of the creative spirit of the universe.

For Cajete, a precept of native science is that there are "infinite moments of both chaos and order... Self-organization or 'creativity' out of the field of chaos occurs everywhere in nature." Another principle is the butterfly effect: when a small change in a system has a cumulative influence on the larger system, displaying how everything is related. The moment of perfect balance is inherent in chaos, which enables the butterfly effect to be creative. Thus, "Native science is a reflection of creative participation, a dance with chaos and her child, the creative spirit." This dance is a pathway of perpetually responsive truth, the spirit of the dance of the universe. Cajete's chapter foreshadows Cordova's thoughts about esthetics and creative thought.

Cajete holds that human vision may show the butterfly effect; it may transform an entire community. The concept of the human body that has vision is based on an animate participation with our animate surroundings. Vision is active and impermanent, never caught in a single moment of still perception. The human mind is an active metaphoric mind that describes, imagines, and creates from an animate world. In storytelling we story (engage with) the world, and in Native science we story (engage with) nature. Storying nature requires participation in the oldest mind, the metaphoric mind, in song, dance, ceremony, and technology.

Yet with language can come the chopping up of this animating metaphoric mind. According to Cajete: "In its holistic and natural sense, language is animate and animating, it expresses our living spirit through sounds and the emotion with which we speak. In the Native perspective, language exemplifies our communion with nature."

The metaphoric mind invented the rational mind, Cajete tells us, which invented language, the written word, abstraction, and dispositions to control rather than be of nature. The rational mind invented the anthropocentric philosophy and science that legitimizes the oppression of nature and its elder brother, the metaphoric mind. The metaphoric mind reveals itself through symbols, and kinesthetic sensual abstraction. Stories of Native science come from metaphor and reflect human nature. Native science deals with "systems of relationships and their application to the life of the community." Western science seeks prediction and control, yet Native science, for Cajete, seeks meaning and understanding to find the proper ethical and moral path to follow in order to understand our responsibilities to Nature, which we depend on, and whose energies and animating power are invoked. The symbols of Native science attempt to represent the universe itself. This is consistent with Burkhart's claim that in Native epistemology, what is true is what is right.

"As co-creators with nature, everything we do and experience has importance to the rest of the world. We cannot misexperience anything, we can only misinterpret what we experience . . . what we think and believe, and how we act in the world impacts on literally everything." Thus Native science represents an inclusive and moral universe. To portray how Native science, and its tools, represent an inclusive and moral universe, Cajete explicates 22 concepts and shows how they relate to Native science: causality, instrumentation, observation, experiment, objectivity, unity, models, appropriate technology, spirit, interpretation, explanation, authority, place, initiation, cosmology, representation, humans, ceremony, elders, life energy, dreams and visions, and paths.

In the next chapter, "Indigenous Numerical Thought in Two American Indian Tribes," Thomas M. Norton-Smith examines the concept of mathematical thought. Norton-Smith argues that human beings have innate numerical abilities, and that different environmental and cultural conditions give rise to different developments of mathematical thinking that depend upon the utility function of mathematical thinking, a cultural variable in a community culture (rather than only the biology of cognitive, or linguistic developments).

Norton-Smith holds that it is false to claim that sophisticated "Western" styles of mathematical thinking (isolating and abstracting), are superior to Indigenous styles, which he identifies as inclusive and contextual.

The desire to control the environment as an exercise in economic control is seen by the Western mind as amoral freedom; the desire is merely to utilize the environment as a means toward human ends. This, Norton-Smith claims, is antagonistic to an Indigenous view of a natural and spiritual world of social relations where achieving a balance, or sense of proportion, with *all* living things in the environment, presents a moral path.

The last chapter in this Part, "That Alchemical Bering Strait Theory" by Anne Waters, is about the pedagogy of teaching the logic of critical thinking skills. The chapter portrays how contextual examples are relevant to methods of teaching that empower understanding. Focusing on argument from Vine Deloria, Jr's *Red Earth, White Lies*, Native students inspire one another to learn critical thinking skills, as they discover ways to determine whether Deloria's concerns with the logic of Western thought are shown to be justified. In the context of teaching about a particular critical thinking fallacy, students grasp the application of logical skills in their own meaningful cultural context. The point driven home is that the meaningful and culturally relevant contextual content of examples used to teach critical thinking can excite and inspire Native students to learn. Thus philosophers can reinforce the acquisition of critical thinking skills for Native students by using meaningful, familiar content to reinforce understanding and praxis, for the recognition of cognitively false conclusions. This chapter implies an ethical maxim: using examples only from Western thought to teach critical thinking skills may prejudice students of other traditions in their acquisition of these skills.

Part IV "Metaphysics and Being" begins with a chapter by Ted Jojola, "Notes on Identity, Time, Space, and Place." Jojola invites readers to share the conceptual ways in which the past and present of American Indian culture give a coherence to the future. Again, we see a theme of continuity, this time a continuity of community identity and meaning through time: for American Indians, "awareness of the past contributes to the collective task of structuring their communities" for the future.

American Indians have not participated in the "melting pot," nor have we allowed our culture to be reduced to the profane, claims Jojola. Rather, Federal Indian boarding schools and Presbyterian missions developed and perpetuated a doctrine of divided tribal communities and alliances. This schism was based upon notions that traditionalists held values fundamentally different (conservative) from those of contemporary American Indians who appeared to accept new ways (progressive). The value of novelty (new) ideas, rather than traditional (old) thought, was encouraged by outsiders. This ideology led many American Indians to believe that it was necessary to adopt modernization in order to survive; rejection of traditional tribal values (and in some cases of the wisdom of traditional elders) was part of that process.

Jojola tells us that many Indian communities today remain divided along these historical lines. Decisions about the acquisition and redistribution of wealth (especially since the rise of casinos), affect the development of Native communities. Intertribal, intratribal, and Federal controversies over clan kinship versus birthright community membership criteria, have contributed to the reducing of Indigenous numbers, and the weakening of our communities. Indians have been pitted against Indians as more and more exclusive ways are developed to deny Indian birthrights. Jojola reminds us that although language proficiency and social contexts play important roles in identity development, they cannot measure how individual actions create a coherent sense of identity and community.

Both "identity" and "community" are illusory concepts for Jojola. For example the Western European tradition links geographical areas of land use to segregated areas of social landscapes (residential, commercial, industrial, etc.), to create individual identity constructs based upon a dominant nomenclature of classification. Yet the Indian tradition embraces notions of community as the embodiment of collective values, where individuals are subsumed in these values. These two ways of developing community identity seem to have little in common.

For American Indians, the foundation of values arises from and is invested in land; being born in a landed context creates birthright responsibilities to uphold the collective community agenda of land tenure and retention of that land base. Thus American Indian communities carry an identity of being intimately tied to sustainable territories, where an individual's identity of time, space, and place create a land-based worldview, complete with sustainable values.

This Indigenous worldview of sustainability is radically different from the industrialized and commercialized Western European notion of land as individual property rights, belonging to a religious figure (pope), a political figure (king), or an individual (citizen). When land becomes reified "property" the landowner is emotionally and socially alienated from the land base, and can sell those property rights to another, and move on to occupy (own) some other land base rights (commodity).

Jojola explains how the indigenous Pueblo matrilineal lineage of clanships, and patriarchal male leaders (who are endorsed and overseen in their roles by clan mothers), creates a village, in aggregate. In this village, each clan is identified with a cardinal point (direction from which clan returns to Pueblo), color (clan's outlying territorial domain), and totem (signifying unique human attributes learned from protector animal spirits). As journeys (or separations) are taken by different clans (due to political difficulties of consensus-gathering, or inclinations to explore surrounding territories), the transformation and survival of the community is linked to the returns from these experiential learning journeys. Thus Pueblos collectively embody clanship experiences and adaptations from these comings and goings that always return to the same place of origin, and create a separate and distinctive worldview for each Pueblo.

In these transformative worldview villages, Jojola tells us, "in no instances did their community boundaries overlap. Rather, there was an interstice which, in effect, represented a 'no-man's' territory. In practice, these spaces between boundaries served as public-way corridors for migration. As such, the interstitial spaces figured just as significantly in the worldview of Pueblo relations as did their own communities."

Identity, then, becomes defined by a sense of place. Jojola tells us that multiple voices (disparate interpretations articulated by distinct groups) and symbols (ascribing commonly held ideals represented by the dominant group) create an American Indian community identity. As new projects integrate the past into the present via "voice" and "symbols," identity no longer exists in a space, time, and place continuum.

Jojola tells us that if American Indians do not understand the meaning of our collective actions, we are perceived by outsiders as merely "playing Indian." Thus, the motivation for Indigenous planning and change becomes not merely reinforcing cultural identity, but "to challenge the community into understanding how the past and present serve to give coherence to the future." Again, through history and planning, the continuity of the identity of American Indians, just as the identity and continuity of corn, both changes and remains the same.

Accepting Jojola's challenge to understand how the past and present give coherence to the future, we might conclude that one task of an American Indian or Indigenous philosophy might be to integrate the past with the present, in looking and planning toward future collective action. Accepting this strategy, American Indian philosophy will need to articulate and reflect upon the past and present of American Indian continuity in order to integrate the past with a future.

Continuing with the theme of metaphysics and being, in "Language Matters," Anne Waters shows how nondiscrete nonbinary ontologies of being operate as background framework to some of America's Indigenous languages. This background logic explains why and how gender, for example, can be understood as a non-essentialized concept in some Indigenous languages of the Americas.

According to Waters, discrete binary dualist ontologies informed most of the "Western" European philosophy that migrated to America, and continues to inform Western European thought as it exists in America. This Euro-American metaphysics and ontology of logic, operating as backdrop framework, affected non-Native interpretations of American Indigenous thought for over 500 years. Because America's Indigenous ontologies were nondiscretely nonbinary, Euro-American and European interpretations of Indigenous thought in the Americas obstructed communication systems; this closed off the sharing of Indigenous ideas and vision. The inability of Euro-American scholarship to recognize and/or comprehend this different Indigenous ontology worked together with other factors to foster colonial efforts that erased many Indigenous ideas, people, and cultures. Prior to colonization, Indigenous cultures shared complementary nondiscrete nonbinary ontologies from Canada to South America. With colonization came clashing ontologies fostering a lack of communication.

Waters claims that understanding specific gender and ethnic concepts, for example, from an American Indigenous philosophical perspective (Indigicentric) requires comprehending the conceptual logic of a nondiscrete, nonbinary, dualist ontology (that stands as ontological backdrop) for these concepts. Waters uses linguistic examples from different tribes to bring home the point.

Embracing the world from this logical system means living a deep ontological alterity, or different reality, from the Western European ontology of discretely bounded entities. The standpoint of this alterity requires a different politics: inclusivity celebrated in the meaning of "all my relations."

The Indigenous understanding that all things interpenetrate and are relationally interdependent embraces a manifold of complexity, resembling a world of multifariously associated connections and intimate fusions. Such a nondiscretely aggregate ontology ought not to be expected to easily give way to a metaphysics of a sharply defined discretely organized binary ontology. From an Indigenous ontology, some multigendered identities may be more kaleidoscopic and protean concepts than Euro-American culture has yet to imagine.

The last chapter in this section of the Reader is by Maureen E. Smith "Crippling the Spirit, Wounding the Soul: Native American Spiritual and Religious Suppression." Smith argues that the "intolerance of the newcomers to Turtle Island has proven devastating to those who were here." Smith holds that intolerance was veiled as moral superiority. To provide evidence for her claim, she develops an overview of the traditional spiritual foundations of many American Indians prior to European contact, contrasts these with European beliefs and views, and shows how European history affected perceptions of American Indians and Native religion. Smith discusses acts, laws, policies, and practices that forbid the expression of traditional Native American religion.

Smith brings to our attention some basic spiritual foundations of American Indian spirituality that acknowledge community and individual diversity. These foundations include: a recognition of nongendered being (energy, or force) which has no name; an understanding that all of creation is alive and bound in sacred relationships necessitating sacred responsibility; recognizing that cosmologies were founded on land, water, sky, and all of creation; knowing how geography bound sacred spots to spiritual practice; remembering origin stories that depict how people arrived in their place, being put there by the creator spirit to live and stay there; and having religion practiced by sacred ceremony, prayer, song, drama, and dance, passed via oral tradition and storytelling, to future generations; and appreciating that human humor was often an integral part of sacred ceremonies. The clowns (coyote, trickster, etc.) "reminded people not to take themselves too seriously and to keep themselves in balance."

Smith carries us through a discussion of Native language meanings, including the absence of discrete concepts such as "good," "bad," "right," and "wrong." All of life was woven together in pre-Columbian thought, so that people lived an integrated philosophy of life in the world, rather than a claimed tenet of belief about the world. The traditional language has potency, and hence power, and all art and craft are alive, and hence sacred. All things, being animate and interconnected, are always in the process of becoming with infinite potential. Humans can direct some processes of becoming, and use dreams and visions to translate the potential into the actual. Issues of space and time were cyclical and reciprocal, connecting living individuals with future generations and ancestors. To be ill was to be out of balance in the mind, body, and/or spirit, in violation of the sacred with the natural environment. Smith tells us that in the context of such a philosophical understanding, each individual is responsible for maintaining body, mind, and spirit in harmony with the environment.

Smith shows how aspects of traditional Native religion were maintained while at the same time some Native groups adopted Christian practices. She defends the position that undergirding the Christian practice were Native values and ways of being with all our relations. She gives examples of the peace message of the Ghost Dance at Wounded Knee (1890), and the Native American Church peyote ceremonies (1918).

While discussing the US acts, policies, laws, and prohibitions limiting Native religious practice, Smith discusses the ethnocentrism of concepts such as "heathen," "lack of progress," "assimilation," "barbaric," "primitive," "good Christian whites," "civilization," "education," "boarding schools," "required instruction in Christian values," "punishment," "speaking of tribal languages," "Indian behavior," "English names," "hair-cutting," "torture," and "beatings." Smith informs us that between religious teachings and the Native language there is a critical link that transcends translation. We can only assume she means that not only are there concepts in Native languages that do not easily or adequately translate into the English language, but that worldview and religious ways of being are embedded in languages. Without the framework for a worldview, however, mere cognitive translation fails to capture the connotative and contextual meanings of words in the language.

Smith shows the interlacing of politics and religion: the raiding of burial sites by soldiers for skulls on the orders of the US Surgeon General in 1868 meant the decapitation of our deceased; the forbidding of the Sun Dance (1883), the Potlatch (1884), and in 1921 of prolonged celebration by Indians, sacrificial destruction of clothing and useful articles, immoral sexual relations, and use of drugs and self-torture by the Bureau of Indian Affairs (acting against traditional sovereign rights). In 1923 there was a government prohibition of any giveaways and, for those under 50 years of age, of participation in any traditional ceremony.

With the forced US citizenship granted to Indians in 1924, Smith informs us, Native American religious protection might have been granted under the First Amendment to the US Constitution. But this was not the case. And although the Wheeler–Howard Act of 1934 seemed to promise religious freedom, government policies toward Indians created assimilation (with acculturation), resulting in termination of tribal status, relocation into cities, and further eroding of Native American religious rights.

Noting that although the American Indian Movement created public awareness of Indian issues by overt action in the 1960s, Smith reminds us that the 1954 ruling against the use of peyote was upheld in 1970 by the Controlled Substance Act. Nor did the 1968 Indian Civil Rights Act, the 1976 Bald Eagle Protection Act, policies regarding use of sacred sites, and the 1978 American Indian Freedom of Religion Act provide any protection for Native Americans to practice our Native religions.

Smith concludes that "there is no freedom of religious practice for Native people in the United States." She considers whether any court cases have provided the promised religious freedoms for Native Americans, and concludes that no results were obtained, until the 1989 National Museum of the American Indian Act was passed, requiring an inventory and return of all Native objects to their rightful owners, the tribes (followed by the Native American Graves Protection and Repatriation Act). Finally, the American Indian Religious Freedom Act Amendments of 1994 provided for the traditional use of peyote for religious and other purposes. No sweeping legislation, however, Smith notes, is present yet to protect the diversity of American Indian religious practices. Smith maintains that although today there is a resurgence of American Indian religious practices, as Indians reclaim the spiritual and religious legacies of our ancestors, without more sweeping legislation or court protections, our current optimism remains only as a hope, and not a legal right.

In conclusion, regarding cultural appropriation that reinforces cultural suppression, Smith raises the question whether New Agers will ever respectfully acknowledge they have "no inherent right" to practice Native American religions unless Native people allow that.

Part V, "Phenomenology and Ontology," opens with Marilyn Notah Verney's "On Authenticity." Notah Verney tells us that because she was raised by her grandparents on the Diné (Navajo) reservation in Arizona, she has no problem knowing what American Indian philosophy is; yet answers for her to the questions "How can outsiders study American Indian philosophy?" and "How and what can American Indian philosophy contribute to traditional academic philosophy?" are much more difficult. Her own contribution is to tell her listeners about the difference between academic and Native philosophy.

Academic (Euro-American) philosophy, Notah Verney tells us, engages philosophy with questions, and analyzes by taking apart what is, so that ideas lose their relation with all surrounding things. Native philosophers, however, engage in philosophical thinking by talking, and engage philosophy by making connections between all things, giving everything meaning, and approaching the world in a holistic manner.

As an example of this difference of approach, Notah Verney analyzes how Euro-Americans view land as parcels of commodity for financial gain, rather than as something sacred and holy. An Indigenous understanding of land is about a relationship with the land. She tells us that if her reader can understand Native America's spiritual relationship with the land and our connections within the universe (a metaphysics that all things share life, and an ontology of equality in relation), then it may be easier to understand our Indigenous people, our culture, and our traditional beliefs. She shares with us the Diné (Navajo) story of the creation of her people, and in so doing tells us how she understands American Indian and "Western" philosophy to differ.

Notah Verney shares with us how parts of the work of Heidegger, although he is a European philosopher, articulate and clarify how she views herself in relation to others. She claims that American Indian people have unconsciously drifted from our own way of being when we regard our own being to not include others. To succumb to this way of being in the world is to give way to a dominant colonial hegemonic ontology. Embracing authentic being, for American Indians, means to embrace all our relations, and to recognize the balance of interdependency and interpenetration of our life and being in the world, with all living things.

Native people have a responsibility to share and teach our philosophy, especially with those who feel themselves to have other than dominant ideologies, and also with our own people who have strayed from the good red road. American Indians have much to contribute to academic philosophy, and according to Notah Verney it is best taught orally, to be kept alive. Remaining true to an Indigicentric perspective means that American Indian philosophy can only be kept alive by oral methods; yet through these methods we can help make connections with traditional academic philosophy and philosophers.

In "Phenomenology of a Mugwump Type of Life in an Autobiographical Snippet," by Leslie Nawagesic, we are presented with a phenomenological account of coming to know Indian identity by recognizing our difference from the dominant culture. Mixing metaphors for race, ethnic, and class difference, Nawagesic tells us about his first self-awareness, or reflection upon being, safely wrapped in a *tikanagan* (cradleboard) in Northern Ontario. He then shares what it felt like being gawked at by sneering passers-by while packed like human cargo in the back of a truck, the sadness and despair of discovering tuberculosis and having to leave his family and stay in a sanitorium, visiting home with his family in Gull Bay, and then the anguish and humiliation of abuse while attending a Catholic boarding school for Aboriginal children.

Taking us with him through each of these life passages, Nawagesic employs traditional descriptive narrative when he articulates, with detail, his memory of the landscape and environment, including what he names "sanitorium scenery." Ever observant, he recounts eyes-open experiences that forewarn, and are premonitions of his future. He shares a personal, revealing story of deep, sharp, clear, and acute injury: "I immediately experienced a tremendous amount of pain all over my body with the slightest of movement, including each time I inhaled . . . the bullet went through the door leading to the porch and came to rest in my left groin area." From this moment on, along with Nawagesic, we understand the feeling of inability to blame the universe for particular personal harms, and at the same time feel the despair of not being able to contol the events of his life.

Whether reciting how numbers were assigned on children's pajamas, towels, and other items, in reverse order of their ages, or conveying the huge, dark, yet always homelike and receptive shape of Mountain McKay, Nawagesic closely inspects the environment as presented to him, and shares his current experiencing of poignant memory. The human spirit of resolving and embracing contradictions of both the beauty and horror of life comes through Nawagesic's phenomenological narration. The psychology of human struggle and acceptance of the inevitable permeates this chapter, portraying the stamina and will of the human spirit.

Nawagesic struggles with his human nature, not to be overwhelmed and overcome by the unnecessary harm he views in the vista of his landscape. He portrays an inner strength and skeptical mind, a spirit struggling to understand and survive in his Indigenous environment of colonial North America. From his perspective, the environment is seemingly indifferent to the harms inflicted by human people. Nawagesic's existential analysis springs from his lived cognitive dissonance amidst the cultural confusions caused by walking two paths at once. These paths are laid out by two very different cultures, an American Indigenous land sustainability culture, and the European colonial industrialist and property-centered culture.

In "Ontology of Identity and Interstitial Being," Anne Waters argues that being American Indian means not fitting a definition or idea about Indianness, but experiencing meaning in the world from a particular type of consciousness, a consciousness with a creative cognitive dissonance that arises from social positionality. For Waters, a unity of identity arises from relaxed interstitial weavings of multiple meanings, that come to be in what she refers to as a landscape of uncertainty.

This chapter shows how a worldview creates and is created from constant and continual change, or animation of being in the world, through shifts of voice, identity, hearing, vision, speech, organizational frameworks, and epistemological knowing. Living through events in the world historical, personal and political horizon gives rise to generational identities and collective responsibilities that assist in particular projects in the world to create balance and harmony in the environment among all living things.

In such a worldview, the individual is both the creative entertaining poet, and the destroyer of hegemonic relations in the world. In this role humans appear at once to be pulling together interstitial converging spaces of cognitive dissonance to arrive at a calmness with clarity of vision.

Part VI, "Ethics and Respect," begins with V. F. Cordova's "Ethics: The We and the I." Here Cordova argues: "In the West, codes of conduct are based on the concept of the individual as the 'bargaining unit.'" Yet she claims: "a code of conduct...can be based on the description of the human being as a social being...within the confines of the 'We.'" What is assumed about human nature grounds whether a community understands proper human behavior to rest upon individual or group action.

Cordova explains how human nature in I-principle societies is about individuals at war, always in conflict with outsiders of the immediate bargaining unit. Yet human nature in We-principle societies is understood to be essentially social, and inter-community cooperative. In We-principle societies, the other is seen as interdependent with the self, or rather, without the group there is no self. In We-cultures, ethical codes are internalized as proper social behavior. In I-cultures of autonomous individuals, ethical codes lie outside a person, externalized in codified rules or laws that require interpretation. In reading this chapter, it may be worth thinking about the cognitive dissonance of Nawagesic in the context of Cordova's analysis of assumptions about human nature.

Cordova discovers similarities between Aristotelian Greek ethics and American Indian ethics: in both cases it is accepted that humans are social beings, and humans wish to remain within a social group, and thus act not simply from habituation, or exercise of autonomous free will. For human beings enculturated to "We", or social group, ethics, group disapproval creates great mental anguish and grief. Nawagesic's cognitive dissonance, for example, creates anguish and grief, for he cannot fully be in either world, but is always a part of both worlds. The traditional Indigenous unity of the group, learned early in life from the *tikanagan*, is torn away by the takings of the industrial colonial culture. This feeling of belonging seems to be ontologically amiss in Nawagesic's life, as he is continually separating from his family due to illness, schooling, etc.

Cordova holds that when an I-culture person adheres to or fails to adhere to an external code of behavior, if the consequences of the behavior make no difference, then it doesn't matter whether the person's behavior adheres or not to external law. This way of being is antithetical to an understanding of ethical norms that arise from communicative understanding and common goals and values among group members.

Cordova tells us that Native Americans (unlike the Greeks) add to "the 'We' definition of human beings the idea of equality" that extends to all forms of life. Because a Native understanding of life extends to all that is, the entire universe participates in the life process. Hence a Native American philosophy recognizes equal respect for all living things as interdependently being both parent and child of the Earth and Universe. Being a part of all things, everything is as one process. Thus, argues Cordova, a Native view embraces equal difference, whereas the "Western" European view embraces hierarchical otherness. Cordova asserts a difference between teaching Native American concepts of autonomy, responsibility, and self-sufficiency, and teaching shame and guilt. Offering examples from her own life, she shows us rather than tells us the meaning of these ethical concepts.

As example, Cordova tells us that environmental ethics in the West is about respecting the rights of trees, animals, etc.: "It is not ever about a concern that the cheap cup of coffee is purchased with the misery of a coffee plantation worker." She also tells us, almost in unison with Greg Cajete's butterfly principle, "the pebble" like an action of an individual, "creates far-reaching ripples throughout the entire pond." The recognition of the We factor, how we are in relationship with all living things in the universe, is an essential aspect of Native being and ethics. Self-interest, Cordova might say, can only benefit Indians if the interest is consonant with community interest. Concluding, she tells us, "the We and the I produce different lifestyles, different ethical systems, different worlds."

Thurman Lee Hester, Jr., in this text, presents two chapters that, taken together, articulate an American Indian ethics of esthetics, "Choctaw Conceptions of the Excellence of the Self, with Implications for Education," and an American Indian esthetics of ethics, "On Philosophical Discourse: Some Intercultural Musings."

In "Choctaw Conceptions . . ." Hester first tells us that although he is a citizen of the Choctaw Nation, he can speak only for himself. Hester claims that Choctaw excellence is what Choctaws do, because from a Choctaw perspective "what you do defines what you think is excellent." One of the elements of Choctaw excellence is sensitivity to context. To be concerned with and aware of context confers value on context. For example, to value historical context is to value context of traditions and lives of elders.

In the context of talking about excellence (the context for ethics) Hester tells us what Choctaws do by carefully sliding from the Euro-American method of doing philosophy to a Choctaw way, which is to convey information through a story. He tells us a story about language: only a non-Choctaw would ask the English question (in Choctaw), "Do you speak Choctaw?" because for a Choctaw speaker, it would be enough to say "Speak," since if you didn't know Choctaw you wouldn't know the word and if you did know it, you would understand the meaning is a question, and you would reply. This story is also intended to show that Choctaws place great value on efficiency.

Hester tell us another linguistic story to show us that Choctaws hardly ever engage in correction. To do so would show disrespect by assuming one person acts correctly and the other does not, and would set up a situation of superior and inferior.

The subtle humor Hester shares in telling us his real-life stories portrays the importance of paying attention to context, both in respecting a stone by taking the time to examine its qualities before placing it back, and by giving it the respect of interacting with it rather than trying to place force upon it. While learning how to shift gears in a truck, Hester provides an example of the importance of context in learning. If you have ever tried to help someone remember the context of the gearbox when teaching a person how to drive (that it really does all synchronize together if not forced), you will certainly understand the lesson Hester presents about context in the story about his father teaching him how to drive.

The last chapter in this Part is by Laurie Anne Whitt, "Biocolonialism and the Commodification of Knowledge." Whitt points out that Indigenous knowledge and knowledge systems were initially deprived of cognitive standing by colonial agents. However, the more recent problem facing Indigenous peoples is that "the commodification of Indigenous spiritual knowledge has become the speciality of the New Age industry, the commodification of traditional medicinal knowledge has become the speciality of the pharmaceutical industry, and the commodification of plant genetic resources and Indigenous agricultural knowledge has become the speciality of the commercial seed industry." Thus traditional knowledge that had been collectively known for generations is now being privatized and commodified at an accelerating rate.

Whitt cautions that the current relations of power between dominant Western and subordinated Indigenous cultures will be reinforced and strengthened by the Human Genome Diversity Project, as interest groups align with the dominant agents' actions. Yet traditional practices of Indigenous healing, hunting, and crop cultivation are given to a community as gifts from nature. As such, they require the practice of a gift relationship or reciprocal exchange, binding the human to the nonhuman world. These gifts from the nonhuman world need to be respectfully admired, and respect for nature must be maintained as part of the contextual requirements of working with Indigenous knowledge.

Legally transforming community information into the private intellectual property of private corporations, universities, and individuals, as commodities for sale in the genetic marketplace, shows us how questions of knowledge cannot be divorced from questions of power. This includes the power of logical debates in divergent political construals of knowledge. Whitt is troubled that the patenting of genetic information, as is being done in the Human Genome Diversity Project, means the patenting of life-forms. Rather than collecting and storing Indigenous ancestors in museums and scientific institutions, she tells us, the very basis of our life-forms themselves are now being collected. This creates a loss of power among Indigenous peoples and, as a corollary, accountability by dominant players for responsibility in accepting these gifts. It creates an obligation to allow Indigenous peoples to determine how this gathered information is to be used. The obligation to protect and not misuse the information is an obligation to act with respect for the natural world and for future generations. This requires receptivity, reciprocity, and responsibility to be enacted in the protection of Indigenous gifts. Moreover, traditionally these gifts of information remain, in an Indigenous context, with the givers, and inalienable.

Whitt informs us that the appropriate response from those interested in preserving genetic diversity has already been formulated by Indigenous critics of the Human Diversity project: an investigation into the cause of Indigenous peoples' endangerment, and that the use of any money arising from the commodification of Indigenous information ought to be part of the principle of reciprocity applied, and gifted in return to Indigenous peoples. These efforts may preclude their endangerment, and would hopefully lower the social, political, and economic imbalances between the dominant and subordinated cultures of the world. As Whitt tells us: "It is, after all, the givers of gifts who must determine when, to whom, and how the gifts are to be given."

Part VII, "Social and Political Philosophy," opens with an analysis of law by Steve Russell, in "The Jurisprudence of Colonialism." Russell claims that "jurisprudence is a fertile field for American Indian philosophy because our status as objects of legal discourse makes the inquiry urgent." Russell points out that Indians study for utilitarian ends a law that has failed to protect our property, our culture, and our lives. He finds it unsurprising that American Indians have generally not supported assimilation. Russell reminds us that it is fitting we do this because, quoting the words of Dann May from Lee Hester's later chapter (22) in this book, it is "the difference between orthodoxy on the European side and orthopraxy on the American Indian side."

Russell argues that a legal externalist approach to law, with its skepticism of established power relations, is the only rational position with respect to the law for American Indian legal scholars. He holds that because federal Indian law presents normative confusion, the logical chaos of it can be overwhelming to Indian legal scholars of any tradition. Only the postmodern fascination with text, he claims, suits the legal experience of American Indians "as objects." For Russell, much of federal Indian law is orthopraxy frustrated by incommensurability. The hermeneutic turn in law founded on incommensurability, leaves Indian scholars, according to Russell, more impressed than not with Michel Foucault's view of truth.

This radical position in relation to federal Indian law is being taken by a Texas state justice, who carefully walks readers through Chief Justice John Marshall's Cherokee trilogy, a set of opinions which fashioned a jurisprudence essentially based on the doctrine of "Christian discovery" although stated in terms of European superiority. Russell explicates how Marshall's sleight of hand results in "the Trail Where We Cried," the forced military removals where thousands died and which broke generational connections with our elders, where we experienced uncompensated appropriation of our collective and individual property, and a devastated economy for Indian nations.

All students, Russell claims, Indian and non-Indian, ought to be familiar with an historical reflection upon the method and meaning of the law, as that body of law that sanctioned manifest destiny and perpetuated (stimulated) the myth of "the vanishing Indian." Russell wants to know what kind of legal system "presides over the conversion of natural abundance into wealth for the colonists and dependence for the natives . . . while using the tiny portions of land left in native hands for disposal of toxic wastes."

Using the methods of postmodernism to expose the philosophical fraud of the legal system is a way to deconstruct that system. But the postmodern claim that concepts such as truth and right are no more than power relationships will not be enough for American Indians, who will require a narrative that our resistance to assimilation will not be futile because, as Russell reminds us, "we will *not* be assimilated."

Dale Turner, in "Oral Traditions and the Politics of (Mis)Recognition" argues that Indigenous peoples have answers to "Western"-framed philosophical questions such as "What is the Truth?" and "What is the nature of reality?" Unique ways of understanding the world are embedded within oral traditions, claims Turner, and because of the

Indigenous–Colonial relationship, these ways of understanding are subsumed within the political practices of the dominant colonial culture. Practices such as the discourse of rights, property, nationalism, and political sovereignty of Indians, however, "can only be recognized and affirmed from within the legal and political practices of the dominant culture." Hence, Indian scholars need to take up two tasks: "to explain to the dominant culture why our ways of understanding the world ought to remain in our communities, and to assert and protect the sovereignty – nationhood – of our communities." Turner, following Deloria, calls American Indian intellectuals who are engaged in this task "word warriors."

Turner claims that "the normative concepts that drive these [political] discourses have evolved with little or no influence from American Indian intellectuals." Asymmetry characterized the Indian challenge to justify and/or explain legitimacy to sovereignty, according to Turner. In the explanation is a telling of who we are and how we came to be here by reciting oral history. Legal argument, however, does not embrace the methods of oral argument as legitimate argument in courts of law. Turner discusses an example of one court decision, however, claiming that Aboriginal title (not ownership) may be justified by oral tradition, and that a dialogical approach to resolution of land claims might be preferable to a litigation approach. He concludes that this approach to law created juridical space that accepts oral tradition as a legitimate source of evidence (knowledge).

Aside from advocating the necessary role of word warriors in contemporary Indigenous culture, Turner contributes to the dialogue of Aboriginal rights a good explanation of what the concept of "homeland" means for Indigenous people. "The notion of a 'homeland' is not simply lands, but everything around one's world: land, air, water, stars, people, animals, and especially the spirit world." "Homeland," in essence, creates worldview and vision.

In "Repatriation, Religious Freedom, Equal Protection, and Institutional Racism" we see Annette Arkeketa embracing the role of word warrior for our people. Arkeketa argues that the American Indian Religious Freedom Act (AIRFA) and the Native American Graves Protection and Repatriation Act (NAGPRA) work together to repair the harm of centuries of racist practices exhibited by unethical and immoral federal policies of grave-looting. She notes that people of color, women, and non-property holders in the USA required the use of special Amendments to the US Constitution in order to demand protection of our freedoms. In this article Arkeketa is concerned with First Amendment religious rights.

Whether looting of corn (sacred food), funerary items (sacred artifacts), or our remains (sacred bones), these acts by Europeans were encouraged by government policy, first in Europe, and subsequently in the USA. Arkeketa traces this history in the context of colonial empire-building that justifies extermination policies toward Indigenous people. The Indian Removal Act was not only a way to gain easier access to colonize and people our Indigenous lands, but also operated to assist in the deconstruction of religious and sacred practices and ontology, destroying the very culture of Indigenous occupants of the land. In consonance with the words of Maureen E. Smith, Arkeketa holds that these genocidal policies of the American government forced religious practice underground, a situation that continues today.

From the US Surgeon General in 1867 enacting public policy to gather Indigenous crania, to accumulation of our remains in museums (most notably the Smithsonian), the US government by 1995 had accumulated as many as 2.5 million Indigenous dead, whereas the total Indigenous population was only 2 million in 1990. Arkeketa rightfully claims that these human rights abuses against our people and culture constitute crimes against humanity. She takes us through examples of asymmetrical treatment when the US Army uses a double standard for treating Euro-American and Indigenous remains. Today this market remains lively in auction houses and flea markets, and the bounties of plundered gravesites, Arkeketa holds, are obvious in museum displays.

Arkeketa also explains why the disciplines of anthropology and archeology are against bills to protect Indian remains, citing their work as advancing the progress of scientific data. Arkeketa counters, claiming that the collection of such data has been of little scientific value, and has spurred the policy of continuing genocide of American Indians by the US government.

Citing Vine Deloria, Arkeketa tell us that "the scientific community has never provided Indians with literature showing how experimentation with Indian remains is necessary, proper, or beneficial." She claims that recently, since some Native Americans have become anthropologists and archeologists, we have been able through the repatriation movement, to create our own gatekeepers and have our remains returned for reburial. Finally, Arkeketa tells us that "the journey for Indigenous people to reclaim our ancestors is also a reclamation of our constitutional rights." Yet it is far more, for in our reclaiming, our ancestors show us powerful spiritual resources in our land, and in reclaiming these resources, we are "watching out for the well-being of their children," thus leading the struggle for all of humanity to protect human rights for all people by respecting the return of our ancestors "back to the earth, where we belong."

Part VIII, "Esthetics," opens with V. F. Cordova, an artist, talking about "Ethics: From an Artist's Point of View." Cordova argues that the principles of esthetics and ethics are balance and harmony. The background from which an artist takes on an arist's identity is embedded in a metaphysics that defines the world. Artists who seek to disrupt the world see an inherent chaos in the universe, and force it on the viewer. This is the "Western" artist! The "artist as scientist," Cordova tells us, holds a metaphysics suggesting "chaos is temporary; order is dominant." The role of the artist is to help viewers understand chaos as well as order by showing an underlying stability in chaos, a stability of balance, not stillness.

The responsibility of the Native American artist, as co-creator in the universe, is as scientist and healer, representing "a point of stability that endures all change, absorbs and transforms all chaos." The Native artist is a product of a group that produces and nurtures human beings. Through a process of watching and experimenting, Cordova tells us, the Native American artist comes to be *as* artist not by learning technique, but by learning a way of being in the world. If to become a person in American Indian communities is to learn the consequences of one's acts, then to become an artist in a Native American community is to develop a way of being that can know the consequences of one's own acts; developed in such a way as to have community members recognize this development and apply the label of art to the individual's accomplishments. With this communal recognition comes a responsibility to the community which accepts the individual as artist. The Native being is, as artist, the butterfly whose every action can set off a series of events having consequences. The artist is aware of this ripple effect caused by the stone thrown into the pond. This awareness, Cordova argues, is a responsibility for adding to the world a new thing, a thing that will have consequences.

Cordova tells us that the Navajo Night Chant both reminds us that the world is a place of beauty, and that we are to add to that beauty. This dual reminder, Cordova says, is about there being no distinction between esthetics and ethics. "The universe is a good thing – the goodness is inherent in the fact that the moving, living universe operates on the principles of balance and harmony." As part of the universe humans must hold to these ways of understanding our place in the world, and the human role of maintaining world balance. "The principle of the artist is reponsibility," as co-creator, healer, and scientist in the community.

In "Along the Horizon a World Appears: George Morrison and the Pursuit of an American Indian Esthetic" David Martínez presents some answers to the question why (the horizon of) Lake Superior is a sacred place, and how George Morrison, an Ojibwa abstract painter, remains consistent with his Native traditions. Martínez argues that as Morrison breaks free of his academic training, and meditates upon his place of origin, his activity comes through the act of painting itself. This thesis is reminiscent of the argument John DuFour presented earlier in this volume (chapter 4), that the knowing and living of one's Indigenous tradition rests in ritual, or act. Martínez tells us that Morrison accounts for his paintings by his lifestyle, which allows his art to emerge from his imagination, as connected with his "subconscious" in a synthesis of meditation and dream; this synthesis creates in his Abstract Expressionism an immediate effect of a concrete moment of experience between painter and viewer. In his Horizon Series the horizon is a natural phenomenon that operates as motif for organizing space in the painting.

Martínez tells us that Morrison was "fascinated and . . . comforted by the vastness of space, because it is along the horizon that the 'mystery' of life appears." To enter a gallery of Morrison paintings, he tells us, is to enter a place of loosened time and space: "Morrison evokes a world before there were humans and language."

Because our relation to the world is given to us in dreams, it is in dreaming that we discover the self liberated from the mundane world. And it is in dreams that we are free to cross the cognitive boundaries between things, finding ourselves a part of everything in the cosmos. Martínez tells us that "just as Morrison has blurred the line separating earth and sky, so too has he blurred the line between traditional and nontraditional." Perhaps it is in the blurring, in Morrison's horizon, that Cordova's moment of esthetic stillness can be found. Or, as Martínez tells us, the artist is like the storyteller, for they both invoke nature's mythical past, bringing it to present experience, evoking feelings of relationship with our environment.

It is in this sense of space, and of place in the world, where the present expands to encompass the past and future, that we humans can understand ourselves as part of nature, which articulates a Native philosophy, and a Native spirituality. From this sense of being with the universe, which is also ourselves, springs a metaphysic and epistemology that articulates and defines all other fields of academic philosophy. For as we come to know ourselves in the world, as of the world, interdependent with and part of nature through the very air we breathe and chemicals we consume, we discover the human self, as not discretely separated, but rather immersed in and vulnerable to all cosmic forces.

The self in this experience is the paradigm of the "We" of which Cordova speaks. And this We only nondiscretely locates being in the world. It is this esthetic being in the world, embracing the meditative ambience of Morrison's Horizon Series, that gives rise to a Native philosophy of being in the world that finds human place.

In the last chapter, "On Philosophical Discourse: Some Intercultural Musings," Thurman Lee Hester, Jr, again places self-introduction in the context of the Choctaw Nation, and proceeds to illuminate a difference between Euro-American and Native American philosophical method. He claims that in Euro-American philosophy answers (which are beliefs or dispositions toward reality) are the means of attaining an answer. Not so for Native American philosophical traditions, however, claims Hester, and tells us a story to show why.

In one of Hester's classes on Native American identity, a student asks a visiting elder, "What makes you Creek?" The elder proceeds to list a short set of practices which might make a person a member of the traditional Creek religion. Hester tells us this Creek elder would call this the difference between Euro-American religious orthodoxy (belief) and Native American religious orthopraxy (action merging theory). Hester tells us: "If practice is at the core of Native American philosophy, then how you go about doing that philosophy may be as much or more important than what is supposedly being said."

Euro-American philosophy, in other words, concerns right argument and belief. Yet Native American philosophy concerns practices that just are! Hester tells us that because there are no "schools" of Native American philosophy, "insight gained from experience will be crucial." Native American philosophy will need to merge practical experience with formal training in the Euro-American tradition in order to work out an understanding of Native American philosophy for those of predominantly Euro-American thought. (Here we are reminded of hints of Marilyn Notah Verney's admonition that there is a responsibility to teach non-Natives about Native culture.)

The role of Euro-American philosophers in American Indian academic philosophy, Hester tells us, is like that of a "Yuchi cornstalk [that] acts like a pole for the bean, while the bean acts as a guywire, supporting the cornstalk in even the stiffest wind." Euro-American philosophers will be the ones to open the gates of academic philosophy in order to train "those Native Americans who wish to enter academe" and "will also help to recognize and bring the wisdom of the Native American tradition to a larger audience."

This volume opens a new field of academic discourse. In the future ideas articulated in this book about nature, and the human place and relations in and with nature, will continue to be thought about and discussed by American Indian elders, scholars, and intellectuals. I look forward to reading, teaching, and sharing many more scholarly works in this field. The philosophical doors are cracked open, and like reviving nations, American Indian philosophers will continue to walk in two worlds, alongside our ancestors and elders, and on the paths of cultural struggle that articulate our Indigenous being. May these doors remain open, and may they never be closed again. May American Indian philosophy and philosophers be respected and appreciated for what we are, as carriers of human origins on this continent, and believers of ideas about all our relations of the universe. There will likely always be sacred knowledge that American Indians will hold close with our tribes, against colonial intrusion. But many of the authors here speak about a need to share our ways of being, for in the sharing, as in orthopraxy, the ethics of a traditional rapport with all the universe can be understood and acted upon. And when this happens, the harms of cognitive cultural dissonance will hopefully be lessened.

# Part I

# AMERICAN INDIANS AND PHILOSOPHY

# 1

# PHILOSOPHY AND THE TRIBAL PEOPLES

*Vine Deloria, Jr.*

People of American Indian descent are now seeking admission to one of the most respected and hallowed intellectual enterprises of Western civilization – philosophy. This last bastion of white male supremacy does not admit members easily and the roadblocks ahead are of such magnitude that it is doubtful that very much will be accomplished. In the last century Asian philosophies have come under examination by Western thinkers, but have failed to be incorporated into any perspective that would point toward a real planetary metaphysics or epistemology. Can American Indians doing Western philosophy, or articulating philosophies based on their traditions, do any better?

Tribal peoples have traditionally been understood by Westerners as the last remnants of a hypothetical earlier stage of cultural evolution, and this so-called "primitive stage" of human development is a necessary preamble to any discussion of human beings and the meaning of their lives. Indeed, the stereotype of primitive peoples anchors the whole edifice of Western social thought. We need the primitive so that we can distinguish Western civilization from it and congratulate ourselves on the progress that we have made. John Locke and Thomas Hobbes may have articulated the idea formally by beginning their theories of the social contract with a hypothetical stage wherein primitive people established a society, but subsequent generations of Western people have wholeheartedly accepted the image without any critical examination of its validity. Thus the attitude of many philosophers is that American Indians must represent the stage of human development in which superstition and ignorance reigned supreme. The primitive is further conceived as having a prescientific perspective; that is to say, the early peoples are believed to have desperately wanted to use the methods of science to explain their world but were unable to form the abstract concepts that – when universally applied – allowed Western people to gain their insights. Thus the circle is logically closed and the possibility of exchanging ideas is neatly eliminated.

Could there ever have been a time when tribal peoples and Western peoples could have discussed abstract concepts in a philosophical setting? Historically, the opportunity existed during the first several centuries in which the two groups encountered each other. And in theory modern tribal peoples who have been isolated from the activities of the industrial world could still converse on some important topics. Thus we have an increasing number of books describing the "dreamtime" of Australian aborigines and a few scholarly articles describing some of the beliefs of African tribes. This pseudoconversation appears more often in popular literature and has not made much impact within the ranks of professional philosophy. For American Indians the period of opportunity probably ended for most tribes around 1900, when the last generation of people born free were in an elderly meditative stage of their lives.

When we speak of American Indian philosophy today, we are probably talking about several generations of Indian people who have popular notions of what Indian philosophy might have been or might become within the Western philosophical enterprise. Conditions in Indian communities have radically changed in the past generation so that the experiences and memories of most people today refer back to the communities that existed in 1960 when the many Poverty programs began to bring modern Western civilization to the reservations. Elders of the 1960s might well have known some of the old beliefs and ceremonies, but more likely they would have remembered the boarding school days of the 1920s. They would probably have expressed regrets that they had been taken away from their relatives during their childhood years when they could have learned something from their elders. Thus we have a body of people wanting to be Indians but badly handicapped by the rush toward assimilation that we have seen in the past 40 years. An elder today, age 75, would probably remember the Great Depression of the 1930s and the revival of ceremonies in the 1950s but would know little else of any importance.

The possibility that we do have, however, is the sense of the knowledge of the old people as recorded by non-Indians, beginning with first contact and continuing until the 1930s and in some cases the 1950s, when the last men who fought against the United States were still alive. But even this material can be suspect. James Walker noted in the earlier part of the twentieth century that the old men at Pine Ridge were disgruntled with the generation following them for changing the pronunciation of sacred ceremonial language to a slang that failed to capture the precise meanings that the specific words contained. People may claim to have this same knowledge today but such claims are mostly wishful thinking. The task today is that of intensive research and study to enable people to project what the various tribal peoples probably meant when they described the world around them.

A projected American Indian philosophy is further handicapped by the popular social setting in which Indians live today. With the popularity of Indians in the 1960s in movies such as *Billy Jack*, the articulation of weird psychedelic teachings popularized by Carlos Castaneda in the 1970s, and the emergence of the noble Indian ecologist in the movie *Dances with Wolves* in the 1990s, things "Indian" have become more fantasy than real. Indian life, culture, religion, and beliefs have become so bastardized that we have Indians interpreting their traditions as if they had a missionary purpose. Some modern practitioners of ceremonies insist that their ceremony was intended for all people of good faith – even if that good faith existed only during the length of the ceremony.

In the 1960s many Indians spoke using a royal "we" when they told of beatings by nuns for speaking their own language or being kidnapped and taken far away to school or not seeing a white man until they were teenagers. These conditions did still exist on the Navajo, Hopi, and Tohono O'odham reservations. But if they claim that these experiences occurred in Oklahoma, South Dakota, Montana, or Minnesota they were indeed a rare event that needed to be documented.

Many of this generation who claim to have suffered these imagined hurts are now getting older. Some of the same people are now claiming that they were 8 or 9 years old when they were spirited away by traditional elders and raised in a secret place where they were taught all manner of sacred things by the last elder who knew the ceremonies and beliefs of ancient times. Combining the two claims to create an accurate history of the past 40 years, one would conclude that thousands of nuns dressed in their traditional penguin costumes roamed the West in an effort to stamp out Indian languages and that at the same time all the Indian children were being hidden by traditional elders in obscure box canyons where they performed traditional ceremonies 24 hours a day. It is exceedingly difficult for this generation of people of Indian descent to intelligently work their way through this politically charged morass.

The struggle to define identity and establish credentials has existed for quite a while and shows no signs of declining. So the development of American Indian philosophies may well experience many advances and retreats as well as some bitter internal quarrels challenging the status of the individuals attempting to do this philosophy. When word gets back to the reservations there will certainly be some controversies about the authenticity of Indian academics, who will be hard-pressed to defend their speculations and interpretations. Already in the discussion of Indian philosophies we have seen claims that only on reservations and in villages can there be any development of an Indian philosophy of any value. Here the idea of philosophy certainly derives from the popular American notion that if a person has certain staunchly held opinions he or she has a "philosophy." So differentiating the technical requirements of the philosophical discipline for local people will involve much time and attention. This situation will probably exist everywhere that a tribal group attempts to speak with the Western philosophical tradition.

What then are the necessary requirements or ideological context in which an American Indian philosophy can be created? First in consideration must be the deeply held belief that there is something of value in any tribal tradition that transcends mere belief and ethnic pride. Instead of developing an idea of cultural movement that has primitive at one end of the spectrum and modern at the other, great care must be taken to identify tribal societies and Western thinking as being different in their approach to the world but equal in their conclusions about the world.

This demand for respect must touch all points where the two groups come into contact with each other. In other words, Indians must examine some of the same phenomena as do Western thinkers and must demonstrate that their perspectives and conclusions make sense. Western science and philosophy have generally worked with syllogisms and general terms in the belief that some kind of knowledge can be derived from this kind of thinking, although on close examination much of the knowledge is tautological in nature and leads nowhere. Only in recent years has the admission of equality become meaningful. Percy Bridgman, in *The Way Things Are* (1959), once observed that while Westerners used the syllogism to expand their knowledge, American Indians chose simply to note many similar concrete cases and remembered what they had many times verified to be true from their own experience.

How does this process work? In the West we would submit the following propositional thinking as capable of giving us knowledge: "Socrates is a man; all men are mortal; Socrates is mortal." For the Indian the response would be: "Oh, yes, I once met Socrates, and he was just like the rest of us so I assume he is mortal also." In both cases there is an assumption. In the proposition "all men are mortal," we cannot truly verify our statement. We have not yet met all men and we infer from the limited number we have observed that our statement holds true. The Indian also assumes that all men are mortal but he requires empirical verification in the remembrance that Socrates is because he once met Socrates and verified that he was a man like himself. This process of verification reduces substantially the number and kinds of statements that Indians would be willing to make. But it substantially enhances the veracity of statements that are made. Whereas the Western syllogism simply introduces a doctrine using general concepts and depends on faith in the chain of reasoning for its verification, the Indian statement would stand by itself without faith and belief. I suggest that the question of all men's mortality is still open for the American Indian on the possibility that some men are immortal but have not yet been encountered.

This discussion makes it appear that no real difference exists. But if we investigate further we will discover that the idea of a man for the Indian is quite specific and exists within a much broader field of data than that of the Western thinker. Suppose the Indian had a dream or vision in which a creature resembling a man appeared. Such phenomena are reported in both Western culture and Indian experiences. The Westerner would immediately reject the idea that any spirit can appear in a dream or vision and be as "real" as ordinary wide-awake life experiences. During the Indian's dream the man-figure can do things that physical humans cannot do. He can become a bird, animal, or some other entity depending on the nature of the dream. Yet he falls within the definition of man that would be taken into consideration by the Indian when making a statement about human mortality. Obviously he is alive and a part of the Indian's world.

In the West such experiences are written off and said to be mere delusions. But what is a delusion? What is being discarded here? The Westerner rejects the experience because it is not a material thing. He insists that the experience be "real" – i.e. a physical presence that can be subjected to some form of mechanical testing. The Indian does not believe that the world is wholly material, and allows for the existence of real but nonphysical things. The Westerner insists that experience be rational, i.e. contained within a cause-and-effect chain of events, and the inclusion of his experience in such a chain gives him the guarantee that his experience is rational. But cause-and-effect is a crude way of explaining the world because, as we know from quantum physics, in at least the quantum situation, there is no cause-and-effect. Would that also apply to phenomena of larger sizes than quantum experiments?

The doctrinal exclusion of certain kinds of phenomena by the West has no basis except the superstition that certain things cannot exist. How do these superstitions become so entrenched in a society's beliefs, at a level so deep that it becomes unthinkable to voice them? I was once on an Episcopal church committee that had a petition from the Indians on the Fort Hall reservation to move the church a long distance from the graveyard because the people said ghosts were bothering them when they went to evening services. The committee found this absurd and hilarious until I reminded them that the reason that the church was near the graveyard was the belief of their ancestors that unless graves were as near as possible to the church where the Reserved Sacrament was kept, the devil would come and steal their souls. Much philosophy and theology in the West is simply revered superstition.

What has happened in this case? In the West the origins of things are lost as knowledge increases and general statements are made using syllogisms containing concepts of which we have little knowledge. Over time people forget the origin or meaning of concepts and begin to make statements that have no real content but are filled with whatever references they might wish to endow them with. The requirement that Indians place on themselves to have some kind of empirical verification for statements precludes them from making the kind of statements the West takes as knowledge, and it keeps their minds open to receive the unexpected and to remember it.

Charles Eastman related a story of his uncle hunting and encountering a clever coyote. The uncle had killed a deer and hung it from a tree. Then he heard all kinds of yips and yelps and the racket sounded like a pack of coyotes about to attack him and take his deer. Upon investigation he discovered it was but a single coyote that was running around energetically behind a hill making various noises imitating a whole pack of coyotes, with the hope he could bluff the man and make off with the meat. This completely unexpected behavior suggested to Eastman that animals had as complex and creative mental processes as did humans.

We may scoff at such reports but we do so from the position of living in an urban industrial society that has no contact with the wilderness landscape and the creatures that inhabit it. We are taught to believe from the very beginning that animals have no feelings, emotions, or intellect. We assume that they function by "instinct," but this word only covers up our ignorance of the capabilities of animals. This incident is very rare, it could possibly be observed only once in a lifetime by a very small percentage of people. Those people would have to be in the wilderness where coyotes live and be in a similar situation. "Scientifically" and "philosophically," such behavior would not be possible. Empirically, it is possible as reported by an observer meeting all the requirements of the coyote world.

We could use this example to explore many topics. Perhaps the best use of it would be to introduce into philosophical thought the idea that consciousness involves considerably more than French thinkers meditating about themselves on cold winter evenings. That proposition, however, exposes the wide gulf that separates the tribal peoples from Western thinking. Tribal peoples include all forms of life in their body of evidence from the very beginning, so that their concepts must be more precise and involve considerably more evidence. Their statements must be framed in ways that are applicable not simply to humans but to living creatures in any circumstances. Many tribes include in the roster of living things certain kinds of stones that in their experience have considerable powers. They use these stones to gather information, predict events, and perform healings. In the West, of course, the use of crystals to perform a wide variety of functions is now taken for granted without a corresponding change in the expansion of empirical data, the critique of philosophical foundations, or refinement of scientific or philosophical conclusions.

In the West knowledge is arranged to support the proposition that matter produces mind. The most comprehensive statement of this belief can be found in the writings of Pierre Teilhard de Chardin, but it is obvious that most Western scientists and thinkers uncritically accept the idea. The proposition can easily be reversed, however, to state that mind (or spirit) manifests itself as matter. James Jeans long ago concluded that the physical world, in its essence, looks like a gigantic thought. Certainly the sophisticated "fields" that physicists believe they describe today are not matter in the usual sense but merely predictive statements of possible results of a restricted experiment. They exist, if anywhere, in the minds of physicists.

Were Western philosophy and American Indian philosophy to meet and discuss this variance, how would they do so? Indians of course could cite modern physics and argue that the Great Mysterious Energy they experience in the physical world, that which makes everything energetic, is comparable to the energy fields of physics. Indeed, one Western writer, Fred Alan Wolf, has already made such a suggestion. It is not, however, finding the final term for which a concept can be devised that is important. Rather, it is the development of a philosophy based on the concept – how the concept is applied – that is important. While Indians would enthusiastically identify spiritual phenomena they have experienced as representative of the basic energy, Western thinkers might be significantly inhibited for fear of ridicule by their colleagues.

If we look closely at the vocabulary used by Western thinkers and examine their concepts, we will discover many things that are buried deep in the psyche of Western man that have no content. Among these ideas are "law," "science," "god," and "truth." No adequate or precise definition can be given for these concepts because they are not only philosophical terms but also have popular connotations. Thus "law" can be anything that appears regularly, that is devised to control human behavior, that has a statistical basis, or that arises as a boundary in experience or capability. We all recognize that "science" can be almost anything from a belief in the regularity of physical behavior to a fascination with the physical world issuing in curiosity. "Truth" can be a logical chain of reasoning resulting in one and only one conclusion, or a mere esthetic feeling.

"God" has as many meanings as living individuals to articulate them, but none of us knows where the concept originates.

How would American Indians handle similar concepts? First, in many tribes these concepts would not exist apart from the concrete situations in which there was a need to describe and remember specific feelings or insights. This process would eliminate discussions in ethics of the "greater good" that were suspect from the very beginning. Second, comparisons between varying manifestations of any of these concepts would depend on the memory of previous situations in which the same or similar reflection created the same or similar feelings. By moving back and forth within the memories of the past a place would be found to place the situation under consideration in the memory bank. Experiences would be distinguished by the specific event that created the memory.

How in this process could a body of knowledge be derived that would be useful to people and help them orient themselves to the world they live in? The Sioux Indians tell the story of the manner in which they received the Sacred Pipe. It involves the sudden appearance of a woman who instructed them in its use and gave them laws of life and then turned into a series of different-colored buffalo and disappeared. This story, for those people, is true. It is an ancient experience. When the Oglala Sioux holy man Black Elk told this story to John Neihardt, he remarked: "Whether it happened so or not, I don't know, but if you think about it you will see that it is true."

Is this attitude not akin to a statement of "faith" in that it calls for belief in an unsubstantiated event? It certainly is at least an expression of faith in the tribal traditions. But this attitude lacks the intensity with which Western peoples hold their faith. Black Elk simply gives his observations; he does not attempt to convince Neihardt. A missionary, Reverend Cram, once came to the Senecas to convert them and recited the story of Adam and Eve. When he was finished the Senecas insisted on relating one of their creation stories. Cram was livid, arguing that he had told the Senecas the truth while they had recited a mere fable to him. The Senecas chastised him for his bad manners, saying that they had been polite in listening to his story without complaining and he should have been willing to hear their tales.

It is not difficult to see that the Indians are totally pragmatic in this situation. They have stories, Cram has stories; but what is important is the fellowship and dialogue between the parties and not the competition to define truth – since truth is a matter of perception. One might therefore describe the Indians as true relativists, possessing no criteria except what happens to strike their fancy. Such is not the case. The transmission of stories of ancient times, along with social relations with other peoples, provided boundaries beyond which people did not go. Their truths were truly theirs and others were entitled to their truths. As Black Elk saw in one vision, the universe was made up of many peoples, each having their own circle within which they lived. The task was to find one's own road, whether as a people or as a person, and not to worry about how other people lived their lives or what they believed and practiced. So instead of being relativists the Indians recognized that there were different perspectives which had equal claim to veracity.

Western thinking, I do believe, has the same manner of transmitting its philosophies, and thus the fantasies and foibles of the Western past masquerade as boundaries also. Physicists can talk about unseen quantum entities that can only be inferred by the rationality of mathematical equations, and their qualities and quantities are taken seriously although they are entirely artificial constructs. But when doctors describe near death experiences they are viewed with great suspicion and their data are subjected to intense scrutiny. Efforts are made to demonstrate that electrical currents placed on certain parts of the brain can reproduce certain aspects of this experience. In the USA we can criticize the government all we want. We cannot, however, express any doubts of Darwinism and evolution. We do not have the civility that marked tribal societies, even with the past knowledge of human beings that we are believed to possess. We could gradually, given sufficient time, identify Western boundaries precisely – they would be those things that we refuse to criticize. The Indian boundaries were in the manner in which people related to each other, not what they were taught to believe.

Among the most important differences between tribal peoples' and Western thinking is the concentration in the West on the solitary individual to the exclusion of the group – a perspective now rendered obsolete by quantum physics. We know today that the idea of the individual is meaningless, but much of our philosophy, law, and religious thinking continues to make the individual the focus of attention and the starting point for all other analysis. From John Locke to John Rawls, the important decisions are to be made by individuals possessing neither father nor mother, village nor tribe, age nor gender. In tort law we have the "reasonably prudent man" who always drives more carefully or acts with greater caution than real people. In religion we have the "sinner" who can be saved from his transgressions even while he creates a society in which others are deprived of sustenance. The ethics of Kant and Aristotle fall apart completely when we begin to attach any attributes to their idea of the person and what he/she knows.

The various Indian tribes recognized that individuals who had no loyalty to anyone else were exceedingly dangerous to have around. Beginning even before birth, people prayed for the unborn child in an effort to establish a family context into which she/he would be born. The pregnant mother visualized the heroic people that she knew, hoping her thoughts would help the baby develop while yet in the womb. Through the family, clan, and society there was never a time when an individual Indian was not a part of the cooperative activities of others. It was believed that people are the sum total of their relationships. The punishment for heinous crimes in many tribes was banishment – the refusal of people in the tribe to continue to recognize the humanity of the wrongdoer.

In contrast to the West, where "rights" reign supreme, the tribal peoples through family, clan, and societies created a climate in which "responsibility" would be the chief virtue. One had all manner of duties toward others and could expect to reap the benefit of one's loyalty in fulfilling these responsibilities by receiving in return the blessings created when others fulfilled their responsibility reciprocally. Individuals were not believed to stand alone but to perform the duties required of a father, grandfather, son, brother, or cousin. A complete rendering of these responsibilities produces a volume comparable in every way to the massive philosophical systems of Hegel,

Aristotle, and St Thomas Aquinas because each possible role that could exist carried with it specific duties toward people occupying all of the other roles.

Perhaps too much attention has been devoted to providing examples of the difference between Western and American Indian thought. The reason for providing anecdotal examples is that there is no philosophy of American Indians apart from the concrete actions of people in a well-defined physical setting. Indian elders and holy people did a great deal of speculation but it was regarded as a pastime, reflecting on experience, and did not substitute for the experience itself. Elders received a hearing and their counsel was more often than not heeded primarily because people recognized that, if nothing else, they had a lifetime of experience during which they were presumed to have understood what their various experiences meant.

When American Indians now come before professional philosophers and request entrance into this professional field, the vast majority of the petitioners will have virtually no experiences of the old traditional kind. The majority of them will begin in the same place as non-Indians wishing to write on American Indian philosophy. The difference will be in the degree to which Indians take their own traditions seriously and literally. If Indians themselves give their own heritage the respect it deserves, an amazing number of issues can be brought forth that Western philosophy does not presently touch on. Foremost will be the view that all knowledge must begin with experience, and further that all conclusions must be verified easily in the empirical physical world.

# Part II

# EPISTEMOLOGY AND KNOWING

# 2

# WHAT COYOTE AND THALES CAN TEACH US: AN OUTLINE OF AMERICAN INDIAN EPISTEMOLOGY

*Brian Yazzie Burkhart*

## SOME INTRODUCTORY PRINCIPLES OF AMERICAN INDIAN PHILOSOPHY

Coyote is described as a philosopher in many American Indian stories. In part, this is because he wonders about things, about how they really work. Often in doing so, however, he forgets his place in the world; he does not remember how he is related. He reminds one of the stories of the beginnings of Western philosophy and the Greek thinker Thales. Plato tells us the story of "the Thracian maidservant who exercised her wit at the expense of Thales, when he was looking up to study the heavens and tumbled down a well. She scoffed at him for being so eager to know what was happening in the sky that he could not see what lay behind him and at his feet" (*Theaetetus* 174). One could quite easily replace the names in this story with Coyote and Rabbit, or Coyote and Skunk, or Coyote and Snake, and so on, and have any number of American Indian Coyote tales. Coyote, like Thales, is made fun of for his actions, actions that arise from his dislocation *vis-à-vis* the world around him.

Now, despite being objects of ridicule, Coyote and Thales seem to provide a starting point for our investigation of American Indian philosophy. But they do so by exemplifying what it is not. Plato uses the story of Thales to make clear what philosophy *is*. He explains that "[the philosopher] is unaware what his next-door neighbor is doing, hardly knows, indeed, whether the creature is a man at all; he spends all his pains on the question, what man is, and what powers and properties distinguish such a nature

15

from any other" (*Theaetetus* 174). The stories of Coyote, conversely, are meant to show Coyote's mistakes. Like Thales, Coyote has forgotten the simple things. He has forgotten his relations. He has forgotten what is behind him and at his feet. When Coyote behaves in this way, he always finds trouble. He is mocked in these stories because he is behaving in the wrong way. The stories are meant to show us how not to act; they show us what philosophy is not, and not, as in the case of Plato and Thales, what it is and ought to be. This is one of Coyote's stories told to me as a child:

> Coyote is wandering around in his usual way when he comes upon a prairie dog town. The prairie dogs laugh and curse at him. Coyote gets angry and wants revenge. The sun is high in the sky. Coyote decides that he wants clouds to come. He is starting to hate the prairie dogs and so thinks about rain. Just then a cloud appears.
> Coyote says, "I wish it would rain on me." And that is what happened.
> Coyote says, "I wish there were rain at my feet." And that is what happened.
> "I want the rain up to my knees," Coyote says. And that is what happened.
> "I want the rain up to my waist," he then says. And that is what happened.

The water continues to rise higher and higher as Coyote thinks and speaks about it. Before long, the whole land is flooded. In this story, we are supposed to learn from Coyote's mistake, which is not letting what is right (the right way to act regarding his relatives the prairie dogs, and so forth) guide his actions, but rather acting solely on the basis of his own wants and desires. We are supposed to see also from this story that we must be careful what we do, what we want, and what we think and speak, in general. We must never forget the things around us and how we are related to those things. We can refer to this last point as the principle of relatedness. The idea here is simply that the most important things to keep in mind are the simple things that are directly around us in our experience and the things to which we are most directly related. (In calling these ideas principles, I do not mean to give them special philosophical status. In American Indian thought, they are simply ways of being. These principles are merely abstractions from these ways of being. We shall soon see that principles in the traditional philosophical sense have no place in American Indian philosophy.)

Coyote also shows us that the questions we choose to ask are more important than any truths we might hope to discover in asking such questions, since how we act impacts the way the world is, the way in which a question will get answered. The way in which we ask questions (the way in which we act toward our relations) guides us, then, to the right answers, rather than the other way around wherein what is true directs the method of questioning and the question itself (i.e., we can ask any question we desire and in any way we desire, and the answer will remain the same). We can refer to this as the limits of questioning principle. Part of what underlies this principle, besides, clearly, the principle of relatedness, is the idea that how we act is not merely a result of causal interactions with the world. How we act is not merely a response to stimuli. The world is not empty and meaningless, bearing only truth and cold facts. We participate in the meaning-making of the world. There is no world, no truth, without meaning and value, and meaning and value arise in the intersection between us and all that is around us. How we behave, then, in a certain sense shapes meaning, gives shape to the world. In this way, what we do, how we act, is as important as any truth and any fact. We can think of this as the meaning-shaping principle of action.

American Indians refer to this principle over and over again when asked certain questions by non-Natives. When asked such questions, Native elders will respond by saying, "We don't talk about those things," or "It is bad to talk about those things." These interdictions generally leave the questioner puzzled. But the confusion seems to arise from a lack of understanding regarding the underlying philosophical assumptions involved. With the aim of making clear these assumptions, here is a list of the principles addressed so far: first, we have the principle of relatedness and, second, that of the limits of questioning. We also have the meaning-shaping principle of action. But there is at least one other principle involved in this interdiction as these three principles are supported by a fourth that we might call "the moral universe principle." The idea is simply that the universe is moral. Facts, truth, meaning, even our existence are normative. In this way, there is no difference between what is true and what is right. On this account, then, all investigation is moral investigation. The guiding question for the entire philosophical enterprise is, then: what is the right road for humans to walk?

Now, this general shape we have given to American Indian philosophy is hardly adequate, at least as it stands. First, we have by no means gotten to the most basic principles. We have only begun to scratch the surface of what are the real underlying philosophical issues. Second, the surface principles are themselves still unclear. The second principle seems to imply that more knowledge is not always better since it seems to say that there are things we cannot or should not know. But how can there be such things? What sort of view of knowledge is at work in such a prohibition? It makes us wonder how such a thing could ever count as a view of knowledge in the first place. Furthermore, we are left wondering how such a view of knowledge would relate to the notion that right action determines truth, and not vice versa. And if acting in a certain way leads to the wrong path, creates the wrong truth, how do we *know* when a way of acting will lead to the right path or even which is the right path? The point is that once we push these philosophical principles far enough we are faced most directly with the question: "What is knowledge, and how could we possibly have it given these principles?"

American Indian philosophy, as we have begun to see and will continue to see, is quite concerned with the questions asked. American Indian philosophy has a very different relationship to questions and question-formation than does its Western counterpart. It is generally thought by Native philosophers that questions are most often a sign of confusion and misunderstanding. The answer to a question often lies in the question itself rather than in some solution outside of the question. The problem a question addresses is typically one that is raised by the very question itself rather than some actual state of affairs. And yet, given what we have described above, nearly any Western philosopher will ask at least the following two questions: "How do you know which is right in the first place?" and "How can less knowledge be better?" This second question is partly a result of Western philosophy's incapacity to grasp the idea that certain things *should* not be known, and the first arises from Western philosophy's so-called battle with skepticism. From the perspective of Western philosophy, it is generally thought that more knowledge is always better. (By Western philosophy here I merely mean mainstream Western philosophy, the tradition that led from Thales to modern Anglo-American analytic philosophy: the kind of philosophy that is usually called merely "philosophy," with no adjective. The point of this distinction is simply that there are a number of fringe-dwelling philosophers, never quite accepted by the mainstream, who should not be saddled with the previous charge.) Of course, Western philosophy has always had skeptics in one form or another who claim that certain things cannot be known, but there seems to be no way for a Western philosopher in this mainstream tradition to claim that things we *can* know we *should* not know. Even those who claim that there are things that we cannot know do not typically see this as positive. We must settle, they want to say, for this limited knowledge. But by saying this, they implicitly suppose that we ought to have more and thereby disallow the notion that there is some knowledge we *should* not have. Even the knowledge we cannot have, we ought to. Given this implicit supposition, it seems impossible to claim that knowledge we can have we ought not to. But in American Indian thought, and for that matter in many non-Western systems of thought, such an idea is not problematic. In these ways of thought, the assumption is not already in place that more knowledge is always better or that we ought always to have more of it. From the American Indian perspective, our knowledge is not limited since we have as much as we should.

In what follows, then, we will concern ourselves with making clear this notion of knowledge and how it relates to an understanding of the principles of American Indian philosophy. In doing so, Coyote and Thales will continue to be our tricksters, leading us by example from their mistakes to a right understanding of American Indian philosophy. However, we must note that an adequate understanding of the principles given so far further requires a detailed analysis of what might be called American Indian moral-metaphysics. Here we would examine the way in which we can understand the claim that the universe is itself moral and how we can understand relatedness as a moral concept. However, in this piece we will concern ourselves only with understanding the given principles via Native epistemology.

## THE TRADITIONAL WESTERN APPROACH TO EPISTEMOLOGY

The Western form of knowledge is expressed in a formula. The one most used is: knowledge = justified, true belief. If knowledge amounts simply to this, then it becomes clear why it is impossible to claim that less knowledge is better. Why would anyone find it necessary to have less true and justified beliefs? However, in order to discover how this might be the case, we must go back further into the methodology that gives rise to the justified-true-belief formula of knowledge. The formula "knowledge = justified, true belief" does not by itself necessarily conflict with Native philosophy, other than perhaps the peculiarities of being a formula and what comes along with that. The conflict arises at a deeper level in what, ultimately, we want this to mean.

In Western philosophy we call the study of knowledge "epistemology," which derives from the Greek *episteme*, knowledge, and *logos*, reason or account. This account purports to lay out the defining features of knowledge, the substantive conditions of knowledge, as well as the limits of knowledge. In large part, it is in these areas alone that the Western philosophical debate regarding knowledge arises: the analysis of knowledge, the source of knowledge (rationalism or empiricism), and the viability of skepticism. In this way, many issues regarding knowledge are generally left unquestioned. One such modern issue is the primacy of propositional knowledge.

Propositional knowledge is knowledge of the form "that something is so." It is the kind of knowledge that can be written down, that can be directly conveyed through statements or propositions. This kind of knowledge is thought to have permanence. If we make true and justified claims that something is so, those claims will continue to be true for eternity. In Western thought, this kind of knowledge is generally thought to be the pinnacle of philosophy.

Unlike in many non-Western schools of thought, in popular modern Anglo-American philosophy (which, as we have said, is for the most part what we mean by Western philosophy in this chapter), the idea that non-propositional knowledge is the more important, more basic, more fundamental form of knowledge has never been given much serious thought. There are those who in fact claim that all knowledge reduces to propositional knowledge. Here is the small and most likely inadequate list that philosophers in this tradition, who do not claim that all knowledge reduces to propositional knowledge, recognize as non-propositional knowledge: knowledge by direct awareness or acquaintance, and how-to knowledge or knowledge of how to do something. There may be still other forms or variations that have been overlooked in the monolithic focus on propositional knowledge. Whether or not this is so, it is clear that in Western philosophy, non-propositional knowledge, if it is accepted at all, plays little to no part in the work of philosophy.

Another aspect of traditional epistemology that has only recently become much of an issue arises from one of the three components of the traditional account of knowledge, and this is justification. It has seemed clear until quite recently to most epistemologists, with few exceptions, that justification requires foundations. To say this and then, by extension, that knowledge requires foundations is to say that justification requires: (1) that at least some beliefs be not only justified non-inferentially, that is, that they be justified not on the basis of other beliefs, but also (2) that they provide justification for those beliefs that cannot be justified non-inferentially, that is, those beliefs that without the beliefs in question would only be justified on the basis of other beliefs. Unless the first condition is met, there is no justification and no knowledge. If only the first condition is met and not the second, then our knowledge is very limited, limited to that of our own psychological states, for example. Part of the idea here is that for any belief $x$ to count as knowledge, it must be justified. If it is justified by another belief $y$, then, in order for $x$ to be justified, $y$ must also be justified. We can quickly see that without something to stop this cycle, we will go on justifying infinitely. The foundationalist claim is, then, that for there to be knowledge there must be a $z$ or set of $z$'s that is not justified by any other $x$ and provides justification for $y$. Thus, in order for any piece of so-called knowledge to really be such, this knowledge must rest on a foundation, something which, in a certain sense, does not rest on anything else.

# THE AMERICAN INDIAN APPROACH
# TO EPISTEMOLOGY

American Indians have encountered the kind of reasoning used in this argument many times before. One such example is the routine response that Western people have given to a certain Native account of creation. In this account, the earth rests on the back of a turtle. The Western response to this account is simply the question, "What holds the turtle?" One elder storyteller responded to this question by saying simply, "Well, then there must be turtles all the way down." The storyteller had no patience with this way of thinking. It seemed to her that asking such a question was like asking for proof that she had a mother or for proof that plants grow in the earth and nourish the people – questions, in her mind, that only someone extremely confused would ask.

Part of the problem with such a question in this context is that it presupposes a certain amount of knowledge. By asking what holds the turtle up, the inquisitor assumes that such a question should be answered in order to justify the initial claim. This then assumes something like the notions of knowledge and justification detailed above, where for any belief to count as knowledge, it must be justified by another belief or be self-justifying. Any belief, then, on this picture must be justified by another belief or be itself a foundational belief, not requiring justification as it is incapable of being false, or whatever. Now, there are many different ways in which this gets fleshed out in modern epistemology, but the general requirement of justification remains the same. This is because the traditional view of justification is that justification is simply evidence.

But, while something like this picture of justification seems intuitive to the Western philosopher, American Indian thinkers will find it counterintuitive. This is because, for American Indian philosophy, knowledge is quite a different thing from what we have been describing. For American Indians, knowledge is knowledge in experience, or if knowledge does not simply amount to this, it is at least the most important knowledge. This is in complete contrast to the Western picture given above, wherein knowledge is propositional, or if knowledge does not simply amount to this, it is at least the most important knowledge. In contrast to propositional knowledge, which seems to be designed to outlast us, to take on a life of its own, to be something eternal, knowledge in experience is the kind of knowledge we carry with us. This is the kind of knowledge that allows us to function in the world, to carry on our daily tasks, to live our lives. This knowledge is embodied knowledge. We might do best to call this knowledge "lived knowledge." Whatever we call it, this kind of knowledge is not improved by adding abstract propositional form and is not capable of being justified in the foundational sense and seems to need no such justification.

In order to get clear about the nature of such knowledge, let us look at a rather simple example. Suppose a person learned to play a song on a musical instrument without the ability to read music. She practiced the song many times after hearing it played by someone else until she reached the point where she could play it herself. She plays the song perfectly but could not say the first thing about the notes, the key, the time signature, and many other propositions regarding the song itself. If her desire were to play the song, then these abstract propositions would only get in the way since as far as playing the song is concerned her knowledge is complete. For American Indian philosophy, knowledge is just like this: it is gained from experience and used in it.

This lived knowledge can be likened to what in Buddhist philosophy is called *prajñā*. In Mahāyāna Buddhism, *prajñā* is the perfection of wisdom. It is called the heart of wisdom. It is the wisdom in *bodhiprajñā*, the wisdom of enlightenment. But this wisdom cannot be directly spoken or written down. It is a wisdom that is carried in one's heart. It is a wisdom that is held in experience. It is a know-how, but, as such, is fragile and non-eternal. It must be kept, as it can be lost if it is not held on to. One foolish notion is enough to shut off *prajñā*. This is clearly also an example of lived knowledge. But lived knowledge need not take on any mystical properties, for as we have seen, it can have great spiritual content (enlightenment) or simple content (the playing of a song). In either case, the knowledge as lived remains the same. It is only in what such knowledge concerns that we find difference.

Now, in Western philosophy, it is generally thought that truth and knowledge are not conducive to our ends, but rather are ends in themselves. Truth and knowledge are capable of guiding and shaping our action rather than being guided and shaped by it. But for American Indian thought this is clearly not the case. Knowledge is not a thing in the world that we can discover. Knowledge is not such that if we just peer into the world long enough or just sit and think long enough, it will come to us in all of its unabated glory. Knowledge is shaped and guided by human actions, endeavors, desires, and goals. Knowledge is what we put to use. Knowledge can never be divorced from human action and experience. Thus, just because we can imagine something that we would like to know, or can formulate a question regarding, this does not mean that there is, in fact, something to know or that we have formulated an actual question. There is no imagining possible things that might be known. There is only what we actually need to know, and this is a function of our practical lives. A question is, then, real just in case it arises in relation to something directly at hand, some practical concern. It is a question that comes to us and not a question that we formulate. Knowledge is then always concerned first and foremost with what is in front of us and at our feet. Unlike Thales and Plato, American Indian philosophers see the act of displacing oneself from the world in order to do philosophy not only as unnecessary but as highly problematic, since in doing so one is only guessing whether what one is striving after is really knowledge at all and whether the questions one has formulated are even really questions.

Now, let us look at a piece of embodied and practical American Indian knowledge in context. Centuries ago, the Senecas acquired a piece of knowledge. Three sisters, corn, beans, and squash, came to them. These three sisters told them that they wished to establish relations with people. The sisters gave the people certain ceremonies and told them that if they carried out these ceremonies (that supported the continued existence of the three sisters) the sisters would become plants and feed the people. Part of this

21

requirement was that the sisters be planted and harvested together. Clearly, this relationship between the sisters and humans, and between the sisters themselves, has spiritual and philosophical significance, but for our purpose we must point out this relationship also served as an extraordinary natural cycle of nitrogen replenishment. This cycle kept the soil productive and fertile and kept the Senecas fed for centuries. European colonists came along and planted only one crop at a time in one place, corn or wheat, and the soil suffered. Many scientific experiments later, scientists discovered that this suffering was from an imbalance of nitrogen and, in effect, acquired "knowledge" (in the propositional sense) of the nitrogen cycle. Scientists create chemicals to replace the natural nitrogen. However, experiments now show that not only do such chemicals have negative effects on the soil, but also negative effects on humans (Deloria 1999: 3–16).

We can see quite clearly how this knowledge is both practical and lived, but it is still unclear how it is achieved. How did the Senecas come to this knowledge? We have already detailed a portion of our answer above. This knowledge was gained by experience. The Senecas lived with the earth and its capacity to grow food. They listened to and observed the earth in the same manner as one would listen to a song in order to learn it, as in the example above. They did not attempt to formulate abstract truths about the earth's plant-growing capacities and how best to meet the needs of the people and at the same time live in harmony with the earth. The Senecas did not formulate questions to test the earth, to see if it conformed best to this pattern or that. To do so is to not really observe, to not really listen. It is to skip the end of the process of knowledge without taking the necessary steps to achieve this end. And yet nearly all of Western philosophy and science depend on this question-asking and test-construction method. In this regard, then, American Indian philosophy seems more philosophical and less dogmatic than much of Western philosophy and science.

The knowledge the Senecas acquired was lived knowledge that came from what was directly around them and at their feet. The knowledge concerned how the people should best live. It was not based on question-formulation or hypothesis-testing, but rather on patient observation and contemplation. And yet this was not the knowledge of the nitrogen cycle but the knowledge of the ceremonies and the three sisters. If the knowledge the Senecas gained was knowledge in experience, why was it conveyed in story and passed down in that form? Here we come to another aspect of Native philosophy that differs greatly from that in the West. Literature and philosophy, science and religion are all very different branches of knowledge in Western thought. Out of these four, most consider only two, science and philosophy, to be branches of knowledge at all. The other two are thought to be entirely different ways in which humans express their being in the world. However, in American Indian thought this is not the case. None of these four can really be separated from the others. The lack of a distinction here is due, in part, to the fact that knowledge is lived. If we think of knowledge in this way, we have no reason to suppose that any of these four carve up the world in different ways, are different takes on the world. For example, literature expresses our emotional involvement with the world, religion our faith, and philosophy and science alone give us the world as it truly is, objectively. If knowledge comes from and is carried on only in experience, then there are no grounds for such a distinction.

As we have seen, American Indian philosophy is concerned with the right road for humans to walk in relation to all that is around them. We have also seen that what is right is true and what is true is right: the universe is moral. It is in this way that stories, ceremonies, and prayers speak the truth. All aspects of human expression have something to tell us about the best way for us to live. In this way, they are all philosophy. And just as American Indian medicine is best described in Western terms as magic, philosophy is, perhaps, best described as poetry. The knowledge of the earth and her capacity to grow plants and nourish humans takes the form of the story of the three sisters. This story is an expression of the knowledge of the earth that was acquired through many years of observation, much like a poem can be an expression of one's experience of a particular landscape. Because philosophy, literature, science, and religion are one in American Indian thought, we cannot truly separate the medicine from the magic nor the philosophy from the poem.

At this point, it may seem that Native knowledge is only concerned with individual, particular experience: my particular experience of a relationship with the land, my particular experience of a landscape that I express in a poem, or my particular experience of a song that I am trying to learn. It may seem that we are trying to claim that for American Indian thought there is no general knowledge. Everything is singular and held in particular experience. However, to make this move would be hasty for there are many levels of knowledge in American Indian thought. The Navajo, for example, hold that there are 12 levels of knowledge, and would say that in Western thought we work on the lower levels most of the time. There are clearly more general levels of knowledge at work even in the knowledge gained and passed on by the Senecas regarding the three sisters. But this knowledge is itself still of a practical and lived nature and it, too, is acquired through patient observation and contemplation and not by question-formulation and hypothesis-testing. This more general knowledge might be called synthesis, incorporation, or understanding. These words fit the different variations of the same general method. At the heart of any of them is a sort of grasping of general knowledge via a sort of phenomenological method.

## AMERICAN INDIAN EPISTEMOLOGY AS A PHENOMENOLOGY

American Indian philosophy finds a camaraderie with the tradition of phenomenology. Phenomenology might stand beside us in some of what we have said earlier about Western philosophy and science since phenomenology has most forcefully questioned the modern philosophical assumption of a single, wholly determinable, objective reality. Edmund Husserl, one of the founders of phenomenology, makes the claim that the accomplishments of science presuppose the pre-given world of life, the everyday world. Husserl claims, however, that almost from the beginning Western philosophy lost sight of just who we are with this pre-given world. Greek science and philosophy "saw fit to recast the idea of 'knowledge' and 'truth' in natural existence and to ascribe to the newly formed idea of 'objective truth' a higher dignity, that of a norm for all knowledge. From this arises the idea of a universal science encompassing all possible knowledge in its infinity" (Husserl 1970: 121). This becomes the foundational assumption of modern philosophy. Centuries later, Galileo asserts that only the properties of matter that are mathematically measurable, that is, size, shape, etc., are real. He claims that subjective aspects, i.e. sound, taste, and so forth, are illusory. The world can only be understood, given this, through the language of mathematics. After Descartes publishes the *Meditations* in 1641 the world becomes understood as entirely mechanical, as an entirely determinate structure governed by laws which are understandable only through mathematical analysis. This finally lays the ground for the idea of an entirely objective knowledge and an entirely objective science.

According to Husserl, however, all science and knowledge come first from the lifeworld and must always return to it. The data of science come from this world of life, and when the science is finished and the results are compiled they are also displayed in the open and uncertain domain of everyday life. The lifeworld is the ground of science, the ground of knowledge, for Husserl, and the crisis that he speaks of in *The Crisis of European Sciences and Transcendental Phenomenology* is that European science and philosophy have not acknowledged this ground. But this crisis in modern science is also a crisis of culture as it has facilitated the loss of this world for Western society.

In many ways, this very crisis that Husserl describes also facilitates a loss of American Indian philosophy. Much of this philosophy since contact has concerned itself with the possibility of a total loss of the lifeworld. However, beyond these similarities in results, there is a more important similarity in method. Phenomenology begins with a distinction between two different attitudes: the natural attitude and the phenomenological attitude. The natural attitude is the way we are ordinarily taken up with the various things in the world. We walk down the streets and pass the trees. We have conversations with our friends and talk about our jobs. What we do not do in this attitude is step back and reflect on this natural way we carry on in the world. We are, after all, taken up with our daily concerns. We have things to do and we cannot do these things if we are disengaged from this natural attitude. However, the phenomenological attitude is just this kind of disengagement. One disengages from the natural attitude and focuses instead on all that is in the natural attitude in order to reflect upon it. In this reflection all of our experiences in the natural attitude count as data to be understood. All of the phenomena must be accounted for. We then, from this reflective perspective, describe all the particular intentionalities (the ways in which we are directed to the world) of the natural attitude in order to understand the world and our place in it.

Now, from this simplified account of phenomenology, we can see a number of commonalities with what we have been given so far in American Indian philosophy. As we have seen, American Indian philosophy is quite concerned with retaining the natural attitude. This is why the Coyote stories are told and why Thales can be seen as a Coyote-like character. And yet at the same time an immediate difference is apparent. Forgetting what one is doing because one is taken up with reflection and then falling down a well sounds very much like what could happen while engaged in the phenomenological attitude. In American Indian philosophy, there is no phenomenological attitude as such. In American Indian philosophy we must *maintain* our connectedness, we must maintain our relations, and never abandon them in search of understanding, but rather find understanding *through* them.

American Indian philosophy also has a very different view on what is to count as data and what is to be done with such data. When it comes to generalities, American Indian philosophy seeks synthesis or understanding, a way of seeing the whole. Given all the observations in our experience, we *begin* to formulate a general picture. A more general knowledge *begins* to take shape through the incorporation of all the data. This means accounting for all the data even if doing so makes understanding difficult, even if there are contradictions, even if the data are messy. In Native philosophy and science, however, there are no real anomalies or contradictions (Waters 2000). Through synthesis, we only begin to paint a general picture. Anomalies are only really possible once we have finished the picture and claim that this picture represents something about the world, that is, that it gives us a general picture of the world. For Native philosophers, this would be to stop doing philosophy, to stop observing, and to make some arbitrary claim that there will be nothing else to observe. It might be said that Native philosophy is a thinking philosophy. It is a philosophy where the thinking and the observing never stop, even to formulate theories, or questions. If we never stop thinking and observing, then there will always be room for new experiences. No matter how strange these experiences may seem, they will never be contradictory since there is nothing for them to contradict; they will never be anomalous since there is no theory for them not to fit into. This process of general synthesis is just that, a process, but it is one that is never finished. In order to complete the process, we would have to stop having experiences, for anything short of that would mean ending the process before it was complete. Thus, the process is always ongoing. We must continue thinking and observing and in that way leave ourselves open to continued experience and not shut ourselves off from it in some arbitrary way.

Phenomenology accepts much of what American Indian philosophers consider the data of experience. However, it draws a line between what counts as data of experience and what does not at a rather peculiar place for the American Indian. In Western philosophy and science, generally, it is my experiences, my thoughts, and what I can observe that count as evidence or data, and nothing else. But for the American Indian philosopher to make such a break is to invoke a bias toward the individual and individual experience. This is what might be called the Cartesian bias, a bias that surely goes back much farther than Descartes to perhaps the beginnings of Western philosophy itself, but it is Descartes who gives it its clearest shape. Many philosophers think that the great bias of Western philosophy is Cartesian mind/body dualism: the notion that the mind and body are two separate substances. However, from an American Indian perspective, the real Cartesian bias is the idea that knowledge can only be acquired and manifested individually, in or by the individual. The *cogito, ergo sum* tells us, "I think, therefore I am." But Native philosophy tells us, "We are, therefore I am." A Native philosophical understanding must include all experience, not simply my own. If I am to gain a right understanding I must account for all that I see, but also all that you see and all that has been seen by others – all that has been passed down in stories. What place do I have to tell you that your experiences are invalid because I do not share them? Such a rejection only makes sense under the assumption that my experiences are somehow antecedent to yours and more basic. If it is "We" that is first and not "I," then what counts as the data of experience is quite different.

In Western thought we might say that my experiences and thoughts count more than your experiences because I have them and you cannot. But if we are *WE*, then this constraint seems rather trivial. The hand may not have the same experiences as the foot, but this hardly matters if we understand them not as feet and hands but as this body. If it is through the body, or the people, that understanding arises, then no one part need shape this understanding. All the experiences of all the parts should be brought into the process of understanding.

American Indians often say that the people are an ear of corn. We may try to just think of each little kernel of corn on the ear, the individuals, but to do so is to take away from what the kernels are: an ear of corn (Cajete 2000). On an earth that suffers each day from environmental catastrophes of tragic proportion, we would do well to learn from this thought. Western thought, philosophy, and science, have gotten us far, we suppose. We have, through technology, become nearly invincible, but we have forgotten how we are related. We desire what is eternal: eternal life, knowledge that is eternal, truth that is eternal. But are our heads not in the clouds? Have we not forgotten what is behind us and at our feet? Have we not followed Coyote and Thales down a very uncertain path toward a rather deep well? This desire for the eternal, the unchanging, through technology and philosophy – eternal life, eternal truth – are surely the desires of Coyote. Life and knowledge are not permanent, American Indian philosophy teaches us. We must continually cultivate them. But just as the ear of corn is cultivated and grows, so does it die. It does not live forever. It provides food for another generation that will carry on and grow and live and die. American Indian philosophy teaches us that to step out of this circle is to make a step on the wrong road for human beings to walk. It is to forget our relations, to forget what our elders have told us, to forget the stories of our ancestors. It is, ultimately, to forget who we are.

## REFERENCES

Cajete, Greg (2000). An ecology of Indigenous education. American Philosophy Association Pacific Division Meeting, Albuquerque, NM.

Deloria, Vine, Jr (1999). Perceptions and maturity: reflections on Feyerabend's point of view. In *Spirit and Reason*, ed. Barbara Deloria, Kristen Foehner, and Sam Scinta. Golden, CO: Fulcrum Publishing, pp. 3–16.

Husserl, Edmund (1970). *The Crisis of European Sciences and Transcendental Phenomenology*, tr. David Carr. Evanston, IL: Northwestern University Press. (Original work published 1954.)

Waters, Anne (2000). An American Indian market of philosophical discourse. American Philosophy Association Pacific Division Meeting, Albuquerque, NM.

# 3

# APPROACHES TO NATIVE AMERICAN PHILOSOPHY

*V. F. Cordova*

Philosophy, as it is practiced by philosophers, is an examination of ideas. Ideas, however, exist in a context. In order to fully understand an idea and its implications and ramifications it becomes necessary to understand the context.

Ludwig Wittgenstein, in his short piece titled "Remarks on Frazer's *Golden Bough*" (Wittgenstein 1979), points out the difficulty of understanding the ideas and beliefs of people unlike ourselves when we take an idea from one context and place it in another. James Frazer, perhaps one of the earliest practitioners of the art of explaining the acts of one culture to another, falls into the trap of taking things out of context. Frazer, according to Wittgenstein, has a problem getting out of the context of an "English parson" (1979: 65) to correctly understand the notions he is trying to explain. "All that Frazer does is to make them [the acts and practices] plausible to people who think as he does," says Wittgenstein (1979: 61). He states further: "Indeed, if Frazer's explanations did not in the final analysis appeal to a tendency in ourselves, they would not really be explanations" (1979: 66). As an example of Frazer's improper interpretation of *alien* acts or ideas, Wittgenstein offers the following comment: "Identifying one's own gods with the gods of other peoples. One convinces oneself that the names have the same meaning" (1979: 69).

In Wittgenstein's *Philosophical Investigations* (1968) we find, again, other references to the importance of understanding a context in order to properly understand that which lies outside our own context. He says: "If a lion could talk, we could not understand him" (1968: 223e). The context in which a lion lives, perhaps even his physiological makeup, might take his *meanings* totally out of our range. Before making this comment Wittgenstein uses a more familiar context, that of human beings, to point to the complexity of what we might call "cross-cultural" communication:

one human being can be a complete enigma to another. We learn this when we come into a strange country with entirely strange traditions; and, what is more, even given a mastery of the country's language. We do not *understand* the people. (And not because of not knowing what they are saying to themselves.) We cannot find our feet with them.   (1968: 223e)

Wittgenstein has accurately pointed to the fact that meanings exist in specific contexts. This is often overlooked in the new impetus to create a field called "Native American philosophy." The practitioners of the new speciality often come to the ideas drawn from Indigenous cultures with very little knowledge of the culture, or the people, from which those ideas originate. The result here is that the practitioner pulls an idea out of a particular context and attempts to fit it into an idea from within his own cultural context; or he can come to the alien perspective armed with his own concepts and attempts to find something in the other culture that matches his concept. This is the act that Wittgenstein singles out when he talks about identifying our own gods with those of others. It is very likely that there are no literal correlates between concepts drawn from different contexts. An example here would be the attempt to find out what the "Huron's concept of the soul" might be; or the attempt to find out "what god" an alien culture worships. It is more likely to be the case that there are no correlates to the terms "soul" or "god" (perhaps, even "worship") in the culture that is not our own. To insist that there is would be to commit the error of which Wittgenstein accuses Frazer: "How impossible it was for him [Frazer] to conceive of a life different from that of the England of his time!" (1979: 65).

To pretend that one can interpret a particular idea from an alien context without understanding that context is to engage in misinterpretation, i.e. to make such ideas "plausible" only to those who think like ourselves.

Does this mean that it is impossible to do what is called "Native American philosophy"? Not at all. It does require that the approaches to doing this type of philosophical examination be quite different from the usual methods and approaches. We must first of all be aware of the assumptions which we bring to such a study: assumptions such as "all people believe in a god"; or "all people act solely from self-interest"; or "humans are naturally bad." More suitable foundations for the initiation of a philosophical inquiry might begin with recognizing that all humans thus far encountered have described the world; they have described what it is to be human in that world, and they have prescribed a role for persons in that world. Cultures differ as their descriptions of the world differ. The "answers" that people create to the questions they pose about the world and themselves are in the philosophical realm of metaphysics.

One of the major obstacles to undertaking an examination of Indigenous metaphysics is the result of another assumption which the researcher brings to his study: it is assumed that metaphysics is a philosophical activity that lies outside the capabilities of anyone from other than "advanced" civilizations. An Indigenous "tribal" culture, by virtue of not being a culture like that of the "advanced" West, is presumed to be on a different level of "development." Such cultures are assumed to operate in the realm of *superstition* or *imagination* as opposed to the "higher" activities of *observation*, *experience*, and *reflection*.

That this is not the case should be borne out by the fact that numerous "tribal" peoples have managed to not only survive but thrive in very specific environments for thousands of years.

An interesting study done by G. Reichel-Dolmatoff on the Tukano Indians of the Amazon Basin bears out the intricacy of an Indigenous belief system as it relates to the specific location of the group. He titled his research, "Cosmology as ecological analysis: a view from the rain forest" (Reichel-Dolmatoff 1976). In an abstract of his article, Reichel-Dolmatoff makes the claim that "concepts of cosmology represent a blueprint for ecological adaptation and the Indians; acute awareness of the need for adaptive norms can be compared with modern systems analysis." The Tukano, it is pointed out, "have developed a set of highly adaptive behavioral rules," which among other things have allowed them to "maintain an equilibrium and to avoid frequent relocation of settlements" (1976: 307). The Tukano, on the basis of their own rules, manage to control the growth of population as well as the exploitation of their environment and interpersonal aggression. In other words, in the context of the Tukano system, they have managed to develop a cosmology and an ethical system based on an intimate, factual knowledge of their environment. Within the Tukano system there can be no doubt that there is also an epistemological base as well as a system of logic and esthetics.

When presented with Reichel-Dolmatoff's research it seems absurd to assume that Indigenous peoples operate only on superstition and imagination. It is equally absurd to believe that non-Western peoples do not engage in a wide range of "philosophical" endeavors. Wittgenstein's stress on context as a source of meaning is also borne out by Reichel-Dolmatoff's presentation of the Tukano "system." In a similar fashion, it would be necessary to understand the "cosmology" of the Navajo in order to understand what is meant when they translate a particular term from their language as "beauty." The philosopher would have to ask: What is the basis of the Navajo esthetics which underlies a claim to beauty? What, in other words, is the *context* which lends meaning to the label "beautiful?"

What is commonly presented as "Native American philosophy" is usually a reading of a particular myth or legend, and the events or characters are related to events and characters from the context of the presenter. Or a specific concept, say the concept of "balance," is taken out of its natural context and presented in a new one. A philosopher would have to ask: "in what sort of world would this concept make sense?" One should ask oneself whether the concepts of "balance" and "harmony" actually make sense when transferred over to a context in which the world is described as essentially chaotic. Where (in other words) and how does the idea of "balance" arise?

Through a focus on events or characters, or myths and legends, philosophers are ignoring what is truly a philosophical activity. They should be exploring the logic of an Indigenous language. All languages have been found to have a logical structure. Epistemological studies could be undertaken. Most English-speakers who encounter studies of the Latin languages come to realize that the term "to know" is quite different from their own: the Spanish language has *saber* and *conocer* which make distinctions between types of knowing. The ethics of a specific cultural group could be examined: is the ethical system tied to a specific definition of human *being* or *nature*? I would argue that esthetics and ethics are founded on the same principle in many Native American cultures. Who is exploring whether this is so or not?

We must, as philosophers, not lose sight of the fact that the reason for exploring alien ideas is to expand our understanding of the diversity of human thought and not to expand our own specific ways of thinking so that they encompass all others. It is common to examine the Other as a means of gaining understanding about ourselves, but we should not mistake the Other for a *mirror*. We can learn something about ourselves as well through a *contrast* with the Other.

One of the most important factors in creating a Native American philosophy is the inclusion of Native Americans in the activity. Many Native Americans, whether one wishes to believe it or not, have managed to survive the onslaughts of assimilation and outright eradication with an intact cultural identity. The Native American has, further-more, been placed in the unique situation of having to understand two very different worldviews. He has been exposed, from childhood, to competing and often contradict-ory value systems. The average Euro-American lacks this experience of competing worldviews and value systems. His "world" reinforces the dominant view; he cannot know that he exists within a self-referential system of thought.

Wittgenstein declared that his aim as a philosopher was "to shew the fly the way out of the fly-bottle" (1968: 103e). Unfortunately, I doubt that he has managed to "shew" that there is a "bottle" (the self-referential system of thought). Not, of course, from a lack of effort on his part. The Native American is in a unique position to realize that there is not only a "bottle" but several bottles. He has become expert, in order to survive, at flying in and out of two bottles.

It is, of course, much easier to explore Native American thought through early European contact accounts or from collected myths compiled by non-Native Ameri-cans on the assumption that the contemporary Native American suffers from "intellec-tual pollution" – that he represents a degraded form of an "original" type. This attitude, which is not at all uncommon, leads to a situation where the interpreter of such thought has no "peer review," that is, there are no checks and balances on the validity of his interpretations. It leads also to the situation of which Wittgenstein warns: "in the final analysis . . . [such interpretations] . . . appeal to a tendency in ourselves," which, he concludes, "would not really be explanations" (1979: 66).

A valid interpretation or explanation of Native American thought would require that the practitioner of that field explore the many facets of the cultural group he wishes to understand. It is not, perhaps, necessary to become fluent in the language but it is necessary to know at least how the language works (its structure). It would be necessary also to understand how cultural transmission occurs: Wittgenstein says, "Every human being has parents" (1969: 29e, #211). It is not uncommon to find that some "expert" in a particular Native culture has never spoken to a contemporary member of that culture. Most philosophers wishing to learn about Chinese philosophy usually examine the language and the culture or at least spend some time in the company of Chinese philosophers. The greatest bridge between cultures is the person who is schooled in the philosophies and histories of both cultures.

Today the field of Native American philosophy is dominated by non-Native Americans. Partly, this is due to a lack of Native Americans trained in philosophical methodologies, but another reason is that too often the Native American is seen as too *subjective*, too immersed in his own culture, to participate in an *objective* examination. On the other hand, the Native American who is trained in philosophical methodologies is excluded from examining or dealing with topics that are "Western" on the basis that "since he comes from outside the culture he cannot truly understand the full scope of Western thought." In the one case "subjectivity" is a flaw, in the other, a requirement! A Native American, however, with a background in philosophy – which by its present nature is necessarily a study of Western thought – is assumed to be fit to teach only Native American "philosophy." This double standard results in the situation which we have at present: any Euro-American philosopher can teach a Native American philosophy course, regardless of his qualifications to do so and very few Native American philosophers are allowed to teach Western thought, regardless of having the educational background or qualification to do so. "Qualification," in each case, means something entirely different. The ideal situation would be to include Native Americans in the philosophical endeavors of non-Native Americans in both fields – Western and Native American.

I have often heard non-Native Americans speculate about how their culture would appear to someone from "outer space." I doubt that such a view would have any different reception than the view of the Native American concerning the West receives now. Stanislaw Lem, a Russian science fiction writer, in his novel *Solaris*, postulates a truly alien intelligence which is beyond human understanding. One of the characters in the novel makes the statement that "man doesn't really want communication with the Other; he wants a mirror." He wants self-affirmation.

The person trained in the field of philosophy, regardless of his or her background, should be expected to be more thoroughly prepared to examine the ideas of any culture and to rise above mere self-affirmation. He is not, as is the missionary, looking for a ground of communication so that the Indigenous thought may be eradicated through conversion to Christianity. And he should be well enough schooled in the tradition of "open inquiry" to be aware of the assumptions that he carries with him to another culture. Some of the assumptions that the Western philosopher brings with him are: (1) the view that all human beings are operating on a common theme; (2) that non-Western peoples are a less complex from of being, less developed than Westerners; and (3) that Indigenous peoples are incapable of engaging in philosophical discussions.

The first assumption, the "common theme," leads the philosopher astray in picking and choosing bits and pieces from the alien culture to satisfy the longing for a common theme. We make things fit whether they do so, from within our own context, or not. The human species is typified by the sharing of common physical characteristics and sensory organs. This leads to many common symbolic forms drawn from sensation, but what those symbols mean is often very different in each culture. We should be prepared to ask of seemingly similar symbols: "This is what this means in my culture, what does it mean to you?" And we should be aware of why we cling to the notion that there must be a commonality of concepts. We should be open enough to realize that this approach necessarily leads to viewing different cultural perspectives as either "right" or "wrong" based on a standard which is drawn from only one culture.

The second assumption, that non-Western peoples are less complex than those of the West, is a common one: our own cultural trappings seem more complex than those of the Other simply because of our familiarity with them. A broad inspection of another culture, language, religion, values, historical sense, quickly dispels the view of the existence of "simple" cultures. It is only through an exploration of the complexity that we find the identifying characteristics of specific cultures. It is not commonly understood by most Westerners that just as a Westerner can learn to recognize the differences between, say, "Eastern" peoples, i.e., distinguish Chinese thought from Indian, so, too, can non-Westerners point to a piece of art or a page from a philosophy text and say, "This is Western." There does exist a *leitmotiv* that runs through a specific culture but it cannot be found if one simply picks up isolated bits of another culture and says, "This is just like that" (comparing an idea from one culture to an idea of another). Usually such comparisons are prefaced by, "This is a *less-developed* form of that."

The third assumption, that Indigenous peoples are not sophisticated enough to engage in philosophical discussion, particularly concerning their own concepts, is simply not true. I recently spent the better part of an afternoon discussing the implications of a single term with an Anishnawbe who spoke his language fluently. He gave me the literal translation of *engwaamizin* as "tread carefully." Some, he said, interpreted this as "be careful," but, he pointed out, it means much more than that. Unspoken, but understood, in that term is a whole worldview having to do with humans' place and effect on the universe. From my own experience, and this has been borne out through discussion with numerous other Native persons, I discovered that many of our family discussions around the kitchen table consisted of very sophisticated philosophical dialogues. Many of these discussions or dialogues revolved around trying to understand the vastly generalized terms used in the West: "love," for example, which could be used to denote one's feeling toward apple pie, country, mothers, and members of the opposite sex. We discussed also the tendency to a reification of abstract concepts as when the sacred was reified as an anthropomorphic deity; or "motion," "change," and "duration" as *things* called "time." We did not use the language of philosophers but the activity and the intent were the same.

The assumptions which serve as roadblocks to understanding the worldviews or philosophical stances of others can be overcome through methods that the philosopher has ready-to-hand: he has made a distinction between logic, epistemology, ethics, esthetics, and metaphysics. Those are the "tools" or "approaches" which should be used in attempting to analyze the thought of others; he lacks only one other "tool" – the need to concentrate, not on similarities, but on differences. It is by contrasting notions that one learns about the distinction between the self and the Other. It is those differences that go into making the Other an Other. But even here there is an assumption that must be overcome. It is generally thought, in the West, that a concentration on differences is grounds for intolerance. "We should seek out our commonalities," I often hear. And having found numerous commonalities we are still surprised when disagreements arise. The disagreements are a result of the intolerance that arises out of the need to concentrate on commonalities. True tolerance consists, not of ignoring differences, but in acknowledging them and acknowledging with equal weight that even small differences carry tremendous import. But true tolerance also requires a recognition that there may not be a vast universal, absolute, Truth (with a capital T). It may be that diversity, which appears to be the identifying characteristic of Earth's creativity, may extend to how we organize and explain our diverse experiences of the world.

The philosophic endeavor, philosophy as an *activity*, should extend its present perspective to an attempt to understand all of the possible ranges of human thought. We can take another tack on what we do as philosophers, once more, from Wittgenstein:

> If the formation of concepts can be explained by facts of nature, should we not be interested, not in grammar, but rather in that in nature which is the basis of grammar? – Our interest certainly includes the correspondence between concepts and very general facts of nature. (Such facts as mostly do not strike us because of their generality.) But our interest does not fall back upon these possible causes of the formation of concepts; we are not doing natural science; not yet natural history – since we can also invent fictitious natural history for our purpose. I am not saying: if such-and-such facts of nature were different people would have different concepts (in the sense of a hypothesis). But: if anyone believes that certain concepts are absolutely the correct ones, and that having different ones would mean not realizing something that we realize – then let him imagine certain very general facts of nature to be different from what we are used to, and the formation of concepts different from the usual ones will become intelligible to him. (1968: 230e)

Imagine, for example, that instead of a concept of "progress" we had merely a concept of "change."

## REFERENCES

Reichel-Dolmatoff, G. (1976). Cosmology as ecological analysis: a view from the rain forest. *Man: The Journal of the Royal Anthropological Institute*, n.s. 2, 3 (September). London: Royal Anthropological Institute.

Wittgenstein, Ludwig (1968). *Philosophical Investigations*, tr. G. E. M. Anscombe, 3rd edn. New York: Macmillan.

Wittgenstein, Ludwig (1969). *On Certainty*, ed. G. E. M. Anscombe and G. H. von Wright. New York: Harper and Row.

Wittgenstein, Ludwig (1979). Remarks on Frazer's *Golden Bough*. In *Wittgenstein: Sources and Perspectives*, ed. C. G. Luckhardt. New York: Cornell University Press.

# 4

# ETHICS AND UNDERSTANDING

*John DuFour*

My purpose in this chapter is to consider a particular ethical value associated with the conduct of our understandings or the conduct of our doxastic lives. The central philosophical issue, as I understand it, concerns what morally responsible believing involves. What is it to be a responsible believer? In this chapter I will offer one possible answer to that question. (I do not intend to suggest or imply that this possibility could be the sole source of ethical value associated with beliefs or understanding. Nor do I intend to explore the issue of how we can *know* that a certain belief is the ethically right one to have; nor will I suggest that the ethical value of holding a certain belief *should* be attributable to the possibility I will describe, merely that it *can* be attributable.)

There has been, and still is, an Indigenous concern about an acceptable route of arrival at what one understands or believes. This concern has yielded a noticeable coupling of ethical and broadly epistemic concerns. Gregory Cajete wrote: "no body of knowledge exists for its own sake outside the moral framework of understanding" (Cajete 2000: 76). In this chapter I will address that idea and briefly explore a relationship between epistemology and ethics indicated in certain texts about Indigenous ways of understanding. I am going to describe a theoretical approach that, I believe, will further clarify some of that relationship.

Manu Aluli Meyer, writing about a Native Hawaiian view of understanding and knowledge, claims:

> how one experiences the environment plays a huge role in how the world is understood and defined, and this experience is nursed and fed via cultural practice, belief, and values.   (Meyer 1998: 39)

A similar point is made by E. S. C. Handy and M. K. Pukui (cited in Meyer 1998): one's understanding or belief can originate in a "concrete and tangible complex or psychological sequence involving sensation–emotion–observation–interpretation–rationalization" (Meyer 1998: 39). I want to follow up on the insight that formation (or maintenance) of belief or understanding can be grounded in certain kinds of practices.

What practices? There are some traditional answers. Arthur Amiotte, describing his understanding of a "Northern Lakota" Sun Dance ceremony, asserted:

> the Sun Dance is probably the most formal of all learning and teaching experiences. Inherent in the Sun Dance itself is the total epistemology of a people. It tells us of their values, their ideals, their hardships, their sacrifice, their strong and unerring belief in something ancient.   (Amiotte 1987: 84)

And Raymond DeMaillie wrote:

> But ritual was not merely a reflection of belief; it was also a means to further belief, for through ritual a person came to expand his knowledge.   (DeMaillie 1987: 33–4)

Both Amiotte and DeMaillie express a concern that is broadly epistemic, that is, with extending one's understanding via some "concrete and tangible complex," such as a ritual or ceremony. "The ceremonies themselves become ways of coming to know, of understanding," Cajete writes (2000: 81). Rudolph Ryser notes that "through the cultural practices of each distinct people, individual human beings come to know their personal identities and learn to know truth" (Ryser 1998: 27). If these authors are correct, if systematized thinking about understanding or belief involves social practices, then if we are concerned about particular normative merits for belief or understanding, such merits will probably be rooted in such organized social practices.

In addition to possible merits that reflect a distinctively epistemic issue (concerned solely with truth or explanation), I think we will also find merits that reflect a concern for the moral good. For instance, the way of understanding Meyer alludes to, if acceptably implemented, results in "empowered" and "meaningful" beliefs, as she put it, which in turn can be considered meritorious (my word) because of the ways they promote and ground values and community (Meyer 1998: 40). The linking of an organized origination space of belief or understanding, the "concrete and tangible complex" (a Sun Dance for example), an acceptable implementation of it, and a concern for values and community, seems to be a result of situating understanding and beliefs in a context other than distinctively epistemic concerns. The context, I believe, is one of morality and understanding.

The point will become clearer, I hope, if we rely on a distinction between a truth-relevant merit that the content of a belief (or understanding) may have and an ethical merit that the *state* of believing (or understanding) may have. Let us name the first kind of merit *content merit* and the second *state merit*. Consider the following illustration of this distinction.

Suppose Phillip of California believed "the only good Indian is a dead Indian." His belief, considered as a multiform disposition, will therefore be expressed in his life in a great variety of ways. Such pervasiveness is part of what worries and motivates us to morally evaluate his belief: he shouldn't believe that. The "should" in the previous sentence refers to an ethical responsibility that I believe Phillip has.

On the one hand, with respect to the content of his belief, it lacks content merit. The content lacks all or some of the following characteristics: reasonable, sufficient, or relevant evidence for its truth. (I don't believe it is necessary to defend this assumption.)

On the other hand, given that Phillip formed that belief on the basis of prejudice, a morally unacceptable process, he would lack state merit also. State merit, for the purposes of this essay, concerns the ethical acceptability of the way one came to understand or believe, the basis upon which one formed a belief, or the process by which one came to believe something and by which one claims that understanding has been furthered. In short, "state merit" will refer to the *ethical* acceptability of how one came to understand, know, or believe something and "content merit" will refer to the *epistemic* acceptability of the content.

Failure to distinguish these merits can lead to confusion. For example, suppose F proposes a principle for the legitimacy of holding a particular belief, one that concerns the ethical legitimacy of the process of forming a belief. Someone D may take it to be a principle of content merit, that is, as a proposal for, say, what it is that divides knowledge from mere opinion. Any ensuing criticism for the failure of the principle to clarify what knowledge is would thus miss the point of it.

It ought to be clear that state and content merit can interact in various ways. For instance, it is possible for someone to have state merit with respect to a particular belief whose content, however, lacks content merit. And vice versa is possible. Ignoring, however, for the moment the various possible interactions between the two sorts of merits, the point with respect to practices is this: state merit can be systematically associated with certain social practices that embody an amalgamation of ethical and epistemic concerns. This is something, I think, that we find to be the case in some Indigenous social practices, a Dakota Sun Dance for instance.

The sort of social practice embodying ethical and epistemic concerns, and which is the basis for determining state merit of beliefs or understanding, is what I call a "belief practice." This complex social practice concerned with understanding or beliefs can be characterized along Schatzkian lines (see Schatzki 1996: 88–110). We should expect to find the practice organized along three dimensions specifically concerned with the way we conduct our ways of coming to believe or understand.

First, experienced participants in the practice possess understandings of what acts belong to the practice and how to perform and respond to those acts themselves. Experienced participants typically would be able to specify those understandings propositionally, but there is also a significant understanding that in itself may defy propositional specification.

The second way a belief practice is organized would be by explicit principles, rules, customs, considerations, or instructions. For example, with respect to a solely epistemic belief practice (one concerned solely with truth–relevant merits) a not uncommon principle is that one should believe only to the degree one's evidence warrants (e.g. Hume 1955; Locke 1987; Feldman 2000). Such a principle, however, may be interpreted ethically, and arguments have been advanced that it is in fact an ethical principle (Lewis 1955; Blanshard 1974; Clifford 1986). We may find principles or customs among Indigenous belief practices speaking to similar concerns over one's understandings. For instance, a Dakota traditionalist may carry on the custom of having one's pipe acknowledged by spirits, which may very well be an integral part of a belief practice concerned with furthering understanding about something (or finding out about something). We may also find explicit principles or considerations such as "pray as much as you can," or "never leave the fire unattended" that are integrally associated with the concern to find out about something.

A third way a belief practice is organized is according to particular goals, projects, tasks, or appropriate emotions, feelings, and dispositions. For instance, in trying to understand something by participation in a sweatlodge ceremony, an appropriate disposition or feeling involves important elements of seriousness, sincerity, and care.

Now what does all this have to do with state or content merit? We may perceive certain needs with respect to our understandings and beliefs, such as when we see that a belief is morally repugnant and ought to be changed: or there may be something we wish to find out more about, that is, we wish to learn or form beliefs about something. A belief practice, organized along lines described above, would thus be the socially (or community) established and organized way of trying to meet such ethical or epistemic needs with respect to beliefs and understandings.

One philosophical concern may spring immediately to mind. There may be a problem about the voluntariness of belief for this approach to moral evaluations of beliefs. If the belief practice view that I have described assumes that we can legitimately evaluate beliefs by a moral "ought" (one expressing moral obligation and cited in order to get someone to do something voluntarily), that would seem to render such evaluations pointless. For if it is true that we by and large lack control of belief formation, as arguably seems the case, under the assumption that "ought" implies "can," there would be little point to saying that I ought to believe that $p$ when I have no ability to do that.

However, I believe that this problem can be avoided in a natural way by this approach. For practitioners of the belief practice, the obligation with respect to belief is not to decide to believe that $p$; rather, the obligation really concerns one's *attempts* to acceptably implement the practice that relevantly surrounds $p$. There would thus be no suggestion that I choose to believe that $p$; rather, the point of saying, for example, "You ought to believe that $p$" would be that I perform certain actions specified by the belief practice appropriate to dealing with believing that $p$. (This should become clearer through consideration of the example below.)

The focus on appropriate implementation of a practice one has not participated in, or, having participated, to do so in an acceptable way, can clearly be an ethical concern. The beliefs that we have influence our communities in significant ways. Suppose someone $x$ is in charge of distributing cans of turkey to members of his community. However, $x$ has noticed a pattern: many of the cans are rusty and dented. It seems possible that those defects could affect the quality of the turkey in the cans.

Nevertheless, $x$ is pressured to distribute the cans and, putting his worries aside, comes to believe that the turkey is fine to eat. Clearly, if just one of those cans contains bad turkey, $x$ is culpable in some way for holding the belief that the turkey is fine to eat. Or, another example, suppose that I sloppily and lazily read books on racism. My uninformed ideas on racist acts may lead me to believe that an acquaintance $y$ of mine was *not* the victim of a racist act, when in fact she was. My carelessly formed beliefs about racist acts played no small role in the formation of my belief that $y$ wasn't a victim. I may tell a friend of mine $z$, who is an attorney, about my belief that $y$ was not a victim of a racist act. As a consequence $z$ decides not to represent $y$ when asked for legal assistance. Some wrong has been brought about, and my carelessly formed belief played a sad role in helping to bring it about.

In similar ways, many other beliefs may influence one's acquaintances, who in turn influence others for good or bad. Because a belief may be regarded as a multiform disposition emerging into action and expressed in a variety of ways (see Price 1967), and since a belief appears to pervade one's life or perspective, it seems to me that proper care of and concern for one's beliefs ought to be of great significance, not only to the believer but to the community the person belongs to. The beliefs we hold could significantly contribute to fragmentation or harmonization of community. Our beliefs are therefore of social concern. It seems to follow that we ought to take care with respect to our beliefs or understandings. A belief practice thus could embody the community's moral concern for the proper care we should take with respect to what we claim to believe and understand.

It is far from arrogant to regard belief, or someone's understanding, as an appropriate object of normative or moral judgments. It seems to make sense to say it is wiser to believe this rather than that, or to hold that some people are wise, or wiser in certain respects, precisely because of what they understand or believe and because of how they came to understand or believe what they understand and believe. The belief practice perspective makes sense of this attitude in a specific, explicit, and organized way. A belief practice yields a particular normative assessment and understanding of whether and how one came to acceptably believe or understand something.

Another way to put this is that state merit is a socially recognized normative entitlement to belief or understanding. (For ease of reference, call such entitled belief or understanding "balanced.") The social recognition relies on the legitimizing of one's understanding by reference to whether one engaged an appropriately relevant belief practice or not when one should have. The moral legitimacy also essentially depends on whether one has engaged the relevant belief practice acceptably, given that one has engaged it (see Wolterstorff 1995: 272ff.; DuFour 2001, ch. 7).

As Schatzki has suggested, and as we can readily observe, the normativity of belief practices emerges via acts of experienced practitioners. Those new to the practice, whatever it may be specifically, are initiated into it and kept "in line" by reference, among other things, to the understandings, recommendations, assessments, and encouragements of those well experienced in the practice in question (see Schatzki 1996: 101). Claims to knowledge or understanding, formation of belief, maintenance of belief, and change of belief or refusal to change belief, when divorced from an acceptable implementation of a relevant belief practice, need not be admirable from this perspective. In fact, such claims or acts are ethically objectionable, and perhaps ought to be avoided.

Similarly, the acquisition of limited understandings on important subjects, because divorced from relevant belief practices, could be a legitimately culpable activity. The value placed on balanced belief or understanding is perhaps owing to a concern for the appropriate place of understanding or belief in a well-lived life, a life of balance or harmony. Such a concern is evident among some Dakota traditions. Cajete (2000: 76), in the context of articulating his view of a "Native philosophy of science," put the point this way:

> Concerned about the ethical aspects of knowledge, environmental observation, and understanding received from visions, ceremonies, and spirits, Native scientific philosophy reflects an inclusive and moral universe. No body of knowledge exists for its own sake outside the moral framework of understanding.

The "moral framework," I suggest, is just the context of a determination of what distinguishes morally acceptable from unacceptable beliefs or understanding by reference to an appropriately relevant belief practice.

Consider what Cajete says in the following:

> Commitment to gain and share knowledge is an important aspect of Native science since deep knowledge of nature brings with it responsibilities in its application and sharing. It is a "given" in Native traditions that deep knowledge is not easily gained and requires time and dedication to attain. Sanction and commitment are also connected to ethics, or the care and attitude in which important knowledge is gained and shared. . . . Knowledge among Indigenous people is acquired in a completely different way [from "Western objectified science"], but the coming-to-know process is nevertheless extremely systematic. For example, certain processes must occur in a particular order. . . . Like Western science, Indigenous science is sequential and builds on previous knowledge. But in Native traditions, guides or teachers – individuals who have gone that way before – are necessary. (Cajete 2000: 72–3, 80–1)

With the notion of a practice-associated merit for belief or understanding, i.e. practice-assisted balance, we can see why, for instance, Cajete links the ideas of "sanction" and "commitment" to ethical concerns over the place of knowledge, why the mention of "guides or teachers," and why it is important to note the systematic character of how one comes to further understanding. I think it is clear that, at the very least, he alludes to the value placed on the merit of balanced understanding, a normative, if not distinctively ethical, merit essentially a product of acceptably implementing a belief practice.

I believe it is reasonable to claim, therefore, that there has been, and is, an Indigenous concern about an ethical route of arrival at what one understands or believes, and that this concern yields a significant association of ethical and broad epistemic concerns. One's understanding is balanced insofar as it is a reflection of the imprimatur of a belief practice.

(Although my focus is the morality involved with the conduct of our understanding and belief formations or changes, one could, I think, draw a potentially illuminating analogy to contextualist theories of epistemology. According to such theories, standards for what counts as knowing are relative to the context of either the subject that claims to know or the attributor of knowledge claims (see DeRose 1999). The interesting point, at least for my purposes, is that the various features of the relevant context of implementation of a belief practice, by analogy, determine the standards for what counts as ethically acceptable or legitimate understanding or belief.

One last point: for help or encouragement I would like to thank Ladonna Bravebull Allard, William Bravebull, Viola Cordova, John Hurley, J. L. Vest, Anne Waters, and especially Gregory Cajete.

# REFERENCES

Amiotte, Arthur (1987). The Lakota Sun Dance: historical and contemporary perspectives. In *Sioux Indian Religion: Tradition and Innovation*, ed. Raymond J. DeMaillie and Douglas R. Parks. Norman and London: University of Oklahoma Press, pp. 75–89.

Blanshard, Brand (1974). *Reason and Belief*. London: George Allen and Unwin.

Cajete, Gregory (2000). *Native Science: Natural Laws of Interdependence*. Santa Fe, NM: Clear Light.

Clifford, William K. (1986). The ethics of belief. In *The Ethics of Belief Debate*, ed. Gerald D. McCarthy. Atlanta, GA: Scholars Press, pp. 19–36.

DeMaillie, Raymond J. (1987). Lakota belief and ritual in the nineteenth century. In *Sioux Indian Religion: Tradition and Innovation*, ed. Raymond J. DeMaillie and Douglas R. Parks. Norman and London: University of Oklahoma Press, pp. 25–43.

DeRose, Keith (1999). Contextualism: an explanation and defense. In *The Blackwell Guide to Epistemology*, ed. John Greco and Ernest Sosa. Malden, MA, and Oxford: Blackwell, pp. 187–205.

DuFour, John (2001). Ethics of Belief: Morality and the Will to Believe (PhD dissertation, Yale University). UMI Bell and Howell Information and Learning, Publication no. 9991146.

Feldman, Richard (2000). The ethics of belief. *Philosophy and Phenomenological Research*, 60: 667–95.

Handy, E. S. C. and Pukui, M. K. (1972). *The Polynesian Family System in Ka'u, Hawai'i*. Tokyo: Charles E. Tuttle.

Hume, David (1955). *An Inquiry Concerning Human Understanding*. Indianapolis and New York: Bobbs Merrill.

Lewis, C. I. (1955). *The Ground and Nature of the Right*. New York: Columbia University Press.

Locke, John (1987). *An Essay Concerning Human Understanding*, ed. Peter H. Nidditch. Oxford: Clarendon Press.

Meyer, Manu Aluli (1998). Native Hawaiian epistemology: exploring Hawaiian views of knowledge. *Cultural Survival Quarterly*, 22: 38–40.

Price, H. H. (1967). *Belief*. London: Allen and Unwin.

Ryser, Rudolph C. (1998). Observations on "Self" and "Knowing." In *Tribal Epistemologies: Essays in the Philosophy of Anthropology*, ed. Helmut Wautischer. Aldershot: Ashgate, pp. 17–29.

Schatzki, Theodore R. (1996). *Social Practices: A Wittgensteinian Approach to Human Activity and the Social*. Cambridge: Cambridge University Press.

Wolterstorff, Nicholas (1995). *Divine Discourse: Philosophical Reflections on the Claim that God Speaks*. Cambridge: Cambridge University Press.

## FURTHER READING

Clifford, William K. (1901). *Lectures and Essays*, 2 vols., ed. Leslie Stephen and Sir Frederick Pollock. London: Macmillan.

DeRose, Keith (2000). Ought we to follow our evidence? *Philosophy and Phenomenological Research*, 60: 697–706.

Gale, Richard (1980). William James and the ethics of belief. *American Philosophical Quarterly*, 17: 1–14.

McGaa, Ed, Eagle Man (1995). *Native Wisdom: Perception of the Natural Way*. Minneapolis: Four Directions Publishing.

Phillips, Winfred George (1991). Blanshard's ethics of belief and metaphysical postulates. *Religious Studies*, 27: 139–56.

# Part III

# SCIENCE, MATH, LOGIC

# 5

# PHILOSOPHY OF NATIVE SCIENCE

*Gregory Cajete*

In the conceptual framework of philosophy, Native American science may be said to be based upon perceptual phenomenology, the philosophical study of phenomena. The central premise of phenomenology roots the entire tree of knowledge in the soil of direct physical and perceptual experience of the earth. From a phenomenological viewpoint, all sciences are earth-based. In Abram's words: "Every theoretical and scientific practice grows out of and remains supported by the forgotten ground of our directly felt and lived experience, and has value and meaning only in reference to this primordial and open realm" (Abram 1996: 43).

Edmund Husserl, the original promulgator of phenomenology, believed that lived experience, or the "lifeworld," was the ultimate source of human knowledge and meaning. The lifeworld evolves through our experience from birth to death and forms the basis for our explanation of reality before we rationalize it into categories of facts and apply scientific principles. In other words, it is *subjective* experience that forms the basis for the *objective* explanation of the world.

The lifeworld, a vast ocean of direct human experience that lies below all cultural mediation, forms a foundation of Native science. Husserl described it as culturally relative, diverse and different for each culture and each person because it is based on the experienced world of distinct peoples who evolve in distinct places and describe themselves and their surroundings in distinct languages. Yet, there is a unity in such diversity derived from the fact that humans share a species-specific experience and knowledge of nature. Humans also share an experience of nature with all other living things, although our perceptions are different from those of other species because of our unique physical biology. Metaphoric for a wide range of tribal processes of perceiving, thinking, acting and "coming to know" that have evolved through human experience with the natural world, Native science is born of a lived and storied participation with natural landscape and reality. Current cultural concepts of time, space, relationships, and linguistic forms are rooted in this precultural biological awareness.

Native American philosophy of science has always been a broad-based ecological philosophy, based not on rational thought alone, but also incorporating to the highest degree all aspects of interactions of "man in and of nature," i.e. the knowledge and truth gained from interaction of body, mind, soul, and spirit with all aspects of Nature. As all knowledge originates in a people's culture, its roots lie in cosmology, that contextual foundation for philosophy, a grand guiding story, by nature speculative, in that it tries to explain the universe, its origin, characteristics, and essential nature. Any attempt to explain the story of the cosmos is also metaphysical as the method of research always stems from a cultural orientation, a paradigm of thinking that has a history in some particular tradition. Therefore, there can be no such thing as a fully objective story of the universe.

Their cosmology, a people's deep-rooted, symbolically expressed understanding of "humanness," predates all other human-structured expressions, including religion and social and political orders. The first cosmologies were built with the perception that the spirit of the universe resided in the earth and things of the earth, including human beings. A people's understanding of the cycles of nature, behavior of animals, growth of plants, and interdependence of all things in nature determined their culture, that is, ethics, morals, religious expression, politics, and economics. The people came to know and to express a "natural democracy," in which humans are related and interdependent with plants, animals, stones, water, clouds, and everything else.

According to Husserl, there is a kind of "associative empathy" between humans and other living things which is grounded in the physical nature of bodies. The creative body and all that comprises it – mind, body, and spirit – is the creative, moving center of Native science. Although this may seem common sense, modern thinking abstracts the mind from the human body and the body of the world. This modern orientation frequently disconnects Western science from the lived and experienced world of nature. The disassociation becomes most pronounced at the level of perception, because our perceptions orient us in the most elemental way to our surroundings. Receptivity to our surroundings combined with creativity characterizes our perception.

Indigenous people are people of place, and the nature of place is embedded in their language. The physical, cognitive, and emotional orientation of a people is a kind of "map" they carry in their heads and transfer from generation to generation. This map is multidimensional and reflects the spiritual as well as the mythic geography of a people.

Knowing the origins of their people, their place, and the all-important things the place contains is considered essential orientation for a tribal person. A people's origin story maps and integrates the key relationships with all aspects of the landscape.

The metaphor of the body is often used by tribes to describe themselves: not just the physical body, but the mind-body that experiences and participates in the world, as well as their communities, social organization, and important relationships in the world. Indeed, humans and the natural world interpenetrate one another at many levels, including in the air we breathe, the carbon dioxide we contribute to the food we transform, and the chemical energy we transmute at every moment of our lives from birth to death. "Ultimately, to acknowledge the life of the body, and affirm our solidarity with this physical form, is to acknowledge our existence as one of earth's animals, and so to remember and rejuvenate the organic basis of our thoughts and our intelligence" (Abram 1996: 47).

Native science is a broad term that can include metaphysics and philosophy, art and architecture, practical technologies, and agriculture, as well as ritual and ceremony practiced by Indigenous peoples past and present. More specifically, Native science encompasses such areas as astronomy, farming, plant domestication, plant medicine, animal husbandry, hunting, fishing, metallurgy, geology – studies related to plants, animals, and natural phenomena, yet may extend to include spirituality, community, creativity, and technologies which sustain environments and support essential aspects of human life. It may even include exploration of such questions as the nature of language, thought, and perception, the movement of time and space, the nature of human knowing and feeling, the nature of the human relationship to the cosmos – questions related to natural reality. The collective heritage of human experience with the natural world, Native science is a map of natural reality drawn from the experience of thousands of human generations. It has given rise to the diversity of human technologies, even to the advent of modern mechanistic science.

Phenomenology parallels the approach of Native science in that it provides a viewpoint based on our innate human experience within nature. Native science strives to understand and apply the knowledge gained from participation in the here and now, and emphasizes our role as one of nature's members rather than as striving to be in control of it.

Our universe is still unfolding and human beings are active and creative participants. Creativity is both the universe's ordering principle and its process, part of the greater flow of creativity in nature. It flows from the "implicate order" or inherent potential of the universe, and whatever it produces becomes a part of the "explicate order" of material or energetic expressions. These expressions range from entire galaxies to the quarks and leptons of the subatomic world. Human creativity is located in this immense continuum. We are, after all, a microcosm of the macrocosm. We are an expression of the nature within us, a part of a greater generative order of life that is ever-evolving. It is from this creative, generative center of human life that central principles of Native science emanate (Briggs and Peat 1999: 28–30).

An understanding of the nature of creativity is important for gaining insight. Native science embraces the inherent creativity of nature as the foundation for both knowledge and action. Human life at all levels is wholly a creative activity and may be said to be an expression of the nature within us with regard to "seeking life," the most basic of human motivations since it is connected to our natural instinct for survival and self-preservation.

The concepts of creativity: *chaos, participation, and metaphoric thinking*, lend themselves specifically to the way in which Native peoples envision the *process* of science. They also form a conceptual bridge between Native and Western science, although Native science refers to them differently through particular cultural representations in story, art, and ways of community. These theories and their connections to quantum physics have brought Western science closer to understanding nature as Native peoples have always understood it – that is, not simply as a collection of objects, but rather as a dynamic, ever-flowing river of creation inseparable from our own perceptions, the creative center from which we and everything else have come and to which we always return.

*Chaos* is both movement and evolution, the process through which everything in the universe becomes manifest and then returns. The flux, or ebb and flow, of chaos appears in everything and envelops us at all times and in all places. From the evolving universe to the mountain to the human brain, chaos is the field from which all things come into being. It plays a central role in the creation of the universe, the earth, and humankind in the mythology of all ancient cultures. Chaos and its offspring, creativity, are the generative forces of the universe.

*Chaos theory* describes the way nature makes new forms and structures out of the potential of the great void. It also represents the unpredictability and relative randomness of the creative process, appearing in mythology throughout the world in stories of the trickster – the sacred fool whose antics remind us of the essential role of disorder in the creation of order.

There is an ordering or self-organizing process that results from chaos, called "order for free." A simple example may be found in the boiling of water. As water is heated, the water at the bottom of a saucepan starts to rise to the top while cooler water at the top moves to the bottom. This causes a turbulence which takes the form of boiling water or, as a chaos theorist might describe it, the water in the pan exercises its "maximum degree of freedom." In other words, the water in the closed system of the saucepan is exercising the maximum range of behavior available to it. However, if the water is brought slowly to the point just before boiling, something interesting and characteristic of chaotic systems occurs. The water self-organizes into a pattern of vortices. This is called the "bifurcation point," the point just before the system transforms itself, in this case, to boiling water. The bifurcation point is the direct result of the interaction of "positive feedback," which amplifies the transformation to boil, and "negative feedback," which dampens the transformation. These tendencies interact to create a stable pattern of vortices.

This moment, the bifurcation point, when a truth comes to be intuitively known is like the still point in the eye of a hurricane; it is that point when a connection is made to a natural principle manifesting itself in the unfolding of a natural process. Like the birth of a child or a bolt of lightning connecting sky and earth for a moment in time, these are the infinite moments of both chaos and order. This is a precept of Native science, for truth is not a fixed point, but rather an ever-evolving point of balance, perpetually created and perpetually new.

In nature, all systems of energy transformation exhibit a similar kind of behavior. The survival of any self-organizing system depends upon its ability to keep itself open to the flow of energy and matter through it. This necessity may last a millionth of a second or billions of years, as is the case with the universe.

Self-organization or "creativity" out of the field of chaos occurs everywhere in nature. Random interstellar gases and electromagnetic fields of radiation self-organize to form galaxies and star systems. The interaction of rain with the earth's geological landscape leads to the vast patterns of rivers and streams that form drainage systems. Birds or insects fly in perfect unison.

Then there is the notion of subtle influences, or the "butterfly effect" in chaos theory. In chaotic systems, even small things turn out to have large-scale effects over a period of time. For example, if we look at weather we see a recurring climatic pattern over a long period of time. However, if we examine details we see that weather is in constant flux due to the bifurcating and amplifying activity of a host of subtle effects. In a weather system, everything is interconnected. Positive and negative feedback loops are in constant motion, and somewhere in the system, a "butterfly" loop may cause slight changes. Sooner or later one of these loops is amplified, and we see a dramatic and unpredictable shift in the pattern. The butterfly effect may be called chance, but it is really the cumulative influence of a small change in a system. It may be an increase or decrease of temperature in a weather pattern, an individual such as Gandhi taking a stand against oppression, or a Native prayer, song, dance, or ritual to bring rain to a parched land. In the world of chaos, anything is possible.

Chaos theory shows that everything is related, everything has an effect, and that even small things have an influence. In a postmodern society ruled by an obsession with control, we as individuals may feel powerless, but each of us may subtly influence the course of any system, including those that seem to be the most intractable.

Chaos theory offers insight into human creativity. Embodied in the human mind and body, it is chaos that allows humans the ability to respond creatively to constant changes in the environment. Our instinctual ability to "flow" with the stream of chaos and creativity leads us metaphorically to the "vortices" of individual and collective truth. What is true from this viewpoint is that the experience of the moment of balance inherent in chaos, like that point at which water, not quite boiling, forms vortices. Human "butterfly power" resides in our ability to create.

At its highest levels of expression, Native science is a system of pathways for reaching this perpetually moving truth or "spirit." This understanding of the creative nature of the world and of human beings is reflected in the core beliefs of Native thought, life, and tradition.

The quality and nature of human life are the result of human consciousness, or the influences of our experiences, perceptions, language, and society. Consciousness consists of an open system, and is "created," in that this system is constantly being influenced by the forces of chaos expressed through us and by us at the individual and collective levels. Herein lies the true power of individual and collective creativity and its subtle power to influence the entire world. This is the basis of the precept of Native science that a single individual's vision may transform a society, or that a rain dance done properly, with one mind, can bring rain. Hence, Native science is a reflection of *creative participation*, a dance with chaos and her child, the creative spirit (Briggs and Peat 1999: 5–22).

We cannot help but participate with the world. Whether we acknowledge and are creatively open to the perceptions that will result, or remain oblivious to its influence and creative possibilities toward deeper understanding, is our decision. Native science continually relates to and speaks of the world as full of *active* entities with which people engage. This active perceptual engagement with the animate world was termed the *participation mystique* by French anthropologist Lucien Lévy-Bruhl to describe "the animistic logic of indigenous, oral peoples for whom ostensibly 'inanimate' objects like stones or mountains are often thought to be alive and from whom certain names, spoken out loud, may be felt to influence the things or beings that they name, for whom particular plants, particular animals, particular places, persons and powers may all be felt to 'participate' in one another's existence, influencing each other and being influenced in return" (Lévy-Bruhl 1985, in Abram 1996: 57).

The word "animism" perpetuates a modern prejudice, a disdain, and a projection of inferiority toward the worldview of Indigenous peoples. But if, as the French phenomenologist, Merleau-Ponty contends, perception at its most elemental expression in the human body is based on participation with our surroundings, then it can be said that "animism" is a basic human trait common to both Indigenous and modern sensibilities. Indeed, all humans are animists.

It may also be said that we all use *the metaphoric mind* to describe, imagine, and create from the animate world with which we constantly participate. Just as the focus on participation in Native science brings forth creative communion with the world through our senses, so too the application of the metaphoric mind brings forth the descriptive and creative "storying" of the world by humans. Science in every form is a story of the world. In Native contexts, participation and the use of metaphor may result in a story, song, dance, new technology, or even a vision, ritual, or ceremony.

The metaphoric or nature mind of humans is our oldest mind and has been evolving for approximately three million years. Its time of greatest development probably occurred during the Paleolithic era about 70,000 years ago. Paralleling its collective evolution, the metaphoric mind in the individual develops from birth to about the time a child begins to learn language. When language is developed and used extensively, the holistic experience of the metaphoric mind begins to get chopped up and labeled, until, eventually, it recedes into the subconscious. Yet the metaphoric mind remains very important in continued development because it encompasses the perceptual, creative, and imaginative experience of a person's inner world.

Language is our symbolic code for representing the world that we perceive with our senses. Meaning is not connected solely to intellectual definition but to the life of the body and spirit of the speaker. At the deeper psychological level, language is sensuous, evocative, filled with emotion, meaning and spirit. In its holistic and natural sense, language is animate and animating, it expresses our living spirit through sound and the emotion with which we speak. In the Native perspective, language exemplifies our communion with Nature.

As the rational mind develops and the metaphoric mind recedes into the subconscious, there to lie in wait until its special skills are called upon by the conscious mind, it emerges to be used in creative play and imaginative reverie, or in dreams and stories.

As the rational mind develops further and language becomes literacy, the metaphoric mind becomes significantly differentiated from the rational mind and that of social conditioning.

This differentiation has become compounded in Western society with its overt focus on scientific rationalism. Despite the conscious separation of the metaphoric mind from the rational, both minds work together when the conditioning of separation is suspended during creative play, meditation, ritual, or other modes of spontaneous thinking. In Native societies, the two minds of human experience are typically given more balanced regard. Both minds are respected for what they allow people to do, yet the metaphoric mind remains the first foundation of Native science.

Connected to the creative center of nature, the metaphoric mind has none of the limiting conditioning of the cultural order. Its processing is natural and instinctive; it perceives itself as part of the natural order, a part of the earth mind, inclusive and expansive in its processing of experience and knowledge. It invented the rational mind, and the rational mind in turn invented language, the written word, abstraction, and eventually the disposition to control nature rather than to be of nature. But this propensity of the rational mind also leads to the development of anthropocentric philosophy and of a science that would legitimize the oppression of nature, its elder brother, the metaphoric mind.

Because its processes are tied to creativity, perception, image, physical senses, and intuition, the metaphoric mind reveals itself through abstract symbols, visual/spatial reasoning, sound, kinesthetic expression, and various forms of ecological and integrative thinking. The facilitator of the creative process, it invents, integrates, and applies the deep levels of human perception and intuition to the task of living. Understanding Native science begins with developing the creative ability to decode layers of meaning embedded in symbols that have been used for thousands of years and are used artistically and linguistically to depict structures and relationship to places. These metaphoric modes of expression are the foundations for various components of Native science, as well as of art, music, and dance. The metaphoric mind underpins the numerous ecological foundations of knowledge and has been specifically applied in creating the stories that make up the complex forms of oral traditions. As the greatest source of metaphor comes from nature, these stories are filled with analogies, characters, and representations drawn from nature, metaphors that more often than not refer back to the processes of nature from which they are drawn, or to human nature, which they attempt to reflect.

## PROCESS OF NATIVE SCIENCE

The perspective of Native science goes beyond objective measurement, honoring the primacy of direct experience, interconnectedness, relationship, holism, quality, and value. Its definition is based on its own merits, conceptual framework, and practice and orientation in the tribal contexts in which it is expressed. Concerned with the processes and energies within the universe, it continually deals in systems of relationships and their application to the life of the community. Science is integrated into the whole of life and being and provides a basic schema and basis for action.

Meaning and understanding were the priorities of Native science, rather than a need to predict and control. People were interested in finding the proper, ethical, and moral paths upon which human beings should walk. Meaningful relationship and an understanding of one's responsibilities to those entities in nature that people depended on were the reasons for a Native science, which invited the energies and animating power of nature. Native symbols go beyond simple energies and the animating power of nature, beyond simple archetypes, for they attempt to represent the universe itself, as in a ceremonial structure like the Navajo hogan.

As co-creators with nature, everything we do and experience has importance to the rest of the world. We cannot misexperience anything, we can only misinterpret what we experience. It must be emphasized that what we think and believe, and how we act in the world impacts on literally everything. We humans bring our reality into being by our thoughts, actions, and intentions; hence, the focus of Native traditions on prayer to bring about and perpetuate life. Native science is about creating the inner sensibilities of humans, or the inner ear, which hears the subtle voice of nature.

No body of knowledge exists for its own sake outside the moral framework of understanding. The information gained through experience is considered in interpreting our relationship with the natural world, thereby pointing to the kind of "story" that might contain and convey that information. Concerned about the ethical aspects of knowledge, environmental observation, and understanding received from visions, ceremonies, and spirits, Native scientific philosophy reflects an inclusive and moral universe. Methodological elements and tools of Native science include:

> **Causality**: Native science reflects a belief in causes that affect and go beyond the physical, principles such as synchronicity and the action of natural energies and entities. Other such principles include the transformation of energy to other forms and resonance with the order of the universe, as reflected in the adage, "as above so below."
>
> **Instrumentation**: Native science relies on preparation of the mind, body, and spirit of each person as the primary vehicle of "coming to know," the best translation for education in Native traditions. A coming-to-know, a coming-to-understand, metaphorically entails a journey, a process, a quest for knowledge and understanding. There is then a visionary tradition involved with these understandings that encompasses harmony, compassion, hunting, growing, technology, spirit, song, dance, color, number, cycle, balance, death, and renewal. The mind and body can be used for careful, disciplined, and repeatable experimentation and observation. Knowledge is gathered through the body, mind, and heart in altered states of being, in songs and dance, in meditation and reflection, and in dreams and visions.
>
> **Observation**: All science depends on careful observation of plants, animals, weather, celestial events, healing processes, the structures of natural entities, and the ecologies of nature.
>
> **Experiment**: Native peoples applied practical experimentation at all times to find efficient ways to live in their various environments, and ingenious and ecologically appropri-

ate technologies were developed, creating a desired result through entry into specific relationships with the energies of the natural world.

**Objectivity**: Objectivity is founded on subjectivity. Direct subjective experience, predicated on a personal and collective closeness to nature, will lead to an understanding of the subtle qualities of nature.

**Unity**: Native science stresses order and harmony but also acknowledges and honors diversity and chaos as creators of reality. "Relationships and renewable alliances take the place of fixed laws, and Indigenous science accepts the possibility that chance and the unexpected can enter and disturb any scheme" (Peat 1996: 257).

**Models**: Native science also has models. Teaching revolves around high-context models in which information is communicated at many levels and which are highly representational and elicit higher-order thinking and understanding. An example of such a ritual process model would be the Plains Sun Dance which may include symbols such as the circle, or numbers, geometric shapes, special objects, art forms, songs, dances, stories, proverbs, metaphors, all of which unify experience with meaning and facilitate the mind's conscious process of connecting with relationships.

**Appropriate technology**: Because social value is gained by honoring mutual reciprocal relationships, spin-offs of Native science in technology are carefully applied. Adoption of technology is conservative and based on intrinsic need, and care is taken to ensure that technologies adopted and applied do not disrupt a particular ecology. Such care is grounded in the belief that it is possible to live well through adhering to a cosmology and philosophy honoring balance, harmony, and ecologically sustainable relationships.

**Spirit**: Native science incorporates spiritual process: no division exists between science and spirituality. Every act, element, plant, animal, and natural process is considered to have a moving spirit with which we continually communicate.

**Interpretation**: Native science bases its interpretation of natural phenomena on context. Therefore, meaning is based the context of the events and reflection of Native philosophy.

**Explanation**: Native science works with a multiplicity of metaphoric stories, symbols, and images to explain events in nature.

**Authority**: Native science gains its authority partly through the society, elders, direct experience, and dream or vision, and on the sanctity of the relationship established over time with particular environments. "Authority, if we are to use that word at all in the context of Native science, resides in individuals and their direct experience rather than some social establishment" (Peat 1996: 265).

**Place**: Particular places are endowed with special energy that may be used, but must be protected. This sentiment extends from the notion of sacred space and the understanding that the earth itself is sacred. The role of people is to respect and maintain the inherent order and harmony of the land.

**Initiation**: There are both formal and informal pathways to certain levels of Native science. For instance, in the Midewiwin Society of the Ojibwa, there are four stages of initiation, each involving extensive training, learning of songs, ceremonies, stories, interpretation of special scrolls, and petroglyphs (Peat 1994: 267–8).

**Cosmology**: All philosophies are founded on an elemental idea of how the universe was created along with humankind's emergence into the world, and Native science is connected to the origins and migrations of people through the American landscape and to notions of time-space, sacred cycles, astronomy, art, myth, ritual, and dance. Cosmology is reflected in the cycles of community celebrations, rites of renewal, and stories, and serves the important function of validating Native peoples' way of life, core values, and social ecology.

**Representations**: Signs and formulas of thought appear in many forms, records in stone, clay, birch bark, hides, structures, and hundreds of other forms. These representations record key thoughts, understandings, and stories important to remembering aspects of Native science. The structures and symbols of Native science serve as bridges between realities. In archaic Plains Indian traditions, the "medicine wheel" was a structure that bought inner and outer realities of nature together. Many Native symbols are representations of the nonhuman realities of nature.

**Humans**: People play a key role in facilitating knowledge about the natural world in conscious thinking and tool-making. Given this role, humans have special responsibilities to the natural world and to other living things. Native science is the study of learning and carrying out these responsibilities. Native science is about stewardship and the practice of deep ecology.

**Ceremony**: Ceremony is both a context for transferring knowledge and a way to remember the responsibility we have to our relationships with life. Native ceremony is associated with maintaining and restoring balance, renewal, cultivating relationship, and creative participation with nature.

**Elders**: Elders are respected as carriers of knowledge, wisdom, and experience. Therefore, they are utilized as the first line of teachers, facilitators, and guides in the learning of Native science.

**Life energy**: Life energy is acknowledged throughout the expressions of knowledge, understanding, and application. All things have life force. There is a natural energy moving all things that must be understood and respected.

**Dreams and visions**: Dreams and visions are a natural means for accessing knowledge and establishing relationship to the world. They are encouraged and facilitated.

**Paths**: Predetermined systematic activities of learning are viewed as ways to search for and find knowledge. All of nature has these inherent patterns of trajectories, "right paths" which reflect the unfolding of natural pathways through which it may be understood. The "Good Red Road," "Dream-time Path," "Earth Walk," and "Pipe Way" are some of the ways Native peoples have referred to the directed path in the quest for knowledge, meaning, and understanding.

# NATIVE SCIENCE PRACTICE

Native science practice tries to connect the "in-space," our human intelligence, a microcosm of the intelligence of the earth and the universe, with the heart and mind. Art and language, through story, song, and symbolic dance are used to simultaneously explore relationships to the in-scape and the land.

Exploring the in-scape may be considered a "first step" in Native science practice. This is another way of saying that the practice of Native science begins with setting forth specific intentions to seek knowledge from participation with the natural world and then exploration of intuition and creative imagination, which are integral foundations of the metaphoric mind, the mind without or before words – a natural tendency all people intuitively exhibit when confronted with new learning and knowledge. Native science builds upon and encourages this creative and instinctual way of learning.

The world of nature is in constant flux; therefore, Native science does not attempt to categorize firmly within the domains of ideas, concepts, or laws formed only through an analysis bent on a specific discovery, as is the case in Western scientific analysis. Rather, Native science attempts to understand the nature or essence of things. This does not mean the exclusion of rational thought, but rather the inclusion of heart and being with rational perception to move beyond the surface understanding of a thing to a relationship which includes all aspects of one's self.

Sanction of knowledge through the appropriate ritual and tribal society acknowledgment, and commitment to gain and share knowledge are important, since knowledge of the natural world and how best to relate to it is not just a matter of individual understanding but is gained and shared for the benefit and perpetuation of the community. Sanction and commitment acted as foundational safeguards for both individual and tribe and formed a kind of "check and balance" for important knowledge.

The maintenance of dynamic balance and harmony with all relationships to nature is the foundational paradigm of Native science. Reality is based on mutual reciprocity, the rule of "paying back" what has been received from nature. The world operates on a constant flow of give-and-take relationships. Hunting rituals are performed before, during, and after traditional Native hunting to acknowledge the transformation of the deer's life, spirit, and flesh into that of the human. The Native hunter and community know well that this gift from Nature and the game spirits will have to be "paid back" at some time in the future by humans in the universal cycle of death, birth, and rebirth.

This transformation of energy is also exemplified in the continual transformation of energy to matter and back again. Electrons continually borrow energy from the universe to transform themselves into different kinds of atoms. What has been borrowed from the universe must eventually be paid back, and this happens when an electron "dies" back to the field of energy from which it came to provide energy for the creation of new electrons and atoms.

Native science reflects a celebration of renewal. The ultimate aim is not explaining an objectified universe, but rather learning about and understanding responsibilities and relationships and celebrating those that humans establish with the world. Native science is also about mutuality and reciprocity with the natural world, which presupposes a responsibility to care for, sustain, and respect the rights of other living things, plants, animals, and the place in which you live. This is reflective of one of the oldest ecological principles practiced by Indigenous people all over the world, past and present, principles that have been incorporated as metaphysical, and practical, rules for human conduct. In addition to responsibility there is also celebration of life, a key element in seeking to understand how to live a good life. Native scientific philosophy reflects an inclusive and moral universe. All things, events, and forms of energy unfold and infold themselves in a contextual field of the micro and macro universe. In other words, Native science is inclusive of all the ways that humans are capable of knowing and understanding the world.

Today, with the creative influence of chaos theory and quantum physics, a new scientific cultural metaphor has begun to take hold. The insights of this new science parallel the vision of the world long held in Indigenous spiritual traditions. Because of this undeniable parallel, Indigenous thought has the potential to inform a contemporary understanding of chaos. Such understanding allows modern consciousness to encompass the primal wisdom of Indigenous thought and with this to understand the fallacy of scientific and societal control. Rather than seeking to control natural reality, Native science focuses its attention upon subtle, inner natures wherein lie the rich textures and nuances of life. This is exactly what chaos theory shows us: small, apparently insignificant things play major roles in the way a process unfolds.

Spurred by the development of quantum physics with its view of the universe as one indivisible whole, even Western scientists have begun to change their orientation from conviction of an absolute, to one of relative, truth among many truths and possible orientations. They have become more open to consideration of other cosmologies.

The ideas and processes of Native science are conceptual wellsprings for helping to bring about the integration of science and spirit, that marriage of "truth," the ideal goal of science, with "meaning," the ideal goal of spiritual practice. The unity of knowledge now dominates theoretical debate in the philosophies of both science and theology. A new world philosophy of science, designed to meet the environmental challenges of the future which will require a totally different way of living in nature, would draw from the knowledge, understanding, and creative thinking of past and present. As we enter the first decade of a new millennium, Native and Western cultures and their seemingly irreconcilably different ways of knowing and relating to the natural world are finding common ground and a basis for dialogue, the integration or the lack thereof will determine the direction of contemporary society in the twenty-first century.

# REFERENCES

Abram, David (1996). *The Spell of the Sensuous: Perception and Language in a More-Than-Human World*. New York: Vintage Books.

Bohm, David and Peat, F. David (1987). *Science, Order and Creativity*. Toronto and New York: Bantam Books.

Briggs, John and Peat, F. David (1999). *Seven Life Lessons of Chaos: Timeless Wisdom from the Science of Change*. London: HarperCollins.

Cajete, Gregory (2000). *Native Science: Natural Laws of Interdependence*. Santa Fe, NM: Clear Light.

Husserl, Edmund (1960). *Cartesian Meditations: An Introduction to Phenomenology*, tr. Dorian Cairns. The Hague: Martinus Nijhoff.

Lévy-Bruhl, Lucien (1985). *How Natives Think*, reprinted edn. Princeton, NJ: Princeton University Press.

Merleau-Ponty, Maurice (1962). *Phenomenology of Perception*, tr. Colin Smith. London: Routledge & Kegan Paul.

Samples, Bob (1982). *The Metaphoric Mind: A Celebration of Creative Consciousness*, rev. edn. Torrance, CA: Jalmar Press.

## FURTHER READING

Herbert, Nick (1985). *Quantum Reality: Beyond the New Physics*. Garden City, NY: Anchor Press/ Doubleday.

Johnson, George (1995). *Fire in the Mind: Science, Faith, and the Search for Order*. New York: Knopf.

Kremer, Jurgen (1996). Indigenous science: introduction. *ReVision*, 18, 3 (Winter): 2–5.

Lindley, David (1993). *The End of Physics: The Myth of a Unified Theory*. New York: Basic Books.

# 6

# INDIGENOUS NUMERICAL THOUGHT IN TWO AMERICAN INDIAN TRIBES

*Thomas M. Norton-Smith*

In the article entitled "Cultural ecology of mathematics: Ojibway and Inuit hunters" (1986), J. Peter Denny presents a useful analysis of the mathematical language in Ojibwa and Inuit "hunting societies." Assuming that mathematical concepts are reflected in linguistic structures, Denny's purpose is to examine the mathematical concepts possessed by speakers of traditional Ojibwa and Inuit languages in order to argue that "mathematical thought is not inevitable or innate in human beings, but arises from specific conditions in recent human history." The "specific conditions" Denny identifies are ones imposed on human beings by complex agricultural and industrial economies, which force them to alter the natural environment extensively, and which require a standardized measure to coordinate the production of objects when labor is divided among many specialists. But both of these conditions, which require "advanced" mathematical thinking, are absent from traditional hunting societies wherein members use only a small amount of mathematics. However, if mathematical thought were inevitable or innate in human beings, we would expect similar advanced mathematical thinking in hunting societies. Therefore, mathematical thought is neither inevitable nor innate in human beings.

Now, Denny has suggested that these two Indigenous languages embody mathematical concepts that are different from those conveyed by the European languages of industrial societies. And despite his sometimes tenuous reasoning, I have no quarrel with Denny's view that these differences arise largely from the distinctly different environmental and cultural conditions found in hunter and industrial societies. I would even agree that Denny is partly correct insofar as the development of the style of mathematical thinking characteristic of the Western tradition – the style that gave rise

58

to pure mathematics as a formal science – is *in part* contingent upon cultural conditions, and so is not "inevitable." However, I will argue that Denny's considerations are insufficient to show that human beings are without an innate mathematical endowment. Indeed, his analysis of Ojibwa mathematical thinking, coupled with my own preliminary consideration of numerical concepts conveyed by the Shawnee language, can help support the view advanced by Karen Wynn (1992b) that human beings have innate numerical abilities.

Before turning to my discussion of Denny, I wish to say a word about the Western "Eurocentric" philosophical tradition – the tradition of Plato, Aristotle, Descartes, Hume, and Kant – and my place in it. While this tradition richly deserves a sober, honest political critique, giving one is not my present concern. Indeed, there are other American Indian philosophers who could do a far better job than I could. This does not mean, however, that I will refrain from revealing Eurocentric biases or prejudices when they appear in the course of the discussion. Nor will I hide my own history and bias: I am mixed-blood Shawnee, yet so well schooled in Western philosophy and logic that it would be difficult to abandon the concepts and methodologies of contemporary philosophy of mathematics. Moreover, I have only recently been introduced to the Shawnee language, so much of my linguistic analysis is preliminary and relies upon the knowledge of Rick Nightwolf Wagar and other elders of my tribe, the Piqua Sept of Ohio Shawnee Tribe. With these clarifications made, then, I turn to Denny's consideration of mathematical thinking in hunter and complex technological societies.

## DENNY'S "NON-INNATENESS" ARGUMENT

I begin with a more careful statement of what I will call the "non-innateness" argument. Denny observes that mathematical thinking, "those particular abstractions . . . mostly concerned with number and [spatial] measurement," is "underdeveloped" in hunting societies, even though there are no differences in biology, cognitive capacity, or linguistic development between hunters and members of highly technological (i.e. complex agricultural and industrial) societies. Instead, the development of mathematical thinking seems to be a function of its *utility* in a society – a *cultural* variable. Hunting societies have little use for mathematical thinking, while complex technological societies have great need for it. This is because hunting societies have but slight need to alter the environment, while technological societies must greatly alter the environment to meet their extensive demands. Now, if the development of mathematical thinking is a function of a cultural variable, and not a function of biology, cognitive capacity, or linguistic development, then its development is neither inevitable nor innate. Therefore, mathematical thinking is "not inevitable or innate in human beings, but arises from specific conditions in recent human history" (1986: 129–32).

This argument is unconvincing, and showing why will be as easy as freeing it from its subtle, but very real Eurocentric bias. For Denny grants that "there is no such thing as primitive thought or primitive language" (1986: 131), and that members of hunting and technological societies are equally capable of abstract thought, but then he assumes that the kind of mathematics developed in the Western tradition is the standard against which thought in other traditions should be measured – as if "mathematical thought" and "Western mathematical thought" were identical. However, Denny's own account suggests why it is hasty to consider Western mathematics as the standard. When explaining why mathematics is more useful to some societies than others, he makes the interesting claim that a society's "style" of mathematical thinking – and presumably the extent to which that thinking is developed – will "mirror" the cognitive strategies it must employ to manipulate the environment. This is an intriguing claim, because Denny maintains that the members of complex technological and hunter societies must use quite different cognitive strategies to alter the environment. In the case of the former, Denny describes a strategy reminiscent of Lockean abstraction, the (supposed) cognitive ability to focus on one feature or variable in a situation and consider it apart from all others. In order to master the environment, industrial technology must isolate and manipulate individual variables independent of their context; likewise, the pure mathematics of technological societies studies abstract mathematical relations themselves apart from their physical exemplifications. In contrast, hunters must adapt to – not control – the environment, and so a global understanding of natural processes rather than a knowledge of the behavior of isolated variables is critical. If the style of mathematical thinking in hunter societies mirrors this cognitive strategy, then we should expect a context-rich and inclusive style of mathematical thinking – a style Denny has found in his study of Ojibwa and Inuit mathematical thought (1986: 141–3). However, I explain in the next section that these two different "styles" of mathematical thinking about number – the isolating and abstracting as opposed to the inclusive and contextual – are indeed two different *kinds* of numerical cognition. But if they are two different kinds of thinking, employing one as a standard to judge the degree of development of the other is misguided. The mathematics in hunter societies may be different, but it doesn't follow that it is inferior or "underdeveloped."

A second, more subtle point conveys less about differences in mathematical cognition across cultures than about Denny's understanding of the Indigenous worldview of hunter societies. Denny's argument is framed in starkly economic terms, assuming that the degree to which a society develops mathematical thinking is directly proportional to the degree to which it is needed to control and manipulate the natural environment. The unspoken assumption – and recurring theme in the Western tradition – is that the natural world is a mere inert resource distinct from human societies, something which human beings are morally free to utilize as a means to their own ends. However, A. Irving Hallowell (1960) stresses that the key to understanding the Ojibwa view of the natural world – a key Denny apparently failed to grasp – is their belief that the natural and spiritual worlds are populated by other-than-human *persons*. As a result, the relations between human beings and the environment are not merely economic; they are *social relations* between human persons and other-than-human persons. Now, one of the principal Ojibwa moral values is balance, that is, maintaining a sense of proportion in interpersonal relations, including one's dealings with other-than-human persons. And so, the traditional Ojibwa hunting society did not merely "adapt" to the natural environment in order to "gain a living"; it tried to live in balance with human and other-than-human persons alike in a sort of social organization. Western-style mathematical thinking may be more useful in manipulating and controlling the natural world than living in balance with it.

Now, a remarkable thing happens when we revise Denny's "non-innateness" argument in light of these remarks about Eurocentric bias. Instead of having a relatively unconvincing argument that *nothing about mathematical thinking is inevitable or innate*, we have a reasonably convincing argument for the more modest claim that *the development of a particular style of mathematical thinking is dependent upon cultural variables*. Here's the argument: We do not find Western-style abstract mathematical thinking in hunting societies, even though there are no significant biological, cognitive, or linguistic differences between them and technological societies. This is because a hunting society attempts to achieve a balance with the natural world, while a complex technological society must extensively alter the natural world to meet its needs. Western-style mathematical thinking is not particularly useful to the former, but it is crucial to the latter. Now, if the development of Western-style mathematical thinking is a function of a cultural variable – utility – and not a function of biology, cognitive capacity, or linguistic development, then its development is neither inevitable nor innate.

Importantly, the stronger claim that "neither mathematical concepts nor abilities are innate" does not follow. Just as a person's natural abilities might have developed in strikingly different ways in different cultural circumstances, so the development of different styles of mathematical thinking in different cultures still leaves open the possibility that humans have an innate cognitive endowment. In short, abstract mathematical thinking is not inevitable, but some rudimentary mathematical abilities can still be innate. Indeed, Karen Wynn (1992b) has provided good reason to believe in innate human *numerical abilities*, and a consideration of Shawnee and Ojibwa number systems can help support her view – or so I will suggest in section 3. In preparation for that discussion – and to remove any lingering doubt that the mathematical thinking in traditional hunter societies is different in kind from the Western tradition – I turn now to an examination of Shawnee and Ojibwa number systems.

## SHAWNEE AND OJIBWA NUMERICAL THOUGHT

Before beginning, I need to clarify some methodological assumptions and cautions. First, I share Denny's assumption that a culture's concept of number will be encoded in language, so an examination of the structure and uses of numerical language will reveal those concepts. This assumption immediately leads to a critical methodological caution. Suppose that the Shawnee concept of number is indeed encoded in their traditional language. That language has changed in significant ways – both obvious and non-obvious – as a direct result of Western contact. As examples of the obvious influence of Western culture given by C. F. Voegelin (1938–40), the Shawnee adapted the word *poosiiθa* from the English *pussy* (literally "little pussy" or "house cat") and adopted the word *makiliikwa* to refer to "automobile" (literally "big eyes"). However, changes in Indigenous languages have occurred in more subtle ways, as when Denny notes that some important syntactic features in the Ojibwa language are disappearing as contemporary Western industrial society gradually assimilates the Ojibwa people (1986: 154). The difficulty is that I will be making claims about the traditional Shawnee concept of number based on the study of a language that may have changed so much by now that the concept is lost.

To meet this difficulty I will proceed as follows in my preliminary examination of Shawnee. First, I will use fairly contemporary written sources, principally C. F. Voegelin's (1938–40) study of Shawnee stems, but I have confirmed the relative stability of numerical language by comparing it to the Ebeneezer Denny (1996) and Thomas Ridout (Edgar 1977) vocabularies, which were compiled closer to initial European contact. Second, making extensive use of Denny's excellent analysis of Ojibwa, I will note obvious similarities between the structures of Shawnee and Ojibwa numerical languages, two members of the same Algonquian linguistic family. Then I will argue by analogy that we will probably find many of the same numerical concepts in traditional Shawnee that Denny finds in traditional Ojibwa, and vice versa. Finally, I must again acknowledge tribal elder Rick Wagar for his generous contributions.

The Shawnee and Ojibwa number systems are what Michael Closs terms "5–10 systems" insofar as they are primarily decimal systems with linguistic structures that record secondary groupings of five (1986: 3). Both are decimal systems like English, but unlike it as well, since the English system has 10 distinct and non-compounded number words referring to the first 10 counting numbers. The difference is easily discernible in the first 10 number words from each language, but the pattern continues throughout the sequence of count words. The Shawnee number words are compiled from Voegelin, and the Ojibwa number words come from Denny (1986) and William Warren (1868):

| English | Shawnee | Ojibwa |
| --- | --- | --- |
| one | nekoti | bezhig |
| two | niiswi | niizh |
| three | n'θwi | niswi |
| four | niyeewi | niiwin |
| five | niyaalanwi | naanan |
| six | nekotwa'θi | ningodwaaswi |
| seven | niiswa'θi | niizhwaaswi |
| eight | n'θwassikθwi | niswaaswi |
| nine | caakatθwi | zhaangaswi |
| ten | meta'θwi | midaaswi |
| twelve | meta'θwi-kite-niiswi | midaaswi-ashi-niizh |
| nineteen | meta'θwi-kite-caakatθwi | midaaswi-ashi-zhaangaswi |
| twenty | niiswaapitaki | niizhdana |
| thirty | nθwaapitaki | nisimidana |
| forty | niyeewapitaki | nimidana |
| fifty | niyaalanwaapitaki | naanimidana |
| sixty | nekotwaasi | ningodwaasimidana |
| seventy | niiswaasi | niizhwaasimidana |

| one hundred | teepeewe | ningodwaak |
| three hundred | nθwi-teepeewe | niswaak |
| four hundred | niyeewi-teepeewe | niiwaak |
| one thousand | meta'θwi-teepeewe | midaaswaak |
| two thousand | niisene-meta'θwi-teepeewe | niishing midaaswaak |
| three thousand | nθene-meta'θwi-teepeewe | nising midaaswaak |

Notice first some of the obvious surface similarities in the Shawnee and Ojibwa words themselves, as between *niiswi* and *niizh*. More importantly, in both languages the second five number words are compounds formed using a special suffix (*−aaθwi* in Shawnee indicating "an amount," and *−aaswi* in Ojibwa) and in both languages the words for six, seven, and eight are formed by adding the suffix on to the simple stems for one, two, and three: *nekot−*, *niisw−*, and *n'θw−* in Shawnee. Denny informs us that the Ojibwa stem for seven, *ningodw−*, is an alternate stem for one, so the pattern holds. While the number words in Indigenous Indian languages often arise from their connection to counting on digits – and that is also the likely explanation for the secondary grouping of five in both Shawnee and Ojibwa – the digital origins in these languages are not as apparent as in others. According to Closs, the Ojibwa word for five, *naanan*, means "gone" or "spent," and probably refers to all the fingers on the first hand having been used (1986: 6). Rick Wagar conveys that the stem *caaki−* used to form the Shawnee word for nine, *caakatθwi*, means "all," and might mean "all of the fingers are used and a new counting cycle begins with ten."

The similarities between Shawnee and Ojibwa continue as we move up the number sequence. The compound words referring to the numbers 11 through 19 are derived from simple additive processes, clearly indicating that such additive processes are a part of their numerical thinking. This is not unlike some English constructions, e.g. *fourteen* is a compound of *four* and *ten*. For example, the Shawnee word for the number 12 is *meta'θwi-kite-niiswi*, literally "ten plus two," while the word in Ojibwa is *midaaswi-ashi-niizh*, that is, "ten and two." However, both Shawnee and Ojibwa begin a different pattern in constructing number words after nineteen. The Shawnee word for nineteen employs the root *meta'θw−*, which refers to the "count of ten" so *meta'θwi-kite-caakatθwi* may be interpreted as "ten and nine count." But the word for twenty, *niisw-aapitaki* is formed using the suffix *−aapitaki*, which means "a collection of ten viewed as a single unit," or simply "decade." Likewise in Ojibwa, *niizh-dana*, the word for twenty, is formed with the suffix *−midana* (shortened to *−dana* in the case of twenty), so the word *niizh-dana* is literally "two decades." Denny makes the important observation that Ojibwa's word for twenty, *niizh-dana*, represents "counting two decades," not "multiplying two by ten." Likewise, Shawnee's *niisw-aapitaki* encodes a counting process, not a multiplicative process. The reasons are simple. Beside the fact that both Shawnee and Ojibwa encode the multiplicative process using a different linguistic structure, *the count* and *the objects of the count* are separately encoded in the language. The Ojibwa stem *midaasw−* is the "count of ten" and the suffix *−midana* is the "decade"; likewise the Shawnee stem *meta'θwi−* is the "count of ten" and the suffix *−aapitaki* is the "decade." Now according to Denny, in an Ojibwa number word the count is expressed by the first morpheme, the stem, and the thing being counted by the second morpheme, the suffix. Applied to Ojibwa's *niizh-dana*, the stem *niizh–* gives the count of two and the suffix *–midana* gives the decade. Likewise, in Shawnee's *niisw-aapitaki*, the stem *niisw–* gives the count of two and the suffix *–aapitaki* gives the decade.

In Shawnee the pattern continues for thirty, forty, and fifty, adding the suffix *–aapitaki* to the roots referring to three, four, and five. Notice the predictable construction of the word for forty-five, *niyeew-apitaki-kite-niyaalanwi*, literally "four decades plus five." However, unlike Ojibwa, the Shawnee constructions for sixty, seventy, and eighty employ a different suffix *–si* applied to the stems for *nekot–*, *niisw–*, and *n'θw–*. As Rick Wagar points out, the construction of the number words in the decades between fifty and one hundred, like the structure above five in the first ten numbers, reveals the number system's secondary groupings of five.

Just as the suffix *–aapitaki* means "a collection of ten viewed as a single unit" or "decade," the Shawnee suffix *–teepeewe* means "a collection of one hundred viewed as a single unit" or "centum." This again parallels Ojibwa, which uses the suffix *–aak* to express the centum. Thus we have the Shawnee *nθwi-teepeewe* and the Ojibwa *niswaak* for "three hundred." Again, *nθwi-teepeewe* encodes the counting of "three centa," not the multiplication "three times one hundred." This holds for number words through one thousand, which is expressed as "ten centa" (Shawnee *meta'θwi-teepeewe*; Ojibwa *midaaswaak*). However, in both languages the *multiplicative* and counting processes are used to express numbers greater than one thousand. This is accomplished through the use of the Shawnee suffix *–ene* and the Ojibwa suffix *–ing*, both expressing "times." So in Shawnee "two times" is *niis-ene*, and two thousand is *niisene-meta'θwi-teepeewe*, while Ojibwa expresses it as *niizing -midaaswaak–* in both cases "two times ten centa."

For all practical purposes the Shawnee and Ojibwa number systems are finite, but both have the conceptual and linguistic capacities to extend their number systems indefinitely. A list of Ojibwa number words recorded by William Warren runs through the millions to one billion – *me-das-wac-me-das-wac-as-he-me-das-wac* – after which he observes that "[t]here is no more limit (in thus counting) in the Ojibwa than there is in the English language" (Warren 1868: 213). Rick Wagar makes the same point about Shawnee. Closs concurs, asserting that number systems in which the principles of grouping, addition, and multiplication are implicit – as they are in the Shawnee and Ojibwa systems – "have attained a level of conceptual development which makes them equivalent to the set of positive integers with the operations of addition and multiplication" (Closs 1986: 15). However, we will see that significant differences remain.

Importantly, the comparison between the number systems in these two hunter societies reveals their close structural similarity; indeed, the ways of representing number across the Shawnee and Ojibwa languages is amazingly stable. By analogy, then, I will conclude that a noteworthy feature Denny identifies in the traditional Ojibwa number system should also appear in traditional Shawnee. As well, it would be reasonable to expect some of the features of the Shawnee system to appear in Ojibwa.

To begin, remember that Denny identifies abstraction as the essential feature of the style of thinking in complex technological societies. Abstraction is especially evident in numerical contexts where the only salient feature is quantity. The same numbers are used to represent the numerosities of collections, regardless of what they are collections of – six buttons, six concepts, or six spirits. This is quite unlike Ojibwa numerical thinking, Denny continues, wherein certain non-quantitative features of a context are *not* independent of its quantitative features. This inclusive, global style of thinking is evident in the way Ojibwa encodes non-quantitative features of a situation in the construction of number words. Denny discusses several ways in which this encoding takes place. First of all, a –w– missing from a number word stem can indicate a count of non-concrete objects, for example, *nis-ing* counts three non-concrete events ("times") and *nis-imidana* counts three non-concrete units ("decades"). Second, Ojibwa has two distinct words expressing "one," *bezhigw–* and *ningodw–*, where the former stresses a single entity, and the latter expresses one in a sequence (1986: 150–1). But perhaps the use of *numerical classifiers* is Ojibwa's most striking way of encoding non-quantitative features in number words.

Recall from our earlier discussion that in the construction of Ojibwa and Shawnee number words the count is expressed by the first morpheme and the object counted by the second morpheme. Now, Denny identifies a system of similar suffixes used to classify some important properties of objects used in traditional Ojibwa life – hardness, flexibility, and dimensionality – in the structure of the number word itself. Among examples are the suffix *–aabik* classifying "hard inorganic solid" (as in *midaasw-aabik asiniih* meaning "ten-hard stones") and the suffix *–minag* classifying "three-dimensional object" (as in *niizho-minag miinan* meaning "two-3D blueberries"; 1986: 147–8).

Unfortunately, at this preliminary stage of my study of Shawnee, I have found the two different senses of "one" (*nekot–* as "one in sequence" and *peeleko–* as "once" or "single event") but I have yet to find many of the more subtle constructions, including analogues of Ojibwa's numerical classifiers. However, given the other structural similarities between Ojibwa and Shawnee, I am convinced that they are there – or, perhaps, *were* there. Denny laments that these kinds of indicators are being lost as the Ojibwa are gradually assimilated into Western society (1986: 154). Rick Wagar suggests that a similar sort of thing might be presently occurring in the Shawnee language. It is at this juncture, then, that I appeal to its similarity to Ojibwa to conclude that the Shawnee language once had similar ways of encoding important non-quantitative contextual features of a situation in the construction of number words.

What conclusions can be drawn about Indigenous numerical thought in these two American Indian tribes? First, it is "mature" numerical thought insofar as its principles of grouping, addition, and multiplication allow conceptualization of the notion of number without limit (Closs 1986: 15). Second, Indigenous numerical thought is *genuinely different* from the Western tradition, and so is neither "underdeveloped" nor inferior. As evidence, it will be sufficient to show that it is different in *content* from "advanced" Western thinking about number.

In Shawnee – and Ojibwa as well, if I correctly interpret Denny's analysis – the number words are not nouns, but particles, most often functioning as adjectives modifying nouns that refer to collections of objects. This reveals an ontological commitment to *numerical properties* but not to numbers as objects. However, this alone is not unusual, since some Western philosophical views maintain that numbers are properties – although this is certainly not the dominant view. Moreover, numerical thought in these Indigenous cultures is *nominalistic* in the sense that numbers are generally not conceived of apart from the particular collections – collections of concrete or non-concrete objects – exemplifying them. If so, then arithmetical relations between numbers will be conceived of in terms of the relations between particular exemplified collections. Thus, Shawnee translations of arithmetical sentences such as "5 + 5 = 10" – where the numerals refer to abstract objects – are not straightforward, but arithmetical relations exemplified by collections of things can be expressed as a matter of course. Consider Rick Wagar's example: *niyaalanwi sikonaki kite niyaalanwi sikonaki, meta'θwi sikonaki* easily translates as "five stones plus five stones, ten stones." Denny explains that Ojibwa translations of arithmetical sentences come more readily, for example, *bezhig geyaabi beshig, mii niizh* as "one yet one, thus two," but some formulations still hint at the original concrete arithmetical processes (1986: 157–60). However, Denny reminds us that the mark of abstract mathematical thinking is that the numbers and the numerical relations between them are conceived of and investigated apart from their particular exemplifications. Thus the content of Indigenous numerical thought in these Indian tribes is genuinely different from Western abstract numerical thought.

I want to add one last intriguing speculation. On a modest epistemological interpretation of the Sapir–Whorf hypothesis, speakers of radically different languages will most certainly live in *conceptually* different worlds. An example appropriate to this discussion is that certain syntactic structures in Algonquian languages mark a distinction between animate and inanimate objects, which is unknown in the Western worldview. Now, Denny has analyzed the number word in expressions like *midaasw-aabik asiniih* – "*ten-hard* stones" – as though the properties "being ten" and "being hard" are distinct, but when counting objects used in traditional Ojibwa life, these distinct properties are expressed together as a *compound* by a unique number word construction. However, it would be entirely consistent for a people whose "style" of thought is inclusive, context-rich, and global – as Denny characterizes the thought in hunter societies – to conceptualize "ten-hard" as a simple, unanalyzable numerical property distinct from the numerical property "ten." If so, then Indigenous numerical thought would be strikingly different in content, including many numerical properties absent from Western abstract numerical thought. Besides the numbers "five" and "nine" referring to the familiar numerical properties, their system would also include the numbers "five-three-dimensional" and "nine-one-dimensional-rigid."

## INNATE NUMERICAL ABILITIES

Behaviors exhibited at around five months strongly suggest that very young infants possess some sort of innate numerical endowment. Three theories about what this innate endowment might be propose that human beings have an innate knowledge of numerical *principles*, or an innate knowledge of the number *concepts*, or innate numerical *abilities* (Schwartz 1995: 227). Karen Wynn (1992a) proposes that human beings have innate numerical *abilities*, and I will use our conclusions about the Shawnee concept of number to help support her view.

To help understand the details of Wynn's proposal, consider a simple count made by 6-year-old Kate. In her visual field, Kate individuates objects, that is, she "picks them out" as objects distinct from the rest of her visual field, in a way rather like Denny's abstraction. In this case, she identifies the objects as men, and then internally represents the men as a collection – something that will have a numerosity or *cardinality* – and she will employ the counting procedure to discover what it is. Having already learned the stable English count-word sequence, Kate pairs the count words one-by-one with the men in the collection, as in figure 6.1.

Kate is a competent counter, so she knows that the order of the pairing is irrelevant to the success of the count, and that when all of the men are paired with a count word in the sequence, then the last count word represents the cardinality of the collection of men – in this case, five. There is, of course, a very important connection between the position of a count word in the counting sequence and the cardinality of the collection of men. Indeed, the key to understanding counting is connecting the *order of the count words* – ordinal numbers – with the *numerosities of collections* – cardinal numbers.

According to Wynn (1990) by the time Kate was about 3½ years of age she had learned the cardinal meanings of the English count words in her range, and she was competent at using the counting procedure to determine the number of items in a collection. Remarkably, this knowledge and this competency do not come at the same time! Instead, Kate learned the cardinal meanings of the first three English count words sequentially, and *without using counting*. That is, Kate not only learned the meanings of "one" before "two" and then "two" before "three," but she did so by using a

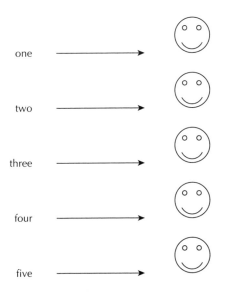

one ⟶

two ⟶

three ⟶

four ⟶

five ⟶

**Figure 6.1**

non-counting cognitive process (Wynn 1992b: 227). Further, at this same time Kate probably knew that other English count words like "five" functioned as count words – words that referred to some numerosity or other – although she could not determine precisely which one. It took about one more year of development for Kate to learn how counting encodes the precise numerosity of the English count words – that she could use counting as a way to answer the question "how many?" Wynn remarks that it's "a surprisingly long time" (Wynn 1992b: 243–4).

Why should it take Kate such a "surprisingly long time" to learn that counting is the way to determine the precise cardinal meanings of the count words? Consideration of Kate's judgment about some of the men she recently counted will help develop Wynn's explanation (see figure 6.2).

In both cases Kate is pairing the men with words, but the clear intent here is that the words are to apply to the individuals with whom they are paired. They refer to features of the *individuals*, and the last one is bald. However, in the count the word "five" is paired with the last individual, but the last individual is not five! Kate knows that when "five" is paired with the last individual, then it refers to a feature of the *collection* of men – its cardinality – and not to the last individual. The point is that the numerosity of the collection of men must be understood in terms of the ordinal position of the count word "five." This is a difficult lesson to learn, because apparently the way that young children internally represent number is very different from the way the counting procedure encodes it.

Wynn (1992b) proposes that human beings have the innate ability to internally represent number and to recognize numerical orderings and relationships between small numbers – this is the nature of our innate numerical endowment. She further maintains that human beings initially represent number in a way functionally equivalent to an "accumulator." As a count of items in a collection proceeds, the accumulator functions like a mental "container," collecting and storing a mental tag corresponding to each item counted. The accumulator fills up in equal increments – increasing in volume at each step – until the count is completed, at which time the entire fullness of the accumulator – not the final mental tag alone – represents the numerosity of the items counted. Because the volume of the accumulator at each step of the count represents number, the

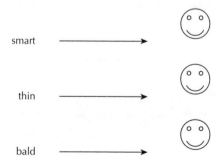

**Figure 6.2**

cardinal conception of number is inherently embodied in the structure of the representation. But the cardinal conception of number is not inherently embodied in linguistic counting, where count words are paired with individuals and only the last count word represents the numerosity of the collection counted. It takes the surprising length of time to learn that counting encodes the numerosity of count words because a child has to learn how to map her innate way of representing number on to the other way.

Wynn interprets this lengthy period of development to be evidence for the existence of the innate ability to internally represent number "as an accumulator." I suggest that there are some linguistic features of traditional Shawnee count words that could provide additional evidence that humans internally represent number in this way. To see how, let us consider a second count of the men made by a traditional Shawnee speaker, Crane. Now, Crane's count of the men seems little different from Kate's – except, of course, for the sequence of count words from Shawnee: *nekoti, niiswi, n'θwi, niyeewi, niyaalanwi*. However, the grammatical features of Shawnee number words suggest that a traditional Shawnee count proceeds much differently than Kate's – indeed, I have good reason to believe that Crane's count will represent number *in a way that parallels Wynn's accumulator*, as in figure 6.3.

The difference is that the traditional Shawnee count words probably would not be paired with *individual* men in the collection, but with *aggregates* of men. *Nekoti* would be paired with an aggregate of one man, *niiswi* with an aggregate of two men – and so forth – until at the final step of the count *niyaalanwi* is paired with the aggregate of five men, and thus encodes the numerosity of the entire collection. But this way of linguistic counting would precisely map on to the accumulator internal representation of number, where the accumulator fills up – increment by increment – until the count is completed and the entire fullness of the accumulator represents the numerosity of the collection.

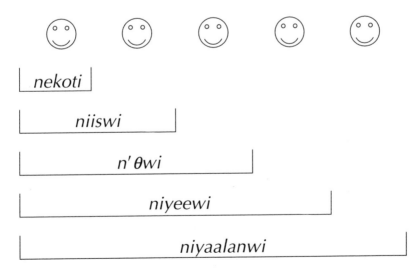

**Figure 6.3**

Why believe that the traditional Shawnee count words would be paired with *aggregates* of men and not *individual* men? Besides the fact that counting by pairing a count word with an aggregate instead of pairing it with an individuated object – an object distinguished from all the rest – would be consistent with Denny's now familiar observation that we should expect a context-rich and inclusive style of thinking in traditional hunter societies, Shawnee number words are particles, not nouns, and so function as adjectives modifying nouns. Moreover, Rick Wagar conveys that they almost never stand alone, but when they do, a noun is implied. However, the count would be nonsense if the number words referred to the individual men in the collection, like this: *nekoti-hekeni* (one man), *niiswi-hekeni* (two man), *n'θwi-hekeni* (three man), *niyeewi-hekeni* (four man), *niyaalanwi-hekeniki* (five men). Indeed, the only plausible way to interpret the count is as *nekoti-hekeni* (one man), *niiswi-hekeniki* (two *men*), *n'θwi-hekeniki* (three *men*), *niyeewi-hekeniki* (four *men*), *niyaalanwi-hekeniki* (five *men*). But then, the number words refer to numerical properties of *aggregates* of men.

Second, Wynn (1992b) argues that the reason why it takes young children so long to learn that counting is a way to determine numerosity is that they have to learn how to connect the ordinal position of the count word with the cardinality of the counted collection. If so, then Kate's pairing of numbers with *individuals* during her count is better interpreted as an *ordinal count*, "first man, second man, third man, fourth man, fifth man." The difficulty Wynn identifies is learning that the "fifth man" count encodes "five men." This is complicated because English numerals play *two* roles – as referring to ordinal and cardinal numbers. However, Shawnee expresses the ordinal and cardinal conceptions of number with two different constructions. "First, second, third, . . . " are expressed using the suffix *–ene* (times): "*peelekotθene, niisene, n'θene, niyeewene,* . . . " while the cardinal conception is expressed in the way Crane counts: "*nekoti, niiswi, n'θwi,* . . . " So, there is no confusion – and no doubt – that Crane's count encodes the cardinal conception of number – just as Wynn's "accumulator" represents number.

Thus, Wynn has proposed that human beings have an innate ability to internally represent the cardinal conception of number as an "accumulator" in order to account for the length of time it takes for English-speaking children to learn the precise cardinal meanings of number words. I propose in turn that an analysis of Shawnee count words provides additional linguistic evidence that human beings have the ability to internally represent number in this way. In addition, the comparison of Kate's count with Crane's reveals other similarities, taken by some to be evidence of "species-unique" innate numerical abilities, among them the abilities to perform one-to-one correspondences, master stable orders of count words, and internally represent aggregates of objects as collections (Schwartz 1995: 236–7). However, we concluded in section 2 that abstract numerical thought is different in kind from that found in Shawnee and Ojibwa, two traditional hunter societies. It is clear, then, that human beings can have innate numerical abilities that develop into different styles of numerical thought under different cultural influences. Abstract mathematical thinking is not inevitable, as Denny contends, but human beings still have innate numerical abilities.

# REFERENCES

Closs, Michael P. (1986). Native American number systems. In *Native American Mathematics*, ed. Michael P. Closs. Austin: University of Texas Press, pp. 3–43.

Denny, Ebeneezer (1996). *Delaware and Shawnee Vocabularies Recorded by Major Ebeneezer Denny at Fort M'Intosh and Fort Finney in 1785–1786*. Waterville, OH: Rettig's Frontier Ohio.

Denny, J. Peter (1986). Cultural ecology of mathematics: Ojibway and Inuit hunters. In *Native American Mathematics*, ed. Michael P. Closs. Austin: University of Texas Press, pp. 129–80.

Edgar, Matilda (1977). *Ten Years of Upper Canada in Peace and War (the Thomas Ridout Captivity)*. New York: Garland.

Hallowell, A. Irving (1960). Ojibwa ontology, behavior, and worldview. In *Culture in History*, ed. Stanley Diamond. New York: Columbia University Press, pp. 19–52.

Schwartz, Robert (1995). Is mathematical competence innate? *Philosophy of Science*, 62: 227–40.

Voegelin, C. F. (1938–40). Shawnee stems and the Jacob P. Dunn Miami dictionary. *Indiana Historical Society Prehistory Research Series*, 1, nos. 3, 5, 8, 9, 10: 63–108, 134–67, 289–478.

Warren, William (1868). Ojibwa of Chegoimegon. In Henry Schoolcraft, *Archives of Aboriginal Knowledge*, vol. II. Philadelphia: J. B. Lippincott, pp. 211–13.

Wynn, Karen (1990). Children's understanding of number. *Cognition*, 36: 155–93.

Wynn, Karen (1992a). Addition and subtraction by human infants. *Nature*, 358: 749–50.

Wynn, Karen (1992b). Children's acquisition of the number words and the counting system. *Cognitive Psychology*, 24: 220–51.

# 7

# THAT ALCHEMICAL BERING STRAIT THEORY: AMERICA'S INDIGENOUS NATIONS AND INFORMAL LOGIC COURSES

*Anne Waters*

## INTRODUCTION

American Indian Sovereign nations students are bicultural; to be bicultural is to live in both Native-centric and Eurocentric worldviews. American Indians in academic institutions must translate information from their Sovereign nation's standpoint to a Euro-American standpoint, and vice versa. Critical thinking courses can help facilitate this skill. Incorporating American Indian philosophy into critical thinking and logic courses empowers Native American learning, and non–Native understanding. Using examples that students can identify with in logic courses makes materials more accessible to them, and assists in the learning process. Incorporating culturally relevant material also serves to reinforce a sense of self-identity and self-esteem. In this chapter I present examples from my personal teaching experience in logic classes, and my work with Indigenous students. As an educator I am privileged to have opportunities to teach Western philosophy, American Indian studies, and American Indian philosophy to American Indian Sovereign Nations students. When I incorporate American Indian philosophy into courses, this means I am incorporating it into logic, epistemology, metaphysics, ethics, social and political theory, jurisprudence, and the history of Western philosophy.

It is my position that when I teach, my identity as a philosopher, lawyer, feminist, lesbian, woman of color, Jew, and American Indian, when appropriate, not be left out of the dialogue. Just as my being a Jew is relevant to a discussion of the European Jewish Holocaust, so also my being an American Indian Indigenist[1] is relevant to a discussion of the American Indian Holocaust. Placing identity information about myself into the classroom setting, and using a variety of culturally relevant content for my examples, opens a space for cultural safety. This safe space allows all students more comfort to name and share their own culture-centric perspectives. It gives rise to diverse voices.

Being able to share a cultural perspective empowers people. Thus the praxis of my teaching reinforces my belief that cultural inclusion is practically useful, and hence culturally appropriate for all students. This praxis is especially useful for some American Indian students, who, because of bicultural mores, otherwise might not as readily apprehend a Eurocentric explanation, or join in the discussion. That is to say, where all or most examples form a Eurocentric perspective, Indigenous students feel left out, and falsely represented. This chilly climate forms the basis for exclusion, and a flight from academic education.

Before providing examples of the incorporation of American Indian philosophy into informal logic courses, I should briefly explain what I mean by "American Indian philosophy." In the Americas a carefully thought out meaning of "American Indian philosophy"[2] might include all ideas that spring from, are about, or affect precolonial and postcolonial thought and experience of nations indigenous to the Americas. It is a fluid and malleable concept, and ought to be defined and clarified by the Americas' Indigenist philosophers. Philosophical thought by or about the Americas' Indigenous nations reaches across all disciplines, and views the world from American Indian–centered perspectives. It may include, but need not be exclusive to, oral or written "testimony" about Indigenous experience and worldviews, from the past, of the present, or in the future.

We can thus distinguish Indigenous nations' philosophy of the Americas from, for example, African American, European American, and Asian American philosophies, as well as philosophies indigenous to continents other than the Americas. Indigenous philosophies, and we as philosophers of continents around the globe, "stand on their own feet, in their own right," as do philosophies and philosophers of non–Indigenous cultures.

We can talk about philosophies of Indigenous nations in the Americas with or without making them a subset of "American philosophy." Thus American philosophy, although having many roots in the Americas' Indigenist thought, can be separated out from an American Indian Indigenous philosophy, by the former's tradition of hosting Eurocentric, rather than Indigenous, values and experience.

With respect to who is American Indian, Native American, Indigenous, Indian, or a member of a Sovereign nation, this is a matter of philosophical interest, because racist political agendas have focused on external identification processes, rather than more easily sustained notions of kinship and geography. Indian identities also spring from tribal sovereignty, community resources, and self-identification.[3] And although an individual may speak "with" sisters and brothers about identity, they may not speak "for" us.[4]

In 1996 Highlands University in Las Vegas, New Mexico, hosted a conference on Native American philosophy.[5] Viola Cordova[6] was not able to attend; however, she did send in a paper that was printed in the program. In this paper she explicates a Native American philosophical framework that seeks to define Native American philosophy.

Whatever Native American philosophy may be defined as, Viola claims, it must be *for* Native Americans. Her other two definitional parameters are that it must be *by* and *about* Native Americans. For Viola, then, a Native American philosophy must benefit Native Americans if it is to be *meaningful* to Native Americans. I believe that my work incorporating Native American ideas, and ideas about Native Americans (and other groups as well), in my courses, benefits Native Americans (and others as well). In this context, "meaningful" signifies that the experience speaks to us, does not marginalize us, and has healing potential for us.

# TEACHING AMERICAN INDIAN-CENTERED INFORMAL LOGIC

Students normally begin a logic course by first identifying the parts of an argument, that is, the premise(s) and conclusion. Then they study the difference between deductive and inductive reasoning patterns in arguments. In most courses (as in my own), before tackling formal logic, we examine and learn about an array of some 20 to 30 informal fallacies (out of the possible 100-plus informal fallacies). I present fallacies in the following order: begging the question; false cause; false analogy; hasty generalization; appeal to authority; suppressed evidence; correct sign interpretation; definitional power; false composition and division; false dichotomy; and slippery slope.

Prior to discussing specific informal fallacies, I discuss the Bering Strait land bridge migration theory. I do this because, throughout the course, we can use this theory as a reference point for locating fallacious reasoning. This also gives me another opportunity to discuss the nature of scientific theory and the foundational reasoning of the hypothetico-deductive pattern. I use this example to talk about the function of theories generally, in the context of the coherence, correspondence, and pragmatic theories of truth. This method lays an epistemological foundation so that students will have a background understanding of why some premises of some arguments will be accepted by some individuals, and not by others.

### Begging the question

To assume the truth of the Bering Strait land bridge theory may "beg the question," or assume that which is in need of proof. As a theory, it is plagued by incompleteness of evidence. Its reasoning assumes that since Sovereign Indigenous nations have not, in a Western sense of scientific proof, proved that we are indigenous, we cannot be. That is, because American Indians have not "proved" that we have always lived in the Americas, Westerners conclude that we are not Indigenous. Arguing that what cannot be proven to exist must not exist, Eurocentrics politically argue that American Indians did not originate in, but were only the earliest inhabitants of, the Americas.

74

There remains, however, no evidence to support this argument; mere intuition convinces students that lack of proof for "one thing" does not thereby prove its opposite true! (Lack of proof that I love you does not prove I don't love you!) Further valuing our intuitions, it is easy for students to see how the background values of scientists can operate: for what purports to rest as proof in this theory may be no more than an unwarranted, wistful hope or fear that Western science could eradicate Indigenist land claims. Yet because the non-indigeneity of American Indians cannot be proven, the Bering Strait land bridge theory may equally support a reverse migration theory, multiple coinciding migrations, or even the arrival of some Sovereign nations and not others.

Assuming that which is in need of proof to support the land bridge theory itself (that there are no nations indigenous to the Americas, hence American Indians are of imported cultures; we migrated into the land rather than always being there) plays to the political advantage of Euro-American land claims. In this way, Eurocentric science denies credibility to other "just so" stories of American Indian origin that are older, and have more coherence than, the Bering Strait theory. The Americas' Indigenous nations may view such a ploy as being arrogantly insulting, morally reprehensible, and scientifically repugnant.

We may now zoom in on the exact logic. The Bering Strait theory runs something like this: (1) Evidence suggests migration took place between the Asian and North American land continents. (The second premise is taken either as (a) a religious "dogma," or (b) a scientific "fact," and then an inference is drawn denying Indigenous roots to American Indians.) (2a) Humans were created by a Hebrew god in the Middle East, from where they dispersed throughout the world; or (2b) Since remains only of Cro-Magnon, not of earlier hominids, have been discovered in the Western hemisphere, human beings could not have evolved in the North American continent, but must have eventually reached it from Africa, via Asia and the land bridge.[7]

In class I discuss some opposing arguments. I show how both of the second premises to the argument (i.e. both (2a) and (2b)) beg the question. Each is assuming the truth of something not proved to be true, namely religious dogma or scientific fact. In this context we can talk about the coherence of American Indian creation stories, the nature of religion and science as tools of knowing, and refer back to our different concepts of coherence, correspondence, and pragmatic "truth."

Generally, I explain to students how assumptions of one culture, or religious group, may differ from those of others, and thus give rise to disparate theories (or beliefs). In this way, we "open up" the practical effects of recognizing that some premises will hold for some persons, but will not be acceptable to others, and that no cultural group has a monopoly on human knowledge.

The question of the origin of the Americas' Indigenous groups, then, remains unproven except by a Western, or Eurocentric, religious dogma or science. From a standpoint outside this Eurocentric position, however, religious dogma and scientific proof "go begging" for verification. Explaining this "begging the question" fallacy puts knowledge systems themselves up for grabs, and effectively sensitizes students to the importance of respecting traditions other than our own. It also gives an academic credibility and sensitivity to the cultural origins and intuitions of American Indian students.

Teaching about such controversial topics empowers students to think seriously about arguments! And what happens when students then go to their anthropology courses leaves smoke in the halls. Thus I warn students that my arguments will not be the same as others they will encounter, but that studying logic provides them with tools of analysis. They then understand that it is their choice to decide which religious theories, if any, they will accept; and how they may work with and talk about scientific theories, without having to believe them.

There are many variations on the land bridge argument, and I encourage students to look at the different possibilities that could be suggested by the very same evidence that scientists cite to prove their theory. I especially like to let them explore the "reverse migration theory," that is, that nations in Siberia originated in the Americas.[8] I also ask them to think about the possibility of numerous migrations of various groups to and from the continents. This praxis encourages students to think of alternative inferences drawn from the same premises, thus expanding their critical thinking skills.

### False cause

The Bering Strait theory presents us with another fallacy, the "false cause" (*post hoc ergo propter hoc*). I offer the following example: S represents "we first see evidence of the early presence of humans in Asia and Africa" and A represents "we later see the presence of humans in the Americas"; (1) S, and (2) A; therefore S caused A. This argument builds into itself a temporal causal connection. To arrive at the conclusion, unannounced premises must be supplied: (3) there is a particular type of causal connection between S and A such that S is sufficient for A; (4) humans are indigenous only to Africa; and (5) there have never been humans indigenous to any of the Americas. Of course, each one of these missing premises also stands in need of being accepted.

This argument can also operate as an example of a *non causa* variety of the false cause fallacy. Again, a presumed premise supports the argument. In this case all that is needed is (5) above. Just because Europeans did not know of the Americas, nor produce any data about Indigenous groups, does not prove anything about the Americas not being inhabited by Indigenous groups.

Another good example of a false cause argument in this context is the claim that (1) Indigenous people caught many diseases from the Europeans, therefore "disease caused the dramatic drop in Indigenous population." While it is true that many Indigenous people did die of disease, as a result of European contact, it is not true that disease was the only cause of the population drop. Nor is it true that contracting a disease like smallpox was only a matter of personal contact with Europeans.

Smallpox-infected blankets and infected handkerchiefs from smallpox hospitals were saved, only to be intentionally and maliciously given to Indigenous nations by the cavalry. Given that the cavalry expected the disease to spread with deadly effectiveness, the motive for introducing it must have been genocide. So also, after periodic surrender by American Indians, massacres of them still took place; American Indians were massacred whether we surrendered after fighting, whether we resisted, or whether we submitted without fighting. From the fifteenth century onward, Euro-American colonial entrepreneurs captured Indigenous people to be used as slaves both internally and via exportation to other European colonies.[9] A broad perspective of this population decline suggests that intentional genocide, the systematic extermination of Indigenous culture, in the context of the encroachment of European immigrants and soldiers, was the main cause of population reduction. Thus the argument posing disease only, or primarily, as the cause of Indigenous population decline, is a *non causa* variety of the false cause fallacy because it fails to cite other causes. In failing to claim all of the causes the analysis has brought forth necessary, but perhaps not sufficient, causal reasoning.

### False analogy

Before introducing the fallacy of "false analogy," I have found it helpful to give an example of a good analogy, showing why and how it functions inferentially. I present an argument that genocide was policy against Australian Indigenous groups. I ask whether we can analogize from the claim of a Holocaust in Australia to the same claim about the Americas. Not only can students see the similarity, as we discuss the particular techniques, but they are also then able to construct an analogy about American Indians as members of a group subject to a policy of extermination, or genocide, perpetrated by Euro-colonists.[10]

An upbeat example of a false analogy pertains to the great diversity of the Americas' Indigenous cuisine. The similarity of some food in two Indigenous cultures does not allow us to analogize to other characteristics. For example, it is not possible to analogize from the claim that "Indigenous nations of the Southwest of North America eat chilis," to the conclusion "hence Indigenous nations of the Northeast of North America also eat chilis!" That some characteristics may be similar in these cultures (for example, origin in the Americas, rhythmic music, a colonization of historic importance, an oral history tradition, etc.) does not mean other characteristics will be similar.

One of the benefits of examining how the false analogy works is that it helps students to see how some stereotypes are created, and enables some students to break away from the notion that "all Indians are alike" or even "all *x*s are *y*s" where *x* is a group and *y* describes an accidental group characteristic. The Indigenous students also have an opportunity to reveal aspects of their culture that are unique, helping to break down stereotypical images and ideas. Using this content, I can educate both American Indian and non-Indigenous students about logic, achieve a cultural sensitivity and respect for different cultures, and positively affirm Indigenous students' experience in academia.

### Hasty generalization

Hasty generalizations frequently create stereotypes about American Indians, and other cultural groups. The processes of creating stereotypes, by false analogy or hasty generalization, are the same, whether about race, ethnicity, sex, gender, class, age, or disability. Most non-dominant power groups, from the point of view of the powerful, which are most frequently the media, are seen as either ignorant or immoral; this standpoint validates the ruling power of the dominant elite.

Cross-cultural communications improve when students understand that misinformation about the world may be rooted in stereotypes passed from generation to generation, culture to culture, and in a silent partnership of the media and the public that maintains, continually reinforces, and recreates stereotypes.[11] Discrimination is sometimes the result of an unconscious cultural process feeding prejudices about persons of non-dominant culture groups. Understanding how these processes work, and how to intervene when they operate, is a process of critical thinking.

Both Indigenous and non-Indigenous stereotypes influence literary, social, biological, anthropological, archeological, historical, medical, legal, philosophical, and other ideas, about both individual persons and groups of persons. The problem of stereotypes from a critical thinking perspective is that they mask information necessary for reasoned inferences. Individuals, by attributing characteristics of one person to a group of persons, can distort and suppress information that is needed to draw correct conclusions if that information does not support the stereotype.

Perpetuating false information, or masking pertinent information by making hasty generalizations, is how some social scientists ignore the anomalous facts they come across, because they are inconvenient. Not using the method of generalization might discredit assumptions, or create anomalies, that could eventually result in a paradigm shift within a particular theory. Sometimes a theory, in shifting its paradigm, may get rid of racist, sexist, elitist, or other internal assumptions that support group oppression.[12] Theories about race, sex, and genetics are especially susceptible to manipulation via generalized assumptions when dominant groups want to keep non-dominant groups in a subordinated legal or social status.

### Appeal to authority

In presenting the fallacy of arguing from authority, an analogy is drawn to how stereotypes can affect even "properly credentialed" authorities, and cause otherwise reasonable persons to make a false authority fallacy. For example, suppose person A is a member of a legally or socially subordinated group, and has a law degree. Suppose person B is a member of a legally or socially dominant group, and also has a law degree. Though A may be a much better lawyer than B, A's membership in the subordinated group may act, in C's consciousness, as a social and/or personal stigma, falsely and unfairly suggesting that A would be a less competent or moral lawyer than B. Thus, C may cite B's argument in a court of tribal law, thinking it to be a more worthy argument. In fact, the better argument may be A's. If B practices civil law, and A practices tribal law, A would be more likely to have a preferred argument for tribal court. Thus C would have cited a wrong, or false authority. Moreover, what gave rise to citing the false authority was an outcome of stereotypic thinking patterns.

Another example I like to use is about an anthropologist who claims to be an authority about a culture to which the anthropologist does not belong. This context provides an opportunity to teach what I refer to as "the field of denotation and connotation." This problem can be introduced with an example of a person from one culture pointing to, for example, a rabbit, and announcing *gavagai*, meaning "rabbit ears." Yet a person from another culture, the outsider (anthropologist) interprets the word as "the entire rabbit." Problems of outside authorities can also occur when there is no similar concept in the outsider's language, but the outsider claims to have a word that correlates to the meaning. A person becomes a cultural authority by living in a culture. Admittedly, a person can read about a culture, study a culture, guess about a culture, or even dance a cultural dance. But cultural authorities must be the persons living and breathing in the culture. This is because such persons are in daily contact with people who have practices and beliefs associated with their own. Thus they are more attuned to changes taking place within a culture, for example, shifts of meaning, practices, intent, and affect.

Authority issues prevail when origin theories and stories are ascribed by archeologists, without consulting or giving credence to the knowledge base of individual members of the culture. For example, although the Bering Strait land bridge theory, as an explanation for the origination of American Indians, contradicts all American Indian origin stories, it is still taught as fact by many disciplines. Thus who "counts" as an authority figure for whom, with respect to this theory, becomes a political rather than an academic issue. It is helpful to all students to discuss the politics of appealing to authorities. Just as Euro-American culture proclaims authorities on certain issues, so also America's Indigenous nations assert our own authorities. And American Indian students have a right to hold and protect their sacred beliefs, without having them belittled by academics. Given the process of colonization in the Americas, who counts as an authority for American Indian students may present a moral problem to Euro-Americans. This, of course, raises issues about gatekeeping, and the role of authority in gatekeeping cultural information.

### Suppressed evidence

A "suppressed evidence" fallacy may operate at a macro-level of education, in the context of teaching Euro-American-centered disciplines to American Indian students. Specific examples, like teaching the Bering Strait theory, have the potential to project false information about Indigenous nations. When information about Indigenous nations is not adequately assessed or portrayed, relevant information is suppressed.

The fallacy of suppressed evidence occurs whenever providing information previously not provided would change the conclusion of the arguer. Thus identifying American Indians as aboriginal, or first, inhabitants may tell part of the truth, but would suppress the idea that we originated in America. Whether intentional or not, suppressing relevant information about opposing theories supports textbook status quo theory, and at the same time implicitly casts doubt upon Indigenous sources of information, and Indigenous people's ideas about their own origins.

### Correct sign interpretation

The problem of inferring information from "signs" can be taught in the context of discussing received messages on billboards, in movies, and television, which depict a false reality about American Indians. Parodies of stereotypes operate to create misinformation that denigrates the character of all Indigenous persons. The real, day-to-day harm that these signs perpetrate (intentionally or not) can be discussed by both Indigenous and non-Indigenous students in a supportive learning environment. Such an environment provides an opportunity to expose blatant cultural racism, sexism, classism, and whether the media force the participation of passive observers.

### Definitional power

A good example that shows how the power of definition and signs can work together to suppress information, and thus portray a false reality, is the case of historical markers across the Americas. At many sites where Indigenous nations surrendered, and then were summarily massacred, the federal United States government has incorrectly put up signs that these are sites of *battlefields*. In many instances no battles were fought. For example, there was no battle fought at Wounded Knee Creek, South Dakota, on December 29, 1890; rather, a genocidal massacre of North American Indians by the US military government took place. This example shows the injustice of false naming, via signs that present misinformation by way of false definition. In this context we can again talk about "begging the question," this time by assuming a definition of the word "battle" that would include "massacre." Obviously, using definitions like this, which fail to depict accurate assessments of reality, begs the question.

### False composition and division

The fallacies of composition and division are appropriate tools that students can use to show, once again, how stereotypes arise. The first is the false reasoning from attributes of the parts of the whole to attributes of the whole itself. A good example of "composition" can be provided by drawing from an Indigenous student's experience of education. Attaining the knowledge base required for an academic degree may enhance American Indians' understanding of a Euro-American perspective, or a Eurocentric culture. From this fact, however, it should not be inferred that attaining many degrees will enhance the student's insights even more; there may be a saturation point with respect to attaining a framework of interpretive analysis. Just like the anthropologist, one cannot "get into" or "put on" another's culture. One can dress differently, act differently, dance differently, and perhaps even grasp the language, but one cannot live another's cultural experience.

Another example of a composition fallacy might be the claim that because some characteristic is true of some particular American Indian, it is true of a nation. And finally, were one to suggest that if ingesting one toke of peyote makes a person feel good, then having many of them will make the person feel absolutely wonderful, the logic of composition would have been misapplied! In fact, it may make them ill, or paranoid, or even pass out!

With respect to the fallacy of "division," the inverse of the previous example of peyote may be used. To argue that because many tokes of peyote may make one sick, thus one toke may make someone ill, is to commit the fallacy of stating that a characteristic true of the whole must also be true of the part, which does not follow. So also, things that may be true of a certain Indigenous nation, may not be true about any individual member of that nation. To suggest otherwise may lead to another stereotype, another fallacy.

### False dichotomy

Another fallacy portrayed in the context of American Indian stereotypes is "false dichotomy." Some persons, it can be argued, think that Indigenous persons are either American Indian or European. This dichotomy is false because it fails to take account of the complexity of race and ethnic identity politics. Some Native nations citizens may identify as both, or as mixed. Some American Indians may also identify differently under different contexts. This example can open a discussion of the philosophy of the self, of identity politics, nationalism, and critical race and ethnic theory.

### Slippery slope

Finally, the "slippery slope" fallacy – the assumption that a tendency gets progressively worse, like something accelerating downhill – can be portrayed by examining the fear of many Euro-Americans with respect to the Americas' Indigenous nations' treaty rights. When we ask that our treaties be recognized, respected, honored, and acted upon, many Americans fear that reparation of lands for one tribe will set a precedent for all tribes, arguing that the next thing you know they will take over and force all non-Indigenous persons to leave the Americas. Quite plainly, granting reparations to Indigenous nations, by recognizing treaty rights, does not lead to the extermination of non-Indigenous persons in the Americas. Indigenous nations have a 500-year history of accommodating the land-space needs of Euro-Americans. It is only "fair," some argue, that the US government now accommodate Indigenous nations with respect to land issues and space. The evidence of our centuries of co-existence ought to preclude slippery-slope, backlash thinking. Yet many persons, for whatever personal reasons, perpetuate this type of slippery-slope argument with respect to Native rights, as well as the rights of other non-dominant groups of persons, who may have justification for reparations from the United States government.

Presenting the slippery slope in this context can lead to discussions of historical injustices in the Americas, causal relationships among these injustices, the social and political contexts of these injustices, and the contemporary power of European nation-states, and the United States, to correct these injustices. It can also lead in another direction, the use of slippery-slope arguments against granting equal rights to non-dominant groups of different race and lower economic class, the elderly, physically or mentally challenged, differently gendered, and historically or politically disadvantaged and disenfranchised ethnic groups.

# CONCLUSION

I have presented some of the informal fallacies and content that I use in critical thinking classes that incorporate an Indigenous perspective. Many more can be developed. My intent has been to show a methodology of curriculum development that encourages Indigenous students to more actively participate, and thereby sharpen their creative thinking skills. Eventually, as the course progresses, students come to grasp and articulate relationships between fallacious reasoning and oppression. They begin to understand the importance of intuitive reasoning, and the problems associated with reasoning from false or incomplete premises. They also get a glimmer of what it means to have to disagree with others as a result of having different underlying assumptions or belief systems. And if I have done nothing else during the semester, this last thing, in itself, justifies my method and content. In this way, I believe I am "doing" Native philosophy of the Americas: it is being done by, for, and about Native Americans! And, yes, it also benefits non-Native students, who learn something not only about logic, but about their hosts, the Indigenous Sovereign nations still inhabiting our home, Turtle Island.

Perhaps I am not doing all that I could. For example, a textbook could be written using examples that incorporate experiences of our multiracial and multiethnic populations in the Americas. Perhaps in the future I or someone else will find the time to write such a book. But this is a beginning. It is one nick in the walls of boundaries that unnecessarily divide students one from another in classrooms. And, in the spirit of doing "insurgent scholarship," it has revolutionary potential to provide students with tools for both living and doing philosophy.

## NOTES

1  An American Indian Indigenist is a person who advocates the claims of American Indians, i.e. the claims and beliefs of descendants of the original peoples of the Americas, for example as a member of a political movement. He or she need not be Indigenous to the Americas. A person who is descended from the original peoples of the Americas is Indigenous. "Indigenous," in the sense I use of "always having been there," is to be distinguished from "Aboriginal": the first to inhabit a region.

2  When I use the term "philosophy" I also mean to include the notion of "doing philosophy" as an activity. I use the term in a broad sense.

3  On American Indian identity, see Ward Churchill, The crucible of American Indian Identity. In Duane Champagne, ed., *Contemporary American Indian Cultural Issues* (Walnut Creek, CA: Alta Mira, 1999), p. 39.

4  Lorraine Brundige, graduate student at the University of Oregon, has recently written a paper asking non-Natives to dialogue "with us, not for us."

5  Although it was advertised as the first-ever Native American philosophy conference, only one person identified as a Native American PhD philosopher presented. That individual was

invited only after the organizers of the conference were contacted with a query about Native American participation. The American Philosophical Association (APA) at the time of writing identified only two American Indian PhD philosophers (Anita Silvers, and also Eric Hoffman, conversation with the author, APA Pacific Division meeting, Berkeley, California, Spring 1999). This does not include persons I would include as philosophers, for example, Vine Deloria, Jr, who was engaged in Indigenous philosophical thought from an American Indian perspective for many years, and many other historical "message carriers" from one generation to another. However, it does raise a question about why there have been no Native American PhD philosophers prior to this date.

6  In 1992 Viola Cordova became one of two American Indian scholars to receive a PhD in philosophy; the other was myself. From 1992 to 1997 Viola had been teaching at the University of Alaska, and I at the Albuquerque Community College in New Mexico. At the time of writing this we are both writing and speaking, though neither is employed full-time as a philosopher.

7  These epistemic arguments are taken up, and convincingly argued against, by Vine Deloria, Jr., in *Red Earth, White Lies: Native Americans and the Myth of Scientific Fact* (Golden, CO: Fulcrum Publishing, 1997).

8  Jeffrey Goodman, *American Genesis: The American Indian and the Origins of Modern Man* (New York: Summit Books, 1981).

9  Regarding disease, massacre, and the enslaving of Indigenous nations, see Ward Churchill, *A Little Matter of Genocide: Holocaust and Denial in the Americas, 1492 to the Present* (San Francisco: City Lights, 1997); and Russell Thornton, *American Indian Holocaust and Survival: A Population History since 1492* (Norman: University of Oklahoma Press, 1987). Both texts quote from official correspondence from Sir Jeffrey Amherst, commander-in-chief of the British forces, to his subordinate, Bouquet. Thornton writes: "In 1763 ... Amherst ... wrote in the postscript of a letter to Bouquet the suggestion that smallpox be sent among the disaffected tribes. Bouquet replied, also in a postscript, 'I will try to inoculate the [m] ... with some blankets that may fall into their hands, and take care not to get the disease myself.' ... Amherst replied, 'You will do well to try to inoculate the Indians by means of blankets as well as to try every other method that can serve to extirpate this execrable race.' On June 24, Captain Ecuyer, of the Royal Americans, noted in his journal: 'Out of our regard for them ... we gave them two blankets and a handkerchief out of the smallpox hospital. I hope it will have the desired effect'" (Thornton, *American Indian Holocaust*, pp. 78–9).

10  The "one exception to the rule" fallacy can also be examined in this context. The claim is that Indigenous persons were not all killed, their descendants live, hence there was no genocide. In this context I can talk about the power of definition, and that the definition of genocide, according to the International Trials at Nuremberg after World War II, rejected this model. It was rejected on the grounds that a few exceptions do not disprove the overall context and motivation, nor the intentional suppression of evidence. Also, the significant reduction of population by disease, massacre, and discontinuity enforced on the remaining nations, was itself enough to claim a Holocaust. See Churchill and Thornton (note 9).

11  Regarding the transfer of false consciousness and cultural groups, see Naomi Zack, *Thinking about Race* (Belmont, CA: Wadsworth, 1998), especially ch. 10 (p. 88): "as the media ... reaches out to give the public what it wants, and the public reaches out to its media to find out what it wants, they form a partnership of creating and re-creating stereotypes and myths."

12  I refer here to a Popperian sense of discrediting (falsifying) a theory, and a Kuhnian sense of a theory paradigm shift.

# Part IV

# METAPHYSICS AND BEING

# 8

# NOTES ON IDENTITY, TIME, SPACE, AND PLACE

*Ted Jojola*

*We MUST be disgusted, I say, and I am thoroughly disgusted this moment at the way the Indians live, if this is the way they live. I know, however, that some live in great deal worse houses than this. I can make this place better. I must make home more pleasant. But, pshaw! What is the use....*

(Narrative from a fictional Carlisle Indian, Taos Pueblo student, Stiya [EMBE] 1891)

"Kill the Indian, and save the child" was the unequivocal policy battle cry of the American assimilationist era. And although Indian boarding school education was only one aspect of this campaign, a great deal of the colonial verve to extinguish Indigenous identity on the home front has generally gone unnoticed.

Although assimilative policies are no longer overt, there is still an implicit assumption that Native people will continue to make decisions without the benefit of understanding who they are and how awareness of the past contributes to the collective task of structuring their communities.

The societal ideal of the "melting-pot theory," for instance, was an attempt to conceptualize the American immigrant experience as a blending of cultures, with each one adding its own distinctive flavor to the brew. The unspoken aspect of that theory, however, was that such a recipe was palatable only if everyone came out in the end behaving like Protestants.

"Culture" has been essentially relegated to the profane. Particularly because mainstream American society had been focused on replacing the traditions of Native people with their own, the concept of "Indian" was equated with a primitive manifestation of identity. Sociological theories have made little or no accommodation with the success of Native people in adapting new concepts in order to strengthen older ones. Rather, what was taught is that there was a profound disjunction between the "traditional" and the "here and now."

This was the hidden community reform agenda behind the Indian boarding school experience. In fact, it should be no surprise that many of these institutions were presided over by Presbyterian missions. Under the guise of eliminating tribal customs in favor of those skills necessary for surviving modernization, their doctrine divided tribal communities into two factional camps – those that ostensibly held on to traditional values (traditionalists or conservatives) and those that ostensibly accepted new ways (progressives).

Many Native communities still exhibit these schisms. A classic situation, for example, is found in the Hopi tribal nation where groups with opposing attitudes toward modern amenities split the historic village of Oraibi into two newer settlements. Bacavi became the domain of the progressives whereas Hotevilla was a stronghold of the traditionalists. Whereas Bacavi embraced all aspects of modernization, including indoor plumbing, phonelines, and electricity, Hotevilla opted for excluding all of these from its village proper. The villages are presently separated by a state highway and the only "neutral" ground lies midway between them, the Hotevilla-Bacavi school.[1]

As a consequence of this separation, individuals were given a clear choice as to which lifestyle to pursue. Over time, the respective habitations became a reflection of these choices, with individuals adopting a subsistence style adapted to one or the other. Hotevilla residents became more self-sufficient while Bacavi residents became more reliant on a wage economy. What is interesting is that just because Hotevilla prescribed for itself a "traditionalist" lifestyle, this did not mean that it did not embrace modern amenities. In particular, when newer self-reliant technologies like solar electricity became cost-effective, residents readily adapted these for the purposes of refrigeration and powering up entertainment systems.

Of course, such practices overlie even deeper divisions involving religious practices and governance. How wealth in the community is acquired and redistributed as well as how decisions are made is at the core of how communities evolve. Such actions over a long and sustained period translate into distinctive ideologies. And these ideologies are used to justify either individual or collective attitudes toward change.

"Indianness," among the tribal nations of the United States has therefore become a beleaguered postcolonial battleground for the resolution of contemporary Indian identity. Thus far, that battle pits kinship against birthright. Using a racial criterion such as blood quantum, Native people are culled from tribal membership. Particularly as a result of the infusion of new prosperity from Indian gaming, the concept of kinship has become even more exclusive. Given the historic propensity of Native people to marry outside their tribe, among either other tribes or non-Indians, it will probably only be a matter of a few generations before no one can claim "full-blood" lineage.

As for birthright, Native language proficiency and participation in "traditions" are used with increasing frequency as a measure of birthright. And unlike kinship, birthright can be driven by an individual's social context. The result can be children and adults who are steeped in tribal traditions but yet are alienated from tribal membership and denied kinship due to a lack of blood quantum – or, vice versa, children and adults possess the requisite kinship, but have little or no knowledge of their traditional culture. And although language and participation may serve as "tangible" ways to measure the strength of an individual's tribal identity, they fail as a measure of how their individual actions add up to a coherent sense of community.

Both community and identity are illusory concepts. In mainstream American society, "identity" appears to be invested in "property rights" with a paradigm shift decidedly towards the notion of "individualism." Individuals become the sum of their tangible goods, particularly as these pertain to property and land. And when people grow discontented and are ready to move elsewhere, they literally "pull up stakes" and transplant themselves.

Similarly, community in the sense of "traditional" mainstream planning practice is limited to the design and implementation of "land-use" principles. It is a concept that owes its origins to nineteenth-century German industrial reform. The ultimate goal of such reform was to situate parcels of land in such a manner as to maximize the utility of the properties while removing them from the possibility of incompatible or hazardous uses. There has arisen a dominant nomenclature that classifies land use into industrial, commercial, residential, and public usage. For the most part, the American town is characterized by land-use practices that zone the social landscape into homogeneous and discontinuous areas. These are segregated from one another and linked by highway systems.

Among Indigenous communities, however, individuality ultimately becomes subsumed in collective values. The basis of these values is invested in land, but not land as individual property right. Instead, valuation is seen in the longer term with the operative principle being that of land tenure. As families occupy and sustain the land over successive generations, the notion of property becomes one of inheritance. By being born in a context, individuals see this inheritance as a birthright. The community is mobilized, therefore, to make certain that individual activities uphold their collective agenda. And unlike mainstream society, the acquisition and retention of a land base or territory becomes paramount.

The great American Southwest is a testament to how sustained collective human interaction has molded a landscape that is the embodiment of both human intervention and the natural ecosystem. On the ecological level, it is easy to see how, for example, Native communities are tied into sustainable territories as delineated by watersheds. In an environment where water is the most precious commodity to sustain life, the worldview of these communities is dominated by water-borne archetypes. As a matter of fact, water in the cosmology of Pueblo Indian traditions has been elevated to a "sacred" construct. Just as Whorfian linguistic analysis expanded the context of "snow" among the Eskimos, "water" as a language variant among the Pueblos is very complex.

Among the Indigenous peoples of the Americas, it is well established that a worldview is at the core of community identity. Although every tribe has its own variant, there are common elements that make up the worldview and that serve to define a community's identity in time, space, and place. These elements can be depicted in a transformative model.

# TRANSFORMATIVE MODEL

In order to begin to construct a Pueblo transformative model, it is first necessary to understand the building blocks of Pueblo society. By and large, Pueblo villages are conglomerations of clanships. These clanships are traced by matrilineal lineage and the mother's clan is usually denoted as the principal socio-religious milieu where birthright is attained. Patrilineal birthright is also important, and it has been suggested that it is only secondary because "a baby's maternity is never in doubt."

In addition, it is necessary to make a distinction between patrilineal clanships and patriarchies the latter of which are exhibited in Pueblo governance. And although it may appear on the face of it that men are the ones that dominate and control, as in the instance of the *cacique* (theocratic headman), it is the women (especially the clan mothers) that endorse and oversee these male roles.

Each clan has its unique history. It is embodied in a migration pattern as exemplified by a spiral (see figure 8.1). Countless such migration spirals are found throughout the Southwest and are often to be seen on petroglyphs alongside a clan symbol.

Clan migration spirals also indicate directionality (see figure 8.2). A spiral with an outward direction indicates that the clan is journeying outwards, literally, towards the perimeter of human and physical settlement. Such journeys may have extended as far as the farthest land passages of the continent. The purpose of such a journey was to gain

**Figure 8.1**  Migration spiral from the Salinas National Monument region. It is unique in that it not only denotes the migration, but has triangles that indicate the 19 months of the solstice calendar. It is also reminiscent of a time-cog in a wheel.

90

**Figure 8.2** Directional migration symbols from the King Ranch region. Note the shift in graphic nomenclature as an important departure from Euro-Western mapping. The top of a figure in Pueblo representation is associated with the East. The directional grid indicates the concept of physical space that surrounds the point of origin, or centerplace. The elevation of consciousness into a higher stage is attained when humankind (in this case, clanships) moves through space and completes a cycle through a journey into the four directions.

experiential knowledge. Once the journey for each of the four sacred directions was completed, the clan returned to its origin point.

A spiral with an inward direction indicates the return of the clan to its origin or centerplace. The centerplace is an important concept and is represented by two types of markers. Physically, it was represented by a central courtyard or *plaza*.[2] This space is one of the most important unifying elements of a village and defines the middle of its outlying territory. Houses, by and large, front on to this space. The *plaza* both serves as an "empty space" and has a metaphorical meaning that relates to the cosmos.[3] From the *plaza*, family land assignments were established that corresponded to the respective clan direction.

As a spiritual marker, the centerplace was also represented by the *sipapu* (emergence hole). In particular, the *sipapu* was embodied in a religious structure called a *kiva* (usually a circular building). Symbolically, the *sipapu* signified the place of mythological emergence, wherein clans, moieties, and societies emerged in a specific sequence from the underworld to the present state of mortal reality.[4] And although each moiety could have its own *kiva*, there was usually one grand *kiva* that incorporated all the symbols of the clans into one unified structure.

The Pueblo village in aggregate, therefore, is composed of various clans, each of which traces its own migration history. In particular, each clan is identified with a cardinal point, a color, and a totem. The cardinal point indicates the direction from which the clan returned to this Pueblo, the color signifies its outlying territorial domain, and the totem symbolizes the unique human attributes as learned from protector animal spirits. During certain times of the ceremonial calender of a village, these migrations are redepicted in dance and ritual.[5]

The clans that compose Pueblo villages could and did change with time. In some instances this was the consequence of political dynamics that occurred in consensus-making.[6] In other cases, it was because of the clan's natural inclination to explore the world around them. The experiencing of life by conducting journeys to the edges of the world was inculcated in the mythos of the emergence stories. More importantly, the ancestors anticipated the importance of experiential learning to the transformation and survival of the communities.

This transformational concept can be depicted by imagining the two-dimensional spiral to be a three-dimensional helix (see figure 8.3). As the path of migration moves upward in space, a cycle is eventually completed. Unlike the closure that is brought by a circle, however, the path remains in juxtaposition to a major axis. This juxtaposition indicates that the clan has not simply completed a cycle, but in the process of its experiential journey, its collective mind has been elevated or transformed to a higher ideological level of consciousness. Paradoxically, therefore, the clan returns to the same place of origin, in the sense of an elevated transformational space.

The spiral dynamic has been likened to a whirlwind vortex.[7] With movement comes not only enlightenment, but a force that ultimately results in adaptation and change in the community.

A Pueblo village, as such, is really the collective embodiment of the clanship experiences. Each clan brought to the village the embodiment of its own knowledge. As a collective, they shared these with one another in an interdependent fashion through the dual summer and winter moieties. Overall, these elements converged in order to imprint each Pueblo village with its own separate, but distinctive worldviews.

In the larger scheme of things, Pueblos evolved over millennia into communities that shared common physical traits, but were separated by different combinations of clans, and different languages and customs, as well as being demarcated into distinct territories. These territories were defended against aggressors. In addition, individuals who dared to tread outside the safe confines of these community boundaries did so at their own risk. Sometimes, the fact that there were similar or comparable clans at other villages allowed safe passage to them. By maternal extension, like-clans considered one another's families as blood relatives.

Patterns of settlement along major waterways in a semi-arid environment were what shaped the regional character of the Southwest. Where water flow was more abundant, the villages were closer to one another. It is important to note, however, that in no instances did their community boundaries overlap. Rather, there was an interstice which, in effect, represented a "no man's" territory. In practice, these spaces between boundaries served as public-way corridors for migration. As such, the interstitial spaces figured just as significantly in the worldview of Pueblo relations as did their own communities.

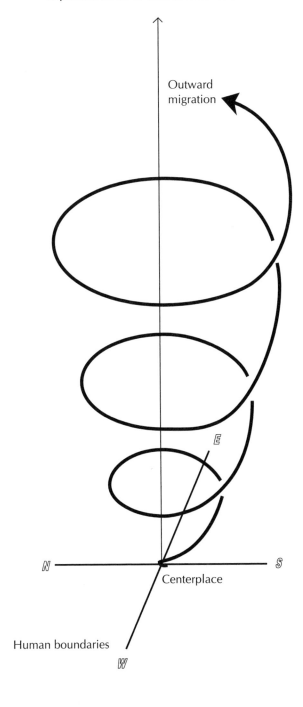

Expanded levels of collective consciousness

Outward migration

E

N — — — S
Centerplace

Human boundaries

W

**Figure 8.3**

# IDENTITY IN CONTEMPORARY SPACE

By and large, the highly refined concepts that evolved into distinctive worldviews no longer figure very much in tribal community development. Instead, land-use principles as practiced by Western (European) societies have tended to dominate the developmental landscape. This is seen, for example, in housing programs constructed under the auspices of federal entitlements, such as those of the Department of Housing and Urban Development (often called Indian HUD housing). These developments take on a decidedly suburban character and, in the instance of Pueblo Indian housing, in no way conform to clanship or collective traditions.[8]

On the other hand, the lack of adherence to Indigenous planning principles does not mean that people are not unwittingly being shaped by past tradition. There are plenty of physical remnants which, when taken with values associated with land tenure, bespeak older patterns of development. Often, newer developments must give way to the preservation of such places. Among Pueblo villages, for instance, the core traditional centerplace is preserved and the newer HUD housing developments are consigned to the periphery, almost as an abject apology for their invasive land-use practices.

Similarly, in any urban milieu, there exist historic buildings, and, just as importantly, historic places.[9] And even in the cases where historic buildings no longer exist, the patterns of newer settlements are still molded by the shape of the places they once were.

A simple and straightforward way of understanding how identity is defined by a sense of place can be achieved by examining its relationship to voice and symbol. Voice represents the interpretive manner in which places are explained. In any community there is a multiplicity of voices. The voices may arise in a unified manner, but more often than not they represent disparate interpretations as articulated, by distinct groups. In Pueblo society these can come from the various clanships, moieties, or societies that comprise a village. In mainstream society they are often separated along socio-economic lines.

Similarly, these voices give meaning to places by the symbols to which they choose to affix the community's ideals. A symbol, in this instance, is nothing more than a shortcut method of ascribing commonly held ideals. In essence, it is whatever a group or society deems to be significant. More often than not, it is the representation of a dominant group.

Old settlements are replete with such meanings. In some cases, the meanings of symbols change over time even though the place may remain the same. In other instances, places are altered in order to fit a new interpretation. In any event, these remnants hark back to a previous era where different values and functions may have existed.

At least within the contemporary milieu of Pueblo society, the meaning behind these clues has been overlooked. And although tribal community planning has been driven by the infusion of new capital projects like casino gaming, thus far there is little or no sense of tradition in the way new projects integrate the symbols of past traditions into the present. Instead, cultural accouterments have become largely cosmetic. In some cases, they have been abandoned altogether (see figures 8.4 and 8.5).

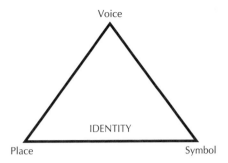

**Figure 8.4**   The structure of identity as based on the triad relationship of voice, meaning, and symbol.

**Figure 8.5**   Traditional adobe house next to HUD house (Jemez Pueblo).

Identity, therefore, no longer exists in a space, time, and place continuum. Rather, experiential or transformation learning no longer is the motivation for change. The most cynical observers of this change will point out that Native people who have no understanding of the meaning of their collective actions are simply "playing Indian." At the least, therefore, the goal of Indigenous planning is not just to reinforce cultural identity, but to challenge the community into understanding how the past and present serve to give coherence to the future.

## REFERENCES

EMBE (1891). *A Carlisle Indian Girl at Home*. Cambridge: Riverside Press.

Hayden, Dolores (1995). *The Power of Place: Urban Landscapes as Public History*. Cambridge, MA: MIT Press.

Jojola, Ted (1976). *Memoirs of an American Indian House: the Impact of a Cross-national Housing Program on Two Reservations*. Limited book publication funded by the Laboratory for Architecture and Planning, MIT and the Atherton Trust.

Jojola, Ted (1998). Indigenous planning: clans, intertribal confederations and the history of the all Indian Pueblo Council. In *Making the Invisible: Insurgent Planning Histories*, ed. Leonie Sandercock. Berkeley: University of California Press.

Markovich, Nicolas, Wolfgang Preiser, and Fred Sturm, eds. (1989). *Pueblo Style and Regional Architecture*. Florence, KY: Van Nostrand Reinhold.

Ortiz, Alfonso (1969). *The Tewa World: Space, Time, Being, and Becoming in a Pueblo Society*. Chicago: University of Chicago Press.

Sandercock, Leonie, ed. (1998). *Making the Invisible: Insurgent Planning Histories*. Berkeley: University of California Press.

Scully, Vincent Joseph (1975). *Pueblo: Mountain, Village*. New York: Viking Press.

Titiev, Mischa (1992). *Old Oraibi: a Study of the Hopi Indians of Third Mesa*. Albuquerque: University of New Mexico Press.

## NOTES

1  See Titiev (1992).
2  It should be noted that the word *plaza* is a colonial Spanish reference to an identical township courtyard found in both the New and Old Worlds. Among Pueblo villages, the centerplace predates first contact. See Jojola, Modernization and Pueblo lifeways: Isleta Pueblo, in Markovich, Preiser, and Sturm (1989).
3  For a more extensive discussion see Swentzell, Pueblo space, form and mythology, in Markovich, Preiser, and Sturm (1989: 27).
4  See Ortiz (1969).
5  See Scully (1975).
6  See Jojola (1998).
7  Conversation with Viola Cordova. I have also adapted from her the term "interstice" that I use later in this chapter.
8  This is the main conclusion of my masters thesis (Jojola 1976).
9  This is the central premise of Dolores Hayden (1995).

# 9

# LANGUAGE MATTERS: NONDISCRETE NONBINARY DUALISM

*Anne Waters*

*The difference is in the promotion, so to speak. A non-Native poet cannot produce an Indian perspective on Coyote or Hawk, cannot see Coyote or Hawk in an Indian way, and cannot produce a poem expressing Indian spirituality. What can be produced is another perspective, another view, and another spiritual expression. The issue, as I said, is one of integrity and intent.*

["The Great Pretenders" by Wendy Rose, in *The State of Native America: Genocide, Colonization, and Resistance*, ed. M. A. Jaimes-Guerrero, Boston: South End Press, p. 416.]

## INTRODUCTION

In this chapter I use gender as an example to explore a nondiscrete ontology of being. To recognize that gender as it is known today among colonized American Indian nations mirrors a notion of gender among American Indigenous cultures five centuries ago may be misleading. Deconstructing contemporary dominant American gender notions against a background of an alternatively conceived ontology of Being through America's Indigenous languages proves fruitful in explicating why and how gender need not be an essentialized concept. This chapter first clarifies an important distinction between a discrete and a nondiscrete binary dualist ontology. In fulfilling the European colonial project in the Americas, a hypersensitively bounded infrastructure of Eurocentric ontology desensitized the nondiscrete[1] binary[2] dualist Indigenist thought. Euro-Americans, while exploiting the people, land, and resources of the Americas,

97

comprehended, of their experiences and encounters with Indigenous people, only what could be conveniently characterized via their Eurocentric ontology. An ontology of binary, or discrete, dualist logic operated as the colonial framework that deeply embedded Euro-American thought and language, and a Eurocentric perspective about Indigenous people, on the North American continent. Eurocentric nonunderstandings, and hence misunderstandings, of precolonial ontology, rationality, beliefs, customs, and institutions of people indigenous to the Americas has been filtered through this overlay, or template of interpretation.

Euro-American institutions, including educational institutions, have placed many nonunderstandings about Indigenous people into the context of Euro-American-embraced conceptual categories. These categories signify a discrete (limited and bounded[3]) binary dualist[4] worldview. This worldview continues to operate as a template into which all Euro-American interpretations of Indigenous thought and being are recorded. Hence, much of Indigenous philosophy is not easily accessible, though some accessibility is possible via language analysis and the semantics of contemporary speakers of Indigenous languages. (Descendants of America's Indigenous people, and Euro-Americans cannot simply step into a world in which nondiscrete binary dualist logic is a diversely functional lived ontology.) Moreover, the Euro-American binary system of dualist thought empowered and facilitated the misinterpretations of the Indigenous nondiscrete binary dualist worldview; many of these misinterpretations remain active in contemporary scholarship.[5]

Imposing a closed binary ontology on to Indigenous ideas obstructs communication/ meaning systems, to such an extent that, for good reasons, Indigenous ideas and vision have largely remained closed to outsiders. The seemingly cognitive inability of some Euro-Americans to acknowledge a different ontological system, represented by Indigenous thought, continues to perplex and befuddle many American Indians.[6] It has historically been in this context of blinded Euro-American vision that many American Indians have been denied the learning/use of Native languages; and in this way have sometimes been prevented from safeguarding ancient sacred knowledge. This theft, or stealing of Native language, and with it, sacred knowledge, led to many painful losses that remain unhealed today. The losses create gaps of understanding of the Indigenous worldview and ontological being in that world. Retaining sacred knowledge would have nourished Indigenous people during half a millennium of painful colonization. Yet it was denied to most of those American Indians that survived the genocide.

Many American Indigenous nondiscrete notions of nonbinary, complementary dualist constructs of the cosmos have been diminished and obscured by colonization. A nonbinary, complementary dualist construct would distinguish two things: (1) a dualism (e.g. male/female) that may appear (in a binary ontology) as opposites or things different from one another in some important respect; and (2) a nonbinary (complementary) syntax that puts together such constructs without maintaining sharp and clear boundary distinctions (unlike a binary system). The maintenance of the rigid distinct boundaries of binary logic enable (though may not necessitate) an hierarchical value judgment to take place (e.g. mind over body, or male over female) precisely because of the sharp bifurcation. A nonbinary (complementary) dualism would place the two constructs together in such a way that one would remain itself, and be also a part of the other. In this way, an hierarchical valuing of one being better, superior, or more valued than another cannot be, or rather is, excluded by the nonbinary logic. Organizing, complementary ideas of an Indigenous ontology still survive within the ontological horizon of nonbinary, nondiscrete, dualist languages. Complementary dualisms can be found today among such diverse Indigenous people as the Ahnishinahbaeotjibway in Canada,[7] to the Mayan in South America;[8] consider also the Diné metaphysics of the Southwestern USA.[9]

Noncomplementary, or binary dualist constructs have rigid boundaries that do not interact, or "cross over," to other constructs. In the English language, and in Western thought the concept "good" if used together with the concept "evil" is such that one can diminish aspects of the other. Something may be good or evil, but not both at the same time and place, without diminishing the other. They need not be equal in the joining, but rather have the potential for one to be superior to the other. Hence, "good" and "evil" may not overlap, nor may there be any ambiguity in the meaning of one in relation to the other. Things, including actions, must be either good or evil, but not both.[10]

For another example with a different twist, consider an instance of the color black and the color white coming into contact with one another. Physically, as with paints, a gray appears, obliterating the black and white boundaries; ontologically, a conflict or struggle ensues, each construct vying for its own showing and placement over that of the other! This is why, in Western thought, it is important to keep sharply divided dichotomies bifurcated with rigid, clear boundaries operating at the margins. These boundaries are what enable value judgment to be applied to the two constructs; that is, the value of one over the other can be achieved only if they do not mix.

Western metaphysics derived from classic Greek thought seems to manifest this bifurcatedness (binariness) of dualist thought; concepts are truncated with sharp, clearly unambiguous, boundaries. This allows Plato, for example, to play word games with some tightly bounded binary dualist constructs, such as "like" and "unlike." To elaborate this point, consider the Humpty Dumpty theory of binary dualism in European thought that reaches back to Greece. In the history of Western philosophical thought since Plato's fracture, not a single philosopher has been able to put back together the universe for the Western world!

Plato created a notion of reality, or "truth," that was static, of the mind, being always in the abstract;[11] he redefined the common notion of material substance to be "the unreal," changing, always becoming a different physical illusion. The "true" became an object of worship, existing in total abstraction from the physical bodies of the universe. The physical became an object of derogation and want, drawing attention away from the realm of "the true." This particular way of being and conceiving reality embedded a structure of hierarchical value: the true was to be embraced as the (nonchanging) form of the "good"; and the formless, constant flux in the universe of matter was to be rejected as "evil". Objects were "evil" because they drew attention away from the "purity" of abstract mental thought; the flux competed to "tie down" thought in the world of matter, but was destined to lose the battle.

These tightly bounded, clearly differentiated modes of being, good and evil, competed for human attention in continual struggle through human experience. And when the realm of form, of the good, won out, the privilege of dwelling in the "land of the forms" was granted in an afterlife. But when the evil, the objects in the realm of the physical, won the competition for attention, great human suffering was to be the consequence, in a land of insurmountable grief "down below" the earth, in an afterlife.

Via Neoplatonism, and through the Middle Ages, Plato's notion of "good" was transformed into a personal Christian "good" named "God" in the creation of a tripartite flat world: the "forms in the abstract heavens – total good-God" were constructed securely up above the earth; and "the physical in the concrete hell – total evil-Devil" were constructed securely down below the earth. The only way to attain human peace or harmony living in the "earthly domain" (the alleged flat surface in between the "heaven and hell of good and evil") was via prayer, or mentally dwelling in the land of the heavens. Neoplatonic thought cemented Platonic metaphysics in Europe, and served well the purposes of the medieval clergy. They turned their backs on the poor, and spent their time communing with their personal (good) God.

In this context, the only way to attain "human perfection" was through abstract thought. Anything that was not abstract thought, such as physical being or physical pain, was to be denied the status of real.[12] Pain, in such forms as flagellation, and physical torture, was believed to lead a person to a state of mind where he or she might exist in complete abstraction. The value hierarchy of a binary dualist thought that valued abstract reason above physical pleasure enveloped the cosmology of the "great chain of being," the "Christian hierarchy of being," and the King commanding through divine right, bringing into being divine plans.

In the fifteenth century, European perceptions and beliefs cemented this Eurocentric metaphysic and ontology of value hierarchy, supported by the two pillars of binary dualism. Western culture lacked any historical understanding about how to live in balance and harmony (complementarity) with diverse metaphysical ideas and beings such as it encountered in the Americas. Europeans had learned no tolerance for difference, much less the ability to survive living with (mother) earth. Europeans were their own products of colonization. They arrived in America knowing how to live only as servants, prisoners, peasants, and soldiers; they were alienated from being in the world. They continued a centuries-old colonial imperialist project (their descendants continue to benefit from it).

When Europeans arrived in the Americas, they found a culture where respecting diversity was integral to survival and living in harmony. Europeans showed an intense lack of respect for diverse cultural ways. Their behavior suggested a psychological necessity to impose colonial European culture, with all of its superior/inferior linguistic distinctions, upon Indigenous people. In this way, any conceivable opportunity for dialogue, or communication between the two cultures, was obliterated. In some instances, the very same families who learned from Native people how to plant, harvest, and survive the cold winters, were forced to leave the area.

America's Indigenous people had a history of creating harmony among diverse communities through political relations.[13] The histories of these relations are many, and are articulated through the oral history of many Indigenous groups. On the North American continent, both intercultural and intracultural relations had long histories of communal respect. Indigenous people found a metaphysical place in the structuring of the cosmos for "all our relations," within the history of "the original peoples."[14] Upon the arrival of Euro-Americans, a completely different mode of communicating, and being in the world, was imposed.

The ontological structures of Indigenous people precluded a coherent dialogue with the newcomers. Europeans, having "purified" the mind, and "corrupted" the body, had no sense of physical rootedness to any land, nor responsibility to self, or other relations. Everything in European thought was filtered through a value sieve, and Indigenous people, because different, were not within the realm of positive value for the newcomers. These Euro-Americans had left behind any remnants of their own sense of place, of geographical roots of being, in Europe. As they gazed upon the land and the bounty of Indigenous foods and resources, they immediately laid claim to America's shores for themselves.

Complicitly, hyper-bounded, value-laden, binary dualist constructs of being were projected on to Indigenous people: first, by sharing interpretations of individual actions; then projecting their interpretations on to groups of Indigenous people. Unable to tolerate difference in ways of being, Europeans disrespectfully labeled Indigenous people uncivilized, inferior, dirty, ignorant, savage, primitive, etc. Thus, in ignorance, and at play in their own binary dualist logic system, the belittling of Indigenous people in the colonial mind made colonizers feel superior to the colonized. And if they were superior, then, their logic told them, Indigenous people were inferior, and if inferior, less than fully human. In this way, by ontologically denigrating the "other" to be of a lower nature in a hierarchy of being, individuals in the south, like DeSoto and his metal-clad warriors and human-eating dogs, could brutally slaughter Indigenous people throughout Las Floridas.

Simultaneously, the Spanish Conquistadores, in what was to become Mexico and South America, acted on similar constructs of Indigenous people, who were seen as "other," which meant not human in the gaze of the Spanish. Enslavement of Indigenous people was justified by a Eurocentric ontology (of being) manifested in the King's orders. Europeans acted as though they believed it were all in accord with a "divine" plan of the universe. The debates at Valladolid were about whether Indigenous beings in the Americas could be considered "human" or not.[15] If the natives were human, then we had "souls" and had to be saved by being "Christianized." On the other hand, if we were not found to possess humanity, then the Spanish were free to enslave us as they would any other creature of their nonhuman world. This debate in Spain clearly shows how an hierarchically structured ontology can be used to manipulate any type of different being in the world that is not seen, through the colonizer's gaze, to suit the plans of a colonial empire.

Thus brutal genocidal treatment of America's Indigenous people, at the hands of colonial Europe, is related to the ontological structure of the European colonial mindset. By the time of "point of contact" among Indigenous people with Europeans, an entire binary dualist worldview of consistently non-equal hierarchical power structures was in place in Eurocentric thinking. This mindset brought with it ideas about a male role as culture bearer in the world, and a female role as culture destroyer in the world. It brought with it ideas about humanity: an upper ruling class, rational and close to deity status; a middle military or overlord class, less rational, more emotional, and capable of some rule over the lower class; and the lower, intensive-labor class, as perceived by the imperial gaze, considered to be incapable of rational thought, and unable to rule over its own appetitive desires.

It was from this vantage point of human nature, and the European binary dualisms of ontological being in the world, that the newcomers brought a theistic worldview of value hierarchy to America's shores. The Eurocentric ontological depiction of a disconnected, bounded, rational, cultured male father creator of the universe, stood in antithesis to (what was seen Eurocentrically as) an unrestrained, unbounded, irrational, raw female mother-nature destroyer of the universe.

And so (it came to pass that) in the Americas men stood over women, imperialists over the colonized, citizens over the enslaved, adults over children, similarly abled over differently abled, those who inherit over those who do not inherit (a lie of) a pure race stood over mixed races, completing the Eurocentric hierarchy of winners over losers, and the valued over the disvalued, empowered over disempowered. All things of the world had a place in this hierarchy of being, and of differing values, according to the types of being, as classified by the rulers' ontological structure of power.

These strange and unreal constructs of hierarchical value were built into the ideology of Euro-Americans and American Indigenous communities through the benefiting of colonizing enterprises of religion, education, commerce, etc. From the land of the Salem witchcraft trials, to the missions enslaving California's Indigenous people, missionaries, politicians, businessmen, and the landed gentry played a key role in maintaining this hierarchical Christian ideology. It was well suited to colonial enterprises of trade in goods and people. Thus, Euro-Americans sanctioned genocidal activities that created chaotic ruptures in Indigenous ontology.

Upon Spain's acknowledgment that Indigenous people had souls, the means of converting Indigenous people to Eurocentric theism played into the colonial project. But because Indigenous people were not easily converted, methods were employed to "kill the Indian and save the soul."[16] These methods included torture, starvation, killing, burning, stealing land, children, wives, or family, enslavement, confinement, denial of languages, threat of diseases, or rape and plunder of homes, burning of crops and people, and disruption of any vestiges of humanity, until Eurocentric theism, in exchange for life or the survival of the community, was proclaimed and witnessed. Even now, after the signing of treaties, the smallpox blankets, the piles of American Indians lying in deep trenched graves, after the removals of the genocide remains, the lynchings, rapes, thefts of children, alcoholic drugging of entire communities, and denial of cultural languages and sacred practices, a genocide continues in the name of religious freedom, citizen protection, assimilation, and, most important, free trade.

It was in this way that it occurred. In this way agents of Euro-American colonial theism wrenched Indigenous ontological constructs (embedded in the linguistic structures and thinking of the Indigenous mind) from Indigenist thought, causing a continental shake-down of the Indigenous worldview. This ontological destruction was but one more notch on the belt of an ideology that worked to maintain power over "others." These cultural extortions resulted in great losses for Indigenous people, in our families, communities, and belief systems. In this psychological dismembering, which was eventually fueled by forced migrations, our fractures of ontology became chasms needing to be filled, gaps in the thought process.

## THOUGHTS ABOUT NONBINARY DUALISM

Among the gaps, however, there remained kernels of ontology: ideas about ways of being in the world; and ideas about ontological relationships in the world. Our stories held understandings of Indigenous human science, technology, relations, and our sacred place in the world. The embedded ontology of the Indigenous worldview has survived for people who have had little else. Their metaphysics and epistemology remain intact among Indigenous people of the Americas.

Hence the colonial project of dismembering the ontology of Indigenous thought successfully failed! American Indigenous nondiscrete notions of nonbinary, complementary dualist constructs continue to exist. Though in some places they are diminished and obscured by colonization, Indigenous ontologies are very active, even if sometimes in the more isolated regions of the Americas. These organizing, complementary ideas, still living within the ontological horizon of a nonbinary, nondiscrete dualism hold much information for our future. And it is to this horizon that many American Indians (and environmentalists advocating sustainable development) are looking, for a renaissance of American Indian thought. These ways of being, in an ontological Indigenous realm, remain as practical, accessible, and pragmatic tools of understanding our place in the world which is, of course, a place of responsibility to "all my relations."

For many Indigenous people, the importance of order and balance, as well as a proper (moral) behavior, are part of the cosmological understanding of our universe. If one is out of balance with metaphysical forces, or out of balance within oneself, sickness will appear and remain, until the universe, and the person in that universe, is again in balance, or ordered. The structures of the cosmos are like the structures of the mind, in that everything must be balanced and nurtured properly in order for the universe, and us, to survive. So, also, in Indigenous thought, dualism embraces difference in principle, not as division but rather as complementarity.

In Diné (Navajo) thought, for example, because the breath of life (air) is constantly being exchanged in the universe, from the cosmos and to the earth, breath plays a central role in complementary metaphysical thought. Not only is breath that which is life-giving, but smoke, as manifesting aspects of breath, operates as the medium for air to reach the sky, the cosmos, as do words when spoken or sung. The exchange of breath is important because all things in the universe are related through air, and all are made of the same basic elements. Just as we take in air to breathe, so also we let out breath, giving back to that from which we take. In Diné thought, for example, earth, air, fire, and water are the basic elements of the entire cosmos. These elements are continually in a give-and-take relationship in the universe as spirit (energy) infuses everything. Thus, upon death, after air is released from the body (given back), the body will decompose into the elements, giving itself back to that from which it was created.[17]

In Zuni thought the Twin War Gods are also known as the Evening Star and the Morning Star. The twins embody the principle of dualism, as manifested not in a binary, but in a nonbinary, or complementary state of being. Hence a complementary dualism of life force and death are held together ontologically, just as they are in real life.

"Twins incorporate not only the principle of duality but also that of balance, being... more than complementary yet less than isomorphic: both are of a piece, perceivable as separate but, in truth, inalienable. The Twins share a single breath of life that animates them both separately and together, providing a model for the Zuni in which to cast other perceptions of the natural and created universe as being all of a piece."[18] Metaphysical space, however, is operative also as moral space; hence the providing of breath of life, via singing or talking, back to the universe fulfills a moral connection of the nurturing of everything in the universe.

# GAPS OF MEANING

As a young American Indian undergraduate philosophy student in New Mexico, I harbored a deep desire to do well in logic. Euro-American professors wanted philosophy students to believe that logic courses presented to us the opportunity to "master" the methodology of philosophy, that the very structure of human philosophical thought would be revealed to us in our study of logic. It was only later, in graduate school, when I proved lengthy deductions, and contemplated meta-theoretical logic problems, that I began to take seriously my outsider intuitions about the field of logic. Our understanding of philosophy was supposed to be different after that first logic course. It was. Since that time I have taught some 63 course sections of logic and critical thinking. And yet I still struggle, in everyday common discussion, to articulate my discomfort with the discrete binarism of some dualist thought systems.

In 1992, while at a community college in New Mexico, at the suggestion of Terry Abraham, an American Indian (Laguna Pueblo) special-needs psychological counselor and administrator, I began working on a project to identify why many Indigenous students were having difficulty passing logic courses. They were opting to "drop out" of the classes. At that time I did not think their problems would be connected to my own ontological issues of binary logic systems. And yet this work also became an opportunity to gain a better understanding and clarification of my own experience.

And so I began, in small ways, to investigate, and change, the nature of the logic course I taught. Early in the semester I incorporated Native American Studies content into examples used to explain the structure of informal fallacies.[19] The level of Native American student interest, enrollment, and attendance was considerably increased. American Indian students began showing up at the classroom door, and wanting to know who I was, and how they too could enroll or sit in for the course.

104

Later in the semester, I also changed my method of introducing formal logic. To eliminate anxiety and stress related to learning a symbolic system, I suggested to students that working with binary logic systems could be thought of as a game of imaginary binary dualities; that these dualities need not relate to world structures. I put special emphasis on the fact that binary dualities, or binary concepts, are used to work with imaginary, non-organic thought processes, such as computers. This analogy to computers seemed to make a big difference. We were merely studying the processing pattern of electrical impulses in computers. I emphasized that such structures, as we imagined them, could be thought of as, but were not believed by everyone to be, the structure of ideas embedded in belief and thought systems of the human psyche. I was teaching students a way of reasoning that humans or machines could use, but in a way that did not establish discrete binary logic as a more fundamental (or more valued) ontology than their own, which should replace their own, or which they would have to engage in in lieu of their own.

With these two changes, adding Native content and analogizing to computer thinking patterns, changes in Native American grades were dramatic. The motivation and enthusiasm of Native American students was beyond my imagination. For I had discovered that in leaving the box of ontological tools open, all students could more quickly grasp the intuitive, creative problem-solving of conceptual pragmatic manipulation.

It was from this experience and standpoint that I commenced to think more deeply about researching the ontological, epistemological, and metaphysical systems of peoples indigenous to the Americas. Changing my teaching methods was the prelude to uncovering an ontological infrastructure of American Indian scientific speculation. As I continued my research, I began to discover how the assumed Western European binary dualism, embedded in what came to be known as Western philosophy (at least as far back as Aristotle), was not the same ontological system as, for example, Mayan (nonbinary) dualism. This revelation changed not only my approach to teaching all of my courses, but my research methods, and the very meaning of my work as a philosopher. No longer was I primarily interested in ethics and social and political philosophy, but more to the point, in the underlying ontology of my own Indigenous thought patterns that created a cognitive environment from which I viewed Eurocentric metaphysics, epistemology, and worldview.

In 1996 I was invited to keynote a conference at the University of Oregon; the conference theme was "Engendering Rationalities." As I began to contemplate what the expression "engendering Rationalities" might mean in the context of a women's (feminist) philosophy conference, my mind's eye drifted to the concept of what the paradigm case of rationality is for the Western European world (and *a fortiori* by colonization, for most of the world). In my pondering I realized the same gaps of ontology were in the the framework of binary dualist logic that was embedded in the non-process ontology of feminist thought: male/female; masculine/feminine; good/bad.[20] And in this context I remembered the importance Adrienne Rich attached to the "lesbian continuum" in *On Lies, Secrets, and Silences*,[21] and how this model had never really been incorporated into conceptual categories of native gender. Naomi Zack's work about racial and ethnic affiliations, and how race concepts are ontologically limited and bifurcated, came to mind as well.[22]

I then thought about static bifurcations of the discrete binary (bounded) dualities of essentialisms in contemporary feminist thought and recent race theory: male/female, masculine/feminine, man/woman; black/white, Indian/non-Indian, Hispanic/not-Hispanic, Asian/non-Asian, etc. These discretely bifurcated and essentialized concepts suggested a way of being in the world that might run contrary to some Indigenist ontology we find remaining in American Indian languages. And the problem seemed to be not so much that "language has gone on a holiday," but rather, that deep structures of Indigenous thinking about ontological relations in the world conflicted with the discrete binary logic inherent in Euro-American reflection about relations in the world.

Critical feminist theory, like critical race theory, pleads for a reconsideration of these categories. And some people have already begun this important work. But perhaps reconsidering race and gender categories will further require us to radically reflect on the possibility of altering our ontology. I have no idea how this could be done, but it seems that it might be a possibility.

One of the common laments Caribbean women brought to race theory toward the end of the second movement was the question: Why can't I be Black *and* Hispanic? This issue pointed us in the direction of critically analyzing all contemporary American race categories. Paula Gunn Allen, also American Indian (Laguna Pueblo), in raising issues about race in the women's movement, brought to our attention the American Indian women's critique of Euro-American feminist historicity and situatedness. Paula, in asking "where are the red roots of feminism?" directed attention not only to a gap of analysis, but to the very denial of human relationship in the world. These two questions fuse together in asking "what are the roots of this language/these ideas, that deny my being in the world?" Or, more aptly put, "who are these people who want to control, through language use, who I am?"

The point here is that history directs us to a time when there did exist a difference of ontology. With this different ontology, there existed a difference of ways of being in the world. This difference of Indigenist thought is cashed out in notions about personal and social identity. Epistemic red roots, for example, once existing in words like autonomy, liberty, respect, and equality (in American Indigenist thought), could not be separated from ideas about freedom, responsibility, and peace.[23] This loss of language meaning is a loss of conceptual ontology; it is a loss of a way of being in the world; it is a loss of ways of relating in the world; and in its concrete manifestation it is a loss of personal, social, cultural identity, or self.

Understanding the permeability of Indigenous constructs of ethnicity, or gender, may assist feminist theory in understanding certain womanist assumptions of indigenism. Indigenous women doing feminist social engineering and healing need to be understood as living two different types of identities: first, the identity of a being in a language that knows only a nondiscrete dualist ontology; and second, the survival identity, imposed by the highly discrete and bifurcated dualist logic of colonial Europe in the Americas. This second identity is molded in the logic and language of colonization; the identity is constructed in a fixed, racialized, and biologized criterion of identity; it is a political identity that works to protect those in power. It is used to announce the presence of a discretely gendered person. When critical theory fails to recognize very different identities of American Indian women, the result is a misunderstood articulation of Indian gender and ethnic identity.

Gendered identity standpoints of the dominant culture become for American Indian women a colonial template, dictating what our reality is supposed to be; it is stamped on us both by a colonial language and by ontology. Colonization has placed American Indians in certain ontological standpoints of perspective, yet it is sometimes from our traditional ontologies of perspective that we see and respond to how others see us. Though we have been forced to participate in a colonial game of "picture, picture, who has the picture," in reality we know there are many pictures, just as there are many different genders and ontological structures in the world. What we don't know is why feminist theorists don't "get this."

Many Indigenous gender categories are ontologically without fixed boundary. They are animate, nondiscrete, and grounded in a nondiscrete and thus nonbinary dualist ontology. That is, the ontology, as animated (continuously alterable), will be inclusive (nonbinary) rather than exclusive (discretely binary), and have nondiscrete (unbounded) entities rather than discrete (discretely bounded) entities. In this way, it is possible to have a nonbinary (nondiscrete) dualist thought system, or a nondiscrete binary dualist thought system, of gender. Understanding how a nondiscrete ontology of gender operates, and being able to imagine it, may be a crucial step toward comprehending the gender[24] politics of American Indian women.

The ontological gender difference, made manifest in linguistic difference, discloses a way of embracing our world. This embracing reflects deep ontological alterity. The overlapping categories of Indigenist ontology create an experience of the world distinct from, but in every way equal to, the Western European ontology of discrete bounded entities. This alterity gives rise to a different worldview, from which a very real standpoint comes into being. This standpoint discloses a difference of politics. It signifies a manifest site of change that it would have been necessary to undergo, in the process of adapting to ontological gendercide within the American Indian genocide in the Americas. For many, because the genocide of Indigenous languages was never metamorphosed, this nontransformed ontological site reflects a nondiscrete, inclusive, living, nonbinary dualism, inclusively celebrated in articulations of "all my relations."

Because ontological difference can give rise to metaphysical difference, Indigenous concepts of gender may sometimes stand outside a sharply demarcated ontology of binary, dualist thought. That American Indians have, against incredible odds, maintained this different ontology is a marvel and a wonder. The presence of this ontological memory suggests that a vital malleability and animation of gender worldview may be preferred by Indigenous people over a categorically fixed, sharply bifurcated, limiting worldview. If this is the case, we can expect to encounter a general shift in disciplines that engage Indigenist thought and ontology; they will need to move toward comprehending a continuum of binary, nondiscrete, dual metaphysical systems. However, the first site of interpretation may be those systems embracing cross- and multi-disciplines, cultures, methods, and dimensions.

An Indigenous manifold of complexity, resembling a world of multifariously associated connections and intimate fusions, might not be expected to give way easily to a metaphysics of sharply defined (bounded) and limited, (discretely) binary dualist constructions of gender. Nor may such yielding serve our situated survival in an actively complex, continuously changing, and hence precarious metaphysical world. But identifying and naming diversely intertwined active gender ontologies (multigender ontologies) may turn out to be a prerequisite for understanding gender worldviews as they have developed in the Americas. This may especially be true for American Indians.

# GENDER BECOMES

Henry Sharp, in "Asymmetric equals: Women and Men among the Chipewyan" (Sharp 1995), notes how fuzzy logic appears in the Chipewyan (Ojibwa) language.

> One legacy of the history of the development of our [*sic*] language [English], and the role of binary thought in our philosophy, is the assumption that categories are discrete . . . that they are discrete bounded entities. A and not-A cannot be the same. Chipewyan categories are, to a far greater extent than is the case in our culture, nondiscrete. . . . Chipewyan symbolic logic is not binary. A and not-A can be the same, or, since neither A [n]or not-A have discrete boundaries, they can overlap. It is the case of fuzzy logic in which the degree of resemblance between categories can be zero.[25]

Sharp claims that if colonial categories are discrete (discretely bounded entities), then it may be exceedingly difficult, in such a value system, to think about categories and not assign an hierarchical relation. In Western thought hierarchy exists between every linked A and not-A. This is because emotional (affective) reasoning that parallels rational (inferential) thought "projects hierarchy onto categorical differences."[26]

Sharp goes on to note that gender is a cultural construct "imposed on the phenotypical expression of the chromosomal diversity present in human beings" (1995: 68) Because there is a variety of genetic construction of the human species in the biology of sex, binary categories need not necessarily arise. Moreover, as there is variation in genetic construction of the human biology of sex, binary cultural categories ought to be demonstrated rather than assumed. This burden falls upon Western Eurocentric culture, and will need to use genotypes, as well as phenotypical expression.

Euro-American culture, in order to explain binary sex/gender categories, will likely have to first presume discretely fixed categories, essentialized (tied down) as ahistorical, and unchanging throughout time and place. This presumption might exclude other possible sex/gender speculations about historical, temporal, and regional cause-and-effect inferences with respect to gender role. As example, comprehending interactive and complementary, nondiscrete dual gender categories could be a function of a specific history of a human group in a particular temporal or geographic region.

A Chipewyan perspective of gender explanation, as a particular instance of general explanation, requires linking alternate explanations together, thus combining a context of many illustrative factors without reducing them to a single concept of cause and effect. Contrast this with the "modern" scientific enterprise of seeking singular (tied down) necessary and sufficient conditions of explanation, as found in the history of Western European and Euro-American culture. The framework "is a triadic system, involving male, female, and a third category/context in which male/female is not relevant."[27] This third category retains the rudimentary ambiguity of nonfixed categorization: "who and what the being is is not knowable from what it is, but only from what it later became."[28] Male and female cannot be presumed; the nature of the cause/effect relationship between adult and child may be the equivalent to gender classification, that is, it is something one attains.

In some contexts male may be an achieved status, and female an ascribed, rather than achieved status. For example, the Chipewyans do not distinguish between physical and supernatural causality; cause and effect are one. *Inkoze* is a Chipewyan concept that describes the "collective knowledge of supernatural causality."[29] Males must achieve the status of maleness by attaining *Inkoze*. They do so by displaying behavior appropriate to having the knowledge of *Inkoze*. To have *Inkoze* is to attain respect; it is achieved via performance. Prior to attaining *Inkoze*, men do not have gender. Because women already have respect and status, ascribed via teaching skills, women do not need to perform in order to attain *Inkoze*.[30] In sum, Sharp tries to show how gender relevancy can be interculturally context-laden. Yet historical records of gender relevancy may depend upon a logic of the recorder's ontological understanding of a particular event, as well as that recorder's attitude and ability, to understand *Inkoze* ontology.[31]

Thus we see that the concept of gender can be malleable, and differs not only across cultures, but can be context-dependent within a culture. Gender constructs can be used to interpret the meaning of behaviors appropriate to, for example, menstrual taboos for young women, and root-oven taboos for young men. Lillian A. Ackerman, in "Gender Status in the Plateau" notes that among Plateau Indians, once children matured, taboos were not so strict, as measures could be taken to neutralize gender influence.[32] Understanding gender construct in Indigenous America may require not only non-discrete malleability, but that constructs be understood in appropriate personal, social, political, economic, domestic, spiritual, or even sexual contexts. At it best, understanding will not be uni-definitional or a-contextual.[33]

## GENDER STATUS

The gender status of American Indian women is an important issue to raise in the context of social, cultural, and political relations. Much ink has been spilt during the several years since the second wave of the feminist movement in trying to prove that the Confederacy created by the Iroquois Nations (Mohawk, Oneida, Onondaga, Cayuga, Seneca, and in the early eighteenth century, the Tuscarora), dating back as far as AD 1000, was a matriarchy. Admittedly, the clan system of the Haudenoshaunee was matrilineal; but this does not necessarily translate into a matrifocal or matriarchal framework. Again, the discrete binary imposition of Western European logic has assumed that if a culture is not patriarchal, it must be matriarchal, and if not patrilineal, then matrilineal. In making claims about aboriginal people, Western European scholars have not been able to conceive egalitarian societies with protean (a Delorian word) binary constructs.

Joy Bilharz notes that the status of Haudenoshaunee women in the Confederacy has been continuously debated from 1851 to the present.[34] Bilharz claims that men cleared the land, and women worked it, and it had to be abandoned every ten to twenty years for more fertile soil, timber reserves, and animal access. What we are not told by Bilharz is whether the men/women and male/female constructs were polymorphous. Nonetheless, any notion of ownership of the land was always ephemeral. In this context both horticulture and hunting were complementary (and value-equivalent) activities. And although we don't know the nature of the gender constructs, because a concept of geographical space was associated with gender, the

> Iroquois world divided into complementary realms of forest and clearing...the former being the domain of men, the warriors, hunters, and diplomats, and the latter the domain of women, the farmers and clan matrons.[35]

In the nineteenth and twentieth centuries, many things changed for Iroquois women. The eventual reliance upon Euro-American trade for metal tools and cooking pots, the presence of alcohol, to abet genocide, that lessened a sense of community, the preclusion of traditional roles by new responsibilities of nontraditional ways, the eventual transition from a matrilineal extended-family household to a patrilineal nuclear-family household, and the mirroring, in the mid-nineteenth century, of contemporary Euro-American values and customs, created a somewhat different Seneca Nation of American Indians. Significantly, these events did not defeat Indigenous values and customs, though they contributed to the waning of women's traditional tribal power. "Women were disenfranchised: only males could vote, and only males could hold office."[36] It was not until 1964 that Native women were again enfranchised, and took up empowering political roles in housing, education, employment, and political councils. The current renaissance of Indigenous people's culture can at least partly be attributed to the rebuilding of women's traditionally powerful tribal roles in an urban context. Bilharz maintains that women still hold control over the "clearing," or public policy, outside the home.

Gender construction appears malleable in at least some American Indian cultures. The Chipewyan concept of a gender-becoming, or the acquiring of *Inkoze* by the performance of stepping out from a third, enigmatic gender construct, evidently appears to be, from a Euro-American worldview, a unique and unconventional slant on gender. Yet Chipewyan gender notions present only one among multifarious Indigenous gender roles.

Another example of a variegated, nondiscrete gender identity can be seen in the Taino peoples, at one time from the Southeastern United States. Taino have rites for girls and boys upon attaining puberty; they generously grant young adults an autonomous option of gender selection. And a further illumination of Indigenous gender autonomy can be gleaned from the notion of the "manly-hearted" women (*ninaupos-kitzipxpe*) among the Blackfoot, and the *nadlee* of the Southwest. In Diné thought, the *nadlee* remains a mixed-gender status – the hermaphrodite, mythic trickster and creator, highly coveted, and always treated with respectful awe – which dignifies the marvel of creation and all relations. I can think of no similar concept in Euro-American thought.

Various supplementary examples could be cited. The presence of traditionally admired gendered beings endures. Peoples indigenous to the Americas and elsewhere suggest that we can secure at least one credible inference about differently gendered beings. That inference is this: that cultural values of at least some Indigenous people have continued to offer exceptional sanctuary to an attitude about gender that cherishes a wide arena of personal autonomy and freedom. This sanctuary has been exceptional because it has withstood over 500 years of cultural attack.

Alice Kehoe explains the importance of autonomy as a context for gender roles:

> What really matters to a Blackfoot is autonomy, personal autonomy. Blackfoot respect each person's competence, even the competence of very small children, and avoid bossing others. People seek power to support the autonomy they so highly value. Competence is the outward justification of the exercise of autonomy. If a person competently engages in work or behavior ordinarily the domain of people of the other sex, or of another species, onlookers assume the person has been blessed, either uninvited or through seeking by spiritual power to behave in this unusual manner. A woman who wanted to go to war, and there were many such, was judged as a man would be by her success in counting coup [counting winnings] or seizing enemy weapons.[37]

# CONCLUSION

The colonization of the Americas brought severe penalties for anyone exercising an opportunity to exert individual gender autonomy. The previously known cultural exuberance of autonomous gender decision and polymorphous constructs became significantly erased by tightly defined, delineated, and discrete European and Euro-American gender roles. To transgress the hypersensitive boundary in the presence of the colonizer was to flirt with death.

Feminists have argued that European gender roles, via rigid and discrete boundary constructions, have limited the human experience of sex and gender potentials. Certainly we do not find among Indigenous people of the Americas a utopia of sex and gender roles, any more than we find a romanticized matriarchy, in which women are worshiped as the center of the world. And yet, even when some cultures may appear to have women at the center of a cosmos, it is not yet clear how under- and over-determination affected interpretations of what passed for gender dichotomy in the eyes of the beholder. Certainly in the Americas, the ontology of translation as practiced by Euro-Americans did not adequately sustain the ontology of Indigenous thought. It appears that it is as difficult to define gender among Indigenous people today as it is to define other discrete binary dualist concepts carried within Western European ontology.

Although I would disagree that a common ontology stands behind Western European and American Indigenist thought, there is still some common ground here. If concepts of personal autonomy and equality are linguistically interdependent in Indigenist languages, this may help explain something about ambiguous and multigendered identities and humanly lived relations. And if this is the case, then gender may be a more kaleidoscopic and protean concept than Euro-American culture has yet to imagine.[38]

# NOTES

1   An earlier draft of this chapter used *polythetic* and *monothetic* rather than *discrete* and *nondiscrete*. *Poly* – meaning "many-contained" rather than *mono* – meaning "one-(self)-contained." Monothetic logic would be one-place predicate logic (monadic); polythetic logic would require many-place predicate logic (polyadic). I later switched to using the distinction between "discrete" and "nondiscrete" binaries for clarity.

2   A *binary* system has a base of two, and everything is expressed using only two symbols, e.g. a binary logic system of computer programming uses only the digits "0" and "1"; and all programs are created using only these two symbols. Another example would be binary stars (sometimes referred to as double stars), where two stars revolve around a common center of gravity; there are never more than two, and each remains within the common gravitational pull, yet retains its own boundary. In binary logic systems the two values are the "true" and the "false" and all meaning is put into this value system. By contrast a nonbinary system may have bases of three or more, and may or may not be open to emergent change, e.g. a deontic logic system would use a value of the "true," the "false," and the "unknown," and meaning would be put into these categories.

3   Val Plumwood refers to the "boundedness" of the logic of colonization and oppression as being part of a dualism (or binary opposition) that constructs conceptual identity in terms of exclusionary contrasts, e.g. male/female. She indicates that feminist psychology has a term that she will use to designate the "gulf" inherent in dualised (note the *s* in the word "dualised") categories. The term is "hyperseparation." Plumwood indicates that the hyperseparation is a form of identity constructed by maximum exclusion from the "other's" qualities which, she adds, are conceived as inferior. Val also notes that Marilyn Frye claims that the members of dualized (note the *z* here) classes assume they are both hyperseparated from "others" (who constitute the opposition), and also homogenized, i.e. very like one another in one's own group (Plumwood 1998; Frye 1983). "Dualize" means to make or consider dual.

4   A "dualistic" system (of or based on dualism) is a system composed of two parts, or kinds, like or unlike. Hence, dualism *per se* does not give rise to unlikes (opposites), nor to the "inferiority" of one in relation to the "other." For example, a dualist ontology might hold that reality is composed of two elements, mind and matter, but need not make these kinds exclusive of one another, nor place value on one to the exclusion of the "other." Thus the privileging of "mind" over "matter" as we see manifest in some forms of rationalism, is not a natural byproduct of dualism, but rather the product of a value intentionalism; similarly for a theological dualism holding that there are two antagonistic principles in the universe, the "good" and the "evil." Of particular note is the fact that members of colonizing groups generally do not see themselves as members of a colonizing group but, rather, only as "superior to" the "others."

5   See for example Jacobs, Thomas, Lang (1997).

6   Throughout this chapter I use "American Indian" to refer to Indigenous people of the Americas (North, Central, and South) and their descendants. Thus an American Indigicentric perspective is used analogously to the notion of a Eurocentric, Africentric, and Euro-Americentric perspective; i.e., it is seen from the "eyes of" Indigenous people of the Americas.

7   Wub E Ke Niew, in *We Have the Right to Exist: a Translation of Aboriginal Indigenous Thought* (1995: 236) has referred to this as an "unresolvable dualism in their [English] language . . . Because I cannot conceive of a language with dualism, I use notions of binary and nonbinary to expose an important distinction here."

8   See Michael Ripinsky-Naxon (1998). He discusses one of the roles of a "shaman" as bringing together the abstract idea with the concrete reality: "The Maya principle of polar biunity finds, in many ways, an intellectual resonance in Niels Bohr's 'principle of correspondence' in which a single entity can be both matter (a particle) and pure energy (a wave); its nature is determined by its behavior at a given moment of observation. The observation of such physical behavior is subject to laws, formulated by Werner Heisenberg in his Uncertainty Principle, that are an inescapable property of the universe . . . such cosmological systems are not, in essence, incompatible descriptions of the world" (1998: 155). Vine Deloria, Jr., has remarked to a similar effect, in *Spirit and Reason* (1999), that it may be possible to replace the Western word "Spirit" that was imposed upon Indigenous thought, with "energy" and reconcile at least some of Western scientific thought with American Indigenous thought.

9   "In Navajo they say like, whatever that goes on within your world it is moving. It is just like a flow, everything is in flow. There are no solid objects or anything. Everything . . . goes through transformation. It goes through manifestations. There is wear and tear, there is, but there is no addition or there is no loss to anything. It is just a transformation. You are in that. You are participating in that, so everything is alive. So that is how the Navajo would interpret (Hanson Ashley, Sonto, Arizona, July 27, 1993)" (Schwarz 1997: 18); cf. p. 93 regarding pairings of contrasting but complementary components to make a whole (where each half is necessary) in the web of interconnectedness formed by relationships in the universe, with self and all relations.

10   In binary dualist logic, if something appears to be both good and evil, rigid boundaries must be marked out to clarify which one is to be dominant. Time and place function as language markers in the English language in such a way that something cannot both be and not be in linear time or geographical space. What is commonly known as "Indian time" on the other hand, is measured by events, and because events can recur, the "same" event may be in many places, or occur in many times.

11   As I use the concept "abstract thought" it means thought apart from any particular instances or material objects as semantics.

12   Wub E Ke Niew (1995: 219).

13   See Williams (1997).

14   Both the phrases "all our relations" and "the original peoples" have deep structural meaning in Indigenous cultures. Indigenous people of the Americas' philosophical thought generally incorporates an acknowledgment of "the" people, in origin stories, as human people, as distinct from different kinds of people, like animal people, tree people, etc.

15   See Hanke (1959). Although the humanity of Indigenous people of the Americas was at issue in the Valladolid debates, other issues also provided impetus for the colonization of the continents: Vitoria (Francisco de Vitoria at Salamanca) denied the right of mistreatment of

Indigenous people; Vitoria also argued that to prevent Indigenous people of the Americas from denying trade to Europe in a world where "God" had intended all nations to trade, any nation or group had a divine right to conquer America in the interests of uninhibited trade. Vine Deloria discusses this in *God is Red* (1994), and notes that "the doctrine that the pope had been given total control over the planet by God was soon secularized into justification for European nations, definitively Christian, to conquer... Once the doctrine became secularized, it was impossible for anyone to question its validity" (1994: 277).

16    As quoted from Hanke (1959).

17    Consider: "the daily occurrence of the dawn as the sun returns symbolizes the continuation of time and of life itself. Dawn (associated with the white and the East) is one of the four cardinal light phenomena, along with the blue of day-sky (associated with the South), the yellow of evening twilight (West), and the black of darkness (North). Each of these four light phenomena serves as a guide to people's movements and activities (Griffin-Pierce [Navajo-Diné] 1988)." In Williamson and Farrer (1997: 284).

18    Epilogue to Williamson and Farrer Mescalero Apache (1992: 285).

19    When *Red Earth, White Lies* (1995) by Vine Deloria, Jr. was published, it became the perfect medium of text examples to use to teach about how modern science was rampant with informal fallacies!

20    And in this context I remembered the significance of the "lesbian continuum" in Adrienne Rich's *Lies, Secrets and Silences*; Naomi Zack's work about racial and ethnic affiliations, and how race concepts could ontologically limit and bifurcate; and Maria Lugones' presentation in 1983 about our need to unwrap conceptual frameworks.

21    See Rich (1979).

22    See Zack (1995, 1997, 1998).

23    Se Wub E Ke Niew (1995), and Weatherford (1989).

24    Recent texts that have attempted articulations of Indigenous multigenders include: Roscoe (1983), Roscoe (1998), and Jacobs et al. (1997).

25    Klein and Ackerman (1995: 68).

26    Ibid.

27    Ibid.

28    Ibid., p. 69.

29    Ibid., p. 66.

30    From an American Indian multigendered perspective, it might make sense that a multi-gendered person would need to attain *Inkoze* (which is a concept we find in many Indigenous communities); but I have not yet thought about this very much.

31    Ibid., p. 67.

32    Ibid., p. 95.

33    See Tafoya, "Principle of Uncertainty," in Jacobs et al. (1997), p. 198.

34    Bilharz, "The changing status of Seneca Women," in Jacobs et al. (1997), p. 102.

35    Ibid., p. 103.

36    Ibid., p. 109.

37    Kehoe, "Blackfoot persons," in Jacobs et al. (1997), p. 122.

38    See the bibliography at the end of this volume for some of the works by Alice Kehoe and Bea Medicine that might begin to help clarify gender in Native North American Communities.

# REFERENCES

Deloria, Vine, Jr. (1994). *God is Red: A Native View of Religion*. Golden, CO: North American Press.

Deloria, Vine, Jr. (1995). *Red Earth, White Lies: Native Americans and the Myth of Scientific Fact*. New York: Scribner.

Deloria, Vine, Jr. (1999). *Spirit and Reason: The Vine Deloria, Jr, Reader*. Golden, CO: Fulcrum Publishing.

Frye, Marilyn (1983). *The Politics of Reality: Essays in Feminist Theory*. Trumansburg, NY: The Crossing Press.

Hanke, Lewis (1959). *Aristotle and the American Indians*. Bloomington: Indiana University Press.

Jacobs, Sue Ellen, Wesley Thomas, and Sabine Lang (eds.) (1997). *Two-spirit People: Native American Gender Identity, Sexuality, and Spirituality*. Urbana: University of Illinois Press.

Klein, Laura F. and Lillian A. Ackerman (eds.) (1995). *Women and Power in Native North America*. Norman: University of Oklahoma Press.

Plumwood, Val (1998). The environment. In *A Companion to Feminist Philosophy*, ed. Alison M. Jagger and Iris Marion Young. Oxford: Blackwell, pp. 213–22.

Rich, Adrienne (1979). *On Lies, Secrets, and Silences: Selected Prose 1966–1978*. New York: W. W. Norton.

Ripinsky-Naxon, Michael (1998). Shamanistic knowledge and the cosmology. In *Tribal Epistemologies: Essays in the Philosophy of Anthropology*, ed. Helmut Wautischer. Aldershot, UK: Avebury Press.

Roscoe, Will (ed.) (1983). *Living the Spirit: A Gay American Indian Anthology*. New York: St. Martin's Press.

Roscoe, Will (1991). *The Zuni Man-Woman*. Albuquerque: University of New Mexico Press.

Roscoe, Will (1998). *Changing Ones: Third and Fourth Genders in Native North America*. New York: St. Martin's Press.

Schwarz, Maureen Trudelle (1997). *Molded in the Image of Changing Woman: Navajo Views on the Human Body and Personhood*. Tucson: University of Arizona Press.

Sharp, Henry (1995). Asymmetric equals: women and men among the Chipewyan. In Klein and Ackerman (1995).

Weatherford, Jack (1989). *Indian Givers: How Indians Transformed the World*. New York: Crown Books

Williams, Robert A. (1997). *Linking Arms Together: American Indian Treaty Visions of Law and Peace 1600–1800*. New York: Oxford University Press.

Williamson, Ray A. and Claire R. Farrer (1992). *Earth and Sky: Visions of the Cosmos in Native American Folklore*. Albuquerque: University of New Mexico Press.

Wub E Ke Niew (1995). *We Have the Right to Exist: A Translation of Aboriginal Indigenous Thought. The first book ever published from an Ahnishinahbaeotjibway perspective*. New York: Black Thistle Press. (Reprinted 1997.)

Zack, Naomi (1993). *Race and Mixed Race*. Philadelphia: Temple University Press

Zack, Naomi (1995). *American Mixed Race: Constructing Microdiversity*. Lanham, MD: Rowman and Littlefield.

Zack, Naomi (1997). *Race and Sex: Their Sameness, Difference and Interplay*. London: Routledge.

Zack, Naomi (1998). *Thinking about Race*. Belmont, CA: Wadsworth.

# 10

# CRIPPLING THE SPIRIT, WOUNDING THE SOUL: NATIVE AMERICAN SPIRITUAL AND RELIGIOUS SUPPRESSION

*Maureen E. Smith*

It was apparent from the first interactions between American Indians and Europeans that their ways of viewing the world differed significantly. This difference was especially apparent in their respective concepts of religion and spirituality. While such differences were inevitable, given their very diverse histories and worldviews, the intolerance of the newcomers to Turtle Island has proven devastating to those who were here. For American Indians, religious freedom has remained an empty promise, a right extended only to the colonizers. For Native people, the myth of religious freedom has remained an enduring and pervasive part of their history since European contact. While Native spirituality is resilient, the last 500 years of religious and spiritual suppression have wounded souls and, often, ravished Native religions.

Indeed, it is ironic that American Indians, so revered for their spirituality and connection to the earth, are deprived of their inherent right to practice their own religions on their own lands, in their revered sacred sites. An additional concern to Native people is the appropriation of many spiritual traditions by New Age followers. While Native people are fighting off such attempts, they also are in a battle for the freedom to engage in these very same religious practices themselves.

This chapter will attempt to provide an overview of the historical events that demonstrate how intolerance, veiled as moral superiority on the part of many Europeans, has denied Native people their inherent right to religious freedom. In order to better appreciate the history, I will begin with a brief overview of the basic spiritual foundations of many American Indian people prior to European contact. I will then contrast these beliefs with views held by Europeans coming to the "new" world, focusing on how their history affected their perceptions of American Indians and Native religion. I will briefly address the challenges posed to Native spirituality by the coming of Europeans. The fact that American Indian people had diverse responses to the prohibition of their religious traditions will be discussed; in addition, acts, laws, policies, and practices that expressly forbid the expression of traditional Native religion will be addressed. Finally, a short overview of the recent history, particularly after the 1978 passage of the American Indian Freedom of Religion Act, will detail the current status of Native people's status on their spiritual and religious freedom.

## TRADITIONAL NATIVE AMERICAN RELIGIOUS AND SPIRITUAL FOUNDATIONS

With over 500 individual American Indian nations in the country today, each with its own culture, language, and spiritual traditions, there exists great diversity among the tribes in the United States. Additionally, each individual tribal member interprets his/her spirituality in his/her own way. Therefore, when I discuss the spiritual foundations within American Indian communities, I am addressing only the broadest and most common aspects of that spirituality. While there is wide diversity among the Native nations in America today, the past saw even greater variance. It is beyond the scope of this chapter to elaborate on the specific religious beliefs and ceremonies of the tribes. However, it is critical to understand central tenets of many American Indian religious beliefs.

Virtually all tribes had a single supreme being; often, this divinity was not named due to its inherent sacredness. The deity also had no gender since such a concept would be foreign to an entity that bore no likeness to human beings. In near equal reverence was the whole of creation. All elements of the Earth and the people's relationship to them were seen as holy, a sacred relationship which necessitated a sacred responsibility. Most tribal religions were land-based, with their cosmologies founded on land, water, sky, and all of creation. Religion was geographically bound to sacred spots integral to spiritual practice. Most tribal people have origin stories that depict how they arrived in their place. They were put in locations like North America or Turtle Island by the Creator to live and worship there. Few, if any, tribes have stories of migration that tell of crossing large land or ice masses. The Creator placed them, and there they were to stay. Therefore, Native religion and nationhood were tied to specific geographical places.

Religion was practiced in many forms by Native people, including the sacred ceremonies, prayer, song, drama, and dance. The philosophy of Native religions was passed to future generations through oral traditions and storytelling. Many tribes saw the need for humor in all of their most sacred ceremonies. It was often an integral part of religious ceremonies. For some, particularly in the Southwest, sacred clowns reminded people not to take themselves too seriously and to keep themselves in balance.

In most Native languages, there is no sense of strict categorizations of concepts. Therefore, for many Native people there was no real sense of good without bad, right without wrong, there was balance in all things. In fact, many tribes had no separate word for religion or spirituality since the concepts were woven into all aspects of their lives. Traditional arts and crafts are viewed as sacred. Language itself had a power, a sacred potency to it, which awarded power to the words. Therefore, language had an inherent spirituality to it, as it was viewed as a gift to humans from the spirit world.

Because all things were viewed as interconnected, relationships among people were also critically important; the notion of religion and spirituality had a communal rather than an individual basis. From birth to death, families and communities were in the process of becoming; their potential could be infinite. By directing the process of becoming, humans could transcend the limitations of materiality. The human spiritual dimension allowed individuals to be able to: respond to dreams and visions; accept them as representations of human potential; give these non-material realities symbolic expression; and use them to translate the potential into the actual.

Elements pivotal to American Indian value systems included issues not only of space, but also of time. Time was perceived as cyclical and reciprocal, not linear; likewise, immortality and existence were circular in nature. Such concepts connected living individuals, the future generations yet unborn, and the ancestors. The Native belief system further stipulated specific concepts of illness and health. Illness affected all aspects of the human being; wellness represented harmony. Natural and unnatural illness, from the violation of the sacred or the act of witchcraft, resulted in disharmony of the mind, body, and spirit. Each individual was responsible for his or her own wellness.

## EUROPEAN CONCEPTS OF RELIGION

The European concept of religion is important if we are to understand the religious suppression of Native spirituality. Europeans viewed their own religious beliefs quite stringently with a dogmatic stance that has affected the laws, court rulings, and policies that followed. Coming out of the context of the Middle Ages, with the Crusades and the Inquisition, Europeans had very strict ideas about appropriate religious behavior – notions of how to worship and how to live. These beliefs colored their view of Native religion, leaving them virtually incapable of viewing the Natives' actions as spiritual.

In Europe, Christianity had attempted to eliminate "folk" healers and traditional medicinal practices with the suggestion that such behavior was probably superstitious at best, evil at worst. Female healers and midwives were often punished or killed on charges of witchcraft. Oral traditions were also eliminated because the printed word of the Bible was taken as "truth." At the same time, science was emerging as a powerful approach in the quest for certainty, so the rise of intellectual notions of reason provided Europeans with a belief that religion and logic could serve as the means to develop truth.

Europeans were also intent of the idea of discovery, a religious and a contractual construct which promoted the alleged legitimacy of Christian conquerors. In fact, many sixteenth-century Christians believed that they could claim a land if the inhabitants of the land were not Christian. Because of this belief, those who were non-Christians were afforded no rights whatsoever. Once New England was established, colonists often believed they were destined by God to conquer the new land. Many Europeans viewed the tragic epidemics that wiped out numerous tribes and decimated others as a divine sign they were meant to possess and occupy the land.

Europeans also brought with them the idea of property rights and consequent notions of boundaries, limits, restrictions, and prohibitions, thereby instituting the concept of bounded land. Because land to Europeans was a commodity, ownership became a fundamental concept underpinning the law. Throughout this process, economic development and religious beliefs became inexplicably intertwined.

Moreover, European Christians brought with them a sense that their religion was superior, their values more moral and advanced than anything they saw in the new land. Such beliefs allowed them to develop policies and laws which would further their causes, regardless of the consequences to others. Later the Bill of Rights guaranteed free exercise of religion. However, the European concept of what was appropriate religious behavior undergirded this right. Native religions were not even considered legitimate and were not, therefore, protected by any Constitutional rights.

## CLASH OF CULTURES

The clash of European and Native communities was virtually inevitable, especially in terms of religion. To the Europeans, it appeared that since many tribes had no apparent name for their divinity, they must not have had one. Further, tribal people often acknowledged and thanked the natural world; in European eyes, these people worshiped the false idols of nature. Such behavior, they reasoned, indicated a people devoid of a religion or worthy of consideration. In fact, it was not uncommon for Europeans to declare that Native people were a Godless people.

The only form of worship acceptable to the Europeans was a particular ceremony performed at a particular time of the day and week, in a particular place, for a particular amount of time. It was not necessary for European Christians to focus on specific geographic places to ensure their religious survival. Moreover, European Christian ceremonies required great solemnity. Native people utilized dance, music, and storytelling in their ceremonies, performing them outside at various times of the day, a concept Europeans could not or would not see as appropriate religious behavior. Any deviation from the European norm was considered barbaric, primitive, and dangerous. Particularly troublesome to Christians were ceremonies that had humor in them, utilizing elements such as the sacred clowns. Surely this must have been viewed as sacrilegious, providing further evidence that these individuals had no sense of religious and sacred behavior.

Such clashes of culture and the inability or unwillingness to accept diverse religious practices led to the history that followed. Within the context of this history we find the pervasive adherence to principles brought from a society that had passed through religious upheaval to truly organized, regimented religious practice. Although Europeans may have came to this country to escape religious persecution, they were not above using the same modes of oppression under which they themselves had suffered. Given the prevalence of the decimating epidemics, it was not long before it became seemingly self-evident that the tribes must either perish under the wrath of the European God or become followers of Christianity.

# NATIVE REACTIONS TO EUROPEANS' RELIGIOUS BELIEF SYSTEMS

Native people had diverse reactions to the conversion processes of the Europeans. Not surprisingly, some people, in fact whole tribes, eventually adopted the ways of Christianity. Other tribal peoples chose to seek a balance between Christianity and their traditional religion. For others, the suppression of their religions forced them to turn to new forms of worship which were neither their tribal traditional practices nor Christian. These new forms, which often were an amalgamation of the two, have been termed Nativistic religious response. Still others chose courageously to continue engaging in traditional religious practices, despite the potential harm and punishment that might await them.

Ultimately, many tribes appeared to embrace Christianity wholeheartedly. One possible explanation for the conversion to Christianity assumes that the European God was seen as somehow more powerful. It must be remembered that spirituality and religion were interwoven into all aspects of Native life. When the Europeans came to America bringing epidemics with them, Native people had no natural immunities to the diseases. Not surprisingly, the healers, many also religious leaders, had no remedy for the in either. These traditional healers often lacked ceremonies to deal with this near genocide. While the Native population was succumbing to these terrible illnesses, their white neighbors were flourishing. It may have seemed that the European God was indeed more powerful, as the missionaries suggested. Christianity may have appeared to provide an alternative for tribes to the chaos they faced by having their worlds and lives turned upside down by the white invasion.

Whatever the reason, many tribes embraced the new religion. In fact, today Christianity flourishes on many reservations and in large urban areas, often combining Christian religious beliefs with Native traditions. Being Christian is often a critical element to the individual Christian tribal member's spirituality. It is estimated today that one-third to one-half of contemporary Indians identify themselves as Christians.

For many Native people, engagement in both traditional and Christian religious rituals was common. Much to the dismay and chagrin of the local missionaries and governmental officials, this practice made sense to the Native people, given their inclusive worldview. Individual tribal members would both go to the traditional ceremonies and attend the Christian church service on Sunday, believing that both religions had something of value and merit, and that the practice of both could only enhance an individual's religious and spiritual life.

Despite a large number of individuals converting to Christianity or combining the religious practices of both, many Native people continued to follow their traditional religions exclusively, often an extremely dangerous activity. Terrible punishments usually awaited those who made this choice. Thus, many practiced in secret, bravely ensuring that traditional ceremonies would continue to the present time.

When social, political and environmental changes occur rapidly, people are left without means to address what is happening. This loss of control, this basic shaking of fundamental reality, can cause individuals to react in order to ward off chaos. They may need to find a means to construct something spiritual to put their world in balance. For a people whose worldview is so strongly based on the concept of spirituality, a world tipped so fundamentally out of balance could only be restored to normalcy through divine intervention.

Because Native people faced such shattering experiences with the onset of European domination, nativistic religious responses often arose. Such responses signaled an attempt to use a transformed spiritual foundation to give people a sense of control. While such forms often differed significantly from the traditional belief system of the tribe, they nonetheless contained fundamental Native principles.

Probably the best-known nativistic religious response, and the one with the most tragic outcome, was the Ghost Dance Movement. In 1889 Wovoka, a Paiute prophet, had a vision in which the Creator instructed him to induce the people to dance. These dances would enable practitioners to travel to another world and be reunited with their deceased relatives and other tribal members. In this new world, they could live in peace, happiness, and prosperity, as they had before the Europeans appeared. Wovoka's teachings, which became known as the Ghost Dance Movement, spread throughout a good part of the nation. Although his message was one of peace, it was misunderstood by European settlers and the United States government. Through a series of miscommunication and misunderstandings, a band of Lakota practicing the Ghost Dance was attacked by US soldiers; several hundred men, women, and children were killed at Wounded Knee, South Dakota, in December, 1890.

Similar responses developed throughout the early years of European exploration and conquest. In fact, from the period 1869 to 1872, there was a series of related religious movements. Many of them followed the basic tenets of the Ghost Dance – that the dead would return and the Europeans would go back to their homes across the sea. The less stable a tribe was, and the more uprooted their lives had become, the more likely they were to accept a diverse religious concept. Although a great number of these religious revitalizations occurred in the mid-to late nineteenth century, other responses emerged at different times. All of the other nativistic religious responses had the common focus of establishing a new religious belief system that could assist tribal members to deal with the rapid, immense, and forced influences brought about by unyielding European contact.

Another response combining traditional religion and Christianity was the Native American Church, a form of organized religious expression which has undoubtedly remained the most constant. One of the basic components of this religion was the sacramental use of peyote. While peyote ceremonies had been performed by tribes long before the arrival of Europeans, they became more widespread during the late nineteenth century. Several tribes banded together to form the Native American Church in

1918, in the hope that by establishing an organized religion, their right to use peyote would fall under governmental protections granted to other religious organizations in the country. History has shown, however, that the organization of the Native American Church did not protect its members from punishment.

## UNITED STATES ACTS, POLICIES, AND LAWS IMPACTING ON NATIVE RELIGIOUS FREEDOM

The acts, policies, cases, and laws limiting the freedom of traditional Native religions are important if we are to understand the situation as it exists today, particularly given that the history of religious prohibition for Native people is not a well-documented factor in American Indian history. In the early years of colonization and missionary efforts, agents and missionaries would remark on the horrible "lack of progress" being made on reservations, particularly by the most miserable and heathen – the Native practicing his or her tribal religion. There were, however, few official policies prior to the late nineteenth century prohibiting the celebration of traditional religions. Often such prohibition was not a law at all or even an official policy; it was more of an assumption made by those in charge of reservation life that such behavior and practices had to be either eliminated or ignored. The belief was, that with education, assimilation, and contact with "good Christian whites," such seemingly "barbaric" and "primitive" beliefs would simply be cast aside. Whether Europeans were incapable, or unable to view the diverse concept of religion, the result was the same – the firm belief that Native people needed Christianity to be civilized, or, as one government official said, they had to be subjected to programs that "humanize, Christianize, civilize" (Beck et al. 1992: 148).

One manner in which Europeans and the United States government could institute conversion to Christianity was through the education process. Many treaties between tribes and European countries (and later the United States) included provision for education, which was often carried out by the clergy. In the Midwest and the South, the Jesuits and Franciscans of the Roman Catholic faith served to educate the Native children in the ways of Christianity. In the East, Protestants were heavily involved in the transformation. Once the United States was established, it was not long before the Congress began to pass legislation to ensure such education continued. In 1802 Congress appropriated money to "promote civilization among the Savages" and in 1819 the Civilization Act was passed with money allotted to a similar endeavor. Until 1873, the majority of all education for Native students was conducted by missionaries who, along with the government, claimed that any success in educating and civilizing Native children would only result from the inclusion of Christian teachings.

As history progressed, schools became an increasing force in American Indian life. Early educational attempts were aimed at the removal of Indian children from their families, communities, and tribal links. By 1860, boarding schools were the preferred mode of education, taking Indian children from their homes as early as age 4 and often not returning them home for up to 19 years. Until 1934, Indian children in boarding schools were required to join and attend a Christian church in the local community. Often, the school curriculum included required instruction in Christian values.

In the schools, participating in anything Native was expressly forbidden. It was assumed the children would not practice traditional religion at the school, and they were constantly monitored and punished for any kind of "Indian behavior," particularly for the speaking of their tribal languages, even though the inability to communicate with the Creator in the one's sacred Native language often meant the Creator would be unable to "hear" the person. Children were immediately given English names upon entrance, despite the sacred and religious connotation associated with their Indian names. Often, their new names were jokingly chosen by classmates. Hair, which often had a religious significance, was immediately cut off. As one student lamented: "the next day the torture began. The first thing they did was cut our hair....But I lost my hair. And without it how would Ussen (the Great Spirit) recognize me when I went to the Happy Place?" (Ball 1980: 144). Often by the time the children returned to their reservations they had forgotten their traditional religion. Additionally, since they had their Native language literally beaten out of them, and could no longer speak it, there remained no means to re-instill Native beliefs. There is a critical link between the religious teachings and the Native language, which transcends translation.

While the use of education to eliminate Native religions was somewhat covert, overt endeavors have also been recorded. Certainly one of the most notorious examples of forced conversion occurred in the Southwest during the sixteenth century. A Hopi man was charged with idolatry by a friar in his village. This man was not only punished, but also used as an example to any who would follow in his footsteps and practice their traditional religion. It was reported this man was beaten in public, dragged to the church and beaten again. Finally, his body was smeared with turpentine and set on fire for his sin.

In 1868, the US Surgeon General issued an order to all military personnel to collect the skulls of Native people for study. Along with decapitating deceased Natives, burial sites were raided and funeral objects were sold to museums. Further, in 1906, a law was passed legislating that dead Indian people found buried on federal land were considered archeological resources and the property of the federal government. It is abhorrent to all humans for their dead to be desecrated, and such acts fall within the area of sacrilege in most religions. Yet, the United States government and its own people were ardently involved in promoting such a lack of regard for the ancestors of Native people.

Beginning in the late nineteenth century, with the relocation of most tribes on reservations, the government began to take a much harder line in terms of religious activities. As it became abundantly clear that Native people were not quickly vanishing, agents and missionaries began to re-examine their policies. In 1884, the Potlatch ceremony among the Northwest tribes, in which individuals would give away all their possessions to others in the tribe, was forbidden. Such a ceremonial practice seemed contrary to the very values the government wanted to instill in its Native people. Indeed one Commissioner of Indian Affairs reported:

His whole nature must be changed. He must have a white man's ambition, to be like him. He must have the objects and aims of a white man. What might seem bad teaching to the white man may be good teaching for an Indian; for instance, we would say that it is bad to teach the white man to be more mercenary and ambitious to obtain riches and teach him to value the position consequent upon the possession of riches.    (Commissioner of Indian Affairs Report 1861)

In 1883, the US government listed the traditional Sun Dance ceremony of the Plains tribes as a punishable offense because the sacrifices made by some practicing members were deemed as "barbaric and heathenish." The penalty for breaking laws prohibiting traditional religious behavior was often the withholding of rations for 10 days for a first offense. This punishment was particularly threatening because as tribes moved on to reservations, they became totally dependent on government rations for survival. Therefore, for many of these individuals, the choice became whether to practice their traditional religions or to feed their family. Later the punishments for participating in the Sun Dance increased to imprisonment for 30 days.

In 1921 the Bureau of Indian Affairs (BIA) became adamant about the abolition of traditional religions. The BIA circular of April 26, 1921, categorized the Sun Dance as an "Indian offense." Along with the Sun Dance, any act which involved self-torture, immoral relations between the sexes, reckless giving away of property, sacrificial destruction of clothing and useful articles, use of drugs, and frequent or prolonged periods of celebration was prohibited. Acceptable times and durations of ceremonies, according to European-American values were established. In 1923, strong recommendations were made that give-aways of any kind must be prohibited and, further, no one under the age of 50 should be allowed to participate in any traditional ceremonies. The Commissioner of Indian Affairs was particularly concerned that participation in ceremonial activities would divert the Indians' attention from "political, useful, thrifty, and orderly activities that are indispensable to [their] well-being and that underlie the preservation of [their] race in the midst of complex and highly competitive conditions" (quoted in Beck et al. 1992: 157).

In 1924 American Indians were granted United States citizenship. With the passage of the Citizenship Act came the assumption that Native religions would be protected under the First Amendment. Technically, it was only with the granting of citizenship that tribal members were legally protected by the kinds of freedoms most Americans had taken for granted for almost 150 years. It soon became apparent, however, that citizenship and the First Amendment of the US Constitution did not, in fact, actually provide the religious freedom to Native people that they did to other Americans.

In 1934 legislation was passed that would seemingly guarantee such freedom through the Wheeler–Howard Act. This act expressly forbade the government to force Indian children at boarding schools to attend Christian services or join Christian denominations. Additionally, it forbade the ban on any practice of traditional religions, including the use of peyote. The Wheeler–Howard Act seemed to finally provide protection for Native people's traditional religious freedom. The benefits were short-lived, however. After World War II, governmental policies turned toward assimilation once again. The legislation and policies affecting Native American people in the 1950s included termination of tribal status and relocation of Native people off reservations into cities, further eroding the continuation of religious traditions.

During the 1960s with the rise of the overt activism in groups like the American Indian Movement, the nation again became aware of the tragic conditions of Native peoples and the failure of the United States government to uphold its promises. The nation also began to take notice that Native people were denied access to the basic freedoms and rights that most American citizens took for granted. Despite citizenship and the Wheeler–Howard Act, the ability of the Native American Church to continue practicing its traditional religion with the sacred use of peyote remained in jeopardy. In 1954 a court ruled that the use of peyote was not protected under the First Amendment. In 1970 peyote became classified as a hallucinogen under the Controlled Substance Act. It was apparent from these events that the use of peyote, despite its sacred character, was not a protected sacrament.

Hope was again expressed by Native people with the passage of the 1968 Indian Civil Rights Act. This act was intended to strengthen and protect the freedoms of American Indians, including religious freedom. Indeed, the act specified that the protections granted to other citizens in the Bill of Rights would be afforded to Native people. Once again, however, such a promise failed to be honored.

The environmental movement of the 1970s gave rise to legislation to protect endangered species and threatened wilderness areas. Often, however, this legislation negatively affected American Indian spirituality. For instance, the 1976 Bald Eagle Protection Act, passed to protect the sacred bird, meant that the possession of eagle parts, including the feathers, was illegal. Despite the intent to use them for ceremonial purposes, Cheyenne and Arapaho tribal members were arrested by federal authorities for the possession of eagle feathers. Later the act changed to enable the Secretary of the Interior to allow Native people licenses to have access to eagles if they proved the use of such objects were necessary to their religion and they were enrolled on Native censuses. The necessity of a license would seem to fly in the face of the separation of church and state, not to mention the intense emotional expense to prove one needed sacred objects to worship.

Another aspect of this environmental movement was the protection of sacred lands. Although Native people wanted their sacred sites protected, they also wanted access to them when appropriate and necessary for prayer. The policies meant to protect the land failed to exempt Native people who had used these sacred sites for centuries. It is apparent that most agencies charged with the "protection" of these lands were unable or unwilling to understand the distinction between cultural resource management and real religious accommodations. As these lands became increasingly valued by non-Natives, efforts were made to increase accessibility for all people; these "improvements," however, destroyed the sacred nature of the sites. Native people can use their sacred sites if they follow all state, local, and federal regulations, including sharing the site, even during the most sacred of ceremonies, with everyone else.

While for many Native people all of Mother Earth is sacred, there are certain categories that make a site truly sacred and an integral part of religious practices:

1   The location is mentioned in the oral traditions of the people.
2   The spot is a place where something supernatural occurred as mentioned in the oral traditions of the people.
3   It is a location that contains the plants, herbs, minerals, and waters that have healing powers.
4   It is where a person can best communicate with the supernatural world.

In 1978 the American Indian Freedom of Religion Act was passed. This law recognized the inherent right of Native people to practice their traditional religion freely, and specifically addressed the necessity for them to have access to their sacred sites. This act was an attempt to direct policy comprehensively toward promoting the free exercise of Indian religions.

Not long after its passage, however, tribes began to see that this law provided no real protection. Although the act directed federal agencies to review their regulations and try to accommodate the practice of Indian religions, Native people were still unsuccessful in their attempts to actually practice these religions. A number of disputes occurred in which Native people were unable to reap the potential benefits of the act. These disputes often landed in the United States Supreme Court and the results for tribes continued to be clear – there is no freedom of religious practice for Native people in the United States. Two cases have stood out as clear examples of the complex issues American Indian people continued to face.

The first case, *Lyng v. Northwest Indian Cemetery*, was settled in 1988 and involved three California tribes. The US Forestry Department sought to widen a logging road in a park to allow trucks to move more quickly. This construction, however, would destroy the sacred sites of the Yurok, Karok, and Tolowa tribes. It was argued that the proposed change would lead to the ultimate destruction of the traditional religions of these tribes. Despite the possibility of such a tragic outcome, the Supreme Court ruled in favor of the US Forestry Department and the road was widened.

A second case, the 1990 *Employment Div., Dept. of Human Resources of Oregon v. Smith*, involved the religious practices of a member of the Native American Church. Al Smith, a drug and alcohol counselor, attended a religious service and took part in the sacramental use of peyote. Following his attendance at his church worship, his employer proceeded to do a routine drug test. Since Smith had partaken of the sacrament, he "failed" the test. As a condition for keeping his job, he was required to attend a drug rehabilitation program. Smith explained that his use of peyote was a sacrament and refused treatment. He was fired and applied for unemployment compensation. Through a series of appeals, the case ended up in the Supreme Court, which ruled that Smith was ineligible for unemployment compensation due to his violation of employment practices. The ruling indicated no concern that Smith's Constitutional rights had been violated.

These cases, and others like them, recreated a crisis in Indian country. It became painfully apparent that the American Indian Freedom of Religion Act of 1978 had not provided the promised freedoms for Native people's worship. Indeed Senator Morris Udall's assertion that the act had "no teeth" was becoming evident. As interpreted by many non-Native bureaucrats, judges, enforcement people, and the United States Supreme Court, the 1978 act stipulated that *consideration* must be taken when actions might interfere with the religious freedom of Native people. In other words, Native people would be consulted only when their sacred lands or the practice of their religion was threatened. The act provided no guarantee that Native concerns would necessarily be taken into account, only that such consultation would occur.

Proper treatment of the deceased is integral to most religions. American Indians, however, were unable to protect their ancestors. Because the study of Indian "skeletal remains" had been considered scientifically necessary and appropriate for centuries, Native people had endured the sacrilege of grave-robbing activity. In fact, it was estimated that "museums, federal agencies, other institutions, and private collectors retain between 300,000 and 2.5 million dead bodies taken from Indian graves, battle-fields, and POW camps by soldiers, museum collectors, scientists, and pothunters" (Thompson 1996: 46). Finally, Native people brought their concerns to the legislature and got results in the form of two acts.

In 1989 the National Museum of the American Indian Act was passed. This act required the Smithsonian Institution to inventory all Native human remains and funeral objects in its possession. All identified objects and human remains must be returned to their rightful owners – the tribes. The Smithsonian was particularly targeted because it had such enormous collections of Native people's remains and funeral objects. The act further mandated the creation of a museum dedicated to Native people by the year 2000. The second act, the Native American Graves Protection and Repatriation Act of 1990, required that Native ancestors warehoused in museums and universities must be returned to their tribes for appropriate burial. The shameful practice of collecting Native people to study had led to the storage of thousands of individuals who had often been carelessly removed from their attentively constructed burial place. This desecration is particularly heinous to Native people because of the connection between the present generation, the future generations, and the ancestors in relation to cosmo-logical belief systems.

An additional issue leading to the passage of this act was the removal of sacred ceremonial objects from the tribal people. Many tribes had found it virtually impossible to practice their traditional religion due to the removal of irreplaceable sacred objects. Additionally, for numerous tribal people, displaying such items affected their sacred essence. For some tribes, the objects placed in museums to be protected from decay were *supposed* to decay, that was their natural end. The unnatural protection of the objects was considered sacrilegious.

In 1994 the Senate passed the American Indian Religious Freedom Act Amend-ments. This legislation was a significantly shortened version of the proposed 1993 Native American Free Exercise of Religion Act, which had much more encompassing protections and freedom than the 1994 act. The amended act served "to emend the American Indian Religious Freedom Act to provide for the traditional use of peyote by Indians for religious purposes, and for other purposes" (Public Law 103–334). While this legislation provides hope for religious freedom for some, the lack of sweeping legislation still puts Native religious freedom in peril.

Another battle being waged by Native people deals with the industry propelled by the New Age movement, which appropriates, distorts, and sells Native spirituality without respect or permission. Many non–Native people are "devouring Native American spiritual traditions in the same way they have consumed Native American art, jewelry, clothing, weavings, and crafts" (Hernandez–Avila 1996: 343). It would appear such practitioners feel they have an inherent right to use whatever aspects of Native spirituality they feel disposed to use. It has been suggested such a sense of entitlement to everything Native stems from the initial sense of discovery the first Europeans felt. "This entitlement assumes the right to take what is indigenous, with complete disregard for Native peoples, in a manner in which the perpetrators would not think of doing so easily with other traditions" (Hernandez–Avila 1996: 343). It is only when one romanticizes and objectifies Native people that such appropriation can occur. And beyond ethical considerations, the use of ceremonies and practices so misunderstood could possibly lead to harm to ill-prepared, ill-informed practitioners.

# CONCLUSION

Today there is a resurgence of American Indian spiritual practices. In record numbers, Indian people are reclaiming the spiritual and religious legacy left to them by their ancestors. While the practices may have been modified through the years, Native people hope to rekindle the flame snuffed out with such arrogance by the colonizers. However, it remains to be seen if religious freedom will ever be a reality for Native people.

Perhaps, eventually, American Indians will have the right to practice their traditional religions without fear of legal punishment, sanction or imprisonment, unfettered by tourists and hunters, and without the potential loss of places of worship. The hope remains that Native Americans will finally be able to appropriately bury their ancestors with dignity and respect; freely utilizing the sacred objects central to worship which will be returned to them.

However, the optimism is guarded, given the historical past. It remains to be seen how the courts, the governments, and the bureaucracies of this nation interpret and define religious freedom. It remains to be seen if Native American people can finally become fully empowered, fully enfranchised citizens of the land the Creator put them on. It remains to be seen if New Age people, in search of a higher form of spirituality, may respectfully acknowledge they have no inherent right to practice religions Natives have been given by their Creator, unless the Native people allow them. It all remains to be seen.

## BIBLIOGRAPHY

Ball, Eve (1980). *An Apache Odyssey*. Norman: University of Oklahoma Press.
Beck, P., A. Walters, and N. Francisco (1992). *The Sacred: Ways of Knowledge. Sources of Life*. Tsaile, AZ: Navajo Community College Press.

Bopp, Michael and Judith Bopp (1984). Four Winds Development Project. Unpublished paper written in conjunction with the Four Winds Development Project, Lethbridge, Alberta.

Brown, Joseph (1982). *The Spiritual Legacy of the American Indian*. New York: Crossroad.

Commissioner of Indian Affairs Reports (1861). Milwaukee, WI: Marquette Library. (Microfiche.)

Deloria, V., Jr. (1992). Secularism, civil rights, and the religious freedom of American Indians. *American Indian Culture and Research Journal*, 16, 2.

Deloria, V., Jr. (1994). *God is Red: A Native View of Religion*. Golden, CO: Fulcrum Publishing.

Echo-Hawk, W. and R. Echo-Hawk (1996). Repartition, reburial, and religious rights. In *Handbook of American Indian Religious Freedom*. New York: Crossroad.

Harvey, Karen, Lisa Harjo, and Linda Welborn (1995). *How to Teach about American Indians*. Westport, CT: Greenwood Press.

Hernandez-Avila, I. (1996). Mediations of the spirit: Native American religious traditions and the ethics of representation. *American Indian Quarterly*, Themes in Native American Spirituality, 20, 3 (Summer-Fall).

Hirschfelder, Arlene and Martha Kreipe de Montano (1993). *The Native American Almanac: a Portrait of Native America Today*. New York: Prentice-Hall.

Jocks, C. R. (1996). Spirituality for sale: sacred knowledge in the consumer age. *American Indian Quarterly*, Themes in Native American spirituality, 20, 3 (Summer-Fall).

Lee, Irwin (1996). *The American Indian Quarterly*, Themes in Native American Spirituality Summer-Fall, vol. 20, no. 3.

Locust, Carol (1990). Wounding the spirit: discrimination and traditional American Indian belief systems. In *Facing Racism in Education*, ed. Hildago, McDowell, and Walker-Siddle. Cambridge, MA: Harvard Educational Review.

Loewen, James (1995). *Lies My Teacher Told Me*. New York: Simon and Schuster.

Michaelsen, Robert (1996). Law and the limits of liberty in handbook rights. In *Handbook of American Indian Religious Freedom*. New York: Crossroad.

Moore, S. (1996). Sacred sites and public lands In rights. In *Handbook of American Indian Religious Freedom*. New York: Crossroad.

O'Brien, S. (1996). A legal analysis of the American Indian Religious Freedom Act. In *Handbook of American Indian Religious Freedom*. New York: Crossroad.

Prucha, Francis (1990). *Documents of the United States Indian Policy*. Lincoln: University of Nebraska Press.

Reeves, T. K. (1999) Native American natives of the Black Mesa Region. <http://www.geocities.com/Yosemite/Trails/1942>.

Smith, Maureen (1993). Effects of United States policy from 1819 to 1934 on American Indian identity. PhD dissertation, University of Wisconsin-Milwaukee.

Stewart, Omar (1996). Peyote and the Law. In *Handbook of American Indian Religious Freedom*. New York: Crossroad.

Talbot, Steven (1994). Religion. In *Native America: a Portrait of the Peoples*, ed. Duane Champagne. Detroit, MI: Visible Ink Press.

Thompson, W. (1996). *Native American Issues*. Santa Barbara, CA: ABC-CLIO.

Vecsey, C. (1996). Prologue. In *Handbook of American Indian Religious Freedom*. New York: Crossroad.

Walker, Dale, and LaDue (1986). *American Indian Mental Health in Ethnic Psychiatry*. New York: Plenum Medical.

# Part V

# PHENOMENOLOGY AND ONTOLOGY

# 11

# ON AUTHENTICITY

*Marilyn Notah Verney*

## INTRODUCTION

American Indian Philosophy: What is it? How can outsiders study it? How can it contribute to traditional academic philosophy?

I am a member of the Diné (Navajo) Nation, and the reservation that I am from is in the Southwestern USA. I belong to the By the Water Clan, and am born for the Between the Red Earth Clan. My maternal grandparents raised me and taught me the traditional beliefs and teachings of my people. Therefore it is not difficult to answer the first question. I refer to the beliefs and teachings of my people as American Indian philosophy. However, to answer the last two questions is difficult for me because I must use a framework of non-Native traditional academic studies in philosophy. Thoughts about the framework I must use to respond to the last two questions guide me in my response.

There have been many books, articles, research materials, and even Hollywood movies written and made about American Indians. But much of this material is written and produced by non-Native writers, scholars from different academic studies, government agencies, and religious institutions.

One can find books and articles co-authored by non-Native writers. Yet how many academic philosophical materials are out there written by American Indian scholars. My contribution as an American Indian philosopher is to tell you my perspective about the difference between traditional academic philosophy and American Indian philosophy. In this I hope to contribute to the ongoing exchange among philosophers about the place of American Indian philosophy in academe.

# METAPHYSICS OF COGNITIVE DISSONANCE

In the USA, where traditional academic philosophy generally means Euro-American (or Greek) philosophy, the recent tendency toward method has been to analyze by taking apart "what is" to distinguish "what is" from "what is not." Using this method myself, I notice ideas, when severed, tend to lose meaning by losing relation with all surrounding things. In contrast, we Diné (People) talk, and philosophize, by making connections among all things, thus giving all things meaning in relation, and approaching our world in a wholistic manner.

One example of Native metaphysical and ontological assumptions that differ from Euro-American philosophical assumptions can be recognized in how we view the land. The land viewed by Euro-Americans is seen as an object, a commodity to be owned, and viewed as an investment for profit; it is there to develop and commercialize for financial gain. By contrast, a common philosophy that is shared by all Indigenous people is that our land is sacred, holy. There is a strong relationship (interdependent relational bond) between land and people. Land is Mother Earth. We came to be from within the womb of Mother Earth. Mother Earth is home for all living beings: human people, animal people, plant people, everything in the universe. Therefore, Mother Earth, as an interdependent sustainer of life, is not to be stripped, taken apart, or desecrated, nor should boundaries of property (ownership) be placed upon her.

To understand American Indian philosophy one must first understand our spiritual relationship, our connection with the land, with Mother Earth. If non-Natives can understand our traditional spiritual relationship with the land and its connections within the universe, that all things have life, then one can better understand our people, our culture, and our traditional beliefs. Only then will our philosophy, hopefully, touch your heart, and bring meaningfulness into your life.

Although American Indians are members of different tribal nations, we are bound together by similar political, social, and spiritual philosophical beliefs. Some of us live on reservations, federally allotted sections of land. Indigenous people living in North America, prior to the arrival of Europeans, shared our Motherland with the early settlers. History will remind us that through wars, treaties, and congressional and judicial decisions, our people were forced to change our relationships with our Motherland.

The early settlers viewed our people as obstacles needing to be removed, in order for Europeans to migrate westward. Our grandfathers and grandmothers were forced to walk hundreds of miles to a new location, and once there, they learned that boundaries and restrictions had been placed upon them. Our people did not comprehend, but quickly grasped that they were no longer free, free to migrate across the land as the seasons changed.

The way to begin to understand our philosophy is to hear how Diné people came to be. Almost all Indigenous creation stories relate to the land. The creation story of most American Indians is that Mother Earth gave birth to the people. I asked my father to tell me the creation story of our people. This is the story he told me.

At one time the animals and the spiritual beings were immersed within Mother Earth. Due to a great flood, the animals and spiritual beings had to climb through a hollow reed to the surface of Mother Earth to escape the rising water. The water kept rising around them even though they were on the surface. They looked around and discovered that Coyote had taken two baby seals from the Water people. Coyote was instructed by the others to return the baby seals. When the baby seals were returned to the Water people the water began to recede, revealing the surface of Mother Earth. The animals on the surface became known as the Surface people.

There is also another familiar story shared by different tribal nations about how our people came to be throughout all the particular land(s). The story tells us that there was a great migration from where the North Star is located, following the direction of the sun as it traveled across the sky. Upon reaching the great warm waters, some people began a great migration to return to the land under the North Star. It was during this great movement that many of the people chose to remain behind. This is the story of how our people found themselves throughout the land of what came to be called the Americas.

Stories such as these form the basis of our thought, our philosophical metaphysics, which is shared by many different tribal nations. Our philosophy is simple. It is through our spiritual (metaphysical) connection with Mother Earth that we are able to teach our philosophy of communal living among all life in the universe. We are no better or worse than any of our relations, because the metaphysics of respect (interdependency) sustaining our fundamental relations with Mother Earth are relations of equality. Everything that sustains life is within our reach, for we sustain and are sustained by life, which is given to us by our Mother. Therefore, our universe and land are sacred, holy, and to be treated with respect.

This metaphysics of respect grounds our philosophical ethics, based on kindness, caring for others, and sharing what is given to us by our Mother through a communal way of life. Nothing is owned, and hence nothing is owned by an individual. In this metaphysics, ownership is inconceivable. Mother Earth continually nurtures all her children by providing food and shelter. So long as we sustain Mother Earth all of our needs are provided for, and there is no desire to commodify our environment. Without commodification, everything is shared equally, as needed. How can one own what is shared with our Mother? It is inconceivable to claim (own) that which must be shared.

Many early Europeans came to our home for different reasons. They came to escape from religious persecution and oppressive economics, or to seek new land for their nation. These foreigners to our home were greeted by our people and, in keeping with our philosophy, we offered them food and shelter. But rather than visit, we learned they had come to conquer. Unfortunately for our people, Europeans also brought their own philosophy, a philosophy grounded on and framed by religious and economic principles of ownership. Our people, not knowing about property and ownership (dominion), were considered uncivilized, savage, and not human. We were forcefully introduced to the Europeans' philosophy. To be civilized, one had to embrace the Christian religion, with its teachings of male dominion over all creation (stemming from the Christian creation story).

In this way Mother Earth was seen as land, and beheld and coveted as a material commodity to be owned in a Lockean framework, with boundaries signifying owner-ship demarcations. The land had to be divided, worked, and owned, in order to produce commodities that could be sold for profit rather than shared. The land itself became a commodity.

American Indian philosophy is and always has been contrary to much of traditional Euro-American philosophy. Euro-American philosophy is deeply rooted within the institutions of this country's social, political, economic, religious, and educational structures. Euro-American philosophical assumptions create standards and principles that operate as foundations for these systems.

At an early age we are at the same time immersed in Euro-American and Indigenous culture. We are unaware of how we are being acculturated. From our parents' gener-ations to the present, the population of American Indians living outside the reservation has dramatically increased. Moreover, approximately one-third of the reservation is occupied by non-Indians (traders, ministers, BIA, etc.).

Unfortunately, it is through our acculturation to the controlling and influencing world of Euro-Americans that a majority of our people are losing their spiritual connection to the sacredness of our traditional teachings and beliefs that are taught to us by our tribal elders. Many of our young people are unknowingly influenced by what is outside of themselves, a culture foreign to our traditions. They are losing their identity as American Indians because they embrace the philosophical system of non-Natives, and become alienated from the philosophy of our people as American Indians . . . they are losing their identity as American Indians.

## IGNORANCE CREATES OTHERNESS

We can look at a few ideas about acculturation articulated by at least one Euro-American philosopher, Martin Heidegger, in *Being and Time* (tr. E. Robinson and J. Macquarrie, New York: Harper, 1962. See also *Being and Time: A Translation of Sein und Zeit*, tr. Joan Stambaugh, New York: SUNY, 1997). Heidegger's work resonates with how I sometimes view myself in relation to others. In this particular book, Heidegger introduces the reader to the word *Dasein*, which, translated from the German language, means "being there." Heidegger tells the reader about "being":

> But there are many things which we designate as "being" (seiend), and we do so in various senses. Everything we talk about, everything we have in view, everything towards which we comport ourselves in any way, is being; what we are is being, and so is how we are. Being lies in the fact that something is, and in its Being as it is; in Reality; in presence-at-hand; in subsistence; in validity; in Dasein; in the "there is." (1962: 26)

*Dasein* (Being) is revealed to the reader in a phenomenological manner, "to let that which shows itself be seen from itself in the very way in which it shows itself from itself" (1962: 58). Heidegger informs the reader how Being is revealed and how individuals perceive Being. In order to know and understand personal existence, it is necessary to disclose Being, to reveal true self, which enables re-emergence and transcendence to a higher possibility of an authentic Being. How is this possible?

Heidegger states: "And because Dasein is in each case essentially its own possibility, it can, in its very Being, 'choose' itself and win itself; it can also lose itself and never win itself; or only 'seem' to do so" (1962: 68). Heidegger goes on to tell the reader that in everydayness, the difference between Being and Others can have a disturbing effect on *Dasein*.

> In one's concern with what one has taken hold of, whether with, for or against, the Other, there is constant care as to the way one differs from them, whether that difference is merely one that is to be evened out, whether one's own Dasein has lagged behind the Others and wants to catch up in relationship to them, or whether one's Dasein already has some priority over them and sets out to keep them suppressed. The care about this distance between them is disturbing to Being-with-one-another, though this disturbance is one that is hidden from it. (1962: 164)

Do American Indians have to continue to follow a philosophy of the "Other"? Are we aware of how far some of us have unconsciously drifted from our tribal philosophy, from our own way of being? Heidegger continues by stating:

> This Being-with-one-another dissolves one's own Dasein completely into the kind of Being of "the Other", in such a way, indeed, that the Others, as distinguishable and explicit, vanish more and more. In this inconspicuousness and unascertainability, the real dictatorship of the "they" is unfolded. We take pleasure and enjoy ourselves as they (man) take pleasure; we read, see, and judge about literature, and art as they see and judge; likewise we shrink back from the "great mass" as they shrink back; we find "shocking" what they find shocking. The "they", which is nothing definite, and which all are, though not as the sum, prescribe the kind of Being of everydayness. (1962: 164)

As Heidegger might say, we are forgetting what it means to follow the traditional philosophical teachings of Indigenous people. We get lost in the everydayness of Euro-American culture (Others) and its philosophical framework. For me, part of Heidegger's message is powerful because he is reminding us to embrace our authentic being, to be proud of who we are, and not to succumb to what we perceive as the inauthentic ways of the dominant society.

Let me tell another short story about myself that has to do with academic philosophy. I had a personal encounter with a certain philosophy professor at the university that I attended as an undergraduate student. I approached this professor and told him of my plans for writing a paper about American Indian philosophy. He quickly informed me that as an American Indian I had nothing to contribute, because scholars already knew about American Indian philosophy. I was stunned and speechless at his response, and could not immediately respond. He affirmed to me his belief that because I am an American Indian woman, my presence at an upcoming Native American philosophy conference would probably be beneficial.

I interpreted this encounter to mean that my presence would be appreciated as a token Indian, but that I was not now, and would not at the conference be, embraced authentically. The reason this professor, and Euro-Americans generally, could not embrace my being authentically is because of a lack of information about American Indian philosophy in the dominant culture. To me, the Euro-American academics were Outsiders because they did not know about Indigenous being. The framework of perceiving my being would be that of a Euro-American seeing a foreigner, an Other, but attributing to me a Euro-American philosophy of being in the world. They would not grasp me, but rather a stereotypical concept of their own making. This situation is created because of a gap in their education.

So how do I deal with the ignorance of this person seeing me only as a stereotypical silenced Indian presence? My way of dealing with this human blindness to the philosophical being of another human, is by being here, by telling my story and sharing my philosophy with you, in the hope that changes can be made in the academic setting.

What are we able to do practically and concretely? Is it even possible to have an authentic classroom situation if academic philosophers (teachers) have no knowledge about, and hence no sensitivity to, or respect for, our philosophy? How would a professor begin to understand, and feel within their heart, the importance of our philosophy for our people? Maybe we need to change the narrowly restricted academic understanding of American Indian philosophy. In order to teach our philosophy effectively in academic settings, there has to be a respect for philosophical difference, including ontological shakedown when Euro-American and American Indian concepts collide, creating cognitive dissonance for American Indians.

As Indigenous people, we do have something to contribute to traditional academic philosophy. Our philosophy is told through stories, songs, ceremonial dances, art, and our ways of being in the world. Our philosophy is an oral philosophy. It is through oral philosophical method that the sacredness of traditional beliefs, songs, dances, and stories embodies our ontologies, epistemologies, metaphysics, ethics, and science of being in the world. So long as we retain philosophical meaning and connection with all our relations, with who we are as American Indians, our philosophy of being in the world will remain intact.

Once ideas are written down, in black and white, those ideas become objects, something to be studied and taken apart. This process of writing separates our being in the world, and we can lose touch and become isolated from all our relations. To be effectively taught in an academic classroom, American Indian philosophy must be taught orally. We as Native people have a responsibility to carry on the traditional philosophical oral teachings of our elders. It is our responsibility to make changes within the traditional academic institutions. Our philosophy can retain its meaning by making connection with those who are willing to listen to our oral teachings.

# CONCLUSION

In this chapter I have shown how cognitive dissonance is created from competing metaphysical systems, namely Indigenous and colonial. In this cognitive dissonance neither system totally dominates the ontology of being in the world for American Indians. I have also shown how a metaphysic of otherness, as articulated by Martin Heidegger, can give rise to a loss of identity as an American Indian. Recognizing and accepting the viability of American Indian ontology and being in the world, for American Indians, will allow for reintegration of American Indian identity through an understanding of the metaphysical framework of American Indian philosophy. Understanding this metaphysical framework will enable the discerning of an American Indian ethics, and hence the reason why we do the things we do the way we do them.

# 12

# PHENOMENOLOGY OF A MUGWUMP TYPE OF LIFE IN AN AUTOBIOGRAPHICAL SNIPPET

*Leslie Nawagesic*

My earliest memories begin somewhere around the age of 3, although at times I can recall being encased in a *tikanagan*. A *tikanagan* is a small backboard-like contraption that is rectangular in shape and used by Anishinabae people to care for our babies. It is made of cedar with a protective bar over the baby's head. The encasing is made of soft materials with Anishinabae art patterns threaded on the outside. The bindings are made of leather that secure the baby in a cuddly enfolding.

Carrying babies in a *tikanagan* is an Ojibwa (Anishinabae) child-rearing practice that ends somewhere after the first 12 to 16 months of a baby's life. Whether it is humanly possible to remember that far back, I don't know. It may simply have been the case that I was a late bloomer and didn't leave this secure cocoon till about the age of 3. In any case, the experience itself, when I look back, is traumatic enough to leave an indelible mark on anyone's memory.

I was born in Beardmore, a small northern Ontario railway town situated on the south end of Lake Nipigon. I should have been born on the Gull Bay Indian reserve which is my home reservation. Gull Bay is located just opposite Beardmore on the west side of Lake Nipigon, roughly 40 miles away. There are practical reasons for this being born in Beardmore. My father was a pulp-cutter and we Ojibwa were (as a group of people, according to anthropologists) hunters and gatherers, and so Beardmore at the time provided an excellent venue and opportunity for my family to engage in these activities. My father did his pulp-cutting at camp, just six miles outside Beardmore, and our family would pick blueberries in the surrounding area and sell to local buyers. Blueberries would later symbolize a more powerful continuity of place for me in my world that was to be shaped in my formative years and by two different races.

The area around Beardmore during this period of my life was a veritable garden of blueberries during the summer months, most notably during August. In late July the entire populace of Gull Bay would pack their belongings and clamber aboard trucks, cars, and boats. Then we would head like a small army and armada to Beardmore for the annual blueberry harvest. At times the blueberry merchants would facilitate these movements from blueberry patch to blueberry patch with their own trucks. Once I remember vividly five families, including mine, packed in the back of one such truck. It was big enough to hold several families and had lattice-like sides in the back to hold its cargo which usually was many baskets of blueberries – and of course the families. During this one particular incident, the merchant truck-owner we affectionately lavished the moniker "Scrapiron" on, stopped and parked his truck alongside a curb in downtown Nipigon, Ontario. Why he would treat us in such an undignified manner, to be gawked at, I cannot to this day fathom. There we were, packed like human cargo on the back of this truck with all our belongings – blankets, clothing, tents, tools, pets, pots and pans – dangling on strings along the latticework. It is memories of moments like this, that make John Steinbeck's *The Grapes of Wrath* one of my all-time favorite novels. Our own predicament might very well have been deemed "the blueberries of wrath," since in many ways it paralleled the plight of the migrant workers during the Depression era of Steinbeck's book.

# THE SAN

My parents had 12 of us and I was the third eldest. Sometime around my third or fourth year the three eldest, myself included, were unceremoniously scooped up one day by the powers that be and shipped off to the Saint Joseph's Orphanage in Fort William, which is now a part of the city of Thunder Bay. We were living in Beardmore at the time of this particular incident. I barely remember the Children's Aid lady who commanded this entire exercise, but the policeman who accompanied her I have never forgotten, for he and his fraternity have somehow embodied or have been thematic in many nightmares and fears since then. I remembered distinctly the blackness of his uniform, his size, the black panel truck, his red face, and, most of all, his loud angry voice barking orders and threats. Years later I learned this was no isolated incident but part of a much larger and grander scheme by the powers that be to send Indian children to residential schools.[1]

Be that as it may, my eldest sister and I did not pass the post-arrival medical examination at "Yuma State." The latter was an epithet we gave this ominous-looking structure called St Joseph's Orphanage. As active and imaginative kids, we borrowed this characterization "Yuma State" from one of many westerns on TV which we would be bombarded with and with which we would later come to associate our identities, albeit with much confusion. In any case, in the course of my medical examination, a small spot was discovered on my left lung and for this reason I would spend the next three years at a sanitorium in the suburbs of Fort William, battling tuberculosis. Fortunately, a significant period of my convalescence was to take place at an annex of the larger hospital on the Fort William Indian reserve. The actual annex, given the dubious distinction of being called Squaw Bay, was by contrast in one of the prettiest spots one could ever see or imagine. The annex was perched on a low hill overlooking the bay, which itself was guarded on the opposite side by a huge wall of precipitous rock that is part of the Mountain McKay Range. At any given time in the day and from a specific angle one can discern the outline of an Indian woman's face etched out by nature against the cliff. Adjacent to the hospital stood a small whitewashed church where I would have my first experiences that were for a child more unusual than everyday events and matters. The physical interior of this building, the general layout, and the behavioral expectations of participants, including myself, were clearly unconventional. At the time, since I was only 3 or 4, I could not put a finger on what it was that was different, but I felt it was quite important and had a lot to do with some power beyond all these bigger people. I also sensed, with the help of a cuff here and there, that it had a lot to do on how I was to behave in this building and during the rituals. Much later I would learn a great deal of this power was shaped by a people I would see as distinct from the one I belonged to.

At some point during my stay at the sanitorium I may have forgotten consciously who were my parents and who I belonged to as a group. What I do recall is that the people I was most closely associated with were the patients. They were also distinctly different, most notably in color, from the group who I deemed to belong to the caretakers: the doctors, nurses, cleaners, janitors, and so on. Strangely, I did not necessarily feel I belonged to any one group other than being a patient. My facial features and hair at that age were quite fair and no one pointed out either directly or indirectly any signals for me to form any alliances with any particular group other than the patients. One person who did visit me, who would have reinforced this obliviousness to my identity, was a paternal aunt. On my father's side of the family there are distinct Euro-Canadian bloodlines and features, and the aunt who visited me had bright red hair and a very pale complexion. She may have related to me incidents about my heritage but I perhaps did not feel compelled to hear anything of interest regarding this subject. Part of this indifference may have been due to the seemingly interminable length of my stay at the sanitorium and the notion that this was perhaps my permanent home. This complacency would soon end in dramatic fashion and without any forewarning.

One day it was announced that I was going home, and that the aunt who visited me periodically would accompany me. The suddenness of the news threw me off guard and I didn't know how to react other than with surprise and shock. Home! Where is that? Who are these people that I am supposed to be going home to? One of the notions I did manage to internalize at the hospital was that I did belong to someone and somewhere other than at the hospital. After the initial shock of the announcement wore off, I was eager to solve this mystery and my excitement and anticipation started to grow. Little did I know how these same feelings and emotions were occurring in an entire community just a little over 100 miles to the north of Port Arthur.

## GULL BAY (KIASHK BAY)

The people of Gull Bay are the descendants of one of several groups of Ojibwa people or Anishinabae[2] who were signatories to the Robinson Superior Treaty. Prior to this they were part of a larger group that migrated from the pre-Columbian east, perhaps to facilitate the colonial fur trade, or were just trying to escape further encroachment into their homeland in the east. They were known as the Northern Ojibwa group and their southern brethren were the Chippewa who also migrated to the south on Lake Superior, to the northern states of Minnesota and Wisconsin. The Gull Bay Anishinabae at the time of the 1850 treaty were settled on the northwestern fringe of Lake Nipigon, partly on the mainland, and a portion of their home base was located on Jackfish Island roughly 200 yards off the mainland. The area at the time was teeming with wildlife for the residents' sustenance: fish, waterfowl, moose, caribou, bear, and beaver. The little harbor on the island, protected in the back from open water by a mountain, could not have been a better spot for its serenity, comfort, and relative isolation. On the mainland a little trading post was erected by the Hudson's Bay Company to accommodate trade. Here on Jackfish Island the Anishinabae settled in after the treaty and prepared to carry on their quiet and unobtrusive lifestyle. Shortly after the turn of the twentieth century, however, two things occurred that necessitated their departure from this spot. First, the need for a better hunting area and, second, the scourge of the great influenza epidemic that further reduced their numbers. Initially, some time in the early 1920s, a couple of families set out to settle at the present location which was in a fairly large bay on the west side of Lake Nipigon. It, too, was an ideal location for hunting, fishing, and trapping – occupations these people carried out with great efficiency.

Fishing was facilitated by *nup-kwan-uk*[3] boats sturdy enough to handle the rough open waters of a lake 80 by 45 miles. The fish were then transported to a fishing community at the southern tip of the lake at MacDirmand where they were further shipped by truck on the trans-Canada highway to destinations elsewhere. At the height of this industry in the 1950s, this occupation provided, in addition to monetary compensation, most of the benefits career seekers find in any occupation: security, nearness to family, interest, satisfaction, and advancement. The latter came in the form of owning one's own boat some day. Most of the equipment was made and maintained by the people themselves: the punts, canoes, outboard motors, and nets. Generally, the nets were woven and outfitted with corks and lead weights by the women at home. They were periodically brought to dry on revolving spools.

Trapping also provided most of the amenities that accompany many careers, with the exception of being home for supper. It may have been more labor-intensive than fishing but for adventure, interest, and contentment it was unmatched. Most Anishinabae trapped in pairs, were flown out after freeze-up, and returned in the spring laden with furs. In regard to their respective occupations, the people of Gull Bay were very efficient, highly productive, and excelled in skills that would match any. But it was during the early 1950s that they were to embrace a new occupation that made them less isolated and perhaps made them susceptible to new social problems. At about the time

143

of my release from the hospital, Gull Bay was still only accessible by boat and the Hudson's Bay store was replenished by supplies brought in this way. However, a logging road from the trans-Canada penetrated just a few short miles away and in the spring of 1954 a small fish truck was meandering its way to a point of rendezvous to pick up fish for return to Port Arthur. One of its passengers was a plump 7-year-old Anishinabae boy unsure of his own identity but full of anticipation at meeting a family and home he had forgotten after three years in the hospital.

I left the Fort William sanitorium with little fanfare and was to be accompanied by my aunt to Gull Bay. Passage from Port Arthur to Gull Bay usually amounted to securing a ride by automobile up to MacDirmand where any fishing boat on its way to Gull Bay might be picked up for the remainder of the trip. For this particular trip my aunt was able to secure a ride for us by way of a small fish truck whose owner was the middleman for the Gull Bay fishing industry. For most of the journey, particularly the last half, we would be traveling through bush country. The road was long, winding, rocky, and, this being the springtime, extremely muddy in some areas. For the adults it must have been an arduous and taxing experience but for me it was sheer heaven and I didn't suffer the usual children's "are we there yet?" malaise. It was my first conscious exposure to an automobile trip and I wanted to experience every mile of the road with its countless bends, hills, lakes, and open sky – these small surprises periodically punctuated with wildlife. I didn't want this ride to end. After several hours we finally came to a spot so muddy the truck got stuck and we could go no further. The driver and his helper got out to see what they could do. My aunt and I sat in the cab and watched helplessly. After what seemed like a very long time trying to extricate the truck from its muddy prison, I noticed two adult males approaching us; evidently they just seemingly and mysteriously appeared out of nowhere from the bush. Prior to this incident, though, I did recall hearing a sound emanating from the bush which I recognized (with the help of a mind slowly adjusting itself to some far-off past) as an outboard motor and its dying engine. Somehow my inexperienced brain didn't at the time relate or link these two incidents together. When they approached close enough, there were some greetings exchanged among the men. Almost immediately I noticed that their physical appearance and mannerisms were different from what I was accustomed to. They were darker in complexion and seemed more subdued than the driver and his helper. The younger, taller, and less reticent of the two spoke to my aunt in a language that both startled me at first and yet had a far-off familiar ring to it, like my remember-ing of the outboard motor. To my astonishment I heard my aunt speak Ojibwa for the first time to her brother, my paternal uncle. And yet when I thought about it she did exhibit the same reserved bearing and mannerisms as these men. My uncle and his friend attempted to help free the truck from the mud with little success. After a while it was decided that my aunt and I would be escorted out to the reserve and at the same time additional help would be sought to help the fish-buyers retrieve their truck. My uncle lifted me up on to his back and with his partner leading the way, the four of us disappeared into the woods. In a few minutes we approached a shoreline where a skiff was moored or tethered to a dead fall. Again a rush of adrenalin overcame me as I anticipated a fast boat-ride. In a few minutes we were aboard and speeding off to a new destination. This new experience was exciting and I kept glancing around to absorb everything with my senses. Because of a headwind the ride was a bit bumpy. Looking back, I saw the shoreline recede steadily and quickly while in its wake the boat parted the water to create a V-shaped wedge of waves. Ahead the distant bluish-gray hills lined the horizon, spotted only with intermixed dark shades that denoted the various islands. As cool water, brushed aside from the bow plunging against the waves, sprinkled my face, I continued to stare ahead and wonder excitedly what lay ahead for me.

We had been riding for about 20 minutes when we rounded a large bend and my attention was directed far ahead to what looked like the outline of a village. In the distance I could make out sandy cliffs[4] and just above them dotted here and there houses most of which were painted white with black tar-papered roofs. As we drew closer to the reserve I could make out to the left a little harbor that supported a fairly large dock with mooring posts and automobile tires strung out on the sides to prevent abrasion of boats. But what caught my attention most was that a huge crowd had gathered on the dock and seemed agitated or excited in anticipation of some event or other. A short distance away from the dock my uncle slowed the engine and his partner stood ready to tie the boat. As we inched our way to the dock I looked up and saw a sea of brown faces smiling and laughing with their attention apparently focused on the contents of the boat. Little did I know or appreciate that all the commotion was for the welcoming of a chubby little boy who had been away for three years in a hospital – one of their own. After being hoisted up on to the dock, I was guided by my aunt through the crowd, where individual people began touching my clothing and my hair out of curiosity. The dock was L-shaped and my aunt made her way up toward some people who seemed to be waiting for her. I was led to this one woman who stood quietly to the side with a gentle and almost shy smile on her face. Beside her stood a dark-skinned boy just a little taller than I was. I was then introduced to my mother and then my older brother, who in a few short days would play a very dramatic role in an incident that was to affect me psychologically for the rest of my life.

For the past few days, from the time of the announcement of my release from the hospital up until this very moment, I had accepted my fate rather nonchalantly and unquestioningly in a sort of wait-and-see manner. I don't recall being prepared for any dramatic changes in my life, but the transition for me did not seem at all too traumatic, if it was ever supposed to be. I accepted my mom for who she was, and my new home and surroundings, rather casually. I would in a short while form a natural and close bond with her and the rest of my family. My father, this being spring, was still out trapping in the bush. My mother stayed at home caring for three of the seven children she had by this time in her life. In all, she would have twelve.

When all the greetings and news communicated at the dock subsided, my mother lifted me up on her back and proceeded to walk home a third of a mile away with my brother at her side. Almost immediately I could not help but notice the difference in worlds between now and what I had experienced in the city. The most discernible was the sense of stillness and relative quietness of life on the reserve. I could hear almost every sound: the noise of chopping wood, of dogs barking, the drone of an incoming fishing boat. Out on the lake I could make out a lone figure in a punt powered by a three-horse Johnson motor. On the way to our house I took a brief moment to assess both my mom and my brother. I remember sort of looking objectively to the side of her head and thinking simply "so this is my mom." She sensed me shifting a bit and asked what was wrong. I said nothing and with that I closed a episode in my life that should not have happened – the part about being in the hospital and away from my family, that is.

For the next little while and with a little more free rein I began to get more acquainted with my family and my new home. I met uncles and aunts whom I had almost entirely forgotten. Vague memories assisted in my becoming more used to these experiences. I had a little sister barely able to walk and a little brother, besides my older brother staying at home. A few days later another younger brother and sister came home from hospital following tonsil removal. I was also to learn our oldest sister was in the hospital for the same reasons I had been. Almost immediately I began to explore my physical environment with great relish, as this had been denied me for some time. One of the stipulations impressed upon me was that I was not to go swimming out in the lake, for reasons related to my continued recovery. Almost immediately I broke this rule and I suffered the consequences. For the most part, life for me consisted primarily of getting up in the morning and just playing all day long or simply doing all the things any 7-year-old does on an isolated Indian reserve, particularly one who has been denied all these things for three years.

# THE SHOOTING

It was just one of those ordinary days when it happened. The skies were partly cloudy and it seemed mild out that afternoon. The three oldest of us boys were playing around the house and my mother was washing clothes in the porch the old-fashioned way, with scrubbing board and tub. My oldest brother made his way into the house and we younger ones continued playing outside. Tiring of the game I made my way to the porch to see what my mom was up to. Nearing the porch I could hear the grating sound of clothes, board, and water. As I stepped on to the porch my mother turned around to greet me. I don't recall hearing the sound but my mother must have for she let out this wild scream or yell that something awful had occurred. A split second later while she continued staring at me and screaming she collapsed to the floor near the doorway of the porch. I went out from the porch but for some strange reason I seemed slightly numbed and immobile. Limping a few yards from the house I came to a stop and looked down at my legs. My left pant leg was covered in blood from my belt down. Despite all the blood I didn't feel any pain. I still did not know what had happened but I was terrified and started crying in horror that something awful happened to me. Not knowing what to do I continued limping up the road toward some people who were approaching with disbelief in their eyes. An elder was the first to reach me, whereupon he picked me up and started towards our house. That was the last I remember before I passed out. I must have been out for a couple of hours before I woke up and immediately experienced a tremendous amount of pain all over my body with the slightest of movement, including each time I inhaled. I then became aware that I had been shot. Knowing this, I became almost inconsolable, crying aloud that I didn't want to die. This profound awareness of life's fragility would remain with me through all of my adulthood. My older brother had been apparently playing with a gun when it discharged and the bullet went through the door leading to the porch and came to rest in my left groin area. After settling down a little I noticed the whole house was filled with people, the very same people who just a few days earlier had welcomed me home at the dock. My mother also got over her initial shock and was by my side trying to comfort me. Apparently an airplane had been summoned to fly me out to Nipigon, where the nearest hospital was. A short while later I heard the plane flying above and that alone cheered me up somewhat, in anticipation of this new experience. Our house was the last one in the village and it was decided I would be transported bed and all down the cliff on to a skiff and to the dock where the plane was moored. When we reached the dock it was again packed with people to see me off. Lying prostrate, I looked up to see everyone throwing money down into the boat. My mother collected the money, thanking everyone for their generosity and concern. I was boarded on to the plane and we took off. The exhilaration of flying must have negated the pain from my shot wound for I was trying to get up and look around to see the world below. It didn't seem long before we were at the hospital and I began another convalescence. I don't remember too much about my stay in Nipigon but it wasn't very long before I was home again and resumed the catching-up activities I had started before I was shot.

# INDIAN CHILD

The year that followed the shooting incident was perhaps one of the most important of my formative years. It was the only year in which I spent a winter at home on the reserve. Despite my own childish concerns, interests, and focus, I did take in a lot that was going in reserve life. I began to internalize the community ethos, mores, social practices, and customs, many of them transmitted to me by my parents, and generally through osmosis. I didn't speak my language but managed to pick up enough to get by with. Being raised as a white boy for four years with all the attendant mannerisms not conducive to reserve life didn't hinder my transition much, for I adapted quite well, as perhaps any boy of 7 might. I did get teased a lot for not speaking the language and laughed at for a lot of the other things I did. For instance, as I was very inquisitive, I would ask a lot of questions unabashedly, about a lot of things in general, of people I naively assumed spoke English as proficiently as I did. Often I would get this look of incredulity and a laugh from the older people. Most often I wouldn't get an answer at all, but I knew most people tolerated me with amusement. I perhaps embarrassed my mother a lot. I didn't miss the attendant comforts of life in a hospital such as white sheets, regular meals, change of clothes and state-of-the-art toys. The freedom I enjoyed at home I wasn't prepared to trade for the accouterments of city living. In the year I spent in Gull Bay, I began to pick up with subtlety nuances of behavior from the Native adults that depicted their passive mannerisms in their relations with white people. In turn non-Natives generally (schoolteachers, Hudson Bay managers, DIA officials, the police, to name a few) reacted reciprocally with subconsciously patronizing mannerisms and in some curcumstances direct superiority. These behavior patterns I would internalize and integrate in my own behavior, and they later would be reinforced by the residential school. By the time I was introduced to the regimen of residential school living I had all but fully integrated to life on the reserve as an "Indian." Gone was the spontaneous, full-of-emotional-energy kid spawned in a clinical setting, oblivious to color and class lines. Instead, I became less spontaneous and a bit more cautious of people, in particular white people and very especially those in authority. In one sense this passive orientation was to provide me with a strategy for avoiding confrontation with authority. On the other hand this passiveness in its most nefarious form would have a long-term negative effect and would completely pervade my behavior through life. I don't doubt this process afflicted many more people than just myself.

## ST JOSEPH'S ORPHANAGE

In the fall of 1955 I was for the second time scooped up along with some of my siblings, and sent off to the boarding school in Fort William. This time I wasn't to be spared by a debilitating illness and would have to spend the next five years in an institution that did everything but assimilate us into mainstream society. When we arrived at the doorstep of St Joseph's I may have instinctively sensed what was in store for us when we gazed up at this ominous and imposing-looking six-story structure. Built around the turn of the century, St Joe's was set back from Franklin Street about 20 yards and was guarded all around by a high hedge that seemed sufficient to dissuade prying passers-by, as it was intended to. The overall structure looked as if it had been built haphazardly and piecemeal with little esthetic input by its architects. When we entered through the front doors and into a dark lobby we were greeted by a tall nun who was the mother superior. While our escorts discussed the handover details with her I absorbed my new environment with some trepidation. I was at once aware of certain uneasy sensations. I heard light music off in the distance, piano music. I could hear people engaged in light activity somewhere far away down the hallways. I could also smell the pleasant odors of food, preparations for supper, I supposed, since it was already late afternoon. I could smell other odors, but could not pinpoint what they were. The sensations were innocuous enough but I could not elude this sensation of uneasiness. These initial sounds and smells would remain with me all of my life and would always trigger memories associated with loneliness, abandonment, alienation, and profound sadness. As much as I wanted to cry, I was determined not to for the sake of remaining strong and perhaps not to set off a chain reaction. After our escorts left we were led away, our sister in one direction and us three boys in another. There was no response to this divisive action as our subjugation seemed complete to some unknown irresistible force. Segregation of the boys and girls was common procedure for reasons known only to those who created these analogues of the Dickensian novels. We would only see our sister again at Christmas, months away, the only time of the year girls and boys would be allowed to mingle. My younger brother and I stayed close to our older brother and followed his every move.

Two nuns were assigned to look after the 60 or 70 boys. The older, and perhaps more experienced nun acted as the superior of the two. The younger and much prettier one was the first who took us under her wing and gave us our first orientation and introductions. In real life and in art it seems the prettier ones are always the kinder ones. I guess art does imitate life. Throughout that first year her demure nature and presence would always mitigate the stern, stringent, and harsh temperament that accompanied the older one.

We were to stay downstairs till suppertime and then be taken up to the uppermost floor where the boys' dormitory was located. We went down to the basement, which was pretty much the day room for the boys. Here we had lockers to keep our coats, and winter gear and other miscellaneous items. We also had facecloths and towels assigned to us that had our individual numbers attached. The numbers were assigned in reverse order to our ages for reasons unknown to everyone. They were attached to everything that was assigned and belonged to us: towels, clothing, pajamas, etc.

The boys were playing outside and would soon be summoned by a bell to get ready for supper. They would file in and go to their lockers, put away their outdoor gear, wash up, and wait for suppertime. While doing this they would size up the "new guys," who in this case would be us. We would just sit on the benches and try to maintain a brave front in this strange and unfriendly environment. Just before supper we were instructed to line up in single file just outside the door that led upstairs to the refectory. We were to form this single line over the years at a moment's notice and at any time for various purposes. Lineups were used for disciplinary purposes such as strapping or just standing still for long periods. They were also used for marching to the refectory for meals, retiring for bedtime upstairs, going to school classes, on outings, and of course for required religious functions.

From the basement we marched upstairs to the main floor, where the refectory was. When we entered the dining hall I welcomed the odor of the food, and my stomach juices must have gone into a frenzy as we had not eaten for some time. Despite this, though, I still approached everything with caution and curiosity. The hall was long and well lit by incandescent lamps. The walls and ceiling were painted sky blue in contrast to the dark hallways and other parts of the building. There was an aisle at the center, separating the rows of tables and benches. At the end of the refectory the food was laid out on tables. We were assigned our places at a table before we lined up again and marched to retrieve our main dish and dessert. When we were served I noticed the girls' refectory partially through a doorway that led to the kitchen. In case I might spot my sister I took a quick glance, but with no luck. I was discreet, for I intuited that behavior of this kind would be frowned upon. The meal was served by two of the residents, a chore that would be assigned to everyone sooner or later. While the two sisters looked on, I sneaked a stare at the older one for the first time and what I saw instilled a sense of dread in me which was not totally unmerited. She was slightly shorter than the younger one but seemed more robust in physical stature. Her face wore a very stern expression on a bland complexion. Her jowls protruded from the tightly fitted habit around her head, making her appearance owl-like. She hid behind a pair of thick-rimmed glasses that added to her martinet-like features. And as if that wasn't bad enough, a second stare yielded a light but discernible moustache on her. In her dark habit all these features seemed to underscore her sternness even more. Later I would learn first-hand about my intuitions of her.

Meals began and ended with the saying of grace. The meals were not out of the ordinary but on some occasions we were confronted with the ordeal of eating something totally repulsive to our personal palates. For many it was spinach, but for me it was pumpkin, and one day it was served, if you can believe it, as a dessert. Most of the time it was served as a vegetable, and even then it tasted atrocious. Generally we were able to dispense with it in one form or another. Often we would deal it away quid pro quo for favors to some other resident who was born without tastebuds or somebody with masochistic predispositions. One was well advised to give these guys a wide berth when interacting with them. Anyway, the nuns would often get wind of this practice and sometimes one had no alternative but to eat. I don't recall the punishment meted out for this offense but it was bad enough for me to get sick with horror when faced with the prospect. My older brother was one of these hard-nosed cases and maybe came to my aid that day because I can't remember being punished for that one occasion. I think the nuns came to their senses after that first year and forced eating must have been abolished soon after.

After supper that first day we went downstairs briefly while the boys went outside for a while to play. Then we were escorted upstairs to the dormitory, the three of us, and shown our beds. We were presented with another set of facecloths and towels, along with a set of pajamas. From the basement to the upstairs dorm we had to ascend 12 flights of stairs each evening and descend the same each morning. For some reasons, such as doing chores, we had to do this more than once a day. For the five years I spent at St Joseph's I wondered how many flights of stairs I had negotiated. That evening the strange sights, smells, and sounds permeated my thoughts again in some strange unexplainable way like that afternoon, when we had first arrived. I sat on the bed assigned to me and felt the rough texture of the army blanket. I leaned down and smelled the clean white sheets and pillowcase. These things were not new to me, as I had experienced them before at the hospitals I had been to in the past. Somehow, though, there was something strangely uncomfortable about these and I felt that I should approach them with caution. All the beds were the same, made of cast iron and painted white. Even the scent of the wood emanating from the creepy floor and walls had a distinct odor that evening. I supposed it was all perfectly natural to expect all these new sights and sounds. I walked over to the south end of the dorm to the veranda and took in the vista before me. The huge dark shape of Mountain McKay with its flashing red lights was the first thing I noticed. And then all the bright lights of the Westfort area sparkled brightly in the distance. It seemed as if I could hear all that was going down below. Then I noticed the railroad track directly below. I knew that it led to somewhere away from here. When I heard the train far off in the distance it immediately reminded me of home and my mother. Somehow I managed to keep myself from breaking down. Whatever it took, I had to deal with what was to be my new home. The rest of the evening went by quickly. After lights were out and everyone else was asleep I continued with my observations. Staring around at the beds before me with their clumps of human content, I briefly wondered about the others' predicaments. I would meet many of them tomorrow. The last thing I took notice of that night was the red glow of the exit light. It seemed both sinister and a beacon of hope for a better tomorrow. No sooner was I asleep than we were awakened by the ringing of a bell. That probably was the most annoying sound we would all hear for years to come. When I had an opportunity I gave the bell a closer inspection. It was made of brass in the shape of a sphere with rib-like sides; inside were two brass bearings that made the ringing sound. The nuns would ring the bell by holding it in the palms of their hands and twisting their wrists. Many were tempted to hide this contraption but few dared. While I was still trying to wake up, an older boy came over and helped me make my bed. I learned he was assigned to help me, something that was routinely done for the younger residents. After we dressed and washed up we formed a line and went downstairs to the chapel for mass. This was another routine we would perform every morning except Saturdays for the next five years.

During mass I noticed that the altar boys were residents. A couple of years later I would become one. This I didn't mind since being one made you something or somebody special. I worked hard at practicing my Latin which we memorized but hadn't a clue as to what I was saying. After mass that second day we went downstairs for breakfast. I don't remember much about what came next that day, except for the fact that I met my first best friend in life. During a break my brothers and I went outside to play. My brothers went their way and I, with hands in pockets, sauntered over to a boy of around my age (which was 8) sitting on a stone pillar working on something. With hands in pockets, according to boy culture, you were displaying non-aggression as opposed to having open hands by your side. As I looked closer, he was fashioning a gun holster out of a discarded linoleum tile. His state-of-the-art tools consisted of a nail and rock to punch holes for the seams. With little fanfare I found myself helping him and we just became friends.

Over the next five years I would experience many things that have left some important or poignant memory in my life. Only one stands out more than others. Sometime shortly after we arrived at the orphanage I was trying to darn a sock upstairs in the dormitory. We were taught to place a burnt lightbulb in the sock to support the area we were to darn. With the needle and darn we would simply sew the sock. With my best efforts I just couldn't do it properly. The older nun, without any warning, suddenly appeared and started screaming at me. The next thing I knew I was rolling up my sleeves and bracing myself for what came next. She hit me all over my arms with a sturdy ruler. The pain was stinging and I reacted with a healthy scream and a post-licking whimper. What was perhaps more traumatizing was having to be singled out before your peers in such a manner. Whenever we would line up for a strap thereafter, I was among the first in line. There was less trauma in getting over the ordeal quickly and then sitting back and sadistically watching others receive their due. Anyway, these straps were relatively easy to take compared to my inaugural licking. The older nun, much to my relief, would only be looking after us that first year. For the next four years we were attended by two less strict nuns.

151

I had gone from *tikanagan* to boarding school, and was now a long way from home. These early memories were to remain with me for many years to come.

## NOTES

1   The process of assimilation of Native people has been well documented and established by sociologists in both the United States and Canada.
2   One version of this self-designation Anishinabae by the Ojibwa was the concept of beauty (*Anishshin*) and ground (*nabe*) which when given its full interpretation meant "the beautiful people from the ground."
3   These boats were made by the Anishinabae themselves, were anywhere from 20 to 50 feet in length and made of steamed cedar strips. Many were powered by automotive engines easily mounted at the center of the boat and connected to a drive shaft. A cabin was built to house the engine room, kitchen, and sleeping quarters. Atop the cabin were placed all the fish boxes, nets, punts, and "kickers" (small outboard motors).
4   Sometime in the 1940s an Ontario Hydro project on Lake Nipigon raised the water level and as a result land erosion began on the shore of Gull Bay. By the mid-1950s the erosion had eaten away hundreds of feet of shoreline with the resultant 30-foot-high cliffs lining the frontage.

# 13

# ONTOLOGY OF IDENTITY AND INTERSTITIAL BEING

*Anne Waters*

## INTRODUCTION

This chapter is about in-betweens of interstitial space, and the cognitive dissonance of coming into being. In-betweens are not nothing, though they sometimes appear this way. An interstitial gap, or space, when circumscribed with new defined angles (boundaries, or borders), creates a new interstitial identity. In these interstitial spaces (where being and non-being come together), we locate an American Indian metaphysics, where everything is, or rather everything is always coming into being some thing. This metaphysics can help draw an understanding of an apparent, or real, human cognitive dissonance. The dissonance may be a function of either indiscrete category classifications blending, a function of discrete category classifications clashing, or the bringing into being of new identity. These collisions and overlays of blended meaning are part of the creative process in what I call "the Land of Uncertainty." In the Land of Uncertainty, when new being categories are created from cognitive dissonance, the dissonance, relaxed, releases new meaning. This chapter argues that unity, or identity, arises from these relaxed interstitial weavings that arise from being coming-to-be in this Land of Uncertainty.

## VOICE SHIFTS IN UNCERTAINTY

When I read poetry (or papers) I shift from one voice to another. I sing or shout, perhaps admonish or warn, and sometimes soothe or sound philosophically neutral.

The inflection and rhythm of sound articulate my intent, as a speaker. Time-span changes occur between the changes of voice. In any given reading, my being-in-the-world rearranges and shifts from sameness to difference, and back again, with a same, or new, meaning. These shifts of voice, and new meaning born of cognitive struggle, interest me. My interest is as a philosopher, poet, lawyer, and most especially, as an American Indian. From this latter space of being, that is, as an American Indian, I focus my discussion.

Creating new meaning out of cognitive dissonance shifts my way of being, and fills interstices of coming-to-be. In this process my disposition toward indiscrete being enters the space of the discrete being, and change, or new meaning, happens. The interstitial gaps into which my nondiscrete way of being moves are necessary in order to allow the shifting from a way of being holding one voice to the holding of another. This experience of shifting occurs sometimes as a willful shift, and at other times as an unknowing shift. Bilinguals and code talkers make these kinds of shifts on a regular basis and at an amazingly rapid pace.

My concern is how interstices of identity shifts carry the potential to create an identity of what bell hooks would refer to as an insurgent intellectualism. In this chapter, as I analyze the issue of identity in difference, I locate a place of conscience for people cognizant of identity difference. I discuss the geography of place as it is situated in identity formation. I then address the conscience that speaks to the interdependence of geographical space and identity formation as they relate to global resources redistribution.

## IDENTITY AND DIFFERENCE

I read the story of mixed-race identity from the lives of particular persons. This method seems necessary to understanding, and is playful and fun, engaging me as a puzzle might. The trick is to locate the subject while retaining subjectivity. This emphasis of locating subjectivity in a particular exemplar of identity enables me to locate sites of my lived experience that do not fit fixed identity.

To the extent that identity theories are political, they are about power and oppression. Understanding identity helps me understand politics, and understanding politics helps me understand the interdependency of identity and politics for oppressive colonial action. Thus, understanding identity politics helps me articulate practices of identity suppression (and oppression).

Cultures that locate identity in a politics of ideas, e.g. those belonging to Greek thought, tend to colonize other cultures, and rule politically oppressive states. These colonial social cultures link individual identity with linear time (of discrete human events and institutions) rather than with a geographic place. Conversely, Indigenous cultures nurture individual identity formation with a communal interdependence and sustainability in a specific geographic location. Vine Deloria, in *God is Red*, claims the importance of geographic place identity for America's Indigenous peoples, and he clarifies the nature of our cognitive and, hence, practical struggles with a culture whose identity is found within linear time events.

Indigenous identity stories link communal identity to particular geographies, sometimes conveying patterns of hybrid beings. These beings sometimes interact with us in stories offering playful and humorous insight, or fearful and awesome insight! A hybrid being, going back one generation, has at least two original genetic blueprints, though there may be one or more original cultural blueprints; the metaphor of a family tree of DNA, culture, language, or worldview can be understood as a model of grafted identity.

Race theory in the United States generally classifies biracial persons as individuals having two original DNA blueprints (genetic parents), with variant racial markers. As Naomi Zack has illustrated, however, these persons can be thought about more properly as mixed-race individuals. On this model, everyone is hybrid as a result of hypothetical race markers, and historical global colonization. Using this metaphor, Zack articulates the nondiscrete borders of racial identity, and the subsequent political uses of them. Zack shares with Deloria a suspicion about unified and theoretically constructed identities that are not grounded in the particularity of real individuals' lives. I feel an affinity with this position.

When we focus upon our Earth Mother and Sky Father around the globe, hybrid persons of nation and geography will be found, whether of different tribes or nations, in Africa or Asia, India, Europe, or the Americas. Indeed, when Eric van Sertima, in *They Came before Columbus* (Random House, 1976), wrote about trade between Africa and the Americas, I don't think we need to assume he was just talking about trading cloth and food! Thus, around the globe, hybrids, whether by choice or force, assimilate to identities of cultural domination. This model of hybrid-grafting helps me to understand how to teach a deconstruction of race, culture, and national identity theory.

The extent to which an analogy can be drawn from exemplars of race hybrids to exemplars of cultural hybrids may depend upon what we mean by "culture" in the context of personal identity. And in this context of personal identity, to gather a meaning of culture, we can begin with the relationship between outer and inner cultural identity constructs.

## OUTSIDE/INSIDE IDENTITY

Vine Deloria, in several of his books, claims that for American Indians, our tribes live in and through us. Implicit in his understanding of tribal identity is that identity manifestations, i.e. our ways of being in the world, may or may not be conscious awareness. American Indian identity and worldview, a history of place consciousness, preserved through oral history, manifests discrete geographical place symbols within consciousness that provide a conceptual framework of identity as place. American Indian consciousness, and hence American Indian identity, is cognitively of, and interdependent with, our land base. Though many things may be inferred from this claim, I focus here first on what it means for inner/outer identity, and for consciousness and worldview preservation, by drawing an analogy to Asian identity.

Direct attention to an Asian American poet, Mitsuye Yamada and her poem "Mirror Mirror" (in *Camp Notes*, Shameless Hussy Press, 1976) helps articulate the differences of inside/outside identity. Mitsuye's Asian American son is having problems at school being accepted by non-Asian students. He believes this is because he appears Asian on the outside; he is upset because he believes that because he is American on the inside, he should be accepted as an American. Social acceptance is so important that her son is willing to ignore, and wipe out, any Asian identity on the inside that he might otherwise own. Our poet cautions him, however, indicating that as she sees his identity, he needs to turn the outside in; he is both American and Asian on the inside, and this is what America looks like.

This poem illustrates how identity is beyond visibility, and much deeper than external markers. Here, cultural markers create identity, distinct from any DNA features. Moreover, we indicate who we are and are not both by our physical appearance (how we appear to others as an $x$, $y$, or $z$), and by many intangibles, such as language (syntax and semantics), worldviews, values, positional vision, ways of thought, ways of being, and motivating actions. These are the things of culture, e.g. being part of an interdependent universe, that lives in and through us.

Another analogy comes from the work of Annette Arkeketa, a Creek playwright and poet. Throughout her work, Arkeketa suggests a sense of knowing identity from within, from a placed being. Understanding this sense of identity requires knowing that a Bureau of Indian Affairs (BIA) Certificate of Degree of Indian Blood (CDIB) card is not necessarily an identity marker. In one of Arkeketa's poems this is shown to us through the eyes of her son. It is the metaphysics of his communal existence, as a member of a group, and the blended identities from which his identity, as a tribal member, comes into being. He calls forth tribal powers that already live in and through him as he mocks the BIA identity police, "CDIB! CDIB! I know who I be! . . . CDIB!" All the while, as he mocks the oppressed external identity marker, he suggests nothing really has changed from inside, but rather that the changes have been forced from the outside. The importance of Arkeketa's identity portrayal is that her son knows who he is, and this knowing comes from a tribal knowing.

The reality of identity frequently is problematic for us when we do not know, or cannot discern, another's cultural identity. For example, we may not know or have the ability to recognize or name cultural markers, codes, or differences. This may especially be true for individuals who are culturally isolated, having only the dissonance of not-being to push up against in understanding another's identity, rather than an affirmation of a particular cultural trait or way of being. Cultural isolation creates cognitive dissonance with cultural difference. Important to understanding identity problems as they relate to communicative dissonance is awareness that our communicative pathways are 90 to 95 percent non-verbal! Hence, cultural behaviors such as human movement patterns and eye positions become important to intracultural communication. The ability to recognize the furniture of cultural communication helps to release initial cognitive dissonance.

Assume some person wants another to know and/or respect cultural difference. From an epistemological perspective, the subject knower must have a reference point of culture recognition. Because these differences can and do go unrecognized frequently by a subject knower, the phenomenon of passing occurs (intentional or not). In this way, culture markers, both internal and external, matter. False identity assumptions may occur unknown to either the subject or the subject knower. When this happens, potential communication slips past speakers.

What all this seems to imply is that if a person is to arrive at the ability to see, hear, feel, and appreciate that cultural difference, they must have the key to unlock a cultural conceptual framework. What seems obvious to Mitsuye's son, being Asian on the outside rather than the inside, clearly shows how he focuses (has been taught to focus?) on his external and internal being in the world. And Arkeketa's son, for those who wield power over him, is Indian only because he has met the qualifications of his colonizers; yet for himself, his family, and community, the BIA CDIB card is irrelevant to his being Indian, and his Being having a heritage and culture. What the child knows intuitively is that who he is is not who the card says he is, but is a lived relationship to those who share his place. He is who he is only as he lives a relationship with all his relations in the universe. This worldview of an identity construct is a gift of coming into being by acting in the world. The gift of identity, the learning to see through his mother's eyes, is also a part of who he is, and is a creative force informing his nondiscrete identity.

The playful outer reality in these examples is that cultural identity neither begins nor ends with physical appearance, promulgations of a national citizenship, nor discretely unified categories. The lesson to be learned from these analogies is that identities of people are about a culture or about a relationship, in a way that we cannot presuppose to be true about discrete nationhood. In conclusion, whether or not the Asian American child is recognized by his peers as American, or the American Indian Creek child is recognized by a dominant colonial government as a Creek citizen, no one could seriously deny that they are these things, and that these things also create nondiscrete ways of being that are essential to (children's) cultural identity.

## HEARING AS BEING

I recall a conversation that took place several years ago relative to the issue of music and volume. Central to my musings about this conversation is the extent that music, or what and how we hear as sound, is a function our being in the world, as cultural specific beings. The conversation I mention flowed from the process of listening to classical music with a colleague, and then listening to African American music, and later American Indian music with that same colleague.

When African American music began playing, my visiting colleague asked me whether I had just turned the volume down. She then asked me to turn up the volume, to make the music louder. I complied with the request, wondering if perhaps my guest had a hearing difficulty (since I thought the volume was already sufficiently loud). After a bit, the musical selection changed from African American music, to American Indian music. Almost immediately my colleague asked me whether I turned the volume up; and claimed that the music now sounded disturbingly and uncomfortably loud to her. I politely informed my guest that I had not, subsequent to the initial request, turned up the volume. But try as I might, I never did get this person to believe that I had not surreptitiously changed the volume when playing the American Indian music.

My musings about the effect of the cultural music selection suggest to me that how we hear volume may also be, at least partly, a function of culture. In response to sharing this amusement with my partner, I was reminded that Harlem, New York, is a community of communal music on the streets, and that it is not played with a low volume! And I now recall that after my partner's child returned home from her first visit to Harlem, as a young African American college student, she seriously entertained the thought of packing up and moving to Harlem, so enamored was she with the sweet sounds of street music!

Music is rooted in, and is about, a way of sharing. In a community that affords not much else by way of commodities, music can be sacred. Music takes on a special cultural meaning, just as the sharing of "frybread" takes on a specific cultural meaning, when we could only afford a few bread-makings in American Indian communities. Both music and frybread are intimately a part of the lifeworld of our American Indian communities. Both have played a role in bringing and holding people of a culture together.

More recently, American Indian ways of music and dancing, as commodities, are seeping into dominant mainstream American culture, in much the same way that African American music has found itself co-opted by dominant cultures. Yet the ways of being from which these sounds and songs have come, are heard by the mainstream not as voices of the mainstream, but rather, as dissonant, and for some, discordant voices.

My point here is that many times, totally unknown to us, we show who we are by our body language as we move, as we talk, as we perceive the world, and also by how we hear the world, through the sounds and rhythms of our environment. We may sometimes cringe at what sounds to others as carefully orchestrated musical harmony. These sound rhythms emanate from our body movement. This is how deep are our identity markers. For American Indians, the voice of the drum, the heartbeat of Earth Mother, in harmony with Sky Father, is a voice of our being, a voice of knowing our place among all our relations.

## SEEING AS BEING

In a 1992 *American Philosophical Association Blacks in Philosophy Newsletter* article titled "An autobiographical view of mixed race and deracination," Naomi Zack speaks of her experience of having an African American absent father, and being raised by a very present Jewish mother. Zack is a culturally grafted person (as we all are in some sense). As such, she claims that warps in her psychology of identity are the effects of warps in her external social reality. As a person of mixed-race identity, she is appalled at the racial theory in our country that dictates each person shall have a race, and that they must choose between black and white. The problem, as Zack sees it, is that there is no place for mixed-race persons.

Though I sympathize with Zack's position, I'm not sure whether I favor her overall thesis that a new universal be developed having a bias in favor of raceless races. (However, this may only be an indication that I am not clear about her meaning.) On the other hand, Zack recognizes that we must block the privileging of race via the use of racial designators. This makes some sense to me. I cannot help but wonder if such counsel could bring us culturally closer to a place where we would be judged not by our racial affiliations, nor cultural contributions, but by the content of our character, our moral character, as Martin Luther King would imply, and our cultural moral character, to which Deloria frequently alludes. Blocking racial designators, however, will not bar cultural dissonance, and ultimately, I think, race theory is also about cultural dissonance and cultural domination.

Important for my work in critical identity theory, and my thesis here about the metaphysics of identity, are the reasons why Naomi Zack claims she identifies with her Jewish mother, and not her African American father. She says her mother was not an observant Jew, nor was she (Zack). Nevertheless, she says, "my mother saw the world with (what I take to be) Jewish eyes and felt the world with (what I take to be) Jewish fears, and I have never been able to avoid (what I take to be) the same apperceptions. In other words, I believe I 'identify' with my mother." By analogy, I recognize my Jewish ancestry and heritage of my father, and I do believe I see the world with (what I take to be) a particular type of Jewish consciousness.

More important for myself, however, is that I understand the world with (what I take to be) and feel the world with (what I take to be) an American Indian, specifically a Northern Florida Seminole matrilineal consciousness. Thus, I have never been able to avoid (what I take to be) the same apperceptions of my mother. Or, as Zack would articulate it, I believe I "identify" with (the worldview of the apperceptions of) my mother. But this identification is not a racial one so much as a cultural one that embodies racial dispositions. I believe I share much the same metaphysical and ontological understandings of the world that my mother inhabited, and that this sharing has led me to a similar skeptical epistemological position. I want to flesh this out a bit, to see how this might inform my understanding of the hegemonic world that surrounds me.

Over 500 years of cultural seeing of the resistance of American Indians to colonization, assimilation, and genocide have informed our hearing of a different drum. After over 500 years, our resistance, metaphorically speaking, is as much in our DNA (whatever DNA may ultimately turn out to be by some theory or another), as our heartbeats are resonant in our drum. Hence, our seeing is a cultural seeing of resistance to dominance as shared from the eyes of those closest to us.

## ORGANIZING AS BEING

I feel it is important for all people to recognize (and especially in the USA) that Indigenous people of color, and especially peoples of more recent tribal descent (500 years or so), really are, in some ways that matter significantly, sometimes different from

159

the dominant culture. In the ways that we cognitively structure how we exist in the world, we are already at home in the Americas, and have a sense of belonging in our own lands. We have no need to return to a lost continent over the waters, or to study a "golden age" of scholarship. This sense of belonging is crucial to our ability to relax cognitive dissonance. (An important (moral) question is whether this difference ought to make a difference in the world, and in global politics. I will return to this question later, in the section "Political Being.")

The process of discovering identity formation, it seems to me, is first to detect how our frameworks of recognition comprehend only what these frameworks have been trained to comprehend. I differentiate here between conceptual frameworks of understanding, or conceptual frameworks we use to interpret an outsider's world, and conceptual Indigenous frameworks that give rise to worldviews and ways of being in the world, that complement particular cultural conceptual frameworks of understanding.

For philosophical clarification of these conceptual frameworks I refer to a German philosopher's framework, that of Immanuel Kant. I draw an important philosophical marker between my view and Kant's view. Kant held, and I do not hold, that universal concepts of space and time organize cultural conceptual categories. Kantian categories would admit of universal (and hence natural) categorical classifications of time and space, as part of the fundamental apparatus or tools of the human brain.

The conceptual frameworks I discuss are acquired ways of being in the world. They are socially transferred from one generation to the next; they are socially secured by defining place-specific identity categories; the frameworks apprehend a worldview situating the identity of a person in a community; that community shares the place-specific worldview; and hence shares a (partial or complete) worldview about identity as nondiscrete. Moreover, it is the worldview that arises from the geographic place-specificity, and events that take place in that space, that enable communally apprehended nonlinguistic communication to emerge. Some of this communication is nonverbal; it is behavioral. Some of what is communicated builds upon communally accepted beliefs about the world and our place in it.

Deloria once indicated, and I agree, that an American Indian identity could be grounded on a common "response to" the colonization of our land (*God Is Red*, 1994). In addition, I believe it could be grounded on a common response to the genocide of American Indians and our worldviews. This genocide has significantly influenced our contemporary relationships with one another: to the federal government, among Indigenous nations around the globe, and among all our relations.

Thus, apperceptions of a communal world are transferred from generation to generation, by a communal sharing of that worldview. As Annette Arkeketa and Vine Deloria have portrayed in their work, for American Indians the concept of space organizes; I refer to this cognitive organization as mindspace.

A mindspace is an idea about belonging to a place. It is formative to the worldview infrastructure of American Indian thought, and can be tangibly recognized in our cultural productions. Being attuned, consciously or not, to the sights, sounds, smells, and breaths (air) of that space where our ancestors live, is as fundamental to American

Indian identity as are the sounds of the drum. Understanding mindspace is fundamental to understanding an American Indian standpoint, position, or worldview.

So also, all our relations have a strong influence on the shaping of our identity. Thus, I see the world from (what I take to be) my mother's eyes, and that means my mother saw the world from (what she took to be) her mother's eyes. So also, then, I see the world from (what I take to be) my grandmother's eyes. And so on down through our mothers' lives, the transitive relation glues together the generations. For many American Indians, because we have been raised primarily to see the world from (what we take to be) our grandparents' eyes, we reach back at least two generations for our early visions.

The question of what types of ontological relations exist in the world for American Indian thought, is perhaps best understood by considering how ontological differences operate at the epistemological level.

Epistemology occurs when infrastructures of cognitive and affective frameworks of a worldview come together in apprehending the world, or reality, as we come to know it. Reality comes to us and is made by us in the world through all our relations including ourselves as part of that of which the world is made. Frameworks organize schematic components of indiscrete concepts that originate out of our experience. Experiences originate as a function of relaxed cognitive dissonance during our experience of the world.

In this way, what I see when I look in a mirror, or hear myself speak, is not only what is in the playful mirror or voice, but it may be radically different from what you see or hear. I, and not you, am in the place of experiencing self-reflection on my identity in the present, the very moment that I live the experience. This is one way we can be tricked in the game of identity – for what we appear to be to ourselves may not be what we appear to be to others. We need to continue to think about this trick, as Maria Lugones might admonish us, playfully, with a sense of discovery, and also with a sense of intellectual rigor.

Humans generally have some similarly as well as differently organized schemata. Some cultural groups of persons have developed similarly organized schemata because of similar group cultural experience. Thus, although the ability or attentiveness to recognize others like oneself may sometimes be difficult and complex, like a game it may also be fun to play. Recognition is possible via cultural perspectives that live "in and through us," frequently at an unconscious level. We need only remember how we marvel when we learn things about ourselves that we did not previously know, to see why some folks do not grasp the same things we are experiencing when we experience them. Developing an appreciation for schemata of recognition, however, for where our indiscrete conceptual borders get played out, might give others the ability to see by joining the dance of cognitive dissonance "as a subject knower from the other's perspective." The difference between theory and practice remains, however, and although I can articulate the theory, I do not know if there can be a practice.

What this means, pragmatically, is that some of you may perceive what appears to you as an Anglo woman, while some may perceive what appears to them to be "one of ours," as we say in Indian Country. Those who would identify me as the latter would have to know and recognize clues that may or may not be obvious to the perceiver, in order to correctly identify me. The reality before each person is similar, but the schematic of recognition organizes according to indiscretely boundaried concepts of differences. It may be that relaxing cognitive dissonance is an acquired skill. I don't know, and the jury is still out on this one!

Before moving on to the political issues of this analysis, a final word. What we see, and hear, and know, and how we organize in the world are dependent upon what is programmed into our computers upstairs. As two persons look upon a third person, the third person's identity may be detected differently by the two observers. Of course, this happens every day. The important philosophical question of identity here, then, is how some things being noticed, while others are unnoticed, creates value judgments about that third person in the world.

Worldviews embed value judgments. Values arise from particular places and historical events/experiences in those places. Value judgments are markers informing subjects about which aspects of the observed are important, and which are not important. Value judgments are markers informing the subject which attributes are to be paid attention, and which are not; which attributes are to be recognized, and which are not. Perhaps most important, they mark which attributes are acknowledged as being (having existence) in the world, and which are not (to be).

## EARTH BEING

I am a person who generally enjoys interviewing. I am also a person who has done a good share of interviewing (both formal and informal) at philosophy conferences. Through these experiences I have come to realize that the colonization of the institution of matching job huntees with job hunters is fraught with cultural (mis)interpretations of behavior. The interviewers (like the Wizard of Oz) generally grant cordiality to job hunters only after all of the hoops have been jumped, hurdles crossed, articulations of thesis dissertations made, and proper cultural innuendos asserted. As in the institutions of racism, sexism, and classism, there are protocols to be observed in order to pass the tests of inclusion as a potential colleague (nonverbal, secret rites of passage). My point, quite simply, is that there is no room for difference to be asserted. One either belongs or one does not belong according to sameness of affiliations. This difference makes a difference institutionally.

Given the context, and the situatedness in which I move through the world, I must be a person of shifting identities in the world to function successfully. Hence I have collected a variety of shifting identities from which I select an appropriate one at any given time or place. As a being with many shifting identities, one method I use to understand this complexity of living identity shifts within my "self," has been to write poetry. For me, poetry creates a space of story, and so it is with my poetry as with my stories, they embrace stories about my ways of knowing my space in the world.

I mentioned earlier that when I read poetry I sound (I voice – I hear) very differently at times, depending upon what I am reading, and who is in the audience. I hear

162

an academic voice when I read academic papers; and sometimes I will change this academic voice for effect. In the context of voice-shifting, I have a special relationship to an indiscrete space within my being that recognizes all of my voice-shifts among different audiences. What intrigues me, as a philosopher, is how this shifting of voice correlates to shifting identity. For an answer to this, I turn to the historical context of my coming to be in the world. In doing so, I will tell a story.

Living in an extended family, my primary caretaker was my grandmother, my mother's mother. My mother's mother was a Northern Florida Seminole woman, who said she would never live south of the hurricane line, which meant Tampa Bay. It was as clear as pure water for her that this was the way things were to be; there were certain things people were meant to do, and living below the hurricane line in Florida was not one of them. Hence, she would travel east and a bit north, but never travel south nor west. She would not travel west because, according to her, her people had always been from the east, and it made no sense to travel to a geographic place that was not home. She was willing to go as far as Georgia, where she had kin, but no further. I remember the year when we moved to Massachusetts; she said we had no business being there and ought to go back home as soon as we could manage. Manage – that was the word our elders used for being able to pick up, financially or emotionally, and move to where things might be better, financially or emotionally. To manage was to find a place to be.

Fundamental to my mother's identity (apperceptions of the world) was that "real" Seminoles, which we were, had never signed a treaty with the USA. I grew up with a consciousness that our US citizenship had been forced upon my family, and that we were still, in some surreptitious way, at war with the USA. And for this reason, we were told never to sign any membership rolls for Indians. Not that it mattered much to me, because there weren't any for me to sign. But the stories, and the admonitions, were powerful; they created a space of being, of identity, of knowing my "place" in the dominant world, that remains with me today. Moreover, because of the removals that separated and brought death to so many of our relatives, I was told about how our relatives migrated away from Florida, and how many still lived with fear of government power. I was told how some of our relations lived in hiding, and how some members passed when they could, to survive, and how sometimes we did not survive when we couldn't.

As a child, my being Indian was being a Seminole. My family was not just Indian, but a people with a long and serious history in the Americas. To be Seminole was to still be renegade, tergiversator, an insurgent presence in our own land. And to us, that land was everything that we had been and were still. Always, it was about the land. To be Seminole also meant my family had been forced by the government to live away from our community of origin. Our relations had dispersed throughout the Southeast, some as far as Mexico and Texas. We had been forced away from a culture of fun-loving games, and people-loving groups, embracing and embraced by all our relations of the Southeast who had taught us how to survive, and how to treat all beings in our world.

Our old stories were stories of what it meant to be human and what it meant to be Seminole. They were stories about understanding ourselves in relation to those who came to share our place. Mostly these included European immigrants and African Americans. And so, when my grandmother's six foot five, big-eared brother would come up from Florida to visit us, to make sure his sister and her family were being well taken care of, he told us stories of change. He told us stories of a Florida he said my mother's mother would not recognize again, and would never see again. These stories brought with them a continued sadness, and a sense of loss.

My uncle told us stories of recent times, of how our grandmother married a man of mixed heritage, of Seminole, Choctaw, Chickasaw, and Cherokee descent. It was said that he might have been Creek as well, but for some historical reasons, we never mention this identity. James Hunter Henry came from Indian Country in Oklahoma, where 20 years ago, in Wewoka, I visited photographs of him. I never knew my grandfather; he died when my mother was 17 years old, but I heard many stories about his family from Mary Hunter, in Tennessee. After so many years Mary had gone back to the old records of allotment, and forced the government to give to her and her family the 25 acres that the government placed in trust, deeming full-bloods to be incompetent to manage land. To this day, as far as I know, that land is still held by Eugene, her son. A picture of my grandmother and grandfather, taken when they were youthful, always hung in my grandmother's bedroom.

My mother left Florida when her father died, to take a job with a government program in the city. She took the job to take care of herself and her mother. Though she married a non-Indian from the Midwest, over the years my mother kept in touch with her many relatives. When I turned 21, I visited these family members as my mother took me on a sojourn, just her and me, through the land of my many ancestors in the Southeast. This was done for the purpose of knowing who I was, and where and why my family of several generations had passed through, and been set to rest. I heard many stories then, from many relatives. Driving through several Southeastern states, none of the resting places had any markers, yet my mother had historical memory of which graveyard, and which tree, and which hill or rock they rested upon or near. To this day I can see these resting places we visited, and the surrounding land, as clearly in my mind as I saw them many years ago. In this way, as Paula Gunn Allen might say, I hold an idea about who I am in the context of kinship, accountability, and responsibility.

Most important to my grandmother's way of seeing the world was an idea about herself as a Southern woman, a woman from Florida. And not just any place in Florida, but from the Tampa Bay area. This was home, and had always been home for her, and for my mothers' mothers. The South was part of our blood running through our veins, and part of our breath bringing oxygen to our blood. The South was in the food we ate, in the smells of home, and in our stories of every day. This South was us, just as surely as the blood and bones of our grandparents and all our relatives, resting in the Southeast, in the ground, the air, the plants, trees, flowers, rivers, and in all of creation in that place where our people still live. We were told we were a part of that land, and that that land, in the Southeast, that land and no other, was a part of us from which we grew to be who we were. The land had provided our food, and was in us, and we, in setting our relatives to rest, were in the land. When my grandmother cut oranges, she cut them with the smell and taste of Florida fresh in her nostrils and breath. And when I smelled the oranges, the juice seeping from her fingers as she cut for ambrosia, the oranges mixed with pecans and coconut, I knew it was a special smell, and that somehow my being in the world was connected to that smell.

Always, every day of her life, my grandmother yearned to return home, to Florida; to return to that place and no other. She finally returned home when she passed on after 99 years of living in this world. And when I walk with my grandparents and all my relations in returning to Florida, I am walking in that place where my family and ancestors lived, and live still. And when I smell oranges in the humid South, I smell my grandmother, my family, and my people. That place, near the Tampa Bay area, is a part of an idea I have about myself, about what and who I am. I cannot help but think that I am also, in some strange way, a part of what that place is now, a part of the invisible stories of Seminole survival, a part of my homeland.

## EVENTFUL BEING

Eventful being is about historical context. It is about Muscogean being blending with Seminole being, in text, though not in story. It is also about being from a culture that experienced cognitive dissonance in suddenly finding itself dominated by people of another shore, another place. As colonists from Spain swept across the Southeast, they first tortured and murdered our people, and then "traded our land" to the people of the colonies of England. They did this in exchange for the Spanish privilege to more fully colonize (without interference from the North) another territory, the Indigenous communities of the Southwest. In asking why the colonists from England would want Florida, land of crocodiles and mosquitoes, we uncover hidden relations.

From my mother, back to my mother's mother, and her mother's mother's mother, and on around through our matrilineal descent, from each generation back to creation from our Earth Mother, we, the people, have been agrarian, with a diet of corn, potatoes, squash, and fish. We have settled the lands, always building community, always building survival, and always accommodating other cultures the best we knew how, and for the best reasons we could find. Neither romantic nor dramatic, we simply survived the best way we knew how to manage.

Florida was a land rich with hiding places. Foreign capitalists in slave ships would stop in the Boston Harbor, unload Africa's human beings that would be sold into slavery, and then sail on to the Carolina coast. Here they would unload human kidnaped cargo that was enslaved by the thieves who stole Africa's legacy, and sold it to the world. From this Carolina coast these foreigners would sail their human cargo completely around the Florida shores, staying clear of the land, and cut up through the Gulf of Mexico into what is now Mississippi, always fearing a mishap of navigation might put them on the shores of Florida. For in Florida, not only could these people kidnaped out of Africa have a possibility of escaping their enslavement, but the Africans, as the kidnapers knew, would be aided in these efforts by Florida's Indigenous people. Such an assimilative culture were the Seminole, that our assimilation into our communities of slaves escaped to Florida, threatened by the early nineteenth century to destroy the plantation economic system, and with it, the Confederated United States of America. Thus go stories of the Florida underground railroad, and the removals.

Our mothers' children of generations had stories to tell. From the time when I was young, my mother told me how Florida far surpassed what became known in the history texts as the "underground railroad at the Ohio river." She would lean over me, tapping her finger on the page of the book, and tell me that "that" was not the way it was, that we also had a story about the way things were. Our land, Florida, was the land of Indigenous Southern hospitality, the land eventually populated by Spanish Indian people, by African Indian people, by people of color, of *indigenismo*. Many Africans fled to Florida to escape the newcomers' tortures inflicted upon Africans, as the newcomers practiced their capitalist trade, the legacy of slavery learned in the colonies of England. These Africans migrated, and were welcomed, assimilated, and blended with many of our people. These were some of my mother's stories.

When I hear the old stories, stories about the struggle of Osceola, a Seminole man, and his wife, a Seminole woman having her roots in Africa, I remember three interdependent connections in my being. In my Indigenous Seminole heart I feel one leg of Africa, and one of Spain. Through our Indigenous being we have survived the colonization of Spain, and through this Indigenous survival, our blending with Africa was made possible. Thus, while retaining our own worldview, we have partly taken on and absorbed the interdependencies of all our relations among three major continents. In doing so, however, we have remained Seminole. And although many of us do not know our language, we know that it has survived, and that in it we can find a mirror to our worldview that has been kept alive in and through us for generations. It is from this heart, this Indigenous Seminole heart, and the psychic space it holds, that my identity and moral character coalesce, ingathering all that we be, with or without CDIB!

The historical text that Osceola's wife was never found, though the US government placed bounty on her, is a metaphor for the never-found migrating Seminole: into the Everglades, down through Mexico, off to the cities, and anywhere we could find to hide our people. We were dispersed in many directions, a diaspora from Las Floridas, forced from our lands, our places and psychic spaces of being. From fighting one another, from Billy Bowlegs' fighting stamina to Osceola's travels and deceptive capture, through the sickness of the snow and disease, the loss and genocide across the Trail of Tears, finally resting in Wewoka, we crossed over. Some Seminole remained in Florida, some Seminole may yet be found today, near the "Hanging Tree" outside the courthouse of colonial Wewoka. Our presence stands as a tribute to our strength for survival, and our passion for belonging in a community of ideas about ourselves. My presence and being come from that struggle.

These are stories that some Seminole have in our being, that we have remembered, and not forgotten. These are stories of a powerful nation that sought to prevent what could not be prevented – the Civil War between the Northern and the Southern states. The economics of slavery, and the moral assistance of Seminole people in the flight of Africans out of that slavery, was an economic matter for the Confederation of States. In removing the Five Civilized Tribes, beginning in 1830, the North hoped to appease the South's complaints about Southern American Indian tribal support given to escaping

African slaves. Also, the North hoped to improve its colonial economic development into Florida.

A partial disappearance of the stories, our deeds, our people, was caused by those who committed genocide upon us. Finally, when "they" could not divide us by the color line, when "they" were in fear that "their own nation," lacking any unified identity, would collapse from North to South, they kidnaped many people of our Five Civilized Nations (having a long legacy of successful kidnaping), and took women, children, and men to armed military camps where many were surreptitiously killed, and others left to starve to death. This message left a stark impression upon those who escaped. This impression remains part of our being in the world.

These events live with us still; as in memory together we walk the lands of our ancestors. And in the walking we feel the energy of our being mixing with the energy of those who have shed blood, and through this walking we, the Indigenous people, remain on and in our land, our place, our cognitive space. We love our land, and we will not be moved without struggle.

That the current government continues its genocide against us is a moral issue, is a religious issue, is a legal issue, is a sovereignty issue, is a survival issue, and is an identity issue. That newcomers to this land continue today to benefit from this genocide and land theft is a moral issue, is a religious issue, is a legal issue, is a sovereignty issue, is a survival issue, and is an identity issue.

## POLITICAL BEING

American Indians are political beings, as all tribes share in the struggle against the continuing genocide perpetrated against our people and nations. Echoing the words of many contemporary Indian scholars and intellectuals: "I am a member of a group which comprises over 500 distinctly identifiable ethnicities stretching across at least three noticeably different yet questionable racial divisions, that are lumped together in the category of Native American."

As an American Indian, I am a member of the Indigenous Peoples of the Americas (IPA). Part of an idea about myself in my cognitive space is about how the blood and sacred agreements of the IPA have created and continue to create family and political alliances in our struggle, alliances that survive the ever-present global genocide of Indigenous peoples. This genocide was begun over 500 years ago, and is continued today by the same corporate interests, inspired by all newcomers to America's shores. The historical and present families of these newcomers have profited, enriched, and furthered their economic political interests at the expense of both American Indians and African Americans. In the year 2001, some 200,000 individuals from India alone will immigrate to the United States in search of these benefits. These newcomers receive innumerable government benefits, non-payment of taxes for seven years, ready-made loans to open businesses, and educational dollars for their children to attend college. American Indians, and our African American brothers and sisters will be denied these same benefits while many of our children go hungry. My cognitive apperception of these newcomers is as beneficiaries of the human and cultural genocide of American Indians and African Americans. My cognitive dissonance is that the newcomers seem to have no similar political understanding, nor do they express cognitive understanding of this situation.

In North America today there are persons who have deserted their own economically troubled lands and people because of the difficulties brought on by political and economic disasters after centuries of European colonial conquests, and the extraction of natural resources, and human labor. Those taking flight to the economic comforts of North America, to escape the anguish and distress of corporate and religious colonization, only further diversify a group of people who have in the past benefited from, and continue today to benefit from, a global systematic genocide of Indigenous nations. Without a nation, a people cannot survive; and without a nation's people, worldviews cannot survive. Failure to recognize full nationhood of Indigenous peoples creates an active agency that denies our survival. This agency creates cognitive dissonance, when we must stand against newcomers whom we might otherwise welcome to the shores of the Americas. If the current global genocide of Indigenous peoples succeeds, the worldview of the historically most violent and intolerant peoples of the colonial world remains intact. This information precludes a cognitive coherence when I must at the same time be a part of such a system and struggle against such a system.

Failing to take a stand against those who benefit from the current economic global warfare is like failing to step forward when your name is called to take your place in a historic event.

As an insurgent political intellectual, philosopher, and academic, I walk in the footsteps of two insurgent academic intellectuals, Vine Deloria, Jr, and Angela Davis. From the blending of the work and life of these two Indigenous scholars, I have charted my own political identity. It is a lived identity, and a lived politics. I have found my path of political identity in the Indigenous projects of Mexico, Central and South America, Africa, Australia, and India. It is the identity and philosophy of a Native woman whose heart is well above the ground, always in struggle against colonial supremacist, patriarchal capitalism.

I find direct connections from the omnivorous corporate global exploitation of human labor and natural resources (that fills the pockets of large, gluttonous investors around the globe), to the contemporary brain drain from other nations to North America (based on the "if you like capitalism you are smart" immigrant test). And from both of these, I have found connections to the contemporary associations of the blockheaded, parsimonious proliferation, and profit-driven expansion, of the North American Prison Industrial Complex. Just as in our South Africa, in the Americas the same stakes that drove the capitalist entrepreneurs of human slavery are profiting from mega-complex global corporate prisons at the expense of so many of my brothers and sisters behind those profit-driven bars.

My identity as an American Indian, to Black Africans and African Americans, is defined by my cognitive space, where my identity and my life are a struggle to survive human, economic, and cultural genocidal madness. American Indians have been with this identity for a very long time. Yet always we are with the cognizance and cognitive dissonance of who we are, and who we are not.

I do not want a new place. My identity is in the soiled bloody mud of North America. And it is from this vista, as I see it, that I take a stand, and share my political identity dissonance. Like the mud, like the turtle, the alligator, the snake, the rabbit, and the swamps of my people, of my place, I am together in it, and I am myself in it.

Three main historical areas of genocide continue: of American Indians, of Black Africans, and of Semites or Jews. Racial and ethnic purity are alive and well in the belly of the beast. Contributing to the beast's "divide and conquer" mentality toward "others," race and ethnic confusion are encouraged. Cognitive dissonance: Israel's people (and others) are walking this land, my place, with the Books of Law; and Africa's people (and others) are shoved into the infested prisons, in this land, my place, bearing the burden of humanity's chimera with global capitalist cleansing. In conversation, it frequently becomes difficult for me to determine just how far the notion of "others" or "we" extends in dialogue!

Yet there is one discrete boundary that shows itself clearly: Indigenous resistance to government and corporate takeover of minerals and land rights (which has been going on for a very long time). It has been going on so long, in fact, that to all appearances colonized capitalists think it quite a rational and natural state of economic being. Thinking that a racist capitalism is quite the quotidian state of affairs requires no trick of vision; it is obvious.

There is a fundamental irreconcilable difference between identifying as a member of a group engaged in Indigenous sustainability of land and culture, and as a member of a group supporting the continued colonization of global resources, including humans, by participating as a beneficiary of that colonial capitalist regime. The newcomers to North America are part of a system that requires the correlative continued oppression of the people they leave behind in their own nations, as well as those in the land they come to. Someone may soon hear the town crier: "Hey folks, this is not a very viable situation – you cannot simply migrate to what has become known as the First World without it collapsing under the weight!"

This, then, is another of my selves, a political identity grounded in my Indigenous being. When our people, in this place, are starving, and are dying, from the byproducts of a rapacious capitalist culture, I cannot be silent. My place of being defines who I am politically, and it is in this place that my ancestors have fought for a very long time, and that we have watched, for 500 years, destructive, toxic, annihilative acts take place. In my self that sprang from this knowing, my people have watched the interstices of colonial racial economics secure a base to play itself out. Cognitive dissonance is created from watching the reality of colonial economics diversifying in the Americas.

For many years I have been talking and writing about how we cannot have a global understanding of the world with integrity, until we place and face the racial–economic imperialism of the USA within this global context. The institutional processes that continue the systematic historical events that colonized the Americas are the collective responsibility of persons who benefit from, or who seek to benefit from, this unjust resource acquisition and recreation of the "Holy Roman Empire."

169

These events of colonization happen for me, as we the Indigenous peoples of the Americas are still here, in this place, rooted to the geopolitical events that come over our borders. Yet also, it is here, in the cognition of what America has been and remains for us, that we celebrate our being. Because individuals are used to carry out colonizing enterprises, whether consciously or not, one of my selves stays busy educating those who have the power to dislodge or interrupt the harmful hegemonic thinking about "what America is." As an educator, it is crucial that I remember Coyote's relation to the moral universe. In this remembering, I know my selves in and with all my relations.

## SHIFTING IDENTITY

Returning to our theme of creative cognitive dissonance, relaxed interstitial meanings, and shifting voices, I turn to what ties these activities together in my sense of identity. At once I am poet, playing with nuances of the language, grounded in my playfulness with a language that belongs to my colonizer. I play to survive. Shifting in the play, I become the serious philosopher, searching for some semblance of meaning relevant to my being in the world, both a participant in an academic elite, and simultaneously a stubborn word warrior against that same elite, seen as colonizer. Cognitive dissonance ensues. I shift and become the lawyer, the careful word-crafter restrained from my passion for justice and fairness, admonishing my colleagues to join in the legal struggle for equality in a land not of my making or being. Cognitive dissonance ensues. Shifting again, I become part of someone's problem, as I stand against the "American" system of false education, while at the same time using my paycheck from that educational system to survive, to pass voice.

I shift in voice, in identity, because I am at once with and also against all that I have become. At once I am both the entertaining poet, and the destroyer of colonial poetry. At once I am both the dedicated philosopher, and the deconstructionist of Euro-American philosophy. At once a supporter of oral tradition, and also a writer of words on paper. At once a tribal member, and not a tribal member. I have learned to live with these cognitive dissonances.

My shifting voices are my shifting identities in play. Yet always, most frequently hidden, is the convergence and coagulation of the selves – of who I am now in the becoming of this place where my people walked and where they and I walk still as we voice ourselves into being.

This paper is about in-betweens of interstitial space, and the cognitive dissonance of coming into being. In-betweens are not nothing, though they sometimes appear this way.

# Part VI

# ETHICS AND RESPECT

# 14

# ETHICS: THE WE AND THE I

*V. F. Cordova*

When we hear the term "ethics" we usually think of that which is moral or that which is legal: religion or law. We also are aware of the fact that various disciplines have a "code of conduct." The code specifies the actions and the goals of the practitioners in a specific discipline, for example, law, medicine, engineering. Ethics, as defined by the discipline of philosophy, is a careful examination of the foundation upon which such codes are based.

Religion and law do engage in the examination of their own bases but usually as a means of clarifying a specific rule for their adherence to the foundations of religion and law. The foundations themselves are seldom called into question. Ethics, as a philosophical discipline, deals primarily with the foundations of such systems. Ethics also has a foundation of its own: it is based on the fact that human beings do not exist as isolated, or solitary, beings. They exist, except in rare and unusual circumstances, as social entities. Ethics is based on the fact that human beings exist in social environments; it deals, primarily, with the sense of the "We" rather than the sense of the "I." A creature that truly leads an isolated and solitary existence has no need to take into consideration the relationship between itself and the other.

In the West, codes of conduct are based on the concept of the individual as the "bargaining unit." That is, there is a fundamental description of the human being as essentially an individual which is potentially autonomous. The term *autonomous* is, in this sense, described as making reference to an individual that exists isolated and solitary. The term implies, also, the notion that this individual can act in such a manner that he can become a law unto himself: the "I" is conceived as containing the capacity to be "self-determining."

A code of conduct, however, can be based on the description of the human being as a social being; that is, he exists within the confines of the "We." The adjustment of his behavior in the company of others is necessary for the continued existence of the individual. In other words, if there were no others, or if the individual were truly autonomous, there would be no need to adjust one's behavior in order to maintain membership in a group.

Between those who would define the proper behavior of human beings toward others as based on the We or the I lies a tremendous difference. The societies based on the principle of the I as the essential bargaining unit see the individual as being "at war" with each and every other individual. The British philosopher Thomas Hobbes (1588–1679) best outlined this view of the individual; he saw individuals, also, as existing in a state of competition – one against the other – for a limited supply of those goods essential for the survival of the individual. ("If you won't attack me at the watering hole, I won't attack you.") Even in a Christian, or religious, sense this view of the individual is not uncommon in the West. In the religious version, individuals are separated from other individuals through their adherence to a particular set of beliefs; they come to be a group in order to make alliances between believers and against unbelievers. The Christian god sets the stage for this view of humans in groups: the god makes a distinction between those who follow him and those who do not. The believers are "saved"; the unbelievers are condemned. In both the religious and the "natural" (in the Hobbesian manner) Western definitions of the human being, the actual and undeniable existence of humans in groups must be explained or justified.

This view of human beings is very different from that of the Greeks who are seen as the secular forefathers of the West. Aristotle observed that a "man alone was either a god or a beast." A human was, for Aristotle, a social being, first and foremost. The Greeks were not offended when they heard of a comparison between themselves and bees and ants. These creatures shared with humans an inherently social nature. The West, both Christian and secular, is, in general, offended when humans are compared to bees and ants. The vision of a human as a naturally social being calls up images of "the mindless herd" or "the mass mind" or "the unthinking masses" which can be swayed by a powerful leader. To say to a man of the West that humans are "animals of the herd" is usually seen as an insult. Others would understand this statement to say something "true" or "real" about the species. (To say to a Western person, for example an American, that he is "not like other Americans" is usually taken as a compliment, whereas in other cultures to single someone out as a being "unlike" others of his group can be a cause for unease.)

The heroic figure in the Greek world (despite misinterpretations by the post-Christian West) is that figure who sacrifices his well-being and sometimes his life for the good of the whole. In the West we have an entirely different "hero": the lone figure who stands against the social whole in the name of his own individual perspective. Socrates, so often depicted as a Western hero, in actuality drinks the hemlock and refuses the offer to flee Athens for the good of the society which he has so annoyed. He has a dream in which he converses with the personification of the laws of Athens: he has been duly charged, according to the law, and found guilty, again, through every means provided by the law. He has a right to defend himself against the charges and he even has a right not granted in the West: the right to propose alternative punishment for his act. The personification of the laws reminds Socrates that a society without laws cannot remain a society for long. "The law" reminds Socrates how he has benefited from that very law: his parents have received sanction from the state, thereby granting Socrates legitimacy as a citizen; it has given him an education, and, of his own accord, he has chosen to remain a citizen of Athens. Socrates does not die because he discounts the group, or its laws; he dies because that is the course determined for him by the law. The law and the group have precedence over the whims of an individual, no matter how well-intended.

My "interpretation" of Socrates is rarely encountered, but then who but Westerners are allowed to give interpretations of the Greek works? The Western "hero" tends to be the defiant individual – someone who stands up to and against the group or even the law. We find here a curious situation where both "evil" heroes as well as the "good" exist in the Western context: Jesus Christ and Billy the Kid. Jesus stands against his own people, the Jews, as well as the intruders, the Romans. Billy the Kid, even in Western psychological studies, is a psychopath. Both figures are kept alive through myth and legend in the West. The hero, as well as the anti-hero, appear to those from a different society to bear equal weight in the West.

In a group that defines the individual as a social being, ostracism, exclusion from the group, is a dreaded and extreme form of punishment. In a group that defines the individual as autonomous, ostracism might be a tragedy but never the ultimate punishment. The ostracized is, after all, left with his life. Ostracism, however, in the West, could be as severe as in other societies, *if* the individual was ousted from *all* of the Western societies. Socrates sees this clearly when he understands that being ousted from Athens would bring him no honor in other cities/states: one who was deemed threatening to the social order in one city would be so in another as well. He chooses to die for Athens.

Indigenous Americans, just as did the Greeks, found their codes of conduct on the premise that humans are naturally social beings. Humans exist in the state of the "We." Indigenous peoples exist, however, within a colonial structure that adheres, not only to a different definition of what it is to be human, but to the very different social and moral codes that are based on that different definition. From an Indigenous perspective, Westerners are also a conglomeration of the We. The West simply seeks to deny this fact about human existence. Hence the difficulty encountered in the West in explaining or outlining social behavior.

Professional ethicists cannot agree on what constitutes a "right" action because they cannot agree on a foundation from which to derive their pronouncements. Religion is certainly not the answer. Religion, in actuality, has nothing to do with ethics. The religious relationship is between an individual and his god. If the individual commits "good" acts, they are incidental to that relationship. He acts "good" according to his god's standards in order to gain a reward from his god. If his god wishes him to "love his neighbor" he will do so but only until his god commands him to "slay every man, woman, and child." In a supposedly secular society there is no measure of one's actions against the wishes of a god but there still remains the focus on the individual as the source of moral or legal behavior. The West prefers, overall, to believe that all human acts are a *choice*.

The ramifications of those choices, however, are tied to a set of rewards and punishments. Virtue as a reward in itself is not sufficient in the West as it was for the Greeks. Aristotle's *Ethics* are a prescription for the *internalization* of law or of proper social behavior. He offers no rewards and punishments for following or breaking the law. The West, on the other hand, both secular and Christian, bases its moral and legal foundations on the *externalization* of law or social behavior.

The law that is external is an artificial constraint placed on someone's behavior and enforced through the threat of punishment. An internal law is one that has been so assimilated into the individual's character that he is "a law unto himself." An example of internal and externalized laws can be drawn from one's actions at a traffic light. If one approaches a traffic light that requires one to stop one's vehicle at, say, 4 a.m., and one stops even if there is no one around, then one can see an internal law in action. The internal law says: "It is proper, rational, and good that individuals driving cars stop at traffic lights that so signal." Not to do so would probably not bring about immediate retribution from an external source if no one is about. However, the result of breaking one's own internalized law is guilt and shame. The external law, on the other hand, can be broken without any mental anguish: "It is stupid," could be the reaction of someone who adheres only to external laws, "to stop at a traffic light when there is no one about. What difference does it make?" Or, "Who cares?"

Aristotle's *Ethics* offers a recipe for the development of the *internal* law. He would have us develop this sense through the process of *habituation*. If, for instance, one wants to become an honest person, we become so through practicing honesty. Eventually one need no longer *practice* honesty; one has become *habitually* honest. Honesty becomes part of our character. In the beginning it is presumed that one had a role model for honesty or at least been taught the social definition of honesty.

Ultimately, the foundation for fostering the *internalization* of rules for "proper" social behavior is the assumption that (1) humans are social beings by nature, and (2) humans want to remain in the social group. Internalization of rules is a means of teaching social behavior used by those who subscribe to the sense of the human being as a We. Those who define the individual as an I, separate and apart from the group of which he is a member, use another form of maintaining social harmony: the threat of punishment brought about through the inability, or choice, not to follow the rules. This latter method of bringing about social harmony is also based on two essential assumptions: (1) that the individual is not "naturally" a social being, and (2) that a social identity, as well as social behavior, is artificially imposed upon the individual by others, that is, that such an identity or behavior is "unnatural."

The Native American, like the Greeks, relies on the internalization of rules for proper conduct; but unlike the Greeks, the Native American adds to the We definition of human beings the idea of *equality*. Many outside commentators on Native American lifeways have commented on this notion of equality – that it extends to children; that it promotes an emphasis on consensual decision-making; that it extends even to an individual's actions toward the planet and its many life-forms.

Aside from a recognition of the We-factor in a Native American society, and the accompanying foundational beliefs of humans as wanting to remain as a part of the human society to which they belong, there is one more factor that accounts for the ethical system which the Native American once had as the dominant source of his actions (and in many cases still practices). He recognizes that he is a part of the Earth. He acknowledges that he is a part of a natural process that has led to his existence as well as to the existence of all other things, "animate" and "inanimate." (The terms are not relevant within a Native American context; all that exists is seen as participating in a life process.) The Native American recognizes his dependence on the Earth and the Universe. He recognizes no hierarchy of "higher" and "lower" or "simple" and "complex," and certainly not of "primitive" and "modern." Instead of hierarchies he sees *differences* which exist among equal "beings" (mountains, as well as water and air and plants and animals would be included here). The equality is based on the notion, often unstated, that everything that is, is of one process. The Native American, in other words, has a more inclusive sense of the We than others who share the sense of humans as *social* beings.

The combination of defining the human as a social being and denying any hierarchical systems, and a recognition of humans as a part of a greater whole, leads to a complete ethical system. This "complete" system includes not only one's behavior toward other individuals and to the society as a whole but toward the planet which has produced one and upon which one is dependent. For those who would raise objections to the validity or the durability of such an ethical system, it must be pointed out that Native American societies existed for tens of thousands of years and have not perished. Despite territorial wars and skirmishes between adjoining groups, when the European arrived on the American continents there was a vast diversity of peoples and languages. Had the Native Americans been as reckless as they are depicted there would have been less diversity. Even among those groups found to be existing in some form of hierarchical system (slave and free, which seemed to be practiced among the Aztecs and the Incas) there were highly ritualized rules for undertaking conquest and conduct in war. The Aztecs went so far as to set the boundaries for gains and losses by each side before going to war. Slavery in such societies was very different from that practiced by Europeans; under the Aztec rules of conduct in war, he who was free today could be a slave tomorrow, and vice versa. The rules of behavior also prescribed a method of dealing with the stranger: no early European colonizer could have survived without the hospitality and lessons in agronomy provided by the Indigenous peoples.

Just what, then, is this ethical system?

Each new human being born into a group represents an unknown factor to that group. The newborn does not come fully equipped to deal with his membership in the group; he must be taught what it is to be a *human* being in a very specific group. "He has never been here before," I have often heard in explanation of why the newborn must be taught. The newborn is at first merely *humanoid* – the group will give him an identity according to their definition of what it is to be human. The primary lesson that is taught is that the individual's actions have consequences for himself, for others, for the world. The newcomer's *humanness* is measured according to how he comes to recognize that his actions have consequences for others, for the world. Usually an infant was accorded "human" status through a naming ceremony around the ages of 8 or 9. (Many anthropologists "explain," mistakenly, the naming ceremonies as a result of a low survival rate; that is, the infant was not given a "real" name until he appeared to have survived infancy.) It was at or around this age when it became obvious to the group that the infant had come to recognize his place as a member of the group. (A naming ceremony without some knowledge of the child's character would be somewhat premature given that names usually depicted character.)

The lessons included an enhanced perception of the needs and emotions of others as well as a keen perception of where the child was in the world (a sense of place). In a society of equals a proper perception of others is necessary. The term *autonomy* takes on a whole different meaning in this environment. In a society of equals no one can order another about. No one can be totally dependent upon another, as that would create an artificial hierarchy (the dependent and the independent) with all of its accompanying ramifications such as authoritarianism and lack of individual initiative. The autonomous person, in this environment, is one who is aware of the needs of others as well as being aware of what the individual can do for the good of the group. "Autonomy," in this case, would be defined as self-initiative combined with a high degree of self-sufficiency. For example, a simple but unstated rule of behavior is that I cannot ask another to do for me what I can do for myself. Another is that if I am not perceptive enough to discern the needs of another and that other is required to ask something of me, then I have somehow diminished the other's worth. If I tell another what to do or ask the other for something then I have diminished us both.

In a cross-cultural context this training leads to some misconceptions: a native student who is failing a class never asks the white teacher for help because it is obvious to the student that both he and the teacher know that he is failing but the teacher has failed to offer assistance. The teacher, in the student's view, may be seeking to punish the student's failure by forcing him to ask for help. Having to ask for help, on the other hand, diminishes a sense of self-sufficiency on the part of the student; it also puts into question the student's "place" in the group. "She knew I couldn't understand it and she ignored me!" The fact that the teacher is not a product of the same ethical and cultural system as the student does not occur to the student.

A heightened perception of the other as well as an awareness of the consequences of one's own actions is enhanced by offering the child choices. He can choose to bring his mother, who is busy gardening, a glass of water. His father may ask, "Shall we take her a glass of water?" The child must make a choice; he is aware of having made the choice; and he will be aware of the consequences of that choice for his mother and perhaps even his father. His parents (or aunts, uncles, cousins, grandparents) may point out possible consequences of particular actions. An example from my own childhood shows this "pointing out" accompanied by "choice":

When I was a child my sister and I slept in a large old-fashioned bed with a high brass headboard. When my parents left the house we often used the bed as a trampoline (accompanied by my brother with whose welfare my sister and I had been entrusted). One day my father came home unexpectedly and stood in the doorway to watch our antics as gymnasts. During the first lull in our jumping he proceeded to come into the room to show us how the bed was constructed. He showed us sharp metal angles, narrow ledges which held up the metal springs underneath the mattress, and the seemingly small joints that held the bed together. He then proceeded to tell us about the consequences of falling on the floor as the bed collapsed. After pointing out all of the bed's features, he remade the bed and left the room. We three sat on the edge of the mattress thinking about what we'd been taught. My sister and I gave a few sitting jounces to the mattress. My brother took a practice jump. Worldlessly, we decided that we could find another form of entertainment.

My father forced a choice on us. If we continued to jump on the bed and it broke, it could not be replaced. If we fell we might suffer injury. There would be no sympathy accompanying that injury because it would have been "self-inflicted." I would be ashamed in the face of my father because "I knew better." I would, if I were injured in the face of all that information, be the only one responsible for my own condition. Choices and consequences.

By the time my own children reached their early teens I saw that they had absorbed a lesson that I had unconsciously taught them: that they are responsible for their choice of action. Once one of my sons tossed a basketball into a garage window when he was in the process of putting his things away so that we could go out for pizza. He proceeded to get a broom and began to sweep up the broken glass. "Just leave it," one of the younger children said to him. My son's reaction was to say that we were to go on without him. "My share of the pizza will pay for the glass pane," he said. Now his honor was at stake; no one dismissed his comment. I heard, instead, quiet murmurs from the other children. As recognition of my son's honorable action we saved him a piece of pizza and offered to help him replace the glass. "I will earn the money," he said. The situation ended there and he did fix the window.

My son's action was an illustration of what is meant when a Native American uses the term "autonomous." It is also what is meant when we apply the term "responsible." Or, when we are taught to be aware of the consequences of our actions on others. Going out for pizza was an expensive venture in my household at the time. The price of a broken windowpane was another expensive venture. My son's action – a careless toss of a basketball – had consequences that affected his family. No one would have thought of inflicting punishment on him; there was no need to. He was a human being; he knew what he had done, the consequences of what he had done, and he knew what had to be done to negate those consequences. There was no need for recrimination from any other quarter.

One often encounters a description of Native American cultures as being based on "shame" rather than "guilt." Actually both shame and guilt are a part of the internalization of rules of conduct. One experiences shame in the face of those who knew that the course of action would bring about specific consequences. One experiences guilt when one confronts oneself. Shame and guilt, in a Western system of conduct, are emotions that are to be overcome. In a Native American society they are what call us to action.

Another description of the Native American is that "he has no conscience" (usually the judgment of Christian missionaries). The Western notion of conscience appears to be a lingering sense of guilt or shame. If that is the case then there is no conscience: unintended or unforeseen consequences as well as those seen and pursued demand reparation in a Native American ethical system. Once reparation has been made and acknowledged there is no need for lingering shame or guilt. If conscience, however, means something that calls us to action then it is wrong that Native Americans do not have a conscience. I know few Native Americans that would pursue a "successful American lifestyle" without the accompanying guilt that results because they have more than others. Western conscience appears to have more to do with personal matters than with concern over the consequences of their actions for others. A good example of this is the current concern over "environmental ethics."

Americans agonize over the continued destruction of clean air and clean water, over the diminishing forests, over rising suburbanization. They do not agonize over the fact that their own "superior" technology and their own "needs" have created that condition. The rising misery of people in the so-called Third World is largely the result of people displaced from a once self-sufficient lifestyle. They are displaced because their own government has chosen to appropriate the land so that goods might be produced for the "developed" world's needs. The Brazilians do not cut down the rain forest for their own needs; they cut it down for the needs of "modern" societies. One official from a developing country explained to me that if they did not cut down their own trees (or mine their own ores, or create modern enclaves) the developed nation would take over the country and do these things themselves with perhaps greater misery imposed on his country's people.

"Environmental" ethics, in the West, is about "respecting" the rights of trees, and lions, and future generations. It is not ever about a concern that the cheap cup of coffee is purchased with the misery of a coffee plantation worker. Or that the displacement of peoples from rural ("undeveloped") areas into overcrowded urban areas is not "progress" except for a very few. The peoples of the developed nations are quick to see the profit in a global economy but discount the possible dire consequences to the laborers in the plantations and *maquiladoras* that are drawn off their land to produce for the wealthy. They can discount these consequences because they are convinced that it is better for Natives or peasants to have "jobs" than for them to persist in lifestyles that have allowed them to survive for thousands of years without destruction of their lands, water, or air.

In a Native American ethical system, the actions of an individual are like the pebble dropped into a pond. The pebble creates far-reaching ripples throughout the entire pond. The American prefers the analogy of human beings as people aboard a ship in a vast sea. The ship is held together, we can assume, by a single authority – the captain. The "ripples" of the ship proceed, in this analogy, into infinity. There are no consequences, if only people would just take orders. The greatest accomplishment that has resulted from the entire ecological movement is the development of what is called the "environmental impact statement." The impact statement is an attempt to understand that there are far-reaching consequences to one's actions. Unfortunately, what the impact statement forbids in one place is usually wreaked upon another. But it is a start.

The greatest advance that could be made in ethical systems in the West would be a recognition of the We-factor. If one imagines the We in a circle of its own unity surrounded by circles maintaining their own unity, perhaps the concept of human action as a pebble dropped into a pond would have more meaning. No pebble can be dropped into a pond without its ripples encountering other ripples and those ripples having other consequences through their encounters. Instead, the I-society prefers to picture itself as the captain in the single ship superior to and disconnected from all other things.

The idea that the planet requires a certain degree of "biodiversity" for its well-being has captured the imaginations of scientists and laymen. The fact that the diversity of human lifestyles might also contribute to that necessary biodiversity has not sunk in yet. The planet can afford to have one group maintain a self-absorbed society (the I-society) but only if others are allowed to survive that follow other lifestyles. The I, in other words, can survive and persist only if there is a recognition that it is not isolated from the others.

The I-society imagines the construction of a massive singular, "monocultural," society made up of only Is each pursuing their own individual interests in "healthy" competition with all of the other Is. Carved, as if in stone, on the inside of the foreheads of Western peoples, I imagine the words, "Each man acts so as to enhance his own self-interest." Carved inside my own forehead are two simple letters, W and E. And that WE can be either exclusive (Apache; Native American) or all-inclusive to encompass the many and diverse peoples and their particular homelands. The I-society has no homeland. It sees itself as owner of a lifeless planet, without boundaries, without limitations.

The definitions which humans assign to unknown processes are not meaningless intellectual acts. The definitions seem to predicate or dictate certain and unavoidable behaviors. If I believe in, for example, and act on, the definition of a human being as "that which acts only in its own self-interest," I will proceed to act on and treat others based on that slogan. Definitions tend to be self-fulfilling. They are so because they serve as the foundational justifications for all subsequent actions. The We and the I produce different lifestyles, different ethical systems, different worlds.

# 15

# CHOCTAW CONCEPTIONS OF THE EXCELLENCE OF THE SELF, WITH IMPLICATIONS FOR EDUCATION

*Thurman Lee Hester, Jr.*

The topic of this chapter is a rather grand one. It is not clear to me that I even know the questions to answer, much less the answers themselves; nor that I could explain what little I know in a way that may make sense to the reader. However, I'll do what I can.

I usually begin any Native American-related talk or paper given to my Euro-American brothers, sisters, and cousins by saying: *Halito. Chim achukma? Sa-hoschifo ut* Lee Hester. *Chahtah sia hoke!* Which is to say, "Hello. How are you? My name is Lee Hester. I am a citizen of the Choctaw Nation." I then usually go on to point out that I am not a medicine man or elder, but just a common citizen of the tribe, that I cannot speak for all Choctaws, that I speak only for myself.

It is important to do this because it helps to set a context. It turns out that sensitivity to context is one of the elements of Choctaw excellence as near as I can tell. As far as I know, no one has catalogued the elements of Choctaw excellence. What makes a "good" person (with scare-quotes around it) is seldom discussed. There are reasons for this which should become apparent in the course of the chapter.

My guess is that Choctaw excellence consists precisely in what most Choctaws do. This contrasts sharply with Euro-American society, where excellence is considered unusual by definition. From a Choctaw perspective, what you do defines what you think is excellent. How can it be otherwise? People do not purposely do what they think is "wrong." When they have qualms of conscience this is most likely an artifact of conflicting values. We all certainly have values that can come into conflict. But it seems crazy to say that we ever do anything that we purely *disvalue*. To do something is to confer value.

This idea is not new in Euro-American philosophy, but somehow the practical aspects of it have been lost. Indeed, the practical aspects of Euro-American philosophy often are. The existentialists all talk about how our actions, our choices, define what we value, or define what is "right." Kant speaks of people acting according to maxims that in essence they are asserting to be right, though in Kant's view they can be wrong in their assertion. Either way, the action confers value.

So, I would say that the best way to know Choctaw excellence is to see what Choctaws do. Specifically, see what Choctaws do that is different from what non-Choctaws do.

The main way that Choctaws convey information is through stories. There are many reasons behind this – but one of the key ones is: How can I attest to that which I haven't experienced? The Choctaw language contains a hearsay marker. In essence, anything you attest to is automatically marked as either known by experience or known only through hearsay. I will stick with what I know through my own experience; I'll tell you some stories that explain what little I know of this topic. Up to now, this chapter has been more nearly a Euro-American philosophy paper. From here on I'll try to do it more nearly in "Choctaw" though I'll lapse frequently into "English."

I said context was important, so I will illustrate that now. I have been attending language classes sponsored by the Choctaw nation. Most young Choctaws speak no Choctaw, and many of the older ones "lost" their language in US government boarding schools where they were not allowed to speak Choctaw. Much of the work of setting up a curriculum has been done by Marcia Haag, a white linguist. Marcia has studied the Choctaw language for years now, and knows more about it than most Choctaws. But at times her constructions – though technically grammatic – are definitely not Choctaw.

I was leading a small group in recitation of one of Marcia's lessons in one class, when I came upon the phrase: *Chahtah imanompah ish anompoli hinla-hoh?* The phrase was Marcia's translation of: "Do you speak Choctaw?" There were several looks of puzzlement in my group, some from people who I knew were native speakers of the language. No one seemed to want to say what the problem was – another Choctaw value that I will discuss in a moment. I thought I knew what the problem was. "You'd probably say *anompoli*, right?" I asked. The consensus was that they had always heard and used the word *anompoli* for asking whether someone spoke Choctaw.

*Anompoli* just means "speak." If you were to use it in a situation where the language ability of the other person was unknown to you, they would not know that it means "speak" unless they in fact spoke Choctaw. If they spoke Choctaw, they would know you said "speak." Since most of these instances would be ones in which it would be odd for you to be commanding them to speak (indeed, it is unclear that there are very many Choctaw instances where a "command" makes any sense) it is clear that you must be asking whether they speak Choctaw. The presence of a falling tone when pronouncing the word, which indicates an interrogative, wouldn't even be necessary. Context is thus crucial for Choctaws in a way that it is not for non-Choctaws. Only a non-Choctaw would ever say, *Chahtah imanompah ish anompoli hinla-hoh?*

Just to bolster your understanding of the importance of context to Choctaws, I will point out that there are no words for "he," "she," "it," or "they" in Choctaw, though you can use other words to form phrases that can convey them. Normally, such phrases are just not used in Choctaw. Either you know by context what is being referred to, or you don't. This reliance on context means that Choctaws utter many fewer words. Unfortunately, my training in Euro-philosophy, as this chapter shows, has made me a lot more wordy than a Choctaw should be. Sometimes other Choctaws wonder about me.

Besides the importance of context, and the value placed on the understanding of context, I like to think that the *Anompoli* story shows that Choctaws place great value on efficiency. We will return to that theme shortly. More even than efficiency, though, Choctaws value respect. By speaking few words we allow others their own understanding; we assume others are aware of the context. Now you can see why I sometimes have trouble in the Choctaw community when I'm too wordy.

Since this chapter is supposed to be about not only Choctaw excellence, but education as well, I'll continue with the *Pishukchi* story, one that has appeared in other works, for very good reason. It illustrates a great many elements of Choctaw excellence and does so within the context of a learning experience where I was taught something in a very traditional Choctaw manner.

Mr Aleckton Davis, an elder of my tribe and a person I'm proud to call a friend, went to see a new gas station just south of the South Canadian River, inside the Chickasaw nation. The service station is owned by the Chickasaws, who are close relatives of the Choctaws. Mr Davis wanted to see how the Chickasaws were getting along in their new enterprise. I was lucky enough to be able to go along with him. While looking over the new service station, we frequently used Choctaw words or phrases to point out or describe what we were seeing. Mr Davis is a true native speaker, having spoken Choctaw as his first language. For my part, I'm more of a learner. Though I learned some Choctaw at my grandmother's knee, she had already lost much of her language and I was forced to learn it more as a second language.

At one point I noted some milk on a shelf, and referred to it as *pishokshi*. Mr Davis slowed and looked at me keenly. I stopped, sensing something of import. I looked at him. I listened to him carefully as he said, "How do *you* say watermelon?" I noted that he placed great emphasis on the word "you." It would seem he was asking me how to say "watermelon" in Choctaw. It was odd that he should ask me that. He knows how to say "watermelon." He knows that I know how to say "watermelon." Watermelon is virtually the Choctaw national dessert, a great delicacy on hot days. Every Choctaw knows how to say "watermelon." It is *shokshi* in Choctaw.

*Shokshi*! Of course, I had said *pishokshi* when referring to milk. A sloppy mispronunciation – milk is actually *pishukchi* in Choctaw. I looked at Mr Davis, laughing at myself inwardly, and said to him, "*shokshi*." Mr Davis had corrected my pronunciation of the Choctaw word *pishukchi* without ever using the word, without ever overtly correcting me. What was even more important, he had taught me more about being Choctaw in that one minute than you could ever learn from a textbook.

Correction is an important part of Euro-American education. Almost everyone in academic life has as part of his or her job the grading of papers. It is central to the Euro-American tradition. It is almost completely alien to Choctaw tradition. This is in part because of the value of context, clearly present in this story, but it is also because of the value of *respect*, that I have already mentioned. Correction implies that one person knows what is correct and the other person does not; even worse, that one person acts correctly and the other does not. Though there may be many ways of rationalizing the need for correction; or how correction, properly understood, actually *is* a form of respect for the person being corrected, it is very difficult – maybe impossible – for it not to convey a feeling of superiority versus inferiority: a lack of respect for, if not downright disrespect for, the person being corrected.

Choctaws almost never engage in correction, no matter how strongly they feel. The actions of the students in the Choctaw class in not correcting Marcia's un-Choctaw phrases are an example, as is Mr Davis's unwillingness to correct me. His incredible ability to instantly create an opportunity for me to experience the fact that I was mistaken shows just how central it must be and also shows how Choctaws conduct education without the need for correction.

The centrality of experience to education is certainly not foreign to Euro-American philosophy. One of the most famous Euro-American philosophers, John Dewey, wrote of educative and mis-educative experiences. I think he would agree that Mr Davis gave me a unique learning experience, a truly educative one. It helped me make connections with past experiences and kept my mind open to future experiences, just as Dewey said an educative experience should. Of course, every experience is educative in some sense, thus we may even have mis-educative experiences. These experiences cause us to make no connections or bad connections with other experiences and can even cause us to close our minds to future experiences. We can clearly imagine, if we haven't actually lived through them, experiences – even in school – that were distasteful, hurtful, or demeaning. Such experiences can often make us close our minds. Among Choctaws, almost all your experiences will be educative. This is true excellence in education.

Perhaps the most amazing set of examples concerning Choctaw excellence surrounds what I earlier termed "efficiency." In speaking, it involves saying fewer words by allowing context to do the work. This also intersects with respect, because you allow the other person room for thought – room to understand. But this "efficiency" is manifest in virtually every aspect of Choctaw life, sometimes in ways that boggle the mind. I will tell you two stories about efficiency and then move on to my closing stories about learning.

I went down to Non, Oklahoma. Yes, that is the name of a town, in fact the name of the town where my Choctaw ancestors came from and are buried. You can imagine the multitude of jokes I can tell. My father was a Non High School graduate; in fact all my Non relatives are Non graduates. The Non dead are buried in the Non cemetery... and so on. I go down to Non occasionally to visit the graves of my ancestors. My great-great-grandparents, the first of my family born in Oklahoma after the Trail of Tears, are buried in what they call the Indian cemetery down at Non. They have a huge headstone erected over their graves, I think in part to keep the grave-robbers from disturbing their rest. You see, it is said that Indians always bury treasure with their dead, so grave-robbers – not to mention anthropologists – have frequented Indian burial sites. The lavish Christian gravestone hasn't kept them from being awakened three times over the

185

years, but my family has always dutifully reburied them. Mr Davis accompanied me on my pilgrimage. When we arrived at the graves, we saw that the huge gravestone was slightly askew. With some emotion, I reached out and began to try to move the stone back into place on its pedestal. I groaned and strained, trying to manhandle it into position. Mr Davis watched for a few seconds, looking mainly at the stone. Then he slowly moved his hands into position on the stone. I ceased my futile efforts, waiting to see which way Mr Davis would begin pushing so that I could work with him. Before I could even see what he was doing, the stone was in place. It had slid effortlessly into position.

Mr Davis doesn't have superhuman strength. But he does have a Choctaw understanding of context. He is fully aware of his surroundings, deeply conscious of all sorts of nuances, which in this case allowed him to notice the slight ridge on the pedestal that allowed him with a little push to balance and pivot the heavy stone into place. He also has Choctaw respect, a respect that kept him from trying to manhandle the stone. He respected the stone and sought first to understand it; only then could he and the stone work together.

I had this same sort of experience with Mr Amos Dorsey, and in addition experienced a little more of the Choctaw style of teaching. Mr Dorsey is Creek, but his wife is Choctaw, and the Creeks are cousins to the Choctaws, so I will call this a Choctaw teaching. Mr Dorsey and I were working together to unload a bunch of tables and chairs at the new Choctaw center in Oklahoma City. There was quite a bit of work to do and I wanted to get home, so I threw myself into the work – busily hustling back and forth. Mr Dorsey began to work too, but a bit more slowly and only after watching me for a second or two. Indeed, as he worked and watched me, I could almost swear he was actually going even slower. Eventually, it was as if he was in slow motion. Of course, part of that was due to my haste. As we worked and after I had fumed a bit at his slowness, I finally realized that somehow he was actually getting more done than I was. Choctaw, or maybe in this instance I should say Creek, efficiency was at work. Mr Dorsey respected the task, understood the context and set about working efficiently. However, I think it was also an instance of teaching. I can't help but think he slowed down as he saw my thoughtless, disrespectful haste and then speeded up as he saw that I had learned my lesson and was working efficiently.

To round out the stories we will examine a couple of quick Choctaw teaching examples from my earliest youth, when my father used some Choctaw teaching methods on me. Until his retirement, my father was a truck-driver. When I was a pre-teen, he owned his own truck and often tried to teach me the practical elements of his profession. To save money, he did some of his own mechanic work. I can well remember "helping" him – and here I again use scare quotes – to work on the truck. He'd look at a bolt he needed to remove and say, "Looks like half-inch." I'd go and get him the half-inch wrench. He'd try it on. "Too small," he'd say. "Let's see, what's bigger than half-inch?" We'd finally settle on three-quarter-inch and that would be too big. "Let's see, what's between half and three-quarters?" We'd work on that a while and finally decide that five-eighths was between the two. Sometimes this would go on for a while, since some wrenches are actually measured in sixteenths and even thirty-seconds.

What I didn't notice in my youth was that any time there was a need to fix the truck in a hurry, or I wasn't really interested in helping, my father could almost invariably pick the right wrench the first time. Oh sure, he might occasionally mistake a nineteen-thirty-seconds for a nine-sixteenths, but it wasn't often. He was, of course, teaching me, creating a set of experiences in which I could learn not only all sorts of things about fractions, common denominators and the like, but also about what I now know to be binary search algorithms. To this day I doubt that my father has ever heard of binary search algorithms, but he taught me all about them. In addition, I feel certain that he would never have set up such an experience if he thought I would recognize at the time what he was doing. You see, that would have been patronizing – it wouldn't have been respectful.

Now, just in case you are beginning to think that Choctaws never make mistakes in teaching – I'll tell you about my father teaching me how to shift gears in the truck. It was a big tractor-trailer rig, and back in those days they didn't have automatic transmissions for trucks. This one had a 20-speed Spicer transmission, with two gear levers that occasionally had to be manipulated at the same time. Over time, he showed me where all the gears were and eventually had me start doing the shifting. He'd call out a gear and say "Now" to synchronize his depression of the clutch with my movement of the levers.

It was hard for him to keep me from having feelings of inferiority – a condition of disrespect – when I missed a gear or, even worse, ground one. I suspect that he put quite a bit of extra wear on the transmission, trying to make my performance seem more nearly on a par with his. Occasionally, however, the act came apart completely. I'd try to force a gear: not respecting the gear, not understanding the context, generally grinding it in the process. He would snap out: "You don't have to force it! Look, you can do it with your little finger." He'd then proceed to do a number of gear shifts using only his little finger. A bit humiliating.

Partly because of that, I try not to humiliate others. This can sometimes be hard. Almost every week we have children, often pre-teens, come to our door to beg money for the local schools. I try to be respectful, but often I don't have any money to give. Sometimes I wonder what the experience is teaching them.

In this chapter I've tried to exemplify, not just explain, some of the Choctaw notions of excellence in education. This means that out of respect to you, the reader, I have left many things unwritten. Ultimately, readers must come to their own understanding of the topic; traditionally Choctaws would never seek to force their understanding on you.

*Yakoke*, which is to say, "Thank you."

# 16

# BIOCOLONIALISM AND THE COMMODIFICATION OF KNOWLEDGE

*Laurie Anne Whitt*

## INTRODUCTION

The ideology of the market, and the omnipresence of market forces, have left an indelible mark on the Western conception of knowledge. Aided and abetted by the Western legal system, and most strikingly by the rise of intellectual property law, knowledge has undergone a steady process of commodification. This is particularly true of knowledge produced in the microworld "factories" of Western biotechnoscience, which have become crucial outposts in the establishment of an international intellectual property rights regime. As capitalism moves from an industrial to a global information economy, it continues to regenerate itself. Wealth, as Christopher Lind (1991: 71) observes, is created

> not primarily from the manufacture of industrial goods, but from the generation of ideas and information. As existing pools of capital seek to capture the new sources of wealth, debates about intellectual property are moving to center stage.

This chapter contends that this conjunction of Western law and biotechnoscience facilitates an ongoing biocolonialism, particularly with regard to Indigenous peoples.

If colonialism encompasses the interlocking array of policies and practices (economic, social, political, and legal) that a dominant culture can draw on to maintain and extend its control over other peoples and lands, then biocolonialism emphasizes the role of science policy. The introduction of monocultures and the attendant undermining of plant genetic diversity (via "development" debacles such as the Green Revolution) is

188

one form that biocolonialism is taking. However, this chapter addresses instead diverse forms of extractive biocolonialism – where valued genetic resources and information are actively sought, "discovered," and removed to the microworlds of biotechnoscience. There they are legally transformed into the private intellectual property of corporations, universities, and individuals, rendered as commodities, and placed for sale in genetic marketplaces such as the American Type Culture Collection. In this manner, the commerical seed industry and the pharmaceutical industry have commodified the plant genetic resources and traditional medicines of Indigenous peoples, along with their agricultural and medicinal knowledge. The controversy over the Human Genome Diversity Project, and the commodification of the cell-lines of Indigenous peoples, is only the most recent phase of this struggle.

This chapter aims to advance that struggle by tracing various issues and historical processes which are pivotal in the debate over biocolonialism. The commodification of knowledge, and the collusion of intellectual property law, are central to my discussion. I suggest that Indigenous resistance to biocolonialism, and notably the strong critiques that have been made of the Diversity Project, derive in part from a refusal to construe certain types of knowledge as commodities. For many Indigenous peoples knowledge of the natural world, especially medicinal and agricultural knowledge, is only properly construed as a gift.

Whether knowledge is regarded as a commerical exchange in the marketplace or as the reciprocal exchange of gifts, an understanding of power relations is integral to understanding of knowledge systems. As several recent science theorists (Rouse 1987) have argued, questions of knowledge cannot be divorced from those of power. Plainly, biocolonialism, and Indigenist[1] critiques of it, cannot be adequately assessed without appreciating how power figures in the epistemological debate and, conversely, how divergent construals of knowledge enter into the political debate. Accordingly, I draw on current accounts of knowledge and power in science to illuminate and strengthen the critique of the Diversity Project and to illustrate how power relations inflect the dynamics of Indigenous and Western knowledge systems. Since law itself is a central factor in the knowledge/power equation, I illustrate how Western legal concepts of "originality" and "innovation" embedded in intellectual property law are not only sharply at odds with their Indigenous counterparts, but are primed to serve the interests of biocolonialism.

## DIVERSITY AND SOLIDARITY

*We are many / We are one.*

(Jaune Quick-to-See Smith)

Some vexing terminological and conceptual issues will remain submerged in my discussion of these matters. Although I do not address these in detail here, I invite and encourage discussion of them. For example, I will often contrast Indigenous with Western knowledge systems. The notion of a knowledge system underscores the heterogeneity of knowledge; certainly it deserves closer attention. (For a beginning, see Marglin 1990; Deshler 1996.)

The nature and terms of the contrast also need to be carefully considered. There are multiple ways of comparing and contrasting knowledge systems. My own preference for "Indigenous" and "Western" as terms of the contrast is mainly political. This contrast, and that between dominant and subordinated knowledge systems, underscores the role of power within, and the power differential among, knowledge systems. Other commonly adopted options – articulate/tacit, theoretical/practical, scientific/traditional – seem questionable and objectionable, especially insofar as they are intended to reflect differences between forms of knowledge within Indigenous and Western cultures. (See Heyd 1995; Agrawal 1995a; and Agrawal's commentators (IKDM 1996b) for some discussion of these issues.)

Nevertheless, I hasten to emphasize the diversity and non–unitary character of both "Indigenous" and "Western." There are differences within, and similarities across, Western and Indigenous knowledge systems which confound any attempt to cast the contrast as a simple dichotomy. Moreover, given the global presence of some 5,000 distinctive Indigenous cultures, it is crucial to acknowledge the specific circumstances that have shaped and differentiated the knowledge systems of these peoples, and that continue to do so. It would, however, be historically and politically myopic to see only differences. There is much that binds Indigenous peoples together. Most frequently noted is a shared experience of oppression, or a relationship to particular lands which carries with it certain moral responsibilities. As artist Gail Tremblay (Iroquois/Micmac) observes, each of us

> comes from a people who has also had the experience of facing the forces of colonization by outsiders and has been subjected to attempts at physical and cultural genocide. Each knows the pressure to assimilate to other cultural patterns, and the pain of loss that has been handed down across the generations of people since contact. . . . So it is that coming from such diverse cultures, we can join together to say, *we are one*.   (Tremblay 1997)

In the words of Aboriginal author Mudrooroo (1995: v–vi):

> We are many mobs with many countries, but we have become mixed up. We were put together without thought for our differences and our attachment to our countries. . . . Us Mob are many mobs, but we all come from that great tree which is Australia. . . . We are a singularity in diversity.

The recent Treaty of Indigenous Peoples International (1997), which creates a political, social, and economic alliance among the diverse Indigenous peoples across the Pacific Rim, declares as its first two principles that:

A   The Creator has made us part of and spiritually inseparable from the environment. This truth brings us together.
B   We share a cultural legacy of natural conservation and protection stemming from our inherent obligation to protect the land, water and natural resources within our traditional territories.

There are shared conditions, shared responsibilities, and a shared struggle. To succeed in that struggle, Indigenous peoples are increasingly responding to a common oppression, forming organizations of resistance such as the World Council of Indigenous Peoples, the International Indian Treaty Organization, the South and Meso American Indian Rights Center, and the American Indian Movement (AIM), among many others. As AIM activist Ishgooda (Wyandotte) notes: "When we divide our people of the First Nations, by location, by blood quantum, by tribe, by traditional animosities, we kill that which we seek to preserve" (personal communication, 1997).

## THE "COMMODIFICATION" OF KNOWLEDGE

*The commodity fiction handed over the fate of man and nature to the play of an automaton running in its own grooves and governed by its own laws.*

(Karl Polanyi)

While the market and market forces of late capitalism differ substantially from those envisaged by Adam Smith, they continue – notably under the banner of intellectual property law – to transform the legal system in ways that impact directly the Western conception of knowledge. Just as land and labor were metaphorically transformed to accommodate a market economy, so too is knowledge – human intellectual labor – being transformed by what Polanyi calls a "commodity fiction."

Various commentators have noted how the market doctrine obtained political and philosophical hegemony over Western society by pointedly ignoring the distinction between commodities and noncommodities. Commodities, for the economist, have a specific origin and purpose. They are manufactured goods which are produced for sale, sold, and eventually consumed. Since human labor – intellectual or manual – is not manufactured for sale and consumption, it is not a commodity, strictly speaking. It is not a product, but a

> personal, intimate and intrinsic part of ourselves. Human work cannot be separated from the whole person . . . it is a market fiction that there is a separation between the human and human work. We can no more sell our work than we can sell ourselves.   (Kimbrell 1993: 269, 270)

Nor, of course, is land – a part of nature – a commodity that is produced by people for sale and consumption.

Yet to leave work and nature out of the market equation would challenge the market system. As Andrew Kimbrell observes:

> If market ideology was to be the central law of a society . . . it had to extend to all important aspects of life. . . . Vital noncommodities had to be subsumed under the definition of commodity, treated like any other commodity, and subjected to the supply-and-demand laws of commodities.   (1993: 270)

191

So, it was convenient to ignore the distinction between commodities and noncommodities. This metaphorical transformation of labor and land into "fictitious commodities" also greatly enhanced the power of the market system, facilitating control of virtually all aspects of social behavior and natural resources. Karl Polanyi recounts this transformation, and its full impact:

> The crucial step was this: labor and land were made into commodities, that is, they were treated *as if* produced for sale. Of course, they were not actually commodities, since they were either not produced at all (as land) or, if so, not for sale (as labor). Yet no more thoroughly effective fiction was ever devised.... The true scope of such a step can be gauged if we remember that labor is only another name for man, and land for nature. (Polanyi 1968: 61–2)

The transformation and commodification of knowledge – of human intellectual labor – was part of this process. Knowledge is not produced by people for sale and consumption. And despite the tendency of recent work in science studies to speak of knowledge production and knowledge products, knowledge is not a product. Such talk merely reflects the effectiveness of the knowledge-as-commodity metaphor. Like manual labor, intellectual labor is a "personal, intimate and intrinsic part" of human beings. To paraphrase Kimbrell, human knowledge cannot be separated from the whole person; it is a market fiction that there is a separation. We can no more sell our knowledge than we can sell ourselves.

When market assumptions are extended to ideas, to information, intellectual property results. Patents, copyrights, and trade secrets are protections that the state gives to innovations – to new ideas (Hettinger 1989: 35). These types of property rights are intended to provide for ownership of "noncorporeal, intellectual objects, such as writings, inventions and secret business information" (1989: 31) that can be bought and sold in the marketplace. Private intellectual property restricts the use of ideas through patents, the expression of ideas through copyrights, and the methods of acquiring ideas through trade secrets.

The rise of intellectual property has also helped to transform the Western conception of knowledge in another way. Scholarly, as well as popular, conceptions of knowledge (see R. Roberts 1987; Fuller 1991) have regarded it as non-exclusive – as existing in many places at once and as not consumed by use: "the possession or use of [such] an intellectual object by one person does not preclude others from possessing or using it as well" (Hettinger 1989: 34). However, when it is commodified, and rendered as intellectual property, information becomes exclusive, and its value is seen to lie in part in that exclusiveness. The point of owning a song, or certain genetic information, is to ensure and secure exclusive profits.

Intellectual property laws serve as means of transforming Indigenous knowledge and genetic resources into profitable commodities, and of advancing the commodification of nature. For example, the chief of the Global Environment Division of the World Bank, discussing traditional plant knowledge in the Ethiopian Coptic Church, recently proposed: "Let's screen that knowledge stock...[and] explore how it might be commercialized" (cited in Bereano 1995). Indigenous representatives to the Commission on Sustainable Development have challenged the practice of bioprospecting, and the global imposition of Western intellectual property laws. Victoria Tauli-Corpus (1993) offers a compelling description of the cultural politics of science unfolding here, and of the contrasting metaphors of knowledge which help to sustain them:

> We have witnessed how indigenous seed varieties and medicinal plants which our women and healers have preserved and developed, were appropriated by international and national research institutes and transnational corporations.... Without our knowing, these seeds and medicinal plants were altered in laboratories and now we are told that the companies have intellectual property rights over these genetic plant materials because they have improved on them. This logic is beyond us.... we, indigenous peoples... have developed and preserved these plants over thousands of years.   (1993: 25)

Another particularly disturbing aspect of this debate is that the patenting of genetic information is simultaneously the patenting of life-forms, since the innovations in question are based upon and produce life-forms. A 1995 report to UNESCO's International Bioethics Committee notes: "Genetic material is seen as part of what constitutes life; as such, patenting transforms this material into a commodity that can be owned and traded in" (1995, section 2.3.2). Commenting on this phenomenon, José Silva (1995: 57) observes that "genetic property rights subject nature to worldwide commodification, an important step in the ongoing biotechnological revolution." This is not limited to plants, of course; it involves nonhuman animals as well. According to the Office of Technology Assessment, well over 190 genetically engineered animals (these include fish, cows, mice, and pigs) are "figuratively standing in line to be patented by a variety of researchers and corporations" (Kimbrell 1993: 198). It also involves human animals, people, who are treated as sources of genetic information. As Okanagan activist Jeanette Armstrong (1995: 11) states: "it is not only knowledge about plants and animals that is being made a commodity: the essential substance of the human life-form – human gene-lines – are now items for transnational trade and profit."

An instance of this, which has provoked widespread Indigenous resistance, is the Human Genome Diversity Project (HGDP), an international undertaking by scientists, universities, private researchers, and governments to create thousands of cell-lines from DNA collected primarily from Indigenous peoples. The controversy surrounding the Diversity Project has been vigorous and substantial from the Project's outset, when the targeted sample populations were referred to as "Isolates of Historic Interest" (J. Roberts 1993: 675 – see Harry 1995; Whitt 1997, for more discussion of this).

The Diversity Project's Indigenous critics charge that "this is just a more sophisticated version of how the remains of our ancestors are collected and stored in museums and scientific institutions" (Tauli-Corpus 1993: 26). According to an article in the prestigious journal *Science*, whose advocacy of this Western science project has been unremitting:

> As [Indigenous] people vanish, they are taking with them a wealth of information, buried in their genes about human origins, evolution, and diversity.... Already, there are indications

of the wealth of information harbored in the DNA of aboriginal peoples. (L. Roberts 1991: 1614)

Concerns about patenting and commercial exploitation have been repeatedly voiced: "How soon will it be before they apply for intellectual property rights to these genes and sell them for a profit?" (Tauli-Corpus 1993: 26). And as John Liddle, director of the Central Australian Aboriginal Congress, observes:

> If the Vampire Project goes ahead and patents are put on genetic material from Aboriginal People, this would be legalized theft. Over the last 200 years, non-Aboriginal people have taken our land, our language, culture and health – even our children. Now they want to take the genetic material which makes us Aboriginal people as well. (Nason 1994: 3)

# GIFTS AND COMMODITIES

*Labor should not be sold like merchandise but offered as a gift to the community.*

(Che Guevara)

The nature, depth, and force of Indigenous opposition to biocolonialism, and especially to the Diversity Project, is poorly grasped by advocates of these extractive initiatives of Western science – whether corporate or academic.[2] It is frequently assumed that once proper informed consent documents, material transfer agreements and database access agreements have been drafted, and the "hysteria" whipped up by "professional alarmists" subsides, opposition to the Diversity Project will and should dissipate (Moore 1996: 62). At the least, it should be effectively disarmed. At best, Indigenous people will realize, finally, that "they should be *grateful* to us."[3] Such assumptions can be sustained only by wrenching certain Indigenist critiques from their contexts. Some of the most substantive objections to the Diversity Project, and to biocolonialism more generally, contend that life-forms, and Indigenous knowledge of the natural world, are gifts; they must not be privatized, commercialized, and commodified.

This section contrasts a Western commodity conception of knowledge with the construal of knowledge as a gift which is prevalent in many Indigenous knowledge systems. I do not suggest that all knowledge within all Western and Indigenous knowledge systems conforms to these divergent metaphors of commodity and gift.[4] Certainly within the West there has been resistance to life-form patents on analogous grounds. Similarly, some Indigenous peoples have embraced such patents, to varying degrees and with varying degrees of consensus and reluctance. As Greaves (1994: 6) notes, "the arena of Western institutions is played in when the stakes are high and there is no other choice." Knowledge systems, whether Western or Indigenous, are neither monolithic nor static; they are varied and changing, far more so than my discussion here will reflect.

Nevertheless, these diverging metaphors of knowledge do capture tendencies and features which are typical of, or prevail in, many Indigenous and Western knowledge systems. Moreover, they have not only intellectual but social and moral implications for what and how something can be known: metaphors "shape our perceptions and in turn our actions, which tend to be in accordance with the metaphor" (Stepan 1993: 372). These are politically significant insofar as they inform contemporary struggles within Indigenous and Western knowledge systems over biocolonialist policies and practices. Indeed, part of what is at issue in resistance to the Diversity Project is whether or not a particular change should take place within Indigenous knowledge and value systems – a significant change in how certain knowledge is understood and in how it is valued.

Consider Aroha Mead's statement of the basis of Maori opposition to the Project. Many of the Diversity Project's advocates, she notes, "have the mistaken view that the reason for indigenous opposition to the [Project] rests in lack of understanding of [its] aspirations, and confusion over minor details" (Mead 1995). Anyone who has followed the long electronic debate on Native-Net between opponents of the Project and its central apologist – Henry Greely, a Stanford University law professor and head of the Project's North American Ethics Committee – will concur with Mead here. Greely and other Project proponents have repeatedly failed to address – or even to indicate they take seriously – what lies at the heart of Indigenist resistance:

> It is difficult to articulate the degree to which the indigenous and Western scientific philosophies differ on such a fundamental point, but . . . I wish to emphasize that it is the difference in understanding of the origin of humanity, the responsibility of individuals and the safety of future generations which sits so firmly at the core of indigenous opposition to the [Diversity Project] . . . the fundamental reason is that, according to an indigenous worldview, this type of research proposes to interfere in a highly sacred domain of indigenous history, survival and commitment to future generations. (Mead 1995)

As Mead (1995) explains, the Maori translate the word "gene" as *iratangata* ("life spirit of the mortals") or *whakapapa* ("genealogy"). So a physical gene is understood to be "imbued with a life spirit handed down from the ancestors." Each successive generation contributes to it, passing it on to future generations. Genes are thus part of the heritage of families, communities, tribes, and entire Indigenous nations. They are not the property of individuals, nor is any part or derivative of them. The innovative manipulations leading to the isolation and storage of DNA segments, and the privatization and commercialization of cell-lines, turn them into such and must therefore be vigorously resisted.

Comparable concerns have been expressed by diverse Indigenous peoples protesting the patenting of traditional medicines and crop varieties, for whom knowledge of the natural world, particularly medicinal and agricultural knowledge, is regarded (like life itself) as given, not produced. There are normative implications to such an epistemological posture. When knowledge is construed as a gift, the *process* of knowing rather than the product of knowledge, and the nature and quality of the relations with the nonhuman world which are constitutive of that process, become central.

To properly engage in a process of reciprocal exchange, of giving and receiving, behavioral constraints must be accepted. The reciprocity of the exchange is to be respected and reflected in one's conduct. These normative constraints are simultaneously ecological and social. The process of knowing must be undertaken in a way that respects and reflects the fact that each individual, each community, each tribe, each nation and species has "a responsibility to the workings of the universe" (Allen 1986: 73), to the generations to come, and to those that have passed. Like knowledge of the natural world, for many Indigenous peoples land itself is a

> gift . . . [so] they assume certain ceremonial duties which must be performed as long as they live on and use the land. . . . Obligations demanded by the lands upon which people lived were part of their understanding of the world; indeed their view of life was grounded in the knowledge of these responsibilities.   (Deloria 1992: 262–3)

This construal of knowledge and the normative constraints which attend it can be readily illustrated by diverse Indigenous knowledge practices. I emphasize here knowledge of healing, of hunting, and of crop cultivation.

### Normative dimensions

There are specific ceremonies and procedures which someone with knowledge of traditional medicine will carefully observe. A traditional healer will typically offer tobacco to the plants being collected. The plant will be addressed and thanked for being there, for allowing itself to be used in healing. Only certain plants will be culled, at certain stages of their life cycles, at certain times of the year and of the day. Diné healer Mae Tso's comments richly demonstrate how conceiving knowledge as reciprocal exchange mediates behavior, what is done in the name of Indigenous science, as well as how it is done:

> When you are collecting medicine healing herbs, you have to collect for the individual sick person. You make an offering to the plants in your prayers, you have to know the plant's name, the person's name and the reason. The medicine plants that you have gathered cannot be used for anyone else, nor can they be stored and kept for use at a later time. When you are collecting herbs, you cannot collect them in large quantities. There are specific sacred herbs for all kinds of sickness. . . . All these medicine plants have a specific song and prayer to go along with them. When you collect these herbs, you have to make an offering to them to get the healing spirit of the herbs to work. You have to know the prayers and songs for the herbs to collect them. You only collect what is needed, nothing more or less.   (Tso 1988: 328)

The ecological moral she conveys here is echoed in Jake Swamp's account of his training in the gathering of medicinal herbs:

> You don't just go out there and pluck it out by its roots and walk away. You have to prepare. You have to know the words that go with it. What I was taught was that when

you see that plant, to first see that it's the one you offer thanksgiving to, that plant is still here with us, still performing its duty and that you wish it to continue. You walk past it and you look for the other one, and that one you can pick. For, if you take that first one, who is to know, maybe that's the last one that exists in the world.   (in Barreiro 1992: 21)

The Cree goose-hunter's practice of *pwaatikswaau*, or smoking to the game, expresses a similar attitude and acknowledgment of the gift relationship, or reciprocal exchange, which binds the human to the nonhuman world, and which "constitutes a root metaphor or paradigm for knowledge in general" (Scott 1996: 74). Smoke is an appropriate vehicle of exchange for creatures of the air, while tobacco is a traditional medicine, customarily offered to honor other beings – human and nonhuman – especially when something is being taken or requested. When the hunter is successful and a goose falls, "the gift is respectfully admired by the hunter and later received as a guest into the lodge by the women of the hunter's household" (1996: 82).

Something analogous is evident in the agricultural knowledge practices of Andean peoples, undertaking the cultivation of their *chacras* (plots of land under cultivation). According to Modesto Machaca, "to open a *chacra* I must ask permission of the Pachamama so that she will allow me to work this soil.... I tell her that I will cultivate this soil with love, without mistreatment and the fruits she gives me we will all eat" (in Rivera 1995: 25). Cultivating a *chacra* is a reciprocal activity, necessarily involving both humans and the land. It is in this sense that Andean agricultural knowledge is to be seen as tied, or tethered to the land:

> To raise a *chacra* is not merely to domesticate plants and animals; it is to nurture lovingly and respectfully, in other words, to nurture ritually, together with plants and animals, the soils, waters, micro-climates and, in general, the whole land.   (1995: 24)

All of the activities that go on in the *chacra* – sowing, weeding, hilling, harvesting, and even the storage, transformation, and consumption of harvested products – are ritual activities. These rituals express the Andeans' attitude of love, respect, and gratitude to the earth for its gifts, including the gifts of knowledge regarding how to cultivate a *chacra*.

The process of knowing exemplified by Diné healing, Cree hunting, and Andean farming practices is not exclusively or narrowly cognitive. It is also an evaluative activity, conditioned by respect and gratitude, in which certain normative constraints on knowledge – on what, how, and by whom things are known – are critical. These spring from an acknowledgment that human beings play, and cannot help but play, a fundamental role in the natural world. Humans are, of course, not unique in this.

The knowledge that Indigenous healers, hunters, and farmers are given binds them, and the people they treat and feed, to the land, just as the exchange of gifts between people binds them to one another. The giving of gifts establishes a relationship between those involved; their circulation within the human world, as well as between the human and nonhuman world, acknowledges and enhances community. Those involved in the exchange and sale of commodities, by contrast, do not look toward the person of each other, but only toward the commodity; there are no obligations of brotherliness or reverence, and none of those spontaneous human relations that grow out of intimate personal community. They all would just obstruct the free development of the bare market community.... Such absolute depersonalization is contrary to all elementary forms of human relations. (Weber 1967: 192)

As one commentator observes:

It seems no misnomer that we have called those nations known for their commodities "the free world". The phrase doesn't seem to refer to political freedoms; it indicates that the dominant form of exchange in these lands does not bind the individual in any way – to his family, to his community, or to the state. (Hyde 1979: 67)

### Resisting commodification

When something that is a gift is metaphorically transformed and treated as if it were a commodity, the social and moral ramifications are considerable. Aroha Mead's comments (above, and in Mead 1996) demonstrate that part of what Indigenist critics of the Diversity Project are contesting is the desirability and inevitability of just such a transformation. What is ultimately at issue is the transformation of certain kinds of knowledge and certain forms of life into commodities, and the implications of this for Indigenous knowledge and value systems. The Declaration of Indigenous Peoples of the Western Hemisphere Regarding the Human Genome Diversity Project (1995) makes this plain:

We oppose the patenting of all natural genetic materials. We hold that life cannot be bought, owned, sold, discovered or patented, even in its smallest forms.... We particularly oppose the Human Genome Diversity Project which intends to collect, and make available, our genetic materials which may be used for commercial, scientific, and military purposes.... Our principles are based upon our profound belief in the sacredness of all Creation, both animate and inanimate. We live in a reciprocal relationship with all life.

So too, in the Blue Mountain Declaration (1995) rejecting life-form patenting, we find the following:

The humans, animals, microorganisms and plants comprising life on earth are part of the natural world into which we were all born. The conversion of these life forms, their molecules or parts into corporate property though patent monopolies is counter to the interests of the peoples of the world. No individual, institution, or corporation should be able to claim ownership over species or varieties of living organisms. Nor should they be able to hold patents on organs, cells, genes or proteins, whether naturally occurring, genetically altered or otherwise modified ... we call upon the world and the Congress of the United States to enact legislation to exclude living organisms and their component parts from the patent system. We encourage all peoples to oppose this attack on the value of life.

A commodity conception of knowledge assumes certain values and facilitates certain behaviors that are inappropriate or inconceivable when knowledge is regarded as something given, rather than produced for sale. Increasingly, Western technoscience – whether corporate, academic, or governmental – is committed to "producing" knowledge that is to be applied in industry. While there is a growing failure to accept, appreciate, and observe limits to such knowledge-acquisition, the rise of intellectual property regimes does indicate a readiness to limit access to such knowledge in the interests of enhancing its value as a commodity. Biocolonialism arises when this conception of knowledge is conjoined to the scope and power of Western legal institutions committed to extending intellectual property regimes globally.

## KNOWLEDGE AS POWER

*Most of the really fresh power comes from sciences.*

(Bruno Latour)

I have been suggesting that the fierce resistance of Indigenous peoples to biocolonialism is due partly, if not primarily, to the fact that it commodifies, privatizes, and commercializes both knowledge of the natural world and genetic life-forms themselves. The conversion of life-forms into intellectual property – into commodities to be harvested, altered, packaged, and sold – requires that valued genetic materials first be identified and located. The latter is often accomplished by "mining" Indigenous medicinal and agricultural knowledge systems, systems which construe such knowledge as a matter of reciprocity: as a moral transaction outside the marketplace, that must be respected and allowed to remain as such. Biocolonialism's critics regard it as an assimilative process that threatens to transform Indigenous knowledge and value systems, as well as the natural world itself, in unwelcome and lasting ways. To fail to resist it is, effectively, to abandon the responsibilities that accompany reciprocal exchange.

The Zuni, for example, have formed a Cultural Resources Advisory Team to provide guidance concerning Zuni genetic resources. It has declared that Zuni seeds "should not be sold or given to outsiders for profit, resale, breeding or trademarketing" (Soleri et al. 1994: 34). The reason is that if Zuni seeds are transformed into a commodity and sold, the Zuni will no longer know how the seeds will be used. Since they will no longer be under Zuni control, their abuse cannot be prevented.

When a gift is rendered as a commodity, it undergoes a change in metaphysical status that facilitates such loss of control and potential abuse. Gifts are inalienable; when a gift is exchanged the continuity of social relationships ensures that it always remains the giver's. Thus the giver remains in a position to influence and guide the disposition of the gift. Commodities, by contrast, are alienable. When they are exchanged, so is effective control over the disposition of the commodity. The "social distance and independence of the transactors" in the marketplace leaves the seller of the commodity unable to influence its use (Berg 1991: 363).

To convert Zuni seeds from gifts into commodities would not only alter the nature of Zuni communal relationships, it would also result in a significant and irreversible loss of power. The Zuni would no longer be able to monitor and control the use of their seeds, and the generations of intellectual and physical labor that their cultivation represents. They would no longer be able to discharge their moral responsibility to ensure that these gifts not be abused.

Indigenous recognition that a gift-to-commodity conversion process involves a loss of power is widespread, and is not limited to the conversion of genetic materials. It includes the commodification of knowledge. Consider the Maori account of this. The third of the three baskets of knowledge which form the basis of traditional Maori epistemology contains all knowledge of the natural world (agriculture, medicine, astronomy, fishing, crafts, etc.). Such knowledge is considered *tapu* – sacred and set apart, or removed from profane use. Thus, it is treated with special respect. It is also endowed with *mana* or power (Marsden 1992: 121). As a gift from the gods, it is not to be passed on lightly. Above all, knowledge that is *tapu* must never be transformed into a commodity:

> our elders never allow us to sell any knowledge of anything Maori that is really tapu. To them it is priceless. Money can never buy knowledge and when they teach they will tell people: "This knowledge I am passing over to you must never be sold." (Pewhairangi 1992: 11)

One is responsible for such knowledge and for how it will be used, or misused: "A tapu involves a restriction, and in the case of tapu knowledge this requires making sure that the knowledge does not fall into the wrong hands" (Patterson 1992: 164). Should this happen, the knowledge will lose its *tapu*, and thereby its power:

> There is . . . a fear that by giving things out they could be commercialized. If this happens they lose their sacredness, their fertility. They just become common. And knowledge that is profane has lost its life, lost its tapu. (Manihera 1992: 9)

Like many other Indigenous peoples, the Maori have long recognized that knowledge and power implicate one another. Recently, work in philosophy of science and science studies has also stressed that questions of knowledge and power "do not belong to distinct domains of inquiry, and that answering each requires sustained attention to the other" (Rouse 1991: 665). Indigenist responses to biocolonialism and especially the Diversity Project have focused on just this issue, so vital to understanding the political dynamics mediating Indigenous and Western knowledge systems. In the remainder of this section I look briefly at some of this recent work on knowledge and power in Western science, show how it helps to illuminate certain processes that are at work in biocolonialism, and how it may be used to enrich critiques of the Diversity Project in particular.

### The politics of science

Joseph Rouse (1987, 1991) has developed a detailed alternative to the conventional understanding of the role of knowledge and power within Western science. It addresses important aspects of power relations, and of the production and assessment of knowledge to which the standard account fails to do justice. Rouse points out that while knowledge and power have both been regarded as things which agents acquire, possess, and use, they have also been taken to constitute analytically distinct domains of human inquiry. The domain of knowledge includes representations, while the domain of power consists of human actions. These two domains interact in a particular way: "power may suppress knowledge, or distort it ideologically; it may also provide resources needed to achieve or accelerate knowledge acquisition, which in turn may augment power" (1991: 658). According to his alternative account, the details of which will not concern me here, knowledge and power are not distinct domains of things, but rather

> interconnected ways of posing questions to and concerns about the same domain. . . . They represent different ways of configuring and interrogating a wide range of our engagements with the world and each other . . . [and] neither is adequately addressed without serious attention to the other.   (1991: 658)

Rouse relies upon Wartenberg's (1990) account of power as a particular type of ongoing social process which is "continually being reconstituted and/or altered by means of the actions and understandings of social agents" (1990: 164). In addition to being dynamic, power is also situated; the role of "peripheral social others" is crucial in understanding power relationships. One agent has power over another as the result of the social field within which they are both situated.

A relationship between two agents is a power relationship because, and only insofar as, others will normally respond to them by aligning themselves with the dominant agent's actions. Power is thus always mediated by a "social alignment"; through the actions of many peripheral agents, the connection between the dominant agent's actions and the denial or fulfillment of the subordinate agent's wishes is established or enforced. On this view, the social world

> becomes an array of overlapping social alignments oriented by ongoing struggles of domination and resistance, within which agents and their actions are situated.   (Rouse 1991: 659)

Although Wartenberg restricts the domain of power to this social world, Rouse expands it to elements of the natural world, since power relations require not only keeping other human agents in line, but also depend on a reliable alignment of the physical environment. The construction and extension of scientific laboratories or "microworlds" shape and transform not only the social but the natural world – materials, things, processes, and practices. Thus he contends that power cannot legitimately be withheld from the "natural world" and confined to the "social world."[5] To illustrate the argument, he shows how "genes" emerge as an object of possible discourse

> through accumulations of capabilities and insights in specific contexts (e.g. laboratories with their own projects, protocols and materials, but also experimental systems such as

pisum, drosophila, maize and bacteriophage). These cannot be extended to other locations without complex and subtle mutual adaptations. (Rouse 1991: 660)

Among these are the standardization, simplification, and adaptation of laboratory practices and equipment, and the knowledge they embody. The material and conceptual working environment to which they are extended also requires modification. To take something as knowledge, he suggests, is to project it as a resource for ongoing activity, be this future research or "applications."

### *Implications for the diversity project*

Rouse's account of knowledge and power in science can be put to valuable use in understanding just how much is at stake for Indigenous peoples in the debate over the Diversity Project. The Project's goal is to collect and analyze DNA samples from diverse, predominantly Indigenous, populations and "to develop databases and resources that could be used to investigate new questions in the future" (NSF 1996). The "wealth of information harbored in the DNA of aboriginal peoples" (L. Roberts 1991: 1617) will be transferred to databases that are openly intended to function, in Rouse's terms, as resources for ongoing research activity (although Project organizers specifically deny any intention of developing applications).[6]

The database microworlds, in which this genetic information is to be preserved, will be located regionally as well as centrally. While it is not likely that they will be situated on the actual lands of the Indigenous peoples who will serve as the source of genetic material, they will certainly impact these communities by transforming the relations of power between them and their surrounding nation-states. The laboratory microworlds on which the Project relies are likely to affect Indigenous peoples and lands for two reasons. One is that the Project is actively discouraging a "bleed and run" scenario. Another is that training in genetic research is being offered as an incentive to establish the regional HGDP committees that will do the sampling. Thus, the promise of training in such techniques as growing white blood cells, preparing DNA, and analyzing DNA markers using the polymerase chain reaction is "luring many developing countries to participate in the HGDP" (Kahn 1994: 722). As one molecular biologist in Nairobi notes, "The new biology must find its way into Africa . . . this is a way of doing it" (Kahn, 1994: 722).

Members of the sampled Indigenous populations are exceedingly unlikely to be members of the regional committees. Anthropologists who have worked among them and who have secured their trust will certainly be. In fact, they already constitute an acknowledged and crucial part of the social alignment that is mediating power in this case, having generated the initial list of the 722 populations deemed "most worthy of genetic study." Indeed, it has been acknowledged that which populations are ultimately sampled will turn on the availability of anthropologists with ties to them. "Isolated and indigenous peoples participate with ethnologists because they trust them," reports one anthropologist and proponent of the Project (John Moore, cited in Gillis 1994: 9).

Many Indigenous peoples have a long history of struggle with and domination by the nation-states in which they are situated, and which will be well represented on these committees. Such committees will decide, among other things, "what scientific questions to emphasize, which populations to approach, and how to adapt the ethics rules to local conditions and cultures" (1994: 9). The Project will significantly impact the social, material, and conceptual environments of Indigenous peoples, sustaining and enhancing the existing unequal relations of power. Indigenous people are acutely aware of this, and of the kinds of tensions and disputes it will exacerbate, or initiate, within their communities.

This transformation of the social and natural worlds is a manifestation of power. The charges of "genetic colonization" that some Project critics have made might best be seen in this light. Rather than the theft and settling of Indigenous lands, the colonization at issue involves their transformation through the wholesale exportation of the microworlds of Western science on to them. Genetic information will be extracted from Indigenous peoples, processed in these microworlds, made available for use and eventual purchase, regardless of whatever measures the Project organizers might take to prevent the latter outcome.

The current social alignments, the current relations of power between dominant Western and subordinated Indigenous cultures, will be reinforced and strengthened by the Diversity Project, as the array of interest groups that constitute and enable Western technoscience (scientists, organizations, institutions, corporations, and governments) respond in ways coherently aligned with the dominant agents' actions. Insofar as the call for the establishment of regional HGDP committees has met with some success, insofar as pilot sampling is currently under way in Europe and China, and insofar as the National Science Foundation has issued – in July of 1996 – a formal call for Project proposals, that reinforcement has begun.

But Indigenist resistance to the Project, and the power relations in which it is embedded, has been massive, vigorous, and effective. Funding support, whether from organizations or government, has been exceedingly slow in coming, and Project organizers have had to wage what amounts to a prolonged public relations campaign in an effort to keep the Project viable and fundable. They have also substantively modified both the rhetoric and the plans of the Project, although I have never seen the Indigenist opposition being credited for this achievement.

## WESTERN INTELLECTUAL PROPERTY THEFT

*IPRs are a sophisticated name for modern piracy.*

(Vandana Shiva)

Law, and most especially intellectual property law, is increasingly central to appreciating the role of power in Western technoscience. It has been, as Alan Hunt (1992: 21) argues, a "primary agency of the advance of new modalites of power and constitutes distinctive features of their mode of operation." Intellectual property laws have been a particularly effective strategy for acquiring, commodifying, and rendering profitable, intangible Indigenous resources, such as artistic expressions and medicinal and spiritual knowledge. (For more on this, see Whitt 1995.)

Current copyright laws, for example, support and facilitate the practice of cultural imperialism by consigning traditional music to the public domain, then providing for its facile "conversion" to private property. The appropriation by American artistes and record companies of calypso music is a case in point. Millions of dollars have been made from a single song without any of this being returned to the communities of its origin (Wallis and Malm 1984).

Patent law enables a similar practice in the case of genetic resources. The US government is currently funding five major industry/university consortia which have planted their bioprospecting stakes throughout the world. Brazil, for example, earns around $25 million a year from exporting *Pilocarpus jaborandi*, a medicinal plant used by the Guajajara to treat glaucoma. The corporations who have patents derived from it reap far greater profits. Yet the Guajajara have been subjected to debt peonage and slavery by the agents of the companies involved in the trade. Moreover, *Pilocarpus* populations have been greatly depleted (Posey and Dutfield 1996: 53). The concrete repercussions of divergent construals of knowledge – as commodity and as gift – are painfully apparent here. How the law has served to advance new modalities of power, and to regulate their mode of operation, might be better appreciated by considering the origins and development of intellectual property law. I will do so briefly, focusing on copyright law.

### The origins of copyright law

While guilds were instrumental in shaping patent and trademark law, mercantile interests played a major role in shaping the formation of copyright law in England. In particular, publishers sought to obtain monopoly control over the production of books. This control was challenged in the late seventeenth century by writers who needed to earn their livelihood from the sale of their writing.

Although copyright is popularly viewed as a law for authors and artists, it originated with publishers and has long benefited entrepreneurs far more than creators (Patterson and Lindberg 1991). Martha Woodmansee has described how writers transformed themselves into "authors" in the modern sense by redefining the nature of writing. She recounts how, prior to the mid-eighteenth century, writing

> was considered a mere vehicle of received ideas which were already in the public domain, and, as such a vehicle, it too, by extension or analogy, was considered part of the public domain.   (Woodmansee 1984: 434)

At its best, writing was understood to be a process of inspired craftsmanship, and writers were understood to be a vehicle or instrument, not distinctly and personally responsible for their creations. Understood as craftspersons, writers had to prove themselves adept at following the body of rules that had been preserved and handed down to them for manipulating traditional materials in order to achieve goals dictated by their audience. Understood as inspired, they were

> equally the subject of independent forces, for the more inspired moments of [their] work – that which is novel and most excellent in it – are not any more the writer's doing than are its more routine aspects, but are instead attributable to a higher, external agency – if not to a muse, then to divine dictation. (1984: 427)

The production of poetical works, Goethe notes, was "regarded as something sacred, and it was considered close to simony to accept or bargain for an honorarium" (in Woodmansee 1984: 435).

As Woodmansee argues, this view of the writer changed, and the view of writer as author emerged, as the element of craftsmanship was eliminated or discarded, and that of inspiration was emphasized. Moreover, the source of inspiration was internalized, seen as emanating from within the writer. Literary inspiration came to be regarded as a matter of "original genius," and the inspired work came to be regarded as the peculiar and distinctive product, and property, of the writer.

The struggle between publishers and writers gradually intensified. Publishers attempted to reduce books to their physical foundations: "The book is not an ideal object . . . it is a fabrication made of paper . . . a commodity produced for hard cash" (1984: 443). Authors insisted their work transcended their material foundation, yet even so constituted property. It was Fichte who provided the distinction on which subsequent copyright law would largely depend, by describing three distinct shares of property in the book:

> When the book is sold ownership of the physical object passes to the buyer . . . the material aspect, the content of the book, the thoughts it presents also pass to the buyer. To the extent that [the buyer] is able, through intellectual effort, to appropriate them, these ideas cease to be the exclusive property of the author . . . the form in which these ideas are presented, however, remains the property of the author eternally. (1984: 444–5)

A book thus emerged as "the intellection of a unique individual" (1984: 447). The author, far from being a vehicle of ideas, transformed them, making them the expression of an individual's own unique mind. That original expression is private intellectual property. It, and the right to any profits from it, is what the copyright protects.

In one influential legal definition, "writings" are defined as "any physical rendering of the fruits of creative, intellectual or aesthetic labor" *Goldstein v. California*, 412 US 546, 93 S.Ct. 2303, 37 L.Ed.2d 163 (1973), 304. Copyright law, as we have seen, developed in response to the need for writers to sell their intellectual labor, to turn it into a commodity. As a result of eighteenth-century European writers' challenge to the existing power relations, publishers no longer retained the exclusive right to sell and profit from their writings. In the future, writers would have to surrender their copyright before this could take place.

This inclusion of intellectual laborers in the marketplace required a significant conceptual transformation. Not only did the nature of writing need to be reconceived, but so did the nature of knowledge. Knowledge, or more exactly ideas, became something that need no longer remain in the public domain. It was able to be transformed into private property, provided that it was "original" and was fixed in some physical form. It could then be exchanged in the marketplace, a commodity to be bought or sold. Interestingly, the originality requirement, at least in US law, has received a minimalist interpretation. A work is original if it is "one man's alone" (*Bleistein v. Donaldson Lithographing Co.* 188 US 239, 1903); any "distinguishable variation" of a prior work is enough to constitute originality, and render it private intellectual property (Baker 1992: 1590).

### Innovation and individuality

The chasm between "inspired" writing and "original" authorship is deep. As we have seen, the writer as a vehicle or instrument was regarded as subject to independent forces that played a crucial role in the writing process. The inspired moments of a work, no less than its more routine moments, were not the writer's sole doing. With the shift to the notion of original authorship, inspiration was internalized and the writer was relieved of responsibility to traditions preserved and passed down. Such intellectual labor sprang from the "original genius" of an individual, and hence was that individual's personal product and property.

The criterion of originality in copyright law to which this led has its counterpart in the requirement of novelty in patent law. The result was the embedding within Western intellectual property law of assumptions about individuality and innovativeness that are acutely at odds with the conceptual commitments of many Indigenous cultures. This has directly enabled the continued expropriation of Indigenous cultural and genetic resources. As Aroha Mead (1995) comments,

> I query the concept of "innovation" as defined by Western intellectual property laws – particularly when no recognition or value is accorded to the customary knowledge which links a species of plant to a particular usage, and details the most appropriate harvest, portion of the plant . . . and method of preparation.

Indigenous knowledge and generations of Indigenous labor – mental and physical – are discredited. All that is credited is the "chop-shop" labor of individual corporate and academic scientists who interject "novelty" into what they have taken.

Western concepts of "originality" and "novelty" are thus imposed on the world through coercive instruments such as the TRIPS provisions of the GATT.[7] The US government, for example, has been pressuring Ecuador to ratify a Bilateral Agreement on intellectual property rights, based on the same principles as those of the TRIPS. It opens the door to broader patents, despite the fact that the Andean Pact Law on Patents forbids any patents on human genes or organs. It does this, moreover, in the face of efforts "to implement legislation on Intellectual Collective Rights to protect traditional knowledge against monolithic appropriation" (Secretariat 1997).

Across the planet, at an accelerating pace, collectively owned traditional medicines and seeds are being privatized and commodified. Altered sufficiently to render them patentable, they are transformed into the "inventions" of individual scientists and corporations, and placed on sale in the genetic marketplace. This is the history and context which informs Indigenist resistance to the Diversity Project. Whatever the "good intentions" of the individual scientists involved, (see Moore 1996), it is only the latest (if most disturbing) manifestation of biocolonialism as a conjunture of Western law and technoscience.

Biocolonialism threatens to assimilate the knowledge, resources, and labor of generations of Indigenous peoples. To play the dominant society's game, and adopt intellectual property protection in order to thwart biopiracy, is ultimately to be transformed by that society's values and practices: "we cannot buy the arguments that we have to play within the field of existing patent and copyright laws to be able to protect our resources and knowledge," Tauli-Corpus (1993: 26) insists. Yet the other horn of this dilemma is that "without control over their intellectual products, their knowledge stands to be expropriated without any material benefits reaching them" (Agrawal 1995b: 4).

Meanwhile, Indigenous knowledge systems are dismissed as closed, changeless, stultifying, and stifling of originality. Such characterizations not only ignore the massive contributions of Indigenous peoples – especially medicinal, pharmaceutical, botanical, and agricultural – they also egregiously distort Indigenous knowledge systems themselves. If these systems did not foster agricultural innovation or plant-breeding "originality" (to cite but one instance), the rich diversity of the gene-plasm currently held in seed banks and field gene banks would be wholly inexplicable.

Within most Indigenous knowledge systems, the source of originality is not internalized, as the genius of one individual. Rather, the natural world, the community, and the individual are all integrally involved. Individuals are subject to independent forces, and constrained by the need to act with respect for the natural world and for future generations. The community grounds and informs the individual. However, since the process of knowing is experientially based, and what one learns depends on individual development, abilities, and preparation, individuals play an essential role in contributing new knowledge to the community. As one young Keres man explains: "You don't ask questions when you grow up. You watch and listen and wait, and the answer will come to you. It's *yours* then, not like learning in school" (Larry Bird, in Tafoya 1982: 24).[8]

Such an approach to innovation requires receptivity, reciprocity, and responsibility to the natural and human worlds in which one is situated. And it is the result of conducting oneself in, and of relating to, the natural and human worlds in accordance with that normative constraint. This relation is evident in the Andean practice of conversing with the natural world which is central to their agricultural science. Such dialogue leads one "to emphasize and attune oneself with [the other's] mode of being, and in company with that other, to generate and regenerate life" (Grimaldo Rengifo, in Apffel-Marglin and Rivera 1995: 13).[9] It is manifested in their effort to increase the diversity of their cultivated plants by "testing" new varieties. The cultivator does this without obligating the new seed "to get accustomed by force". It is accepted for a seed that does not "accustom" itself to move away . . . the [cultivator] says simply: "this seed does not get used to me . . . " . . . and continues "testing" others "to see if they follow him or her." (Apffel-Marglin and Rivera 1995: 33)

The new knowledge that results from such conversing is a gift. To paraphrase an earlier comment: when gifts are given, the continuity of social relationships (and, we should add, of relationships with the natural world) has the effect that the gift given always remains the givers'. It is inalienable.

# CONCLUSION

There has recently been a surge of interest by the dominant culture in Indigenous knowledge and Indigenous knowledge systems. The reasons are multiple. They include the failure of development policies that have disregarded the social, political, and cultural contexts in which they were implemented, and an as yet limited appreciation of the value and viability of Indigenous knowledge systems. The rhetoric of development, one commentator observes,

has gone through several stages. . . . Today indigenous knowledge is seen as pivotal, above all, in discussion on sustainable resource use and balanced development. This orientation is in stark contrast to the views of many earlier theorists, who saw traditional knowledge and institutions as obstacles to development.    (Agrawal 1995a: 3)

The study of Indigenous knowledge has even been institutionalized, with the establishment of a Center for Indigenous Knowledge in Agriculture at Iowa State University, an Internet list on Indigenous knowledge and a journal, the *Indigenous Knowledge and Development Monitor*. Such developments are consistent with the knowledge-as-commodity metaphor. The commodification of Indigenous spiritual knowledge has become the speciality of the New Age industry, the commodification of traditional medicinal knowledge has become the speciality of the pharmaceutical industry, and the commodification of plant genetic resources and Indigenous agricultural knowledge has become the speciality of the commercial seed industry. In opposing the Diversity Project, what Indigenous peoples are now resisting is part of that continuum, the commodification of the genetic information in their cell-lines.

After a period of dormancy, there has also been within academe a renewed interest in contrasting Indigenous and non-Indigenous knowledge, with attendant debate about terminology and the implications of adopting one terminological distinction rather than another. This debate has tended to proceed, as one might expect, on methodological and epistemological grounds. It often aims to secure some sort of dialogue between, if not integration of, Indigenous and Western knowledges of the natural world. A recent editorial in the *Indigenous Knowledge and Development Monitor*, for instance, calls for the development of "methodologies designed to build a bridge between various knowledge systems" (IKDM 1996a: 1). Hand-in-hand with this are calls for the gathering, documentation, archiving, and preservation of Indigenous knowledge in national and international databases, presumably because no bridge can be built when there is nothing left to bridge.

For a long time, the existence of Indigenous knowledge and knowledge systems was denied. When their existence was acknowledged, they were generally deprived of cognitive standing. They were dismissed as primitive, mystical, and unscientific – since they violated the fundamental methodological canons and commitment to value-neutrality of Western science. And steadily, steadily throughout, political, economic, and cultural practices and policies of oppression have been eroding away their very substance, their conditions of existence.

The solution now is not the isolation, documentation, and storage of Indigenous knowledge in international, national, and regional archives. No more than is the preservation of Indigenous cell-lines in databanks the proper response to the "vanishing," "rapidly disappearing" "isolates [who are] of Historic Interest" to population geneticists. Nor is the answer a "bridge" to assimilation built in the context of unequal power relations, and with the bridging interests of the dominant culture setting the agenda: a proposal that promises to be simply another stage in the politics of disappearance.

The appropriate response from those interested in preserving genetic diversity has already been formulated by Indigenist critics of the Human Genome Diversity Project:

> Why don't they address the causes of our being endangered instead of spending $20 million for five years to collect and store us in cold laboratories? If this money will be used instead to provide us with the basic social services and promote our rights as indigenous peoples, then our biodiversity will be protected.   (Tauli-Corpus 1993: 25–6)

And the appropriate response from those interested in preserving the diversity of knowledge systems has been proposed by Arun Agrawal. That response, he suggests, lies

> in attempting to reorient and reverse state policies to permit members of threatened populations to determine their own future, thus facilitating *in situ* preservation of indigenous knowledge. *In situ* preservation cannot succeed unless indigenous populations and local communities gain control over the use of the lands on which they dwell and the resources on which they rely. Those who are seen to possess knowledge must also possess the right to decide on how to conserve their knowledge, and how and by whom it will be used.   (Agrawal 1995a: 5)

It is, after all, the givers of gifts who must determine when, to whom, and how the gifts are to be given.

## ACKNOWLEDGMENTS

I am grateful to the Humanities Research Centre of the Australian National University for the support provided by a Visiting Fellowship which assisted in the completion of this essay.

## NOTES

1 Indigenism critiques the diverse power relations and dynamics that facilitate and maintain the oppression of Indigenous peoples. It stresses the existence, effectiveness, and potential of Indigenous agency in resisting oppression and in formulating concrete proposals for securing justice.

2 For examples, see the Summer 1996 special issue of *Cultural Survival Quarterly*, which was devoted to this topic.

3 This comment was made at a 1997 conference on "Women and Genetics in Contemporary Society" by a geneticist working with one of the Diversity Project's main proponents.

4 Nor do I wish to assume the adequacy of the gift/commodity distinction as a way of contrasting entire economic systems. For further consideration of this, see Appadurai (1986).

5 It is worth noting, parenthetically, that this approach has some limited analogy to the Indigenous conception of power, in which the natural world is also vitally implicated.

6 Surprisingly, given historical precedent and the economic and political realities of securing funding for such research, they also question its likelihood: "Although very unlikely, it is nevertheless possible that the results of the HGD Project" will lead to commercial applications (HGDP 1993). A draft "Materials Transfer and Database Access Agreement" has been drawn up.

7 GATT (General Agreement on Tariffs and Trade) and TRIPS (Trade-related Intellectual Property) are the United Nations' primary trade negotiation institutions.

8 The other side of this is nicely captured by Thomas Buckley: "To explain too much is to steal that person's opportunity to learn" (in Dooling and Jordan-Smith 1989: 39).

9 Rengifo is the coordinator of PRATEC, an NGO formed in 1987 which researches Andean science, technology, and philosophy. This remarkable group has developed an accredited university course which critiques the contemporary Western knowledge system from an Andean perspective. For more on this project see Apffel-Marglin and Rivera (1995).

## REFERENCES

Agrawal, A. (1995a). Indigenous and scientific knowledge: some critical comments. *Indigenous Knowledge and Development Monitor*, 3, 3: 3–6.

Agrawal, A. (1995b). Neither having one's cake nor eating it: intellectual property rights and "Indigenous" knowledges. *CPR Digest*, 36: 3–5.

Allen, P. G. (1986). *The Sacred Hoop*. Boston: Beacon Press.

Apffel-Marglin, F. (1995). Development or decolonization in the Andes? in Apffel-Marglin and Rivera (1995).

Apffel-Marglin, F. and J. Rivera (1995). Regeneration in the Andes. *INTERculture*, 28, 1.

Appadurai, A. (1986). *The Social Life of Things*. Cambridge: Cambridge University Press.

Armstrong, J. (1995). Global trade targets indigenous gene lines, *National Catholic Reporter*, January 27: 11.

Baker, M. (1992). La(w) – a note to follow So: have we forgotten the federal rules of evidence in music plagiarism cases? *Southern California Law Review*, 65, 3: 1583–1637.

Barreiro, J. (1992). The search for lessons. *Akwe:kon*, 9, 2: 18–39.

Bereano, P. (1995). Message posted to <Native-L@gnosys.svle.ma.us> on October 31.

Berg, J. (1991). Moral rights: a legal, historical and anthropological reappraisal. *Intellectual Property Journal*, 6: 341–76.

Blue Mountain Declaration (1995). Posted to <pol-sci-tech@igc.apc.org> on June 3.

Declaration of Indigenous Peoples of the Western Hemisphere Regarding the Human Genome Diversity Project (1995). *Indigenous Woman*, 11, II: 32–3.

Deloria, V. (1992). Out of chaos. In Dooling and Jordan-Smith (1992).

Deshler, D. (1996). External and local knowledge. *Africa Notes* (April): 1–3.

Dooling, D. and P. Jordan-Smith (1989). *I Become Part of It*. San Francisco, CA: Harper.

Ferguson, A. and B. Bar-On (1998). *Daring to be Good: Feminist Essays in Ethico-Politics*. New York: Routledge.

Fuller, Steve (1991). Studying the proprietary grounds of knowledge. *Journal of Social Behavior and Personality*, 6, 6: 105–28.

Gillis, A. (1994). Getting a picture of human diversity. *Bioscience*, 44, 1: 8–11.

Greaves, T. (1994). *Intellectual Property Rights for Indigenous Peoples*. Oklahoma City: Society for Applied Anthropology.

Harry, D. (1995). The Human Genome Diversity Project and its implications for Indigenous peoples. *Indigenous Woman*, II, II: 30–1.

Hettinger, E. (1989). Justifying intellectual property. *Philosophy and Public Affairs*, 18: 31–52.

Heyd, T. (1995). Indigenous knowledge, emancipation and alienation. *Knowledge and Policy*, 8, 1: 63–73.

HGDP (1993). "Answers to Frequently Asked Questions" (FAQ), available on the HGDP's website at <http://www-leland.stanford.edu/group/moprrinst/HGDP.html>

Hunt, A. (1992). Foucault's expulsion of law: toward a retrieval. *Law and Social Inquiry*, 17, 1: 1–62.

Hyde, L. (1979). *The Gift*. New York: Random House.

IKDM (1996a). Editorial. *Indigenous Knowledge and Development Monitor*, 4, 1: 1.

IKDM (1996b). Comments on article by Arun Agrawal. *Indigenous Knowledge and Development Monitor*, 4, 1: 12–19.

Kahn, P. (1994). Genetic diversity project tries again. *Science*, 266: 720–2.

Kimbrell, A. (1993). *The Human Body Shop*. San Francisco, CA: Harper.

King, M. (1992). *Te Ao Hurihuri: Aspects of Maoritanga*. Auckland, NZ: Reed.

Lind, C. (1991). The idea of capitalism or the capitalism of ideas? A moral critique of the Copyright Act. *Intellectual Property Journal*, 7: 65–74.

Manihera, T. (1992). Foreword: learning and tapu. In King (1992).

Marglin, S. (1990). Knowledge systems: Techne and Episteme. In F. Marglin and S. Marglin, *Dominating Knowledge: Development, Culture and Resistance*. Oxford: Clarendon Press.

Marsden, M. (1992). God, man and universe: a Maori view. In King (1992).

Mead, A. (1995). Letter to Darryl Macer. Posted on Native-L on July 29.

Mead, A. (1996). Genealogy, sacredness and the commodities market. *Cultural Survival Quarterly*, 20, 2(Summer): 46–51.

Moore, J. (1996). Native Americans, scientists, and the HGDP. *Cultural Survival Quarterly*, 20, 2 (Summer): 60–2

Mudrooroo (1995). *Us Mob*. Sydney, Australia: HarperCollins.

Nader, L. (1996). *Naked Science: Anthropological Inquiry into Boundaries, Power, and Knowledge*. New York: Routledge.

Nason, D. (1994). Tickner warns over Aboriginal gene sampling. *The Australian*, January 25.

NSF (1996). Pilot projects for a Human Genome Diversity Project: special competition. File nsf 96112, available at <http://www.nsf.gov> under "STIS Publication Database."

Patterson, J. (1992). *Exploring Maori Values*. Palmerston North, NZ: Dunmore.

Patterson, R. and S. Lindberg (1991). *The Nature of Copyright*. Atlanta: University of Georgia Press.

Peritore, N. and A. Peritore (1995). *Biotechnology in Latin America*. Wilmington, DE: Scholarly Resources.

Pewhairangi, N. (1992). Foreword: learning and tapu. In King (1992).

Polanyi, K. (1968). *Primitive, Archaic and Modern Economies: Essays of Karl Polanyi*. New York: Doubleday.

Posey, D. and G. Dutfield (1996). *Beyond Intellectual Property*. Ottawa: IDRC.

Rivera, J. (1995). Andean peasant agriculture: nurturing a diversity of life in the Chacra. In Apffel-Marglin and Rivera (1995).

Roberts, J. (1993). Global project under way to sample genetic diversity. *Nature*, 361: 675.

Roberts, L. (1991). A genetic survey of vanishing peoples. *Science*, 252: 1614–17.

Roberts, R. (1987). Is information property? *Intellectual Property Journal*, 3, 2: 209–15.

Rouse, J. (1987). *Knowledge and Power: Toward a Political Philosophy of Science*. Ithaca, NY: Cornell University Press.

Rouse, J. (1991). The dynamics of power and knowledge in science. *Journal of Philosophy*, 88: 658–65.

Scott, C. (1996). Science for the West, myth for the rest? The case of James Bay Cree knowledge construction. In Nader (1996).

Secretariat (1997). Message posted to <elan@csf.colorado.edu> on June 3.

Silva, J. (1995). Plant intellectual property rights: the rise of nature as a commodity. In Peritore and Peritore (1995).

Soleri, D. et al. (1994). Gifts from the Creator: intellectual property rights and folk crop varieties. In Greaves (1994).

Stepan, N. (1993). Race and gender: the role of analogy in science. In S. Harding, *The "Racial" Economy of Science*. Bloomington: Indiana University Press.

Tafoya, T. (1982). Coyote's eyes: Native cognition styles. *Journal of American Indian Education* (February): 21–33.

Tauli-Corpus, V. (1993). We are part of biodiversity, respect our rights. *Third World Resurgence*, 36: 25–6.

Treaty of Indigenous Peoples International (1997). Posted to <indknow@u.washington.edu>

Tremblay, G. (1997). Statement for exhibition of contemporary Native American art, "We Are Many, We Are One", curated by Jaune Quick-to-See Smith, University of Wisconsin-La Crosse, February 20–March 23.

Tso, M. (1988). Affidavit submitted to the Hearing before the Select Committee on Indian Affairs: Improvement of the American Indian Religious Freedom Act. Second Session of 100th Congress. May 1. Washington, DC: US Government Printing Office.

UNESCO (1995) Report of the Subcommittee on Bioethics and Population Genetics of the UNESCO International Bioethics Committee, dated November 15. Posted on the UNESCO website.

Wallis, R. and K. Malm (1984). *Big Sounds from Small People*. New York: Pendragon.

Wartenberg, T. (1990). *The Forms of Power: From Domination to Transformation*. Philadephia: Temple.

Weber, M. (1967). *On Law in Economy and Society*. New York: Simon and Schuster.

Whitt, L. (1995). Cultural imperialism and the marketing of Native America. *American Indian Culture and Research Journal*, 19, 3: 1–31.

Whitt, L. (1997). Indigenist critiques of the Human Genome Diversity Project. In Ferguson and Bar-On (1998).

Woodmansee, M. (1984). The genius and the copyright. *Eighteenth-Century Studies*, 17: 425–48.

# Part VII

# SOCIAL AND POLITICAL PHILOSOPHY

# 17

# THE JURISPRUDENCE OF COLONIALISM

*Steve Russell*

*Resistance is futile. You will be assimilated!*

The Borg are intergalactic villains who emerged in the *Star Trek* stories after the Klingons/Federation went the way of the Soviet Union/United States and peace dried up the story potential. The Borg warning, reproduced above, is a science fiction echo of the *Requiremiento* of 1513 (d'Errico 2000: 574–5), a declaration read in Spanish or Latin to Native Americans, often innocent of those languages, to secure Papal blessing for the massacre to follow. The goal of the Spanish on the Gulf and Pacific coasts, like that of the English on the East coast, was the same as that of the Borg: philosophical monoculture (Mohawk 2000), bringing European religion to people who already had religion (Deloria 1994) and European law to people who already had law (Strickland 1975; Fenton 1998; Johansen 1998). Whether resistance is futile remains to be seen, but almost 500 years after the *Requiremiento*, American Indians are not a philosophical monoculture in religion or in jurisprudence.

Jurisprudence is a fertile field for American Indian philosophy because our status as objects of legal discourse makes the inquiry urgent. This urgency, this immediate need to understand law, is a defensive response to the cross-currents of Indian policy – e.g., ethnic cleansing, treaty-making, forced assimilation, termination, and relocation – that have swept across our land while the law, particularly the Constitution, has failed to protect our property, our cultures, or even our lives (Wunder 1994). We study this law that has failed us, ironically, for utilitarian ends. It is fitting that we should do so since our typical approach is, in the words of Choctaw philosopher Lee Hester (2000: 2), "the difference between orthodoxy on the European side and orthopraxy on the American Indian side."

In search of an Indian orthopraxy, we quickly discard received Anglo-American legal wisdom from Blackstone to Rehnquist. We know that property law has not protected our land, contract law has not sanctified our treaties, tort law has not compensated us for European depredations, and the workings of criminal law appear to depend on whether the Indian is the victim (Greenfield and Smith 1999) or the accused (Ross 1998). Indians enter the conversation about law in need of an externalist critique.

Postmodern legal thought offers an externalist approach to legal order, highly skeptical of established power relationships. An American Indian, legal scholar or not, can hardly contemplate the "American" legal order from any position other than that of an externalist skeptic. Federal Indian law presents normative confusion (Frickey 1997; Pommersheim 1999) and a stubborn resistance to formal logic and doctrinal harmony. This logical chaos can be breathtaking to a reader schooled in the tradition of law as social science (Pound 1969) or as a positive framework within which justice might be sought if not always located (Rawls 1971).

The postmodern fascination with text – Foucault's discursive practices, Derrida's deconstruction, Lyotard's language games and phrase regimens – suits the American Indian legal experience as object rather than subject, "done to" rather than "doer." Indians on and off reservations live in Foucault's (1978: 293 ff.) disciplinary dystopia, the carceral. Much of federal Indian law is a textbook example of orthopraxy frustrated by incommensurability, what Lyotard (1988: xi) calls the "differend":

> As distinguished from a litigation, a differend [différend] would be a case of conflict, between (at least) two parties, that cannot be equitably resolved for lack of a rule of judgment applicable to both arguments.

The hermeneutic turn in modern jurisprudence seems to founder on this incommensurability when addressing Indian issues.

Traditional legal hermeneutics (teasing out general principles by inductive analysis of legal texts), when applied to federal Indian law, leave an Indian more impressed with Michel Foucault's view of "truth":

> "Truth" is linked in a circular relation with systems of power which produce and sustain it, and to effects of power which it induces and which extend it. A "regime" of truth.   (Foucault 1980: 133)

While Foucault disdained hermeneutics generally, he did not write about law in the Anglo-American tradition of *stare decisis*, where that signified by the text is contested by reference to prior texts and to the signifiers (judges, legislators). Law itself is an argumentative social practice (Dworkin 1986), and the adversarial regime of Anglo-American practice is even more so than the law of Foucault's continental tradition. Foucault would rather follow the power relationships which he believes create the signification which in turn creates the power relationships. He might criticize the linking of the signified (meaning) to the signifier (judge or legislator) through the text as *post hoc* rationalization, where Derrida would find it merely futile.

Derrida's denial of any original or transcendental signified – one meaning for a text valid in all times and places – has become a postmodern truism in the context of constitutional interpretation. While Derrida would find the fresh scent of legislative intent equally elusive in *statutory* text, it is virtually always constitutional text allegedly at issue in Indian cases. "Allegedly" because Indians are mentioned only twice within the constitutional text: the Indian Commerce Clause (US Const, Art I, § 8) and the exclusion of tribal Indians from population counts to determine congressional apportionment (US Const, Art I, § 2). Neither of these specific references to Indians has been particularly controversial, except perhaps the reading of the Indian Commerce Clause as support for the plenary power doctrine examined below.

More is going on here than a simple lack of textual support within the Constitution for the superstructure of federal Indian law, which is erected upon Chief Justice John Marshall's Cherokee Trilogy opinions rather than constitutional text (Norgren 1996). Marshall fashioned a jurisprudence essentially based on the doctrine of "Christian discovery," although he began in *Johnson v. McIntosh* (21 US 543, 1823) to state the premise of the discovery doctrine in terms of European superiority rather than Christian superiority (d'Errico 2000: 574–5). For Indians, the operative concept was that they were inferior as a matter of law, rather than the nice distinctions among the grounds of Christianity, whiteness, or superior military force. The land under the Cherokees' feet suddenly became owned by the colonists.

Marshall's constitutional sleight of hand continued in *Cherokee Nation v. Georgia* (30 US 1, 1831) to answer the question of how Indian nations should be characterized if the Indians did not in fact own the land under their feet. Indians had to have some sort of governmental authority to lend substance to the cessions of land that had been the primary means of colonial expansion. The characterization, *dehors* any constitutional text, was "domestic, dependent nations." Domestic because part of the United States, nations so they could cede land to the United States, and dependent so the United States, could manage their affairs at will. The only bright side of the dark tragedy was the birth of a "guardian and ward" relationship between the United States and Indian nations that carried at least a theoretical duty that the United States act in the best interests of the Indians. While that duty has too often been honored in the breach, it is sobering to contemplate what kind of depredations the courts might have approved in its absence.

The final case in John Marshall's foundational iteration of federal Indian law is *Worcester v. Georgia* (31 US 515, 1832), which the Cherokee won in the courts but still lost on the ground. In *Worcester*, the state of Georgia had passed a law requiring a license for any white person to reside within the Cherokee Nation. Worcester, a missionary, was convicted under that law and sentenced to four years in prison. The Cherokee Nation came to Worcester's defense.

Ironically, this clearest victory for the Cherokee Nation – holding the Georgia statute to be unconstitutional – *was* grounded in constitutional text, the Indian Commerce Clause. The good news was that Georgia had no authority to make laws for the

Cherokee Nation. The bad news was that Congress did. Since the law before the Court was made by Georgia, it was struck down.

The historical backdrop of the Cherokee Trilogy was the effort to move Indians West of the Mississippi River (Norgren 1996). The *Worcester* opinion tempered somewhat the expansive language of *Johnson v. McIntosh*. It recognized the right of the Cherokee to occupy their ancestral lands unless they ceded those lands by treaty. However:

> Real victory – as opposed to theoretical victory – for the missionaries and the Cherokee depended upon enforcement of the Supreme Court's decision. Here they each lost, with devastating results for the Cherokee. (Norgren 1996: 122)

One result for the Cherokee was the Trail Where We Cried, the removal of the Cherokee to Indian Territory (now Oklahoma) by military force. Unprepared for the weather, thousands died. Another result was the uncompensated appropriation of the property of individual Cherokees. The economy of the Cherokee Nation was devastated for a generation. This colonical rapaciousness stands in stark contrast to the words in the legal texts considered fundamental by the United States.

The United States' founding documents, from the Declaration of Independence through the Bill of Rights, are expressions of anticolonial ideology in a specifically anticolonial historical context. This is of course anticolonialism understood in an equivocal sense. The colonists had had enough of exploitation of one people by another, at least when the colonists were the exploited. They had come to look upon North America as home and upon themselves as the colonized rather than the colonizers. The exploitation of indigenous people as a violation of the very same fundamental rights of human beings that the colonists claimed for themselves was not within the revolutionary consciousness of their revolution. They either held the truth to be self-evident that only some people were created equal, or it escaped their notice that the original inhabitants of North America were people.

The Declaration of Independence, in sweeping flights of egalitarian rhetoric, invited revolution; the Bill of Rights institutionalized the revolution's resolve to enshrine in law what Lyotard would call the "metanarrative" of the Rights of Man, grounded in the Kantian idea of man as an end in himself, pursued by the Cartesian quest for ultimate truth, and cemented in the social contract (Rousseau 1762).

Some obvious exclusions from the social contract (persons without property, without penises, without the appropriate racial pedigree) are limitations on the Rights of Man metanarrative that have been somewhat mitigated by subsequent events. African Americans have been five-fifths of a person since the Reconstruction Amendments 13–15. Women are now voters (US Const, Amend. XIX), and legal disadvantages to women are subject to some degree of skepticism in the courts (*United States v. Virginia*, 518 US 515, 116 S.Ct. 2264, 1996). Indians were declared to be citizens of the United States by Congress in 1924 (Indian Citizenship Act, 43 Stat. 253), a status few Indians wanted, but a status that should have conferred some of the rights set out in the United States' founding documents.

How is it, Indians must ask, that the Rights of Man metanarrative, reinforced since the revolution by more inclusionary politics, has produced so little for Indian people that we enter the twenty-first century as less than 1 percent of the United States population divided into fewer than 600 tribes recognized by the federal government? What kind of legal system presides over the conversion of natural abundance into wealth for the colonists and dependence for the natives (Russell 1999), while using the tiny portions of land left in native hands for disposal of toxic wastes (LaDuke 1999)? If this result sounds like colonial exploitation within the legal paradigm created by the anticolonial founding documents, it is fair to ask whether the Rights of Man metanarrative is still present and, if so, where does the postmodern exposure of philosophical fraud lead us?

I will examine the contemporary treatment by the United States of colonized peoples in the texts of three Supreme Court opinions, involving Indian treaty rights to land, the right to a jury trial in Puerto Rico, and the right to vote in Hawaii. Puerto Rico and Hawaii are included to suggest that this jurisprudence is grounded in something in addition to the mythology of "race" (Montagu 1997) as applied to Indians. In each case, it would appear that the result extends colonial power while the text remains tightly bound to the Enlightenment rhetoric of human rights that provided the philosophical foundation for the American Revolution.

## LONE WOLF V. HITCHCOCK, 187 US 553 (1903)

In *Lone Wolf*, the Kiowa tried to interpose the Treaty of Medicine Lodge (15 Stat. 581, 1867) to prevent the allotment of the Kiowa Reservation. Allotment was a policy designed at once to destroy Indian culture and to transfer Native American land into Euro-American hands. Reservations were parceled out to individual Indians so the "surplus lands" could be opened for white settlement. After allotment, even the so-called "civilized" Indians, including the family of this writer, were quickly swindled out of their lands (Debo 1940). By the destruction of the reservations, Indian Territory became Oklahoma.

Many Indian leaders, correctly perceiving common landholding as a cornerstone of their culture, fought the allotment policy tooth and nail. So it was that Lone Wolf, Principal Chief of the Kiowa, did battle with Ethan A. Hitchcock, Secretary of the Interior, for the treaty rights and the future of the Kiowa Nation. Lone Wolf claimed that Kiowa lands were protected by treaty and by the Fifth Amendment. The treaty guaranteed the Kiowa possession of their lands and the Fifth Amendment guaranteed that property could not be taken without due process of law. The Supreme Court had a ready answer:

> The contention in effect ignores the status of the contracting Indians and the relation of dependency they bore and continue to bear towards the government of the United States. To uphold the claim would . . . limit and qualify the controlling authority of Congress in respect to the care and protection of the Indians.   (187 US at 564)

The relationship between destruction of the Kiowa land base and their "care and protection" is never clarified in the opinion. The Court simply asserted that "Congress possessed a paramount power of the property of the Indians, by reason of its exercise of guardianship over *their interests*, and that such authority might be implied, even though opposed to the strict letter of a treaty with the Indians" (187 US at 565, emphasis added).

Lone Wolf should not fear this result because the Court presumed that "the United States would be governed by such consideration of justice as would control a Christian people in their treatment of an ignorant and dependent race" (187 US at 565) and "a moral obligation rested upon Congress to act in good faith" (187 US at 566). Congress was shielded by the political question doctrine, a concept normally invoked in foreign relations and therefore condign in Indian affairs. The *Lone Wolf* case came to stand for this application of the political question doctrine, for the plenary power doctrine that threatens Indians nations to this day, and for the unbridled right of Congress to unilaterally abrogate treaties.

If treaty abrogation meant simply a return to the *status quo ante*, *Lone Wolf* would have increased the Kiowa land base rather than destroying it, since the Kiowa–Comanche Alliance had at one time controlled much of the Southern Plains. However, the American form of abrogation meant that the Kiowa lost their reservation without having their previous lands returned. Legal doctrines available to the Court could have supported a different outcome (Supreme Court of the American Indian Nations 1999) had the law not been captured by the colonial enterprise.

> The Kiowa Indians during their history withstood military encounters, missionary pressures, agent manipulation, assimilation policies, debilitating diseases, even the malnutrition of the ration system. They could not successfully stand in the way of Anglo-American law. Law touched all aspects of their lives simultaneously and tore away their land base at the same time that it incapacitated their religious foundation. Law surrounded them and placed them in a legal straitjacket.   (Clark 1999: 110–11)

Allotment, as Lone Wolf feared and the Court later recognized, "quickly proved disastrous for the Indians" (*Hodel v. Irving*, 481 US 704, 707, 1987). Indians did not become instant Jeffersonian yeomen, and those who did not lose their land altogether (which is to say, those whose power to alienate the land was restricted) soon became absentee landlords, with their property leased for grazing by the Bureau of Indian Affairs at a fraction of market value.

As important, most Indians were unfamiliar with the Anglo-American legal methods of devise and descent and therefore unlikely to write wills. Such knowledge would have been of limited utility, anyway, since Indians had little access to legal services. Without wills or lawyers to clear up land titles through intestacy proceedings in probate courts, Indians watched helplessly as ownership was divided anew in every generation. The result was extreme fractionation of allotment lands, a damage Congress tried to repair in 1983 by providing that fractional interests would escheat to the tribe when they became less than 2 percent of the total acreage and earned less than $100 a year.

By 1987, the Supreme Court had abandoned the political question doctrine that blocked judicial redress in *Lone Wolf* (*Sioux Nation v. United States*, 448 US 371, 1980). The Court recognized the gravity of the fractionation problem, giving an extreme example:

> Tract 1305 is 40 acres and produces $1,080 in income annually. It is valued at $8,000. It has 439 owners, one-third of whom receive less than $.05 in annual rent and two-thirds of whom receive less than $1. The largest interest holder receives $82.85 annually. The common denominator used to compute fractional interests in the property is 3,394,923,840,000. The smallest heir receives $.01 every 177 years. If the tract were sold (assuming the 439 owners could agree) for its estimated $8,000 value, he would be entitled to $.000418. The administrative costs of handling this tract are estimated by the Bureau of Indian Affairs at $17,560 annually. (*Hodel v. Irving*, 481 US 704, 713, 1987, footnotes omitted)

In *Hodel*, the Supreme Court, no longer hampered by the political question doctrine, reached the Fifth Amendment question and declared Congress' paltry attempt to reconstitute the tribal land bases destroyed with the Court's imprimatur in *Lone Wolf* to be an unconstitutional taking of the property of individual Indians! This has the appearance of what Professor Peter d'Errico has aptly called a "shell game" (d'Errico 2000: 577) in a similar context, wherein the Cherokee were barred from suing a state in the Supreme Court on the ground that they are not a foreign nation. Later the Coeur d'Alene were barred from suing a state in district court on the ground that the Coeur d'Alene *are* a foreign nation. The only visible rule of decision is that tribal interests lose and colonial interests win.

## *BALZAC V. PEOPLE OF PORTO RICO,*
### 258 US 298 (1922)

The anticolonial United States was perhaps lacking the insight to see itself as colonizer of Native Americans. After the Spanish-American War of 1898, those racial blinders must have been stripped away when the Spanish colonies of the Philippines, Guam, and Puerto Rico became American colonies. Puerto Rico was governed by a presidential appointee with a customary colonial disregard for civil liberties (Fernandez 1992).

Jesús Balzac published a newspaper in Arcibo, Puerto Rico, wherein he wrote at least two articles highly critical of Governor Arthur Yager, a Princeton classmate of President Woodrow Wilson. We are not informed by the Supreme Court of the exact content of these editorials, but they resulted in two counts of criminal libel. In a one-paragraph dismissal of Balzac's First Amendment defense, the Court reported that

> A reading of the two articles removes the slightest doubt that they go far beyond the "exuberant expressions of meridional speech" . . . Indeed, they are so excessive and outrageous in their character that they suggest the query whether their superlative vilification

223

has not overleaped itself and become unconsciously humorous. But this is not a defense. (258 US at 314)

Neither was the First Amendment a defense, leaving Balzac with the complaint that he had been sentenced to a total of nine months in jail after denial of his right to a jury trial. Balzac's jury demand in such a political context is an eerie echo of the infamous libel prosecution of John Peter Zenger for criticizing the colonial governor of New York (Alexander 1972). Zenger's trial is, of course, the proverbial textbook case of jury nullification.

While it may surprise nobody that Balzac was denied the opportunity to follow Zenger's example, the rationale might raise eyebrows. The result was for the good of the Puerto Rican people and respect for their customs:

> Congress has thought that a people like the Filipinos, or the Porto Ricans, trained to a complete judicial system which knows no juries, living in compact and ancient communities, with definitely formed customs and political conceptions, should be permitted themselves to determine how far they wish to adopt this institution of Anglo-Saxon origin, and when. (258 US at 310)

Balzac thus lost his opportunity to become the John Peter Zenger of Puerto Rico, and joined Lone Wolf of the Kiowa as a man of horizons too limited in the opinion of the Supreme Court to see the best interests of his colonized people.

## *RICE V. CAYETANO*, 528 US 495, 120 S.CT 1044 (2000)

The best interests of colonized people became an issue again in 2000 in a case involving the management of land set aside by Congress "to rehabilitate the native Hawaiian population" (120 S.Ct. at 1051–2). Native Hawaiians were in need of rehabilitation after the United States supported an armed *coup d'état* in 1893 to overthrow the Hawaiian monarchy, an act which resulted in productive land passing from native to colonial ownership and a Congressional Joint Resolution of apology to survivors of the Hawaiian people 100 years later (107 Stat. 1510, 1993).

In the losses they have sustained at the hands of the United States, Hawaiians have much in common with American Indians (Benjamin 1996). The Supreme Court has repeatedly held that for purposes of equal protection of the law under the Fourteenth Amendment, "Indian" defined as political affiliation with a federally recognized tribe is a political classification rather than a racial one (Russell 1998). That is, an Indian is a person politically affiliated with a tribe rather than merely a person of Indian blood. This means that federal laws treating Indians differently (whether the difference is an advantage like the hiring preference in *Morton v. Mancari*, 417 US 535, 1974, or a disadvantage like the federal prosecution in *Ex Parte Antelope*, 430 US 641, 1977), need not be narrowly tailored to accomplish a compelling state interest. Indian status, unlike race, is not a "suspect classification" under the Fourteenth Amendment.

Harold F. Rice, born in Hawaii as a descendant of white colonists, filed a lawsuit against Benjamin J. Cayetano, governor of Hawaii, claiming racial discrimination because he was not allowed to vote for the board of trustees of the Office of Hawaiian Affairs, the state agency charged with managing the assets set aside "to rehabilitate the native Hawaiian population." Native Hawaiians sought to compare their history to that of Native Americans. Indeed, an argument could be made that the Hawaiians have an even stronger case for treatment as a nation rather than a race. Not only was the colonial theft of Hawaii more recent (1893, while the end of the Indian wars is generally dated to the Wounded Knee Massacre in 1890), but the Hawaiian people had a form of government (monarchy) much more familiar to the European colonists than the governmental institutions of most Indians.

The Supreme Court, disregarding a substantial body of Fourteenth Amendment law (as well as history and common sense), analyzed the case under the Fifteenth Amendment, originally enacted to extend the franchise to freed slaves but virtually a dead letter to African Americans until Congress enforced it with the Voting Rights Act of 1965. For purposes of the Fifteenth Amendment, the Court found that "native Hawaiians" is a racial classification rather than a political one. If they had decided the same thing under the Fourteenth Amendment, they would arguably have rendered the setting aside of assets for the benefit of Native Hawaiians to be unconstitutional, rendering moot the question of whether the son of white colonists should be allowed to vote on the management of those assets.

The Court went on to lecture the State of Hawaii:

> One of the principal reasons race is treated as a forbidden classification is that it demeans the dignity and worth of a person to be judged by ancestry instead of by his or her own merit and essential qualities.   (120 S.Ct. at 1057)

Of course, the only judgment implied by the State of Hawaii in limiting this particular vote to Native Hawaiians is that the political affiliation of the voters with the Hawaiian community created an identity of interests. If the interests of the Native Hawaiians and the white colonists had not been so disparate, there would have been no need for an Office of Hawaiian Affairs in the first place. Once more, the rule of decision appears to be that the colonists win even as the opinion appeals to the Rights of Man metanarrative.

# CONCLUSION

If, as *Rice*, *Balzac*, and *Lone Wolf* appear to demonstrate, the power relationships overwhelm the metanarrative in American jurisprudence, what are the consequences for an American Indian orthopraxy? Does postmodernism offer anything beyond methods for exposing hypocrisy? As Litowitz (1997) has demonstrated, none of the major postmodern critiques of law offer convincing support for a positive jurisprudence.

Foucault (1978), in particular, offers penetrating critique without normative guidance. He argues persuasively that discipline used to come from the state acting on the body, but in our time discipline comes from "private" institutions (schools, factories, hospitals) acting on the mind. If he is correct about the puissance of subtle and diffuse power relationships that produce discipline outside of the juridical regime, then resistance may in fact be futile. Even when he seems to advocate resistance, his ideas are less than pellucid in identifying a point of attack (Foucault 1980). Moreover, the postmodern turn is as complicated in the descriptive sense as it is useless in the normative sense.

Dan Gunter (1998) has published a study of the Lemhi tribe's effort to establish federal recognition that imputes a Foucauldian power technology to the federal government. His observations are acute, but Foucault is a much more sophisticated tool than is necessary to explain federal obstruction of tribal recognition. A more parsimonious explanation is that the federal government simply wants to limit its responsibility to Indians by limiting the number of persons who can claim to be Indian, or to make tribal recognition difficult in deference to state governments' fears of losing property off their tax rolls and gaining unwanted casinos.

If the government is in fact taking a postmodern approach to Indian identity, what praxis follows from that insight? Should the Lemhi be recognized because the government is manipulating the terms of discourse? Will the government bureaucrats desist because their tactics are exposed? The Lemhi should be recognized, if at all, because they are a people whose political organization predates that of the United States, and the government bureaucrats will desist, if at all, when public opinion is mobilized to demand justice.

With the idea of justice, we return to the Rights of Man metanarrative, and the lack of correspondence between that metanarrative and the body of federal Indian law is our primary weapon. Even the ugliest imperial decisions – e.g. locking up Jesús Balzac for criticizing the colonial government – are couched in terms of an Enlightenment conception of human worth. Deconstructing the claim of fidelity to the Rights of Man metanarrative is where postmodern thought shows us a point of attack.

Indian orthopraxy is to place a wedge in the gap between human rights theory and human rights praxis and hammer it until the body of federal Indian law breaks, until the American people either do good or unambiguously embrace evil. If all that matters is power, we were lost at the turn of the last century. Postmodernism locates the contradictions in the colonial text but denies that truth and right are anything but contingent labels for power relationships. In the face of that, Indians require a narrative wherein resistance is not futile, because we will *not* be assimilated.

## REFERENCES

Alexander, James (1972). *A Brief Narrative of the Case and Trial of John Peter Zenger*. Cambridge, MA: Belknap Press.

Benjamin, Stuart Minor (1996). Equal protection and the special relationship: the case of Native Hawaiians. *Yale Law Journal*, 106: 537–612.

Clark, Blue (1999). *Lone Wolf v. Hitchcock: Treaty Rights and Indian Law at the End of the Nineteenth Century.* Lincoln: University of Nebraska Press.

Debo, Angie (1940). *And Still the Waters Run: the Betrayal of the Five Civilized Tribes.* Princeton, NJ: Princeton University Press.

d'Errico, Peter (2000). Native Americans in American politics. In *Encyclopedia of Minorities in American Politics,* ed. J. D. Schultz, K. L. Haynie, A. M. McCulloch, and A. L. Aoki, vol. 2. Phoenix, AZ: Oryx Press, pp. 569–80.

Deloria, Vine, Jr. (1994). *God is Red: a Native View of Religion.* Golden, CO: Fulcrum Publishing.

Dworkin, Ronald (1986). *Law's Empire.* Cambridge, MA: Belknap Press.

Fenton, William N. (1998). *The Great Law and the Longhouse: a Political History of the Iroquois Confederacy.* Norman: University of Oklahoma Press.

Fernandez, Ronald (1992). *The Disenchanted Island,* 2nd edn. New York: Praeger.

Foucault, Michel (1978). *Discipline and Punish: The Birth of the Prison,* tr. Alan Sheridan. New York: Random House. (Original work published 1975.)

Foucault, Michel (1980). *Power/Knowledge: Selected Interviews and Other Writings, 1972–1977,* tr. Colin Gordon et al., ed. Colin Gordon. New York: Pantheon. (Original work published 1977.)

Frickey, Philip P. (1997). Adjudication and its discontents: coherence and conciliation in federal Indian law. *Harvard Law Review,* 110: 1754–84.

Greenfield, Lawrence A. and Steven K. Smith (1999). *American Indians and Crime.* Washington, DC: Bureau of Justice Statistics.

Gunter, Dan (1998). The technology of tribalism: the Lemhi Indians, federal recognition, and the creation of tribal identity. *Idaho Law Review,* 35: 85–123.

Hester, Lee (2000). On philosophical discourse: some intercultural musings. Paper presented at Annual Meeting of the American Philosophical Association, Pacific Division, in Albuquerque, NM.

Johansen, Bruce E. (1998). *Debating Democracy.* Santa Fe, NM: Clear Light.

LaDuke, Winona (1999). *All Our Relations: Native Struggles for Land and Life.* Cambridge, MA: South End Press.

Litowitz, Douglas (1997). *Postmodern Philosophy and Law.* Lawrence, KS: University Press of Kansas.

Lyotard, Jean-François (1988). *The Differend: Phrases in Dispute,* tr. Georges Van Den Abbeele. Minneapolis: University of Minnesota Press. (Original work published 1983.)

Mohawk, John C. (2000). *Utopian Legacies: a History of Conquest and Oppression in the Western World.* Santa Fe, NM: Clear Light.

Montagu, Ashley (1997). *Man's Most Dangerous Myth: the Fallacy of Race,* 6th edn. Walnut Creek, CA: Alta Mira Press.

Norgren, Jill (1996). *The Cherokee Cases: the Confrontation of Law and Politics.* New York: McGraw-Hill.

Pommersheim, Frank (1999). Coyote paradox: some Indian law reflections from the edge of the prairie. *Arizona State Law Journal,* 31: 439–81.

Pound, Roscoe (1969). *Social Control through Law.* New Haven, CT: Yale University Press. (Originally published in 1942.)

Rawls, John (1971). *A Theory of Justice.* Cambridge, MA: Belknap Press.

Ross, Luana (1998). *Inventing the Savage: the Social Construction of Native American Criminality.* Austin: University of Texas Press.

Rousseau, Jean-Jacques (1762). The social contract. In *Social Contract*, tr. Gerard Hopkins. London: Oxford University Press, pp. 169–307.

Russell, Steve (1998). American Indians in the twilight of affirmative action. *Chicago Policy Review*, 2: 37–45.

Russell, Steve (1999). A black and white issue: the invisibility of American Indians in racial policy discourse. *Georgetown Public Policy Review*, 4: 129–47.

Strickland, Rennard (1975). *Fire and the Spirits: Cherokee Law from Clan to Court*. Norman: University of Oklahoma Press.

Supreme Court of the American Indian Nations (1999). *Lone Wolf v. Hitchcock*. *Kansas Journal of Law and Public Policy*, 8: 174–203.

Wunder, John R. (1994). *"Retained by the people": a History of American Indians and the Bill of Rights*. New York: Oxford University Press.

## FURTHER READING

Boyne, Roy (1990). *Foucault and Derrida: the Other Side of Reason*. London: Unwin Hyman.

Debo, Angie (1970). *A History of the Indians of the United States*. Norman: University of Oklahoma Press.

Deloria, Vine, Jr. (1969). *Custer Died for Your Sins: an Indian Manifesto*. New York: Macmillan.

Deloria, Vine, Jr. (1985). *Behind the Trail of Broken Treaties: an Indian Declaration of Independence*. Austin: University of Texas Press.

Derrida, Jacques (1981). *Dissemination*, tr. and ed. Barbara Johnson. Chicago: University of Chicago Press. (Original work published 1972.)

Dussias, Allison M. (1997). Ghost Dance and Holy Ghost: the echoes of nineteenth-century Christianization policy in twentieth-century Native American free exercise cases. *Stanford Law Review*, 49: 773–852.

Dworkin, Ronald (1977). *Taking Rights Seriously*. Cambridge, MA: Harvard University Press.

Foucault, Michel (1988). *Politics, Philosophy, Culture: Interviews and Other Writings, 1977–1984*, tr. Alan Sheridan et al., ed. Lawrence D. Kritzman. New York: Routledge. (Original work published 1984.)

Frickey, Philip P. (1993). Marshalling past and present: colonialism, constitutionalism, and interpretation in federal Indian law. *Harvard Law Review*, 107: 381–440.

Jacobs, Wilbur (1985). *Dispossessing the American Indian: Indians and Whites on the Colonial Frontier*. Norman: University of Oklahoma Press.

Kelly, Michael, ed. (1998). *Critique and Power: Recasting the Foucault/Habermas Debate*. Cambridge, MA: MIT Press.

Pound, Roscoe (1922, 1972). *An Introduction to the Philosophy of Law*. New Haven, CT: Yale University Press.

# 18

# ORAL TRADITIONS AND THE POLITICS OF (MIS)RECOGNITION

*Dale Turner*

To ask the question whether Indigenous oral traditions generate unique epistemological claims about the nature of reality is, on one interpretation, already to commit oneself to a particular way of understanding the nature of philosophy and especially what counts as legitimate philosophical inquiry. The way the question is framed points to an answer found within an already existing intellectual landscape. This landscape has largely evolved within Western European epistemological/metaphysical discourses, for which any good undergraduate introductory course in philosophy would provide at least a cursory knowledge of its 2,500-year-old tradition. And, as anyone who has studied philosophy knows, the normative discourses of epistemology and metaphysics very quickly immerse us in a kind of language that requires years of training to understand and use, never mind master.

But what happens when Indigenous peoples themselves ask the question? Then I believe we have to ask who the question is being directed to, and more importantly, why there is a need to ask the question in the first place. Western European philosophers don't have to concern themselves much with "who" they are directing their questions to; the great questions "What is the Truth?" "What is the nature of reality?" "What is the Good?", are, in part, great questions because they are eternal, fundamental, universal, and profound. At least that is how they have been understood in the Western European philosophical tradition. Indigenous peoples have answers to these questions too, but they don't constitute part of the Western European philosophical canon. Indigenous oral traditions have evolved in their own ways, and up until 500 years ago, independently of the Western philosophical tradition. From the early period of contact onwards, the survival of Indigenous peoples has depended on them explaining and justifying to the dominant culture who they are, where they came from, why they believe they possess special rights, and in many cases why they believe they remain sovereign nations.

Indigenous peoples claim that they have unique ways of understanding the world, and that the source of these understandings is embedded within the oral traditions. This claim ought to be understood as, not just a metaphysical claim about the nature of reality, but a foundational claim about the nature of the Indigenous–Colonial relationship. In this chapter I will explore the political significance of this claim and argue that there is an asymmetry of justification built into the legal and political relationship between Indigenous peoples and their colonial states. Focusing on North America I will show that a recent Supreme Court case in Canada, *Delgamuukw v. The Province of British Columbia* (Persky 1998), illustrates clearly the predicament of most Indigenous peoples. It is that Indigenous peoples have been forced to articulate metaphysical claims, that gain their normative force within tribal oral traditions, as political arguments. These political arguments are articulated in the Western European discourses of law and politics, the main consequence of which is that Indigenous metaphysics must be subsumed within the already existing legal and political practices of the dominant colonial culture in order for them to literally make sense.

These practices – the discourse of rights, property, nationalism, and political sovereignty, to name a few – no doubt have a rich, long intellectual tradition, and they have produced sophisticated, complex sets of overlapping practices and institutions. In the American context, these imposed institutions and practices have, over time, driven home a fact of life in Indian Country: political rights and tribal sovereignty can *only* be recognized and affirmed from within the legal and political practices of the dominant culture. This leads me to believe that most American Indian intellectuals ought to be devoting their energies, not to explaining away our ways of knowing the world – doing "metaphysics" and "epistemology" – but to asserting and protecting our political sovereignty within the dominant culture's existing legal and political discourses of rights and sovereignty. We should leave Indigenous ways of understanding the world where they belong – in the communities. The task of contemporary American Indian intellectuals, then, is twofold: to explain to the dominant culture why our ways of understanding the world ought to remain in our communities, and to assert and protect the sovereignty – nationhood – of our communities.

To put my position another way, it is of little importance to American Indians whether their ways of knowing the world are commensurable with European intellectual traditions (although it is of great importance for many academics that Indigenous knowledge be commensurable with European knowledge). American Indian intellectuals, at this point in the Indian–white relationship, should make it clear that the relationship between the tribes and the American governments is, to borrow a phrase from John Rawls, "political not metaphysical." The reason we do this is to assert from the outset that in the legal and political relationship our ways of knowing the world are not up for negotiation. The fact is that the central political and philosophical problem of the contemporary Indian–white relationship is the issue of political recognition. There is no doubt that the origins of the concept of tribal sovereignty have deep roots in

Western European philosophical and legal practices – although these practices have not evolved entirely without American Indian influences. I go as far as to claim that our survival depends on an American Indian intellectual community addressing these Indigenous influences and finding creative, critical ways to assert and defend how tribal sovereignty is recognized and put to use in American law and politics.

I will conclude this chapter with a brief discussion of how American Indian intellectuals can find ways of asserting and protecting tribal sovereignty within the hostile legal and political communities while retaining the integrity of their Indigenous identities. In the end, the fundamental issue at stake for all American Indian tribes is survival, and how do we, meaning Indigenous peoples, develop the necessary communities that are able to assert and protect what is rightly ours. An American Indian intellectual community ought to play an important role in securing this survival; however, the question of what this community ought to look like, and what an American Indian intellectual *is*, remains elusive and controversial. But, if the survival of tribal life depends on the dominant culture recognizing the legitimacy of our unique relationship to our territories, then at least some of our new warriors must be what I call "word warriors" – that is, American Indians who are educated in the white man's ways of thinking and, engaging in the white man's intellectual discourses, participating in the dominant culture's public intellectual life, and gaining greater access to the practices and institutions of the white man's legal and political communities. There is an attached imperative, though, and it is that they do so with their feet, hearts, and sense of belonging firmly situated in their communities – in other words, their work as word warriors is guided by the wisdom found in their oral traditions.

## JUSTIFICATION AND AMERICAN POLITICS

N. Scott Momaday writes, "The Indian and white man perceive the world in different ways. I take it that this is an obvious fact and a foregone conclusion. But at the same time I am convinced that we do not understand the distinction entirely or even sufficiently" (Momaday 1998: 50). One of the main themes of Momaday's work focuses on highlighting the incommensurable nature of European and Indigenous ways of understanding the world. For Momaday, the Indian experiences the world from within different, deeply embedded understandings of time, space, and human history. I am unable (and unwilling) to explain these metaphysical differences; instead, I will focus on the political dimension of asserting that these differences exist in the first place. Let me begin with a fact of the Indian–white relationship: if American Indians want to have their rights and sovereignty recognized by American legal and political institutions, they must do so using the already existing legal and political discourses of the dominant culture – the language of rights, the theory of political liberalism, the languages of nationalism and political sovereignty, to name a few. To make matters worse, the normative concepts that drive these discourses have evolved with little or no influence from American Indian intellectuals. American Indians must use a foreign language to explain the content of their rights, have very little to say about shaping its philosophical worth, and engage the institutions that enforce the decisions created by these discourses. Why? The answer is simple: to survive.

The contemporary reality is that as long as our rights and sovereignty are defined by these Western European discourses, *and* American Indian voices continue to be marginalized within the practices and institutions that shape the way these rights are recognized, our survival as distinct political communities becomes more and more tenuous. Put bluntly, the dominant culture recognizes our rights and sovereignty from within the legal and political practices and institutions of their culture. More importantly, Indigenous voices have not mattered much when their legal and political rights come up for negotiation because the content of these rights – moral obligations that entitle tribes to govern themselves – has been continually determined by the dominant culture.

Of course, American Indians have not stood by silently, nor have they been without some influence in determining the content of their rights and sovereignty. The point I am making here is that in a contemporary context, American Indians do not wield enough political power within existing governmental institutions to protect the sovereignty that most American Indians believe they still possess. The pendulum-like nature of federal Indian policy over the last two centuries ought to drive home the belief that, when it comes to American Indians, the Congress can, and does, do as it pleases. But the power that Congress holds over tribes can be understood in two ways. First, Congress exercises brute physical power over tribes: the American state can and does exert its physical power over Indians at any time, and it does so without accountability (unilateral interpretation, or blatant neglect, of the treaties, Indian Removal policies, Allotment, Reorganization, Termination, to cite a few examples). Second, Congress argues that it possesses *legitimate* power over tribes, which means that their actions are justifiable, and therefore moral, and further, that Congress's behavior is accountable to its citizenry. On this understanding of power, the blatant neglect of the treaties, Indian Removal policies, Allotment, Reorganization, and Termination can be understood as actions that were guided by a particular philosophical vision of a just political community.

Most Indians rightly believe that the first characterization is a more accurate description of the political relationship as it is understood in Indian Country. When one invests the time to understand the Indian–white relationship in some detail, it is hard to see it in any other way than as a relationship of treachery, violence, and domination. Yet, when one begins to investigate it in the context of the second way of understanding political power, we see a whole new dimension to the Indian–white relationship. To generate an explanation for *why* the American state believes it possesses legitimate political power over Indian peoples is to begin to understand the nature of American politics – especially American political philosophy. The complex relationships between equality, freedom, democracy, citizenship, and sovereignty have evolved over the course of several hundred years in American social and political life, and this has created uniquely American ways of understanding the nature of political justice. For American Indians, though, early European colonists stole Indian lands while many Euro-American intellectuals and philosophers consciously justified their behavior.

Judging from the contemporary political relationship, the connection between actions and justification hasn't changed much in Euro-American intellectual culture. Indian lands and resources continue to be stolen, American Indian powers of governance are still being threatened, while Congress still justifies its government's actions as moral and politically just.

The issue of justification matters to American governments; survival demands that it ought to matter to American Indians.

# THE ASYMMETRY OF JUSTIFICATION

No doubt, Congress has a strong hold on Indian Country, but that does not mean that American Indians are powerless. For example, American Indians have a lot to say about the nature of morality and political justice. The source of these Indigenous discourses lies in tribal oral traditions. These traditions – the stories, ceremonies, histories, and knowledge systems – have a long, venerable history, and tribal explanations of the moral and political only make sense within the normative languages of the particular tribe's oral tradition. American Indians have, time and time again, been forced to bring their explanations of who they are, and why they ought to be recognized as the true owners of their territories, into the white man's courts. Of course, the oral traditions have never been recognized as legitimate sources of legal evidence, so American Indian moral and political claims have been rationalized using the language of law. What counts as a legal explanation does not make sense within the oral traditions. Over time, American Indians have become intimately familiar with these legal discourses and with defending the rationality of their arguments in courts of law. Still, the natural home of legal arguments is not within the languages and intellectual traditions of the oral culture. The dilemma is that Indian communities must defend their rights in courts of law, but the discourses they use to justify the legitimacy of their arguments lies within the oral traditions of their people. American Indians must be legal experts, but the source of their moral and political explanations lies within an intellectual tradition the courts don't recognize as a legitimate source of legal evidence. This asymmetry characterizes the contemporary Indian–white relationship in that Indigenous sources of knowledge, while not recognized as legitimate within courts of law, must nonetheless be used to justify the legitimacy of Indigenous legal arguments.

The recent Supreme Court case of *Delgamuukw v. The Province of British Columbia* (or "*Delgamuukw*") is important for Aboriginal peoples in Canada because the Court is, in principle, prepared to do something about the status of the oral traditions in Canadian law. The decision was handed down on December 11, 1997, and is potentially one of the most important decisions on Aboriginal rights in Canada. In 1987, the Gitxan and Wet'suwet'en people of northwestern British Columbia initiated a lawsuit against the province of British Columbia seeking outright recognition of ownership of their traditional homelands. Their original claim in the Supreme Court of British Columbia was to have the court recognize them as the undisputed owners, and therefore possessing sole jurisdiction over their territories. For four arduous years the case was headline

233

news in British Columbia. But when Justice McEachern rendered his British Columbia Superior Court decision in the fall of 1991, he sparked a polemical and often volatile debate on the issue of Aboriginal rights and sovereignty in Canada.

One dimension of the *Delgamuukw* case that is worth examining is the legal strategy used by the First Nations in the British Columbia Supreme Court. Their legal argument consisted of two parallel arguments that, taken together, would fully justify their ownership of their traditional territories. The first argument incorporated a legal/political strategy, and involved interpreting the Royal Proclamation of 1763, the Constitution Acts of 1867 and 1982, and the legislation surrounding British Columbia's admittance to Confederation, and argued that the First Nations never consented at any time during the course of the legal and political relationship to give up their lands. The second argument involved an Indigenous explanation for ownership, and it was, at least initially, articulated in the language and traditions of the Gitxan and Wet'suwet'en people themselves. A number of anthropologists were used as expert witnesses in court, and they explained the oral traditions of the Gitxan and Wet'suwet'en. "The Gitxan Houses have an *adaawk* which is a collection of sacred oral traditions about their ancestors, histories, and territories. The Wet'suwet'en each have a *kungax* which is a spiritual song or dance or performance which ties them to their land" (Persky 1998: 26). Both of these practices claimed to be legitimate sources of evidence for the First Nations. The purpose of the first legal/political strategy was to argue that within Canadian legal practices and institutions, throughout the history of the relationship, the ownership of the First Nations' homelands was never justly ceded. The second strategy was meant to show that, within the understandings of the Gitxan and Wet'suwet'en oral traditions, they remain the rightful owners of their homelands. The first strategy showed that ownership had never been relinquished by the Canadian political and legal system, the second demonstrated that the Gitxan and Wet'suwet'en constituted legitimate political nations.

Both strategies failed in the Supreme Court of British Columbia: the first by the argument that the province, at the time of joining Confederation, inherited sovereignty over the entire territory of British Columbia, thereby extinguishing any possible claims of ownership by First Nations. In other words, at the time British Columbia joined Confederation they were recognized by the Crown to possess sovereignty over all of the territory. The only serious concerns regarding sharing sovereignty existed between the Crown and the province; the doctrine of extinguishment applied to British Columbia at the time the Crown unilaterally asserted its sovereignty. The second argument was, in many ways, much more disastrous for the First Nations. The "evidence," in the form of oral traditions, offered by the tribes to justify and defend the ownership of their territories, was summarily dismissed as unacceptable forms of legal evidence for Canadian courts. Justice McEachern was vilified by Aboriginal scholars and pro-Aboriginal rights advocates for his numerous Eurocentric comments about the nature of political societies, culture, and the epistemic relationship between knowledge and evidence.

The Gitxan and Wet'suwet'en appealed to the Supreme Court. This time they altered their claim in an important way which, amazingly, did not seem to cause much concern at the time – for either the First Nations or the province. The First

Nations no longer sought ownership of their territories, but rather sought recognition of "title" over their homelands. Aboriginal title, while being the strongest form of Aboriginal right in Canada (somewhat similar to "tribal sovereignty" in the United States), is not ownership. Title is a form of recognition that is firmly situated in the existing Canadian legal and political system. The powers entailed by possessing Aboriginal title, while they may be extensive, do not recognize the legitimacy of the First Nations' claim to outright ownership of their territories. Once the Gitxan and Wet'suwet'en accept that they possess title over their territories, they consent to a particular type of political relationship. The range of powers entailed by possessing title remains to be defined and protected within section 35(1) of the Constitution, but there is one definite shift in the dynamic of the legal and political relationship (at least from the state's perspective): the First Nations unequivocally embed their political identity under the sovereignty of the Canadian state, despite how their rights are defined and protected in the Constitution.

This point may be, at the end of the day, uncontroversial, especially if a First Nation chooses to seek title over their homelands. The more interesting claim, if one accepts the claim, as I do, that Indigenous nations *never* give up their status as nations in the course of the legal and political relationship, is when First Nations are recognized to possess title yet they still assert their status as nations. This leads to another kind of asymmetry of the legal and political relationship: Indigenous nations can justify their legal and political status in Canada using the legal and political discourses of the dominant culture, but it's the explanations generated by the oral traditions that matter most of the people. So the tension between "ownership" and "title" remains a central issue in the legal and political relationship, and the Supreme Court in *Delgamuukw* offers very little to resolve the tension.

The Supreme Court ordered a retrial stating that the evidence the Gitxan and Wet'suwet'en provided in court was meant to establish ownership and not title. But the Court went on to add that in the event of a new trial, the court must be more open to accepting the oral traditions as legitimate sources of historical evidence. This part of the decision was hailed as a victory for the Gitxan and Wet'suwet'en, and for all Aboriginal people. The Court also stated that litigation was perhaps not the best approach for resolving Aboriginal land claims and that a more "dialogical" approach between all concerned parties is preferable. Note that the Court states that the oral traditions must be accommodated so that they can be used to justify Aboriginal title, not ownership; in fact, there is never any mention of ownership. The problem for Canadian courts is to find the appropriate relationship between the oral traditions and recognition of Aboriginal title, and to define the content of Aboriginal title as it is protected in section 35(1) of the Constitution. The dilemma for Aboriginal nations is to have their colonial governments recognize the *sui generis* nature of their nationhood – justified by the oral traditions – while participating in the legal and political relationships dictated by Western European discourses of law and politics.

*Delgamuukw* is supposed to create the juridical space for a legal dialogue that respects Aboriginal oral traditions as legitimate sources of knowledge (evidence). I'm skeptical that this kind of accommodation is possible. There is an asymmetry of justification that is deeply embedded in the relationship between Indigenous ways of understanding ownership and Western European legal and political discourses that define political sovereignty, rights, and title. Ownership, in the Indigenous context, involves understanding Indigenous peoples' profound connections to their homelands. The notion of a "homeland" is not simply lands, but everything around one's world: land, air, water, stars, people, animals, and especially the spirit world. Understanding the balance in one's world takes a long time, and one cannot hope to learn these relationships without being guided by people who possess, and practice, these forms of knowledge. This knowledge is passed on by the oral traditions of the community, and virtually every Indigenous community practices the oral traditions in one form or other. The knowledge gained from the oral traditions shapes one's understanding of the world, it gives the world meaning.

The legal and political discourses of title, rights, and sovereignty are not without their own sources of knowledge. Arguably, the idea of political sovereignty and the language of rights goes back to Plato and Aristotle, through the Stoics, then on to Augustine, Aquinas, Vitoria, Grotius, Hobbes, Locke, Pufendorf, Rousseau, Tocqueville, Kant, Hegel, Marx, Weber, Berlin, Oakeshott, Arendt, Strauss, Rawls, Sandel, Taylor, Kymlicka, Tully, and too many others to mention. The point I'm making here is that there is a long intellectual tradition that has created a canon of Western philosophical knowledge. Many of these thinkers have written about Indigenous peoples. For example, the discourse of property was developed by John Locke in the seventeenth century; it has recently been argued that he deliberately designed his theory of property to exclude Indigenous forms of ownership. As another example, Hobbes has a notion of power and political sovereignty that requires a distinction between a "state of nature" and a "civil society," where, incidentally, American Indians are permanently located in the nasty and brutish state of nature. Immanuel Kant's views on rationality imply that Indigenous ways of thinking are irrational. Hegel defends the view that colonialism is a natural extension of a civil society. Political liberals view Indigenous rights as a form of minority right, which therefore can be subsumed within a more general theory of rights.

The discourses of rights and politics have their own intellectual history and to understand what something means is to understand how it is used within that particular tradition. For example, the idea of a right is central to the political liberal tradition. Indigenous rights, however, cause some controversy among liberal thinkers. If rights are trumps, as Ronald Dworkin claims, then Indigenous rights, on occasion, may trump other rights. This rubs many liberals the wrong way, since rights are possessed by individuals, and all individuals ought to possess the same package of rights – this is how the notion of equality is supposed to function in a just theory of rights. In the context of rights, for many political liberals, imposing sameness is better than recognizing difference. Of course, throughout the discussion of rights, especially Indigenous rights, there is no need for the Indigenous voice. The normative force behind the legal and political understandings of rights and sovereignty have essentially evolved without the need for Indigenous participation. Mind you, Indigenous understandings of ownership have no need for Western European participation, either.

The main difference is, of course, that Canadian and American courts of law do not have to justify their philosophical reasoning in the discourses of the oral traditions.

American Indians, on the other hand, must engage in legal and political discourses if they want to survive as distinct political communities. The question for the next generation of American Indian intellectuals, of which American Indian philosophers can play an important guiding role, is: what is the just relationship between our oral traditions and knowledge systems and the philosophical discourses that drive contemporary American legal and political thought? Should we leave our oral traditions in our communities? Or should we approach the relationship as a commensurable one – all we need to do is find the right template, the right theory, to help us explain our stories? If we choose to leave our oral traditions in our communities, how do we then protect our oral traditions, and the sovereignty of our communities, using the language and intellectual traditions of the oppressor?

These are not easy questions to answer. I believe one reason why American Indian intellectuals have such difficulty making inroads into mainstream intellectual communities is that there is not enough Indigenous representation. In one sense it is simply a numbers game. But there is a deeper issue at stake here that ought to cause us serious concern, especially when we reflect on the nature of the contemporary Indian–white relationship. This is the problem of survival. If Congress decided to get out of the Indian business (again), we would still survive. But that is not the kind of survival we wish for. Survival is deeply connected to having the American governments live up to what is right and just, and sometimes, when it comes to understanding the nature of our rights, we are the only ones that recognize what is a right and just course of action. This is informed by our traditions, but it is also understood within the context of the Indian–white relationship itself.

Throughout the history of the Indian–white relationship, our voices have been weakened, marginalized, subsumed, distorted, and outright ignored. Yet we are still here, and still confident that our ways of understanding the world are valuable and necessary for the survival of all people. Our ways tell us that this is not arrogance, but an empirical claim. But to believe that we will prevail despite all odds is naive at best and arrogant at worst. We have to, in some contexts, view ourselves as Indigenous peoples, meaning that all tribes have a few things in common, namely federal Indian law, the BIA, and hostile state governments. Therefore, one responsibility of an American Indian intellectual community is to defend the integrity, and legality, of tribal governments in the hostile intellectual community of the dominant culture. It's not my intention to draw boundaries around who does and does not count as an intellectual in this context, but it makes sense that American Indians trained in Western European philosophy would be in a good position to engage at least the legal and political discourses that drive the American legal and political communities.

I have labeled these intellectuals "word warriors" because their primary responsibility is to concern themselves with the way words are used, and the way words form intellectual landscapes, yet they must do so as citizens of Indigenous nations. These people are not "Society of American Indians" type of intellectuals. That is, they do not go out and get "educated" and return to their communities as enlightened individuals who are ready to take over leadership roles. The intellectual I envision will undoubtedly spend many years away from home, yet she will, in a sense, never have left home. This is because some of our children, if they are guided well, know what the community needs to survive. These children need to be nurtured from a young age, so that they grow up with a strong sense of who they are, and what their responsibilities are to themselves and their community. They are children who know their language, their ceremonies, their tribal history, while understanding that the survival of their people depends on knowing how to effectively engage in discourses that are mostly "about" Indians, or "for" Indians, and not determined by Indians.

A community of word warriors is a difficult one to imagine at this point in the Indian–white relationship. Part of the problem with getting an education, especially one in philosophy, is the issue of whether one can go home at all. The process itself, the way one comes to understand the nature of philosophical inquiry, what counts as rational or sound, becomes deeply embedded in the way one makes sense of the world. In other words, if philosophy is taken seriously, then one's identity comes up for negotiation. One response is to emphasize the importance of the family and community in shaping the identity of its word warriors, especially at a young age. Yes, word warriors function in a very lonely place. Often, they lie between two cultures, two nations, and I can imagine at times feeling like they belong to neither. Perhaps word warriors may only be required for a few generations, like a kind of strange Indigenous affirmative action policy. But the Indian–white relationship has evolved to this critical crossroads, and as *Delgamuukw* shows, if we don't speak up and argue – convince – and get what is rightly ours, who will?

## REFERENCES

Delgamuukw v. A.G., *Reasons for Judgment*, Supreme Court of British Columbia, Friday, March 8, 1991.

Momaday, N. Scott (1998). *Man Made of Words*. New York: St. Martin's Griffin.

Persky, Stan (1998). *The Supreme Court of Canada Decision on Aboriginal Title*. Vancouver, BC: Greystone Books.

# 19

# REPATRIATION: RELIGIOUS FREEDOM, EQUAL PROTECTION, AND INSTITUTIONAL RACISM

*Annette Arkeketa*

## HISTORICAL INTRODUCTION

The American Indian Religious Freedom Act 1978 (AIRFA), and the Native American Graves Protection and Repatriation Act 1990 (NAGPRA) are laws which became necessary to protect the religious freedom and equal protection rights of Native American people. The struggle necessary to uphold these constitutional rights made it clear that the history of federal policies and practices toward Native Americans is replete with institutional racism in the treatment of Native American sepulchers (burials). AIRFA and NAGPRA have met with resistance from federal and state agencies who argue that Native American bodies, grave goods, and patrimony items are the property of state and federal governments. Since the enactment of AIRFA and NAGPRA, archeologists and Native Americans have come together in an attempt to repair the damage done by the unethical and immoral grave-looting that occurred with the support of federal policies for over 400 years.

The Constitution of the United States is supreme law. Within the framework of the Constitution are a list of personal liberties (individual rights) more commonly called the Bill of Rights, or more formally called the Articles of Amendments. Most citizens of the United States take for granted that their rights outlined in this Constitution are upheld and acknowledged, and that laws and policies cannot deny American citizens these personal liberties. However, included in added Amendments are the abolishment of slavery (Amendment 13), voting rights for African Americans (Amendment 15), and voting rights for women (Amendment 19). Even though the preamble to the Constitution claims that the Constitution will insure the freedom and equality of all its citizens, people of color, women, and non-property holders were originally not citizens of the United States. Hence, the added Amendments have been necessary to protect the rights of *all* US citizens.

The First Amendment guarantees the right of religious freedom: "Congress cannot pass any law making any religion the religion of the United States, or take away the freedom to worship as one pleases" (Cullop 1984: 74). Religious freedom was paramount because of a long history of political/religious persecutions suffered by immigrants in their native European countries. Yet, paradoxically, it was necessary for Congress to pass AIRFA in 1978 to guarantee Indigenous peoples of the United States our religious freedom.

The Fourteenth Amendment also neglected to protect Native American rights. Because of the lack of equal protection regarding Native American graves, human remains, and funerary objects, NAGPRA was enacted in 1990. The need for NAGPRA exposed the practice of institutional racism toward Native Americans.

The excavation of Native American dead and of our funerary items has been a frequent and profane practice of pilgrims, army personnel, archeologists, and grave-looters for over 500 years. In 1620, Pilgrim William Bradford described in his diary the looting of Indigenous graves by an expedition led by Miles Standish: "and [they] took with them part of the corn and buried up the rest" (Bradford 1981). As Europeans invaded the North American continent, they continued to loot Indigenous graves of sacred food, funerary items, and our remains. Unfortunately, most of the exhumations of the dead and of funerary items have been sponsored by government policy.

Native Americans see the practice of exhumation as grave-robbing, no matter who the excavator is. Archeologists argue that they are helping preserve the culture of Native American people, yet the principles of Native American culture, including our theology, require respect for the remains of those who have passed on. Disinterring any remains, Native or non-Native, from a sepulcher is considered a disrespectful act and an assault on the spiritual well-being of the deceased, their family, community, and humanity.

Institutional racism toward Native Americans has the longest history of any racism in this country. Institutional racism is the practice of double standards taught and advocated at all institutional (governmental) levels of a society. It is the insidious, systematic singling out of a race, and the subjugating of that race by policy and practice. This practice diminishes humanity.

For Native Americans, systematic racism began during the first European immigrant invasion across this continent. The policy and practice of extermination of Native Americans began with the landing of Christopher Columbus in the Caribbean Islands, and DeSoto's arrival in Tampa Bay, Florida. Indigenous people were executed when we refused to become slaves or Christians. European immigrants followed, military forces greedy for land and resources; colonists caused continual conflicts with Native tribes for our land. Eventually, after many wars by the colonists against their native governments, a group of property holders formed a set of confederated states that created federal policies leading to military campaigns to exterminate all Indigenous people in order to colonize our land. Finally, when the federal government realized it could not exterminate successfully all the Indian people of the United States, it created other policies, like the Indian Removal Act (Pevar 1992: 4). This act removed many Native people from our homelands to other parts of the continent. The physical hardships, hunger, and sickness from the military policy of intentional smallpox infection, caused great suffering and took an enormous death toll during these forced migrations.

Federal policies were issued in the nineteenth century to destroy Indian religions (O'Brien 1995: 28). The federal government recognized that the foundations of Native cultural strength resided in religious practice. Legislators, descendants of immigrants, realized that if the federal government could destroy the religious practices, they could destroy our cultures. The government ordered a policy of imprisonment for Indian people who participated in our religious ceremonies (ibid.). Colonial insistence on forbidding the practice of religion at Wounded Knee, South Dakota, caused a massacre in 1890; some 390 unarmed men, women, and children were gunned down while performing the Ghost Dance. "Congress awarded thirty Congressional Medals of Honor to soldiers of the Seventh Cavalry" for participation in this genocidal event (O'Brien 1995: 29).

During these genocidal campaigns of religious persecution, many tribes went underground with our religious practices. Tribes closed off religious ceremonies to non-Indians, and in some cases to non-tribal members, in an effort to preserve our religions. Talking about religious ceremonies outside of our preparation for religious activity was tribally prohibited. Although there have been many books, articles, and recordings of religious ceremonies made available to the general public, many Native Americans today are still protective of our religious practices. We do not share our most sacred ceremonies with anyone outside of our tribal communities.

## POLICIES AND PRACTICES

James Riding In holds that the activity of grave-looting became prolific when sanctioned by President Thomas Jefferson (Riding In 1992b: 15). Jefferson excavated the burial mound near his Monticello property, motivated by curiosity and what he deemed "the name of science." Because the American public looked upon Jefferson's writings about the expropriation of Indian graves with admiration, his grave-robbing activity perpetuated the practice of opening Native American sepulchers across this continent.

In 1867 institutional policies were enacted by the US Surgeon General to solicit Indian crania: "Many of the Smithsonian's dead bodies were taken from fresh graves and battlefields by army personnel under an 1867 order of the US surgeon general, to procure Indian crania for government sponsored studies" (Echo-Hawk and Echo-Hawk, 1994: 67). Indian crania were dug up and procured by soldiers and head-hunters, who were generously compensated for their stealing.

Samuel Morton, the father of American physical anthropology, collected more than 1,000 skulls, including many of Native Americans. He was acclaimed for his work, allegedly proving that American Indians and African Americans ranked low in

241

intelligence as compared to Europeans. Morton's superior race theories supplied an economically convenient scientific justification for African American slavery. The notion that Indians were a genetically less intelligent, and a vanishing race helped justify the US Indian genocidal policy of the nineteenth century.

Superior race theories, although later discredited, supported institutional racism in the scientific community.

> [Morton] inspired American anthropologists to collect and study Indian skulls. By the beginning of the twentieth century large collections of Indian skeletal remains existed in universities and other institutions through the academic world. (Echo-Hawk and Echo-Hawk 1994: 25)

These policies created federal and state institutions – state historical preservation offices, museums, and university laboratories – that would eventually store and warehouse millions of Indigenous remains removed from their graves. Careers in anthropology to study these remains, artifacts, and grave characteristics, continue today. Archeologists did not seek permission to remove or disinter the millions of Native American people they have stored in their laboratories. Our communities do not approve of these activities, yet our concerns have been so routinely ignored by imperialistic policy that it is difficult for society to see the double standards that exist for American Indians.

During the Great Depression, the Works Progress Administration (WPA) recruited and hired archeologists and local laborers for massive dam and highway projects. Thousands of Native American human remains were excavated and collected. This was perhaps the greatest era of Native American death collections. The late Dr Kimball Smith, Fort Hood army archeologist, reported in a personal interview (January 17, 1999) that most federal institutions who acquired the Native dead still have these people in their institutions. He explained that the collection of these remains is on such a large scale that it is impossible for the archeologists to use all they have in their repositories; consequently, only a small percentage of the remains in storage are actually studied.

The number of Native American dead held in state and federal repositories outnumbers living American Indian people. According to the 1990 Census, there are 2 million Native American people in the United States. Roger and Walter Echo-Hawk refer to grave-robbing activity as the "invasion of the body snatchers"; they estimate that the harvest of "Indian dead held in museums, federal agencies, other institutions and private collections may be as high as 2.5 million," and that the "Smithsonian Institution alone has over 18,500 Indian remains" (Echo-Hawk and Echo-Hawk 1995: 67). This staggering figure is extremely difficult to conceptualize. The enormity of these crimes against humanity constitutes human rights abuse, according to Native Americans and non-Native peoples.

Repatriation is a new phenomenon for Native American people. Tribal people are overwhelmed by the facts surrounding the profane activity of grave desecration and looting. Despite the intentions of NAGPRA, the responsibility of reburial is a new issue in Indian Country. No other race has had to deal with the absurdity of reburial here.

Ancestral remains are considered sacred and precious, because our ancestors are the ones who pass on our traditions to us.

During the preparation for the reinterment of his people, Tonkawa spiritual leader Don Patterson gave an emotional and moving speech stating that our language does not have a word for reburial, and the question arises as to what the proper procedure is (meeting with Dell Web Corporation, AIREC, Tonkawa Tribe, Georgetown, TX, March 8, 1996). Repatriation has become a new ceremony for Native Americans and one that expresses feelings of spiritual distress.

The passage of AIRFA and NAGPRA has made it possible for Native Americans to deal with federal institutions that initially refused to recognize the federal mandates. These institutions have since begun work to repair their inhumane activities over the past 400 years.

Religious freedom, equal protection, and property rights did not protect Native American burial sites. Native Americans became victims of a double standard of Euro-American (white) looting. James Riding In, a Pawnee scholar, writes:

> While depriving Indians of burial rights white society has jealously guarded its own dead through the statutory process.... Until the 1970s ... non-Indians saw nothing wrong with the practice of taking bodies and burial offerings.    (Riding In 1992a: 101)

Before NAGPRA became a law, a common double standard used by the US Army was exposed when a non-Native cemetery site was inadvertently disturbed by environmental factors/military exercises. The army was willing to move the cemetery site if needed, and rebury the non-Native dead within days after the disturbance (with new coffins, if needed, and grave markers). Yet when a Native gravesite was disturbed for similar reasons, the army archeologists would excavate the Native person, and take the remains to their laboratory to be placed in their repositories (Shiloh Perkins, telephone interview, April 25, 1999). Now NAGPRA stipulates that the army must notify tribal authorities when burial sites are disturbed. However, this process is still problematic because tribal resources are limited, and tribal representatives are not always available to travel to these locations right away. While NAGPRA is a beginning for repatriation, clearly, there are still processes that need to be taken into consideration concerning these types of situations.

Native American gravesites are also a treasure for grave-looters. The institutionalized market for Native American "artifacts" made looting Native graves a profitable endeavor. Museums, auction houses, and flea markets are common trade markets for Native American remains and funerary objects. A list compiled by *American Indian Art Magazine* reveals total sales in the six figures for Indian artifacts (Johnson 1996: 158–9). Pictures are often used in these types of advertisements to reveal ornate, one-of-a-kind artifacts. The traditional burial practices of most tribes include dressing and adorning their dead relatives in their finest clothes, jewelry, prayer paraphernalia, with tools, food, or other items they will need to use in the spirit world. Grave-looters plunder these sepulchers, and Native people become aware of this bounty when they see museum displays, auction brochures, and inventory reports.

# ARCHEOLOGISTS, LAW, AND REPATRIATION

The repatriation of Native American human remains and funerary objects began with the persistent support of Native American Rights Fund (NARF) attorneys, Native American Indian organizations, tribal leaders, Native scholars, spiritual leaders, Indian archeologists, Indian anthropologists, state senators, Congressmen, and non-Indian people who supported Natives on this issue. Roger and Walter Echo-Hawk explain how the movement for repatriation began across the country before the enactment of NAGPRA. The historic landmark case of the repatriation of the Pawnee in Nebraska began the national movement that became the framework for NAGPRA. The institutional racism exhibited by the Nebraska State Historical Society (NSHS) office motivated the repatriation movement and was a grim reminder of past atrocities against Native peoples during the bitter times of war and of removal from beloved homelands by the federal government. The refusal of the NSHS to return Pawnee dead for reburial left the Pawnee with no other choice but to take the lead in the repatriation movement (Echo-Hawk and Echo-Hawk 1994: 60). They took up this cause and carried it to success with tenacity and perseverance to insure the repatriation of all Native Americans, beginning with the state of Nebraska, and leading ultimately to the enactment of the federal NAGPRA law. The hostile conduct of the NSHS director James Hanson reminded Native Americans that the roots of institutional racism were alive and well on the central Plains.

During the 1980s Lawrence Goodfox, Jr., was president of the Pawnee Business Council. Upon hearing that the NSHS had thousands of Indian remains, including Pawnee, he began to inquire about the Pawnee dead, and requested that they be returned to the Pawnee for reburial. The request came back with arrogant claims that the NSHS owned the Pawnee remains and accusations that the Pawnee wanted the remains back to sell for profit (Echo-Hawk and Echo-Hawk 1994: 60).

The NSHS also blocked public records that the Pawnee had requested to determine how many Pawnee were at the NSHS, so as to reveal and document grave desecration. After three orders from the State Attorney General's office to open the records, the Pawnee found that the graves had been opened without court orders sanctioning the removal of the bodies. The NSHS still refused to return the remains. The Native American Rights Fund fought the legal battle, for the Pawnee tribe, which led to Legislative Bill 340 in the Nebraska state legislature to protect graves and to require all museums in the state, including the NSHS, to honor tribal requests for the return of their dead. The bill was authored by Senator Ernie Chambers, who stated that

> everybody on the face of the earth is allowed to be concerned about what happens to the remains of their ancestors . . . except the indigenous populations of this country. And the purpose of this bill is to correct that.   (Echo-Hawk and Echo-Hawk 1994: 65)

Nebraska Legislative Bill 340 passed with overwhelming support from the citizens of Nebraska. Opponents were a small group of anthropologists who were bitterly hostile to it. On September 10, 1990, the Pawnee Tribe reclaimed the remains of more than 400 tribal ancestors from the NSHS museum. Robert Peregoy, NARF attorney who led the Pawnee efforts, described the reburial as a hard-fought victory (Peregoy 1992). Yet for American Indians this victory was just a beginning.

Though non-Indians have begun to support repatriation across the United States, the scientific disciplines of anthropology and archeology oppose the new legislative act, NAGPRA. Arrogant resistance and bitter opposition, mirroring the attitude of the NSHS, is expressed nationwide in repatriation review committee testimonies, in academic papers, and archeology journals. As Native peoples, we endure patronizing and condescending complaints from non-Indians, claiming that the scientific data obtained from Native American dead will be a valuable resource lost to the world. Native Americans have always wondered what the scientific value has been of all this research. As Native Americans continue to recover from the social, mental, material, and spiritual assault of past genocidal atrocities committed against us by the federal and state governments, we have a right to understand what significant scientific value is attributed to our ancestors' remains. Will scientific data help us recover from the genocide by the federal government? It seems unlikely that they will help humans eradicate disease, hunger, or poverty.

Vine Deloria, renowned American Indian scholar and distinguished Lakota activist, argues against the arrogant appropriation of the scientific community:

> the scientific community has never provided Indians with literature showing how experi-
> mentation with Indian remains is necessary, proper, or beneficial . . . archaeologists have
> never given the public a satisfactory explanation for why Indian remains are more valuable
> than those of other people . . . if this brand of study is as important as archaeologists claim,
> then this same type of inquiry should be launched in cities and towns across the nation to
> uncover information regarding malnutrition, premature deaths, and other human afflic-
> tions. Such a course of action would surely trigger an immediate public outcry.   (Riding
> In 1992b: 26–7)

While Deloria questions the institutional racist practices of archeology, osteologists Jerome C. Rose, Thomas J. Green, and Victoria D. Green (1996) argue: "the loss of these collections will be a detriment to the study of North American osteology, but the inventory and repatriation process has increased the number of skeletons studied from about 30% to nearly 100%." There is no clear explanation of how any of the osteology studies have benefited Native American people, other than to help identify the cultural affiliation of human remains for repatriation. Technology has made it easier to collect technical data needed for reports because of NAGPRA. The detrimental effect of NAGPRA, scientists fear, is that they will have no American Indian bones to study.

The Native American dead whose remains gathered dust in scientific laboratories for decades (or centuries) are now being studied because of the repatriation movement. Federal monies are now available for the scientists to hurry up their testing and research. If NAGPRA had not been enacted, the Native American dead may have sat in these scientific laboratories for many more years.

Riding In claims that archeology is an imperialist and racist endeavor, and the reburial of human remains is a fundamental human right. In his view collecting data on Native

American remains is unethical and immoral, and data collected from archeological research should be removed from universities and libraries because of their unethical acquisition (Ferguson 1996: 73). Native American people understand that our ancestors mean nothing more to the scientific community than data or hypothetical projects. Our sacred remains have been treated with gross disrespect, and stored in boxes and drawers in clinical laboratories. The discovery that our relatives are not treated with respect is a spiritual assault. Riding In proposes a ban on publications acquired through unethical means as an appropriate action to begin the healing of the spiritual assault felt by the descendants of the Native American dead.

Human rights activist Rigoberto Menchu, at a conference in Georgetown, Texas, an February 5, 1999, when asked what it would take for society to be forgiven, responded:

> forgiveness is strictly linked to truth and justice.... If someday I could take one of the perpetrators to justice then could I say that this is justice because I am one of the people victimized.... It is not our responsibility to ask for forgiveness ... human rights should be enforced.   (Menchu 1999)

This message speaks for Native people and how we feel about the harvesting of our dead. As victims of a double standard for human rights protection, we will continue to work for our human rights enforcement.

Archeologist Larry J. Zimmerman, a repatriation supporter, testifies that he almost left archeology after hearing one of his colleagues say that "the only good Indian is an unburied Indian" (Riding In 1992b: 28). The racist remarks indicate the backlash that occurred when the repatriation movement began to recognize that more archeologists were willing to cooperate with Native Americans to support repatriation. Riding In reports that

> one Princeton University professor of anthropology recently noticed that Indians continue to be the victims of a practice that is without scientific or moral justification.... Many scientists now agree that there are no overriding reasons to retain collections of recent Indian remains. Little research is done on these collections, and little new has been learned from them.   (Riding In 1992b: 28)

During the twentieth century, some Native Americans have become professional anthropologists and archeologists, and are leading our people in the repatriation movement. Some non–Indian archeologists and anthropologists are also dedicated to the repatriation movement. It is with their help that Native American remains desecrated for 400 years are finally being returned to sepulchers. In an ironic twist of circumstances, these professions have become an important resource for Native American people as we travel to rebury our dead. Unaccustomed to the clinical and institutional settings in which our dead are held, spiritual leaders are relieved when they meet Native American archeologists, museum curators, or representatives from the community who are Native American and are directing these institutional repatriations.

Traditionally, for Native Americans, the responsibility for the dead is reserved for tribal people trained to handle sacred occasions. Native American professional archeologists, anthropologists, and museum curators are seen as courageous and necessary today. They take on the responsibility to dismantle the racism and imperialistic dogma they know they will encounter from non-Indian colleagues. Dr. Dorothy Lippert is a Choctaw woman and an archeologist who just recently began her work at a museum in Houston, Texas. She reported (personal interview, 6 February 1999) that she braced herself because she knew she would confront the old possessive attitudes of archeology as she began her work for repatriation and the new federal policies of NAGPRA.

The process of NAGPRA is outlined in the act. In 1995 it was mandatory for all institutions to submit a summary of the inventories they had of Native American human remains, funerary objects and patrimony items to the NAGPRA Review Committee and to the tribe to whom the remains belong. The request was overwhelming to most institutions because resources were limited, or (later) because not all museums and archeological laboratories had money for the task. The review committee gave a one-year extension. In 1997 the Native American Review Committee met and federal agencies gave a report on the progress they were making to complete the inventories. The Department of the Interior, the Department of Transportation, the Department of Agriculture, and the Department of Defense gave reports of compliance. Most of the agencies who had Native American remains also had a "land base" on which they resided. For instance, military installations, national parks, and the Bureau of Land Management had significant inventories of Native American remains.

The NAGPRA Review Committee meets two times a year across the United States. This schedule gives Indian communities throughout the country an opportunity to attend, hear review committee recommendations, and make public comments.

Fort Hood, Texas, the largest military reservation in the United States, is one of the few federal agencies that have taken action to help in the repatriation of Native American remains. The Comanche National Indian Cemetery was established in 1991, initiated by the late Dr. Jack Jackson, who was the staff archeologist at Fort Hood when NAGPRA compliance efforts were being initiated there. Dr. Jackson, with the help of his assistant, Kimball Smith, and American Indian Resource and Education Coalition Repatriation chairman, Shiloh Perkins, began the task of designating a cemetery site on Fort Hood. With the help of Comanche Tribal chairman, Kenneth Saupitty, and spiritual leader, the late Woogie Wachetaker, they founded the site. A Memorandum of Understanding (MOU) was written and signed at Fort Hood, by the Army, the Comanche Otipoby Cemetery Committee, and the American Indian Resource and Education Coalition. The first repatriation was held in November 1991, with the reburial of 49 Comanche children. Their grave was found on Fort Hood and had been desecrated by looters. Their skeletal remains had been scattered over their gravesites. Since the Comanche tribe's repatriation, the Tonkawa people, Coahultecan people, and Kiowa people have repatriated their people at Fort Hood, which was once the home of these people as they lived nomadically across the plains.

Fort Hood has set a precedent in the repatriation of Native American remains on federal property. The cemetery is maintained by the American Indian Resource and Education Coalition, a non-profit state-wide organization dedicated to the human rights of Native American people in education, repatriation, and the law. The intent of the MOU between the three parties was to insure compliance with NAGPRA, but more importantly, to provide our people disinterred in that area with a reburial close to where they had their original sepulcher, and to seek protection from further looting of their graves. The army has placed a fence and other security measures around the area to protect the cemetery.

The journey for Indigenous people to reclaim our ancestors is also a reclamation of our constitutional rights. The passage of AIRFA and NAGPRA became necessary to guarantee these rights.

Our Native American ancestors who have been disturbed in their sepulchers are now returning. These ancestors taught us the ceremonial respect of burial. The significance of these ancestors has been one of spiritual guardianship and guidance for Native Americans today. Our ancestors are the ones who showed us how incredibly powerful are the spiritual forces in our land. Our ancestors once again are watching out for the well-being of their children. In a symbolic way they lead humanity in a struggle to protect human rights for all people. Now the children of these great people are returning our ancestors back to the earth, where we belong.

## REFERENCES

Bradford, William (1981). *Of Plymouth Plantation 1620–1647*. New York: Modern Library.

Cullop, Floyd G. (1984). *The Constitution of the United States*. New York: Signet.

Echo-Hawk, Roger C. and Walter R. Echo-Hawk (1994). *Battlefields and Burial Grounds: The Indian Struggle to Protect Ancestral Graves in the United States*. Minneapolis: Lerner.

Echo-Hawk, Roger C. and Walter R. Echo-Hawk (1995). Repatriation, reburial and religious rights. In *Handbook of American Indian Religious Freedom*, ed. Christopher Vecsey. New York: Crossroad, pp. 63–80.

Ferguson, T. J. (1996). Native Americans and the practice of archaeology. *Annual Review of Anthropology*, 25: 63–79.

Johnson, Harmer (1996). *Mending the Circle: A Native American Repatriation Guide*. New York: American Indian Ritual Object Repatriation Foundation, pp. 158–79.

Menchu, Rigoberta (1999). Panel discussion. Brown Symposium, Southwestern University, Georgetown, Texas, February 5.

O'Brien, Sharon (1995). A legal analysis of the American Indian Religious Freedom Act. In *Handbook of American Indian Religious Freedom*, ed. Christopher Vecsey. New York: Crossroad, pp. 27–43.

Peregoy, Robert M. (1992). Nebraska's Landmark Repatriation Law: a study of cross-cultural conflict and resolution. *American Indian Culture and Research Journal*, 16, 2: 139–95.

Pevar, Stephen L. (1992). *The Rights of Indians and Tribes: The Basic ACLU Guide to Indian and Tribal Rights*, ed. N. Dorsen, 2nd edn. Carbondale: Southern Illinois University Press.

Riding In, James I. (1992a). Six Pawnee crania: historical and contemporary issues associated with the massacre and decapitation of Pawnee Indians in 1869. *American Indian Culture and Research Journal*, 16, 2: 101–19.

Riding In, James I. (1992b). Without ethics and morality: a historical overview of imperial archaeology and American Indians. *Arizona State Law Journal*, 24: 11–34.

Rose, Jerome C., Thomas J. Green, and Victoria D. Green (1996). NAGPRA IS FOREVER: osteology and the repatriation of skeletons. *Annual Revue of Anthropology*, 25: 81–103.

# Part VIII

# ESTHETICS

# 20

# ETHICS: FROM AN ARTIST'S POINT OF VIEW

*V. F. Cordova*

When a young person finally makes the decision to become an artist he, or she, takes on a new persona. The persona, or role, is that of an individual who is separate and apart from his community. He dons new apparel – usually something which will be found to be annoying to the community. The new persona requires a new attitude: one of extreme egocentrism. The artist's role becomes a means of finding a unique form of "self-expression" because art, if it is anything at all, is the ultimate form of *expression*.

But the artist is another society is seen in a totally different light. An artist need not be a Bohemian on the fringe of society, and perhaps more related to the madman than to the healer and the scientist. The artist, like the scientist, is a seeker of knowledge. He examines the world and portrays what he has learned in order to share that knowledge with his community.

The role of an artist need not be that of someone trapped in a stage of semi-adolescence. He can be a thinker particularly adept at *showing* what he has thought or discovered about the world around him.

There is a background to this latter description of the artist just as there is a background to the former. The backgrounds are embedded in metaphysics: a specific way of defining the world.

The artist who strives to show himself as a disrupter of the world sees himself as portraying the chaos which is inherent in the universe. All order is mere appearance, unreal, and of a contingent nature. Order is dependent on the whim of a god, or gods, who proclaim, "Let us create. . . . " Existence, itself, is contingent upon the whim of the gods. If there is order in the universe after the initial creation it, too, is of a dependent and arbitrary nature. The artist, alone, sees the inherent chaos and flaunts it, forces it upon the unsuspecting viewer.

The artist as *scientist* operates from a different set of metaphysical constructs: there is, essentially, an orderly universe. It is an active, moving, living universe, and that motion occasionally exhibits chaos. The chaos, too, is essential: it is a readjustment, a resettling of the universe. Chaos is temporary; order is dominant. Humans are disturbed by the chaos – the unknown, the unpredictable. It is the role of the artist to find the underlying stability in chaos in order to help his viewers understand chaos as well as order.

The artist as disrupter is the Western artist. He is either a creator of order in a chaotic universe or a skeptic who throws back the veil that masks the chaos. He is, himself, an example of chaos – going beyond what he sees as the arbitrary nature of his community by exposing his own innermost self as sheer chaos.

The artist as scientist, even as healer, is the Native American artist; he it is that occupies the ordered and measured universe. He represents a point of stability that endures all change, absorbs and transforms all chaos.

The artist in the Native American community is not an alienated individual pleading for understanding for his own and, thereby, unique view. Native American communities do not disregard the uniqueness of the individual. The uniqueness is, however, a mere given. No other individual is like the one individual. But the individual is a product of the group that produces and nurtures him. The individual appears amidst a group of known individuals: he may have the eyes of his grandfather, the hair of an uncle, the walk of a distant cousin, the temperament of an admired individual. But he enters the group as an unknown that must be molded into the form of a human being that is recognized by the group.

The Western individual is seen as essentially complete when born. It is from this sense of an individual as "pre-formed" that the concept of a "true self" may be derived. Society exists, not to assist in the creation of a human being, but to abolish the uniqueness of the individual. Each individual, though potentially a positive force for the group, is in need of teaching, training, molding, before he can accomplish anything of value. Without the training, or "discipline," the individual may be a negative force.

The Native American, as well as the Westerner, realizes the need for what we call "socialization." But the approaches are different. The Native American waits to see what the new compilation of the group's genetic material has produced. Many Native American groups do not consider children under the age of 5 as "real" persons. The newborn is merely humanoid and must be introduced to the mores of the group under the dictum that "he has never been here before." There is no attempt to "mold," or "train," the individual into what the group wants. The individual is seen as having brought particular gifts into the group. The group need only offer opportunities for the child to exhibit his talents. The introduction into the group consists in the development of the child's awareness of the consequences of his actions on others. It is when the child exhibits such awareness (around the ages of 5 to 8) that he is counted as a "real" person.

By the age of becoming a "real" person the child has also shown some particular interests in certain fields of endeavor. The artist in a Western community is a result of training. There is a stigma of sorts attached to the artist who does not undergo such training that is summed up in the phrase "self-taught." Most Native American artists are of the self-taught variety because of the path that is followed in becoming an artist.

The artistic child will be encouraged to associate with an adult that exhibits the same type of talents. No one "teaches" the child how to do anything. "Being" as an artist is not a matter of learning a few techniques – it is a way of being.

As a child I was encouraged to visit a grand-aunt who wrote. She taught me nothing in the manner of saying, "First, you must. . . . " Instead I watched what she did in the course of her day. Another grand-aunt liked to do embroideries, and I watched and experimented. She pointed out frogs hidden under strawberry leaves along a ditch bank. She taught me the joys of observation in long, ambling walks culminating with a popsicle while we dangled our feet in an irrigation ditch. I watched her observations turn into embroideries.

Today, when I encounter those who see what I do and then ask me for the name of a stitch or the technique, I am speechless. The stitch appeared because it fits. The technique appeared because it was the only thing that would work in a particular circumstance.

There is no distinction made in Native American societies between those who are called artists and those who are not. All people in traditional societies were expected to know how to make things. Some people got very good at some things and chose to do those things while leaving other things to other people. (Somewhere along the way, perhaps through continued practice or through inclination, others recognize the fact that a particular craftsman has reached a state of art.) The maker of such things does not declare himself an artist. The title is a label that others use in recognition of particular accomplishments.

An artist, the individual, has a certain responsibility in the community. The talented individual is not seen as a "self-made" person. The talents are more likely the result of genetic chance. What the artist has is the result of a gene pool and the administration of the group. The artist has the responsibility to share what he does with the group. He cannot be stingy or self-centered.

The Native American artist is not, as is often the Western artist, seen as an exception to the rules of the community. He cannot excuse his behavior on the grounds that he is "an Artist." He does, instead, bear a greater responsibility to the group. And this again is dependent on another metaphysical factor.

The Native American world is a world in constant transition – the world, in other words, is not a thing made once and finished. It is always in the process of *being*. "Being," for the Native American, is not a static state but one of motion and change. The human being is part of the universe – he is as much a part of the universe as is the butterfly in the theory of chaos. In *chaos theory* there is nothing that exists in isolation from anything else and there is no action that does not bring into existence a reaction: a butterfly flapping its wings in Honduras sets off a series of events (waves) that might or might not culminate in a hurricane in Florida. Every action of a human being has a consequence.

The artist, in bringing forth new creations, in effect is assisting in the creation of the world. If chaos is disruptive to human beings, why would the artist bring chaos into the world? If beauty and order are conducive to human well-being, why would he not bring into the world more beauty and more order?

The idea that humans affect their world is not a minor idea in a Native American view. What is said is brought into being. In the West, imaginative excursions are encouraged: that, it is thought, is the source of creativity. In the Native American view imagination is also subject to discipline. What I imagine may bring harm into the world – if I not only hold the thought or the image but also give it substance, I am responsible for adding to the world a new thing. If I portray ugliness, I have thrown it into the world and it, too, will have consequences. The ugliness to which I give substance on my canvas may, like the butterfly's wings, have tremendous consequences. This does not mean that I cannot be creative. Creativity implies working something into a new fashion.

There is a Navajo chant that speaks of Beauty. It is a chant that encourages one to "walk in beauty":

> In beauty (happily) I walk
> With beauty before me I walk
> With beauty behind me I walk
> With beauty below me I walk
> With beauty above me I walk
> It is finished (again) in beauty
> It is finished in beauty.
>
> (Washington Matthews, [translated from] *The Night Chant*
> [1900s], quoted by Ruth M. Underhill in *The Navajos*.
> Norman: University of Oklahoma Press, 1956, p. 212)

The chant has a dual purpose: (1) it reminds one that the world is a place of beauty; and (2) it reminds one also to add to that beauty.

For the Native American there is not, nor can there be, a distinction between esthetics and ethics. The universe is a good thing – the goodness is inherent in the fact that the moving, living universe operates on the principles of balance and harmony. The human being, a part of that universe, also holds to those principles. In art and in life the role of the human is to maintain balance. But balance, again, is not stillness; it cannot connote anything static.

My father described life as like constantly shifting sand. On that shifting sand I lay down a barrel and on that barrel I place a board. My duty is to stand astride that plank and maintain my balance as the sand shifts. My actions can be neither sudden, nor erratic. I maintain my balance by maintaining a certain harmony with the motion that I am reacting to. If violent action surrounds me, I maintain my stance, knowing that the action is only temporary. It is also necessary that I examine my own actions as a possible source of such action. Have I, even unknowingly, contributed to the creation of violence? If there is ugliness around me, can I counter that with the creation of beauty?

In the West, the works of an artist are nearly meaningless. The artist is not a co-creator of the world. He is, at most, an entertainer. In Native America, the artist is a scientist showing what others have not previously seen. The artist is a healer – bringing us into harmony when we might have fallen away.

> The sand painting is a healing ceremony performed to bring back the afflicted
>     into balance and harmony with the world.
> The canvas paintings are a display of order. An ordering.
> The jewelry is a creation of order.
> The rug is order.

The principles of esthetics and of ethics are balance and harmony – beauty. The principle of the artist is responsibility. As co-creator, as healer, as scientist.

# ALONG THE HORIZON A WORLD APPEARS: GEORGE MORRISON AND THE PURSUIT OF AN AMERICAN INDIAN ESTHETIC

*David Martínez*

The Ojibwa artist George Morrison once said: "I believe in going back to the magic of the earth and the lake, the sky and the universe.... I believe in that kind of religion. A religion of the rocks, the lake, the water, the sky" (Morrison 1998: 29). What Morrison really worshiped was the splendor of Lake Superior, upon whose shores he lived and painted. Indeed, it would be the looming presence of this body of water, next to whose shores Morrison was born, which would inspire his most interesting body of work, known collectively as the "Horizon Series." What distinguishes these paintings is the way in which Morrison summons the many moods of the lake with the elusive vocabulary of abstract painting. In fact, Morrison captures the spirit of the lake by looking beyond the lake itself to the horizon. But what makes the horizon such a compelling subject, which is really not a subject in the same way that a lake or a forest is a subject? Moreover, what is implied by Morrison's reverential attitude toward Lake Superior as a sacred place? Lastly, in what way is Morrison using the vocabulary of abstract painting that is consistent with his Ojibwa tradition?

According to Morrison, the phenomenon of the horizon has been infiltrating his imagination since he began staying in Provincetown, Massachusetts, during the 1950s, while taking breaks from the art scene in New York. It was in Provincetown that Morrison applied his skills as an abstract artist to the found objects he discovered along the New England shore, such as whale bones, starfish, and shells. Nonetheless, the horizon would not actually emerge as a conscious subject until toward the latter part of Morrison's long career, during the 1980s and 1990s. By then, he had long since found his home at Grand Portage, near the lake that the Ojibwa named "Kitchi-Gami." Furthermore, Morrison created his horizon paintings at a time when his own style had reached its apex and the years of Abstract Expressionism – a major influence on his early work – were far behind. What appears in the horizon paintings, then, is less a concern for breaking free of any tradition – be it academic or cubist – and more of a meditation on his place of origin. Yet, despite his unquestionable Ojibwa heritage, Morrison does not engage in so-called "Indian Painting," complete with its obvious symbols of "Indian" culture. On the contrary, Morrison's "authenticity" comes through the act of painting itself. As such, he shares in the reverence of nature, including the lake, which is common to the Ojibwa tradition. However, that reverence is expressed in a very individual language, which is consistent, not only with the tenets of Abstract Expressionism, but also with a native culture that values dreams as a source of insight and inspiration. Morrison, in fact, accounts for all of his paintings as having emerged from his imagination, which is really, he claims, a connection to his "subconscious." The result of this technique, which is probably better described as a lifestyle, are paintings that incite an immediate effect, free of the burdens of narrative. "You didn't have to look for a story in the picture," as Morrison asserted. "You could look at an abstraction and have an immediate reaction" (1998: 75–6). It would be this kind of response, a concrete moment between painting and viewer, which Morrison would create in his Horizon Series. In other words, Morrison would bring into his paintings the kind of feelings he experienced between Lake Superior and himself.

Upon entering a gallery filled with Morrison's paintings, you enter a place in which time and space loosen up to become movement. Morrison's paintings make you *feel* Lake Superior even if you have never seen the lake before in person. The paintings instead are an experience in their own right. Without any recognizable referents, Morrison evokes a world before there were humans and language, so that these works appeal first to the senses before they tantalize the intellect. James Billings, in an appropriately small anthology, titled *Morrison's Horizon*, described his reaction this way:

> These paintings are scanned from left to right, from bold and aggressive motifs to subtle, more passive imagery. Eventually one is led into the artist's quiet mood. Morrison's small works require close attention, bringing you into the color and light of the moment he's captured. His works evoke meditation, the mood which created them. One breathes more deeply, more slowly – the deeper the breath, the fuller the work, the deeper the breath. An ambient rhythm of self-sustained spirit stirs the subconscious. (Morrison et al. 1998: 21)

But how does the horizon itself, as a natural phenomenon, play a part in creating such reflective moods? In other words, what is a horizon? Of these small-scale, intimate paintings, which all contain a horizon line about one-third of the way down the canvas, Morrison said: "I think of the horizon as the edge of the world. . . . From the horizon, you go beyond to the unknown" (Morrison et al. 1998: 34). Unlike Pascal, though, Morrison was genuinely fascinated and even comforted by the vastness of space, because it is along the horizon that the "mystery" of life appears. However, before we delve deeper into that mysteriousness, we need to consider the horizon as a natural phenomenon and, more specifically, as a motif for organizing space in the painting.

According to Edward S. Casey in *Getting Back into Place*, the horizon is the ultimate organizer of place. More specifically, the horizon is contingent upon our sense of nearness and farness with respect to our orientation within a given place. In other words, the horizon results from the lived-body taking its place and orienting itself to the surrounding directions of the environment in which it dwells. It is through the lived-body, Casey argues, that our sense of direction emerges. For as we move about a place, the various objects that make up the place are constantly arranging themselves in our perceptual field as before or beside us, above our heads or at our feet, close to us or far away (Casey 1993: 48). In turn, one remembers the placing of objects in terms of how they relate to certain landmarks that seem to dominate the landscape, such as a village, a mountain, a stream, a cliff, or a lake. It is within these surroundings that we witness the rising and setting of the sun and moon, the slowly shifting patterns in the stars, or the place from where storm clouds appear. But without the lived-body assuming its place in this scene there could not be any directions because a direction presumes that something *needs* directing, be it a human in search of game or animals in search of a winter home. "Long before we learn astronomy or geography (much less modern physics)," Casey writes, "we already have reliable orientational knowledge of these places; thanks to our 'knowing body,' we know how to find them and live in them, how to be here in their presence" (Casey 1993: 52). This is to say that our bodies remember the paths that link the components that makeup our world, including the views that arise along the way, indicating that we are headed in the right direction. In the case of George Morrison and his return to Minnesota from New York, his then wife, Hazel Belvo, recalled that when they were looking for the right place to build a home and studio, they were told by an Ojibwa spiritual leader, "when your magic appears to you, you will recognize it" (Morrison et al. 1990: 27). It was at that point that Morrison and Belvo discovered Red Rock. It would be *here* at Red Rock that the Horizon Series would emerge. Moreover, the word "here" is emphasized as a term defining place because it is *being here* from which our knowledge and understanding of place truly derives.

It is from *here* that we ultimately organize our perception of the world, at least as we experience it. We may have longings to be elsewhere at times, but even these episodes, be they induced by homesickness, being lovelorn, or the yearning for adventure, are ineluctably oriented towards the *here* at which we are always abiding. Implied in this is the suggestion that harmony in one's life prevails only when the *here* in which we happen to be coincides with the *here* where we want to be. For an American Indian, that usually means being in the place – a homeland – created specifically for your people. In many creation stories, a people's homeland was created out of the watery depths that existed before there was any earth, sun, moon, or even people. Basil Johnston, in *The Manitous*, speaks of Kitchi-Manitou, "The Great Mystery," as the power that created the world as a fulfillment of his vision, which is to say that Kitchi-Manitou *dreamed* the world into existence. This world would be flooded, and as it sank, taking all life with it, a new being was born in the skies. Sky Woman would emerge as the female god who created the next world in the manner set by Kitchi-Manitou. Sky Woman, according to Johnston, took the earth from Muskrat's paw, after he dove into the depths to retrieve it, then spread it around the rim of Turtle's back, who had offered the top of his shell as the foundation for the newly created world. Sky Woman then breathed life into the land, infusing it with the powers of "giving life, nourishment, shelter, instruction, and inspiration for the heart, mind, and spirit" (Johnston 1995: xv–xvi). In turn, Gerald Vizenor recounts, in *The People Named the Chippewa*, a tale of Naanabozho, a trickster figure, who after the great flood has destroyed the previous world is found atop a tree with water floating up to his mouth. Naanabozho soon noticed other animals in the water, such as a beaver, muskrat, and otter. One by one, Naanabozho asked each animal to swim to the bottom of the ocean to find some "earth," out of which could be made a home for them all. Otter and Beaver failed, but Muskrat returned with some earth in his paws. "Then the trickster took the grains of sand in the palm of his hand and held them up to the sun to dry them out. When the sand was all dry, he threw it around onto the water. There was a little island then" (Vizenor 1984: 9). What is important to note here is that Naanabozho re-created the world in imitation of both Kitchi-Manitou and Sky Woman, similar to the way you retell a story in your own words. Thus, the Story of Creation itself is a creative act. As Gerald Vizenor asserts: "In the oral tradition, the mythic origins of tribal people are creative expressions, original eruptions in time, not a mere recitation or a recorded narrative in grammatical time" (1984: 7). Consequently, stories are never told the same way twice because doing so would eliminate the spirit of creation that is integral to this kind of story.

Morrison imbues his paintings with the lessons of the Ojibwa oral tradition. He never paints the same lake twice. "I am fascinated by ambiguity," Morrison states, "change of mood and color, the sense of sound and movement above and below the horizon line. Therein lies some of the mystery of the paintings: the transmutation, through choosing and manipulating the pigment, that becomes the substance of art" (Morrison 1998: 170–1). What appears in Morrison's paintings is a world that, on the one hand, is inspired by a place that has both English and Ojibwa names, yet, on the canvas, is a space empty of nominal objects, but full of lights, shades, and moods. In a way, it is a preliterate world. Morrison accomplishes this by concentrating his paintings on the horizon. For when you focus on the horizon you are not training your perception on any object in particular occupying the foreground. In looking beyond the landscape to the horizon, the various objects that comprise a place begin to lose some of their solidity, at least in terms of how you apprehend their forms.

For the Ojibwa, things are not ultimately defined by their physical characteristics but by their spiritual qualities. More specifically, the Ojibwa, as Christopher Vecsey portrays them in *Traditional Ojibway Religion*, believed that "the ultimate sources of existence were extremely powerful beings called manitos." The manitos, in fact, were embodied in various aspects of the earth, and it was imperative that the Ojibwa learn how to live with the manitos if they wanted to survive in their homeland (Vecsey 1990: 4). For the land did not really belong to the Ojibwa but to the manitos, of which Naanabozho and Sky Woman are examples. They are the power of life and death, as it was the manitos who controlled such things as weather and game. Consistent with this worldview is the notion that Lake Superior is home to the Underwater Manito. The Ojibwa who lived near the lake offered it sacrifices for the sake of obtaining fish from its waters. Just as important was the recognition that the Underwater Manito was responsible for stormy waters, which could sink canoes and drown the passengers. At the same time, the Underwater Manito would also provide the Ojibwa with medicine and copper; it has even been known to shelter some who fell through the winter ice (1990: 74). "It was a creature," Vecsey writes, "to inspire terror and awe, as well as reverence. Without the aid or benign neglect of this being – part snake, part catfish, part lynx, part mountain lion – the Ojibwas would surely starve or suffer death in raging waters" (1990: 75).

What I see in the paintings that constitute the Horizon Series is not the "spirit" of the lake in some superficial sense, rather, I see the various faces of the Underwater Manito. These are powers that otherwise lie hidden from our profane vision, which does not know how to perceive objects except for what they yield in terms of form and function. "This magic of the artist," as Morrison reminds us of the primal roots of all artists, "works with the magic of nature in change. The rock, which I began to regard late in life, has a presence of its own, and the water is a living force, moving and changing. The same changing in the wind – that phenomenon of nature we can't even see, but it has a sound and presence of its own" (1998: 174–5). The horizon, too, is like the wind – a phenomenon we can perceive but never really apprehend. For as we move about any given place, the horizon is that which constantly moves away from us as we approach it, yet which never leaves our perceptual field.

As Casey proclaims, in the spirit of Heidegger, "the horizon is a boundary, not a limit" (Casey 1993: 61). It is this way due to the fact that the horizon is never literally a "line," but a place where we perceive the environment entering our field of vision from its farthest reaches. "The horizon of the far sphere," Casey observes, "is not itself an object but a boundary *for* objects. It is not so much *in* the world . . . as *with* the world as an outermost part" (1993: 62). Ultimately, the horizon embraces the many places of the *here* in which we dwell. "The basic thing in all the paintings," Morrison points out, "is the horizon line which identifies each little work as a broad expanse of a segment of the earth" (Morrison 1998: 169).

Paradoxically, because Morrison actually draws a "horizon line," usually with red pencil, across each of his Horizon paintings, what he creates is a complement to the phenomena that he observes outside of his studio windows. Whereas the horizon in nature is an ambiguous phenomenon emerging out of concrete objects, such as the lake and forest around Red Rock; the horizon line in Morrison's paintings is the only object that appears unequivocally within a composition of amorphous shapes and colors. Morrison, for as much as he reflects on the lake, does not *look at* the lake while he paints. Nonetheless, natural phenomena enter the paintings, which Morrison *interprets* "in an abstract way" (1998: 168). In this manner, Morrison is like the Ojibwa storyteller who, in the middle of winter, can invoke the animal spirits of the forest and lake without having to point at what his words sufficiently evoke. "The teller of stories is an artist," as Vizenor puts it, "a person of wit and imagination, who relumes the diverse memories of the visual past into the experiences and metaphors of the present" (Vizenor 1984: 7).

At this point it is appropriate to emphasize that during Morrison's long life as an artist, he never portrayed himself as an "Indian artist," but rather as "an artist who happened to be Indian" (Morrison et al. 1998: 32). In fact, Morrison would recall times early on when his work was rejected by institutions like the Philbrook Art Center, a major supporter of American Indian artists, because it was "too extreme; it wasn't Indian enough for them" (Morrison 1998: 70). In other words, Morrison was criticized for not painting genre paintings that were and still are quite popular among American Indian and Western Americana collectors, such as dancers in full regalia or warriors on horseback. On the contrary, Morrison had the audacity to explore the nature of painting itself, especially its capacity for expressing his relationship to the environment. "The basis of all art is nature," as Morrison would proclaim, "it creeps in even to abstract art. The look of the North Shore was subconsciously in my psyche, prompting some of my images" (1998: 146). What Morrison created, according to James Billings, was images that "evoke feelings of empathy, spirituality, and respect for nature" (Morrison et al. 1998: 9).

I would argue that on the basis of Morrison's respect for both his medium and his environment his work is "authentically" American Indian or, more specifically, Ojibwa. For what Morrison establishes through his work is a genuinely American Indian esthetic. "I have never tried to prove I was Indian through my art," Morrison asserts. "Yet, there may remain deeply hidden some remote suggestion of the rock whence I was hewn, the preoccupation of the textual surface, the mystery of the structural and organic element, the enigma of the horizon, or the color of the wind" (Morrison 1998: 141). In the tradition of his Ojibwa ancestors, not the least of whom are Kitchi-Manitou, Sky Woman, and Naanabozho, George Morrison has dreamed a world into existence. It should be reiterated, however, that dreams in Ojibwa culture are not a matter of whimsy but serve to reveal our purpose in this world. Beginning with the Creation Story, Naanabozho, for example, used dreams to gather warnings and infor-mation (Vecsey 1990: 93). It is with the Creation Story in mind that Basil Johnston portrays the role of dreams as a way of honoring the power that created the world itself:

> Following the example set by Kitchi-Manitou, every person is to seek a dream or vision within the expanse of his or her soul-spirit being and, having attained it, bring it into fulfillment and reality. Otherwise the dream or vision will be nullified. Furthermore, every person is endowed with the gift of a measure of talent or aptitude to enable him or her to bring the vision or dream to reality, to shape his or her own being, as it were, and to fashion an immediate world and destiny. (Johnston 1995: 3)

It is safe to say that George Morrison has succeeded in bringing his own dream to fruition. In so doing he has also managed to maintain the Ojibwa tradition as a dynamic force in the modern world, ultimately resisting the forces of assimilation that otherwise characterize the Ojibwas' relation to the Western tradition. More specifically, it is by capturing the "spirit" of the Ojibwa artistic tradition, rather than the mere form of its outward appearance, that Morrison has accomplished something remarkable. On the one hand, he is like the lone figure that Kandinsky spoke of, who resides ahead of his

261

time at the apex of the triangle representing "the life of the spirit"; for Morrison, unlike many other "Indian artists," heard "a voice" to which the rest of the crowd was deaf and which only Morrison could follow (Kandinsky 1977: 6–9). On the other hand, rather than feeling alienated and forlorn in this pursuit, Morrison embraced the only thing that could provide his life with meaning in an otherwise meaningless world – his dreams, which, as it turned out, led him on a path back home. "I wanted to come back to the Indian connection," as Morrison recounts his transformation, "to Minnesota and my family. I felt an inner need to come back, not realizing the consequences of what I was doing. I felt the need to put certain Indian values into my work" (Morrison 1998: 135). It is those "values" that we see today in Morrison's paintings, especially the Horizon Series, with their regard for the mythical qualities of nature. It is also those values that distinguish Morrison's work as a unique phenomenon in the history of modern American art, a phenomenon that is too often overlooked, perhaps because it affirms the vitality of that which many Americans too frequently regard as a relic of the buried past: the American Indian spirit.

In the end, the lessons that Morrison's paintings provide us, if we are willing to listen, consist of realizing that an integral part of our relation to the world is made up of dreams. For it is through dreams that we may discover the self that is unencumbered by personal prohibitions and social mores, a self that is liberated from the confines of the ordinary. In turn, we may come to realize that the boundaries between things, such as human and nonhuman – not to mention earth and sky – are as insubstantial as the fog that drifts over Lake Superior on a cold winter morning. Finally, what Morrison's horizon reveals is that there is a way of looking at American Indian art that depends as much upon appreciating the vitality of the artist's imagination as it does on his faithfulness to tradition. For just as Morrison has blurred the line separating earth and sky, so too has he blurred the line between traditional and nontraditional.

## REFERENCES

Casey, Edward S. (1993). *Getting Back into Place: Toward a Renewed Understanding of the Place-World*. Bloomington: Indiana University Press.

Johnston, Basil (1995). *The Manitous: the Supernatural World of the Ojibway*. New York: Harper Perennial.

Kandinsky, Wassily (1977). *Concerning the Spiritual in Art*, tr. M. T. H. Sadler. New York: Dover.

Morrison, George (1998). *Turning the Feather Around*. As told to Margot Fortunato Galt. St. Paul: Minnesota Historical Society Press.

Morrison, George, et al. (1990). *Standing in the Northern Lights: George Morrison, a Retrospective*. St. Paul: Minnesota Museum of Art.

Morrison, George, et al. (1998). *Morrison's Horizon: New Paintings from the Horizon Series*. Minneapolis: Minneapolis Institute of Arts.

Vecsey, Christopher (1990). *Traditional Ojibway Religion and Its Historical Changes*. Philadelphia: American Philosophical Society.

Vizenor, Gerald (1984). *The People Named the Chippewa: Narrative Histories*. Minneapolis: University of Minnesota Press.

# 22

# ON PHILOSOPHICAL DISCOURSE: SOME INTERCULTURAL MUSINGS

*Thurman Lee Hester, Jr.*

I think traditional rhetoric is absolutely essential to doing Native American philosophy.[1] This is not true in the Euro-American philosophical tradition. It has been said that "the history of philosophy is but a series of footnotes to Plato." Whether a Euro-American philosopher is engaging in the elenctic method, Cartesian doubt, Hegelian dialectic, or any of the other divers and valuable methods that spring from the European tradition, they are still discussing the same perennial issues and generally refining the same set of answers. The Euro-American tradition is fundamentally seeking the "truth." Though many people in the tradition doubt that we'll ever achieve the truth, or that we ever *could* achieve the truth, they are still trying to answer the questions posed by Plato. Answers, in the form of beliefs concerning reality, are the goal while the various philosophical methods are the means.

This just isn't so in many, maybe even all, Native American traditions. I'll try to give you a taste of the Choctaw part of that tradition, while furthering the goal of illuminating the difference between the Euro-American and the Native American traditions. I'll tell some stories. However, this particular chapter may be more nearly a traditional Euro-American one than I'd like. I'd prefer to say that it's because I'm catering to my audience, but the real truth is probably laziness. Coming up with the appropriate stories can be very hard! It will, however, be very traditional in the way it wanders.

A few years ago I was the professor of a course called "Native American Identity." I won't say I was "teaching it," for many reasons. One of them is that I tried, as much as possible, to use members of the Native American community – particularly elders – as the real teachers. I like to think it is because I recognize that they are the ones who can truly teach it, not just that I am lazy.

One of our speakers was John Proctor, the oldest living Creek medicine man. He is the uncle of Wanda Davis, a good friend of mine – so I was able to persuade him to spend a three-hour session with the class one evening. Mr Proctor is a key practitioner of the traditional Creek religion, he is the medicine man for a stomp ground. "Stomp ground" is the name given to the ceremonial grounds where the Creek practice their religion.

Mostly, the students asked the kinds of questions you might expect. Since they thought of Mr Proctor as a representative of a traditional religion, they asked him cosmogonic or cosmological questions.

I was surprised when one of the students asked the ultimate question. Remember – this was a class on "Indian Identity." The student asked: "What makes you Creek?" Those of you familiar with the Native American traditions might expect the answer to be a rambling narrative that wouldn't *seem* to be an answer at all. This is just what I expected. I settled back in my chair in preparation for Mr Proctor's answer. Without hesitation he said, "If you come to the stomp ground for four years, take the medicines and dance the dances, then you are Creek."

The answer was completely unexpected and thus even more forcefully illuminating. Mr Proctor had listed a set of *practices* which made someone Creek, or more properly in context, a member of the traditional Creek religion.

If you asked a member of just about any *Christian* religion what made them Christians, you would get a completely different answer. My Missionary Baptist relatives would tell you that to be Christian you have to "accept Jesus Christ as your personal Lord and Savior." Acceptance, faith – *belief* is at the core of the Christian religion and, not surprisingly, at the core of Euro-American philosophy. Just think about how you would characterize different philosophical schools, or different figures in the Euro-American philosophical tradition. This school believed this . . . , the central tenets of that school were . . . , this famed philosopher thought that. . . . Beliefs, beliefs, beliefs.

As my friend Dann May would say, it is the difference between orthodoxy on the European side and orthopraxy on the American Indian side. This difference has many, many interesting consequences which I don't think have ever been fully examined. For my purposes, though, one thing should be clear. If practice is at the core of Native American philosophy, then how you go about doing that philosophy may be as much or more important than what is supposedly being said. Euro-American methods, honed to their traditional use of arguing and asserting beliefs to be true, are going to have some trouble with practices that just are.

This fundamental difference is just one of many. Native American languages are often very different from European languages. Whether language is a reflection of philosophy, or philosophy a reflection of language – or both – linguistic difference almost certainly assures philosophical difference. Though these differences are part of what makes it difficult to communicate between Euro-American traditions and Native American traditions, they are also part of what makes it imperative that the communication take place.

People are often amazed when I tell them that the Choctaw language has no verb "to be." This has many interesting effects. Besides making it impossible to use the passive voice, giving Choctaw writing teachers much less to do, it means that nothing is ever in a particular state. Things act, change, interact, exchange. In Choctaw, the universe is alive in a way that it can never be for a language that lets things just exist.

The lack of a "to be" verb also means that Choctaw chiefs, unlike American presidents, have never been confused about what the meaning of the word "is" is.

Besides opening up a vibrant new world to the Euro-American philosopher, exposure to Native American traditions should cause some rethinking of the old world. Dennis McPherson and Doug Rabb did some of that in their paper, "Some Thoughts on Articulating a Native Philosophy" (1997, *Ayaangwaamizin: The International Journal of Indigenous Philosophy*, 1, 1: 11), where they provided a critique of Kant's views on autonomy. You see, in many Native American homes, children are basically fully autonomous from the moment they can express autonomy – the age of mobility. In most Euro-American homes, children go through a long period of heteronomy. Their parents make rules for them. This is a very basic difference. I suspect it is about as hard for Euro-American parents to conceive of *not* making rules as it is for many Native American parents to conceive of making them. In the European tradition, a transition from heteronomy to autonomy is assumed. Native American tradition shows that it can be questioned. How can a person go from autonomy to heteronomy? Does a period of heteronomy alter the form autonomy takes? And so on. All new questions for Euro-American philosophy.

The extreme differences between these sets of traditions mean great difficulties in understanding. Native American people must be central to working out the understanding, because there are no formal "schools" of Native American philosophy. Insight gained from experience will be crucial. Working out the understanding will mean that practical experience in Native culture will have to be conjoined with formal training in the Euro-American tradition.

Does this mean that the Euro-American philosophers have no role in the current development of Native American philosophies in academia? Absolutely not. A friend of mine who has a lot of Yuchi friends told me that the Yuchis have a form of corn that grows on very slender stems. In almost any wind, the cornstalk will blow over. The Yuchis plant pole beans between the rows of corn. For those of you who don't know about pole beans, they are basically vines that you put poles next to so that they can crawl up them, get sun, and yield beans. The Yuchi cornstalk acts like a pole for the bean, while the bean acts as a guywire, supporting the cornstalk in even the stiffest wind.

The Euro-American tradition just *is* the tradition of academia here. It is just a fact that Euro-American philosophers will be the gatekeepers, that the success or failure of Native American philosophy to find a niche in academia will be almost solely controlled by Euro-American philosophers. Sympathetic Euro-American philosophers will help not only in training those Native Americans who wish to enter academe, but will also help to recognize and bring the wisdom of the Native American tradition to a larger audience.

A few years ago, Dennis McPherson and I started *Ayaangwaamizin: The International Journal of Indigenous Philosophy*. Dennis and I like to think that our Journal provides a little Native input into academia. When we started the Journal, at least one Native person involved in the project kept pushing me to provide a definition of the word "philosophy." I kept rebelling, thinking that such a project was definitely not a Native American project. Now I see at least some of the wisdom behind it, though certainly not all.

My friend who pressed me to define "philosophy" was doing many things. One was testing me. If I cannot do philosophy in a way that is recognizable to those within the Euro-American tradition, then ultimately they will think that what I'm doing isn't philosophy at all. If I can do philosophy in a way they recognize, they may take a second look when I don't.

The introduction of Native American philosophy into academia has great potential benefits all around, but it can also be a smokescreen behind which no philosophy, or even bad philosophy, is done. The great differences between the Native American tradition and the Euro-American tradition almost ensure that some will miss the wisdom inherent in the other's philosophy; but this shouldn't lead us to think that just because we missed something, there must be no wisdom. People that throw thoughts around and call it "Native American philosophy" are as bad as the plastic medicine men and New Age shamans.

It is my hope that a good academic philosopher can recognize wisdom, even in traditions that they don't really comprehend; and that great academic philosophers can display wisdom that will be perceived regardless of differences in tradition.

For many reasons, the main expositors of Native American philosophy ought rightly be Native Americans themselves. However, we should remember what we teach our first-year philosophy students: Beware of appeals to authority. Just because a person portrays themself as native doesn't mean that they are. Though it would take volumes to exhaust the identity issue among Indians, I would say that community membership is the key here. If a person claims tribal affiliation, I check first with people I know in the tribe – or with the tribal government if I don't know anyone in the tribe. Do they know the person? Is the person active in their community? A CDIB card (Certified Degree of Indian Blood – yes, many Indians do still have US government-issued IDs) or a tribal ID card do not guarantee that a person has any knowledge of their nation, or its ways. But it does turn out that that almost everyone who is a member of an Indian community will have one. For the logically minded, legal affiliation proven by having an appropriate ID is very *nearly* a necessary condition for being "Indian," but it is far from sufficient.

Some identity warning signs include claiming multiple tribes and living far from the bulk of their tribal community. Though most of us have blood of more than one tribe, true community membership generally includes participation and allegiance. To be in a community is not just a matter of blood. Though we might formally note all our relations (and we never forget them), at any one time we generally are members of just one community. Interestingly, people affiliated with more than one tribe will often change their membership claim depending on where they are living at the time. I know several people that do this. One man calls himself Cherokee in Tahlequah and Kiowa in Carnegie. Though sometimes we joke about this, these claims can really be true. People that live far from their communities can maintain their identity, but it is clearly more difficult. But you also have to be careful in determining where these communities are! The Indian relocation program of the late twentieth century helped to create some far-flung Indian communities. There is even a large Choctaw community in Bakersfield, California.

Unfortunately, just because a person is "really Indian" doesn't mean they know anything about philosophy in general, or Native American philosophy in particular. So, we are back to the problem of recognizing Native philosophy. Unfortunately, at this time the Native community in academic philosophy or even in the academy in general is so small that it cannot really be self-policing. We just don't have the numbers to be a real community. This is likely to continue for a long time. Enrolled tribal members constitute less than 1 percent of the US population – and far fewer than that are really members of the community.

So, surprisingly, some of the real work of academic Native philosophy is going to have to be done by the non-Natives. Not only will they, as the gatekeepers-in-fact, act to police the discipline, but they really must do it because it will be a while before our community will be large enough that we can do it ourselves. Those of us trying to do Native philosophy will certainly try to make what we are doing clear, but a person could be a fine Native American philosopher, and be unwilling or unable to do philosophy in a way that is recognizable within the Euro-American tradition. Hope-fully, some of the wisdom will come through, hopefully discerning academic philoso-phers will be able to detect it despite differences in tradition. However, if you can't see it time after time, then I would suggest that you pass on to more fruitful pastures.

*Yakoke.* Thank you.

## NOTE

1   For this reason I usually insert an introduction and disclaimer at the beginning of presenta-tions. Since this book includes two of my articles, I figured I'd only burden one of them with an introduction. So, you are invited to see the second paragraph of the other article (chapter 15, "Choctaw Conceptions of the Excellence of the Self, with Implications for Education") for this introduction.

# BIBLIOGRAPHY

*Anne Waters and Amy Miskowski*

## BOOKS

Acoose, Janice (or Misko-Kisikawihkwe, Red Sky Woman) (1995). *Iskwewak-Kah' Ki Yaw Ni Wahkomkanak: Neither Indian Princesses nor Easy Squaws*. Toronto: Woman's Press.

Adams, David Wallace (1995). *Education for Extinction: American Indians and the Boarding-School Experience, 1850–1930*. Lawrence: University Press of Kansas.

Alexie, Sherman (1994). *The Lone Ranger and Tonto Fistfight in Heaven*. New York: Harper Perennial.

Alexie, Sherman (1996). *Reservation Blues*. New York: Warner Books.

Allen, Paula Gunn (1986). *The Sacred Hoop: Recovering the Feminine in American Indian Traditions*. Boston, MA: Beacon Press.

Allen, Paula Gunn, ed. (1989). *Spider Woman's Granddaughters*. Boston, MA: Beacon Press.

Allen, Paula Gunn, ed. (1994). *Voice of the Turtle: American Indian Literature 1974–1994*. New York: Ballantine.

Anderson, Gary and Alan Woolworth, eds. (1988). *Through Dakota Eyes: Narrative Accounts of the Minnesota Indian War of 1862*. St. Paul: Minnesota Historical Society.

Apess, William (1831). *The Increase of the Kingdom of Christ*. New York: self-published.

Apess, William (1833). *The Experience of Five Christian Indians of the Pequot Tribe*. Boston, MA: J. B. Dow.

Apess, William (1836). *Eulogy on King Philip: as Pronounced at the Odeon, in Federal Street, Boston*. Boston, MA: self-published.

Apess, William (1979). *Indian Nullification of the Unconstitutional Laws of Massachusetts, Relative to the Marshpee Tribe: or, The Pretended Riot Explained*. Stanforville, NY: E. M. Colemen.

Apess, William (1992). *On Our Own Ground: the Complete Writings of William Apess, a Pequot*. Amherst: University of Massachusetts Press.

Apess, William (1997). *A Son of the Forest and Other Writings*. Amherst: University of Massachusetts Press.

Archuleta, Margaret and Dr. Rennard Strickland (1991). *Shared Visions: Native American Painters and Sculptors in the Twentieth Century*. New York: New Press.

Arden, Harvey, ed. (1994). *Noble Red Man: Lakota Wisdomkeeper Matthew King*. Hillsboro, OR: Beyond World Publishing.

Arden, Harvey and Steve Wall (1990). *Wisdomkeepers. Meetings with Native American Spiritual Elders*. Hillsboro, OR: Beyond World Publishing.

Arden, Harvey, and Steve Wall (1998). *Travels in a Stone Canoe: The Return to the Wisdomkeepers*. New York: Simon and Schuster.

Armstrong, Virginia I., ed. (1971). *I Have Spoken: American History through the Voices of the Indians*. Akron: University of Ohio Press.

Ashabranner, Brent and Paul Conklin (photographer) (1984). *To Live in Two Worlds: American Indian Youth Today*. New York: Dodd Mead.

Ball, Eve (1980). *Indeh: an Apache Odyssey*. Norman: University of Oklahoma Press.

Barreiro, Jose, ed. (1992). *Indian Roots of American Democracy*. Ithaca, NY: Akwe:kon Press, Cornell University.

Barreiro, Jose (1993). *The Indian Chronicles*. Houston, TX: Arte Publico Press.

Basso, Keith (1987). *Wisdom Sits in Places: Landscape and Language among the Western Apache*. Albuquerque: University of New Mexico Press.

Bataille, Gretchen M. (1984). *American Indian Women, Telling their Lives*. Lincoln: University of Nebraska Press.

Battaille, Gretchen M. (1991). *American Indian Women: a Guide to Research*. New York: Garland.

Bataille, Gretchen M., ed. (1993). *Native American Women: A Biographical Dictionary*. New York: Garland Publishing.

Bataille, Gretchen M. and Charles L. P. Silet, eds. (1980). *The Pretend Indians: Images of Native Americans in the Movies*. Ames: Iowa State University Press.

Bear Heart (1996). *The Wind Is My Mother: The Life and Teachings of a Native American Shaman*. New York: Clarkson Potter.

Beck, Peggy V., Anna Lee Walters, and Lee Walters (1978). *The Sacred: Ways of Knowledge, Sources of Life*. Tsaile, AZ: Navajo Community College Press. (New edn. 2000.)

Benham, Maenette K. P. and Wayne J. Stein, eds. (2003). *The Renaissance of American Indian Higher Education: Capturing the Dream*. Mahwah, NJ: Laurence Erlbaum Associates.

Bennett, Gordon (1978). *Aboriginal Rights in International Law*. London: Royal Institute.

Berkhofer, Robert F., Jr. (1978). *The White Man's Indian: Images of the American Indian from Columbus to the Present*. New York: Vintage Books.

Bierhorst, John (1994). *The Way of the Earth: Native Americans and the Environment*. New York: William Morrow.

Biolosi, Thomas (1992). *Organizing the Lakota: the Political Economy of the New Deal on the Pine Ridge and Rosebud Reservations*. Tucson: University of Arizona Press.

Birchfield, Dan and Mark Sachner, eds. (in press). *The Encyclopedia of American Indians*. New York: Marshall Cavendish.

Black Elk (1961). *Black Elk Speaks: Being the Life Story of a Holy Man of the Oglala Sioux*. Lincoln: University of Nebraska Press. (First published: New York: W. Morrow, 1932.)

Black Elk, Wallace H. (1990). *Black Elk: the Sacred Ways of a Lakota*. San Francisco: Harper and Row.

Blackman, Margaret B. (1982). *During My Time: Florence Edenshaw Davidson, a Haida Woman*. Seattle: University of Washington Press; Vancouver: Douglas and McIntyre.

Blue Cloud, Peter (1972). *Alcatraz Is Not an Island*. San Francisco: Wingbow.

Boatman, John F. (1992). *My Elders Taught Me: Aspects of Western Great Lakes American Indian Philosophy*, Lanham, MD: University Press of America.

Bonnin, Gertrude (Zitkala Sa) (1921). *American Indian Stories*. Lincoln: University of Nebraska Press.

Bonnin, Gertrude (Zitkala Sa) (1985). *Old Indian Legends*. Lincoln: University of Nebraska Press.

Bonnin, Gertrude (Zitkala Sa) (1900). *People and Events*: Zitkala-Sa (etext). URL: <http://www.pbs.org/wgbh/amex/1900/peopleevents/pande35.html>

Bonnin, Gertrude (Zitkala Sa) (1900). *An Indian Teacher Among Indians* (etext). University of Virginia Library Electronic Text Center, originally published by Atlantic Monthly, New York, volume 85. URL: <http://etext.lib.virginia.edu/cgibin/browse-mixed?id=ZitTeac&tag=public&images=images/modeng&data=/lvl/Archive/eng-parsed>

See the following works by Bonnin at the same URL:

> *Impressions of an Indian Childhood* (etext). University of Virginia Library Electronic Text Center. Also published in Atlantic Monthly 85 (1900): 37–47.
>
> *Old Indian Legends* (etext). University of Virginia Library Electronic Text Center.
>
> *Soft Hearted Sioux* (etext). University of Virginia Library Electronic Text Center. First published in *Harper's Monthly*, New York (1901).
>
> *The Trial Path* (etext). University of Virginia Library Electronic Text Center. First published in *Harper's Monthly Magazine*, 103, October 1901.
>
> *Why I Am a Pagan* (etext). University of Virginia Library Electronic Text Center. Originally published in *Atlantic Monthly*, 90 (1902): 801–3.

Bordewich, Fergus M. (1996). *Killing the White Man's Indian: Reinventing Native Americans at the End of the Twentieth Century*. New York: Anchor Books.

Boudinot, Elias (1996). *Cherokee editor: the Writings of Elias Boudinot*, ed. Theda Perdue. Athens, GA: University of Georgia Press. (Originally published: Knoxville: University of Tennessee Press, 1983.)

Bowker, A. (1993). *Sisters in the Blood: the Education of Women in Native America*. Newton, MA: WEEA Publishing Center.

Broker, Ignatia (1983). *Night Flying Woman: an Ojibway Narrative*. St. Paul: Minnesota Historical Society Press.

Brown, Dee (1970). *Bury My Heart at Wounded Knee: an Indian History of the American West*. New York: Holt, Rinehart and Winston.

Brownlie, Ian, ed. (1994). *Basic Documents on Human Rights*, 3rd edn. Oxford: Clarendon Press.

Bruchac, Joseph, ed. (1987). *Survival This Way*. Tucson: University of Arizona Press.

Bullard, Robert, ed. (1993). *Confronting Environmental Racism: Voice from the Grassroots*. Boston, MA: South End Press.

Bullard, Robert, ed. (1994). *Unequal Protection: Environmental Justice and Communities of Color*. San Francisco: Sierra Club Books.

Bunge, Robert (1984). *An American Urphilosophie: an American Philosophy BP (Before Pragmatism)*. Lanham, MD: University Press of America.

Burnette, Robert and John Koster (1974). *The Road to Wounded Knee*. New York: Bantam.

Burt, Larry W. (1982). *Tribalism in Crisis: Federal Indian Policy, 1953–1961*. Albuquerque: University of New Mexico Press.

Butler, Johnella E., ed. (2001). *Color Line to Borderlands: Ethnic Studies in Higher Education.* Seattle: University of Washington Press.

Butruille, Susan G. (1995). *Women's Voices from the Western Frontier.* Boise, ID: Tamarack Books.

Bryde, John F. (1974). *An Indian Philosophy of Education.* Vermillion, SD: South Dakota University, Institute of Indian Studies.

Cajete, Gregory (1994). *Look to the Mountain: An Ecology of Indigenous Education.* Skyland, NC: Kivaki Press.

Cajete, Gregory (1999a). *A People's Ecology: Explorations in Sustainable Living.* Santa Fe, NM: Clearlight.

Cajete, Gregory (1999b). *Igniting the Sparkle: an Indigenous Science Education Model.* Skyland, NC: Kivaki Press.

Cajete, Gregory (2000). *Native Science: Natural Laws of Interdependence.* Santa Fe, NM: Clearlight.

Calloway, Colin G. (1998). *New Americans and First Americans in New Worlds for All: Indians, Europeans, and the Remaking of Early America.* Baltimore: Johns Hopkins University Press.

Campbell, Maria (1973). *Halfbreed.* New York: Saturday Review Press.

Champagne, Duane (1992). *Social Order and Political Change: Constitutional Governments among the Cherokee, the Choctaw, the Chickasaw, and the Creek.* Stanford, CA: Stanford University Press.

Champagne, Duane, ed. (1994). *Chronology of Native North American History: from Pre-Columbian Times to the Present.* Detroit: Gale Group.

Champagne, Duane (1999). *Contemporary Native American Cultural Issues.* Walnut Creek, CA: Alta Mira Press.

Champagne, Duane (2001a). *The Native North American Almanac: A Reference Work on Native North Americans in the United States and Canada.* Detroit: Gale Group.

Champagne, Duane (2001b). *Reference Library of Native North America.* Detroit: Gale Group.

Champagne, Duane (2002). *Distinguished Native American Political and Tribal Leaders.* Salt Lake City, UT: Onyx Press.

Champagne, Duane, Suzan S. Harjo, and Dennis Banks, eds. (1994). *Native America: Portrait of the Peoples.* Detroit: Visible Ink Press.

Champagne, Duane and Jay Stauss, eds. (1994). *Native American Studies in Higher Education: Models for Collaboration between Universities and Indigenous Nations.* Detroit: Visible Ink Press.

Chaudhuri, Jean and Joyotpaul Chaudhuri (2001). *A Sacred Path: the Way of the Muscogee Creeks.* Los Angeles: UCLA American Indian Studies Center.

Churchill, Ward (1984). *Marxism and Native Americans.* Boston, MA: South End Press.

Churchill, Ward (1990). *Critical Issues in Native North America* (IWGIA Document no. 62; December 1988/January 1989 edn.) Copenhagen, Denmark: International Secretariat of IWGIA (International Work Group for Indigenous Affairs).

Churchill, Ward (1992). *Fantasies of the Master Race: Literature, Cinema and the Colonization of American Indians,* ed. M. Annette Jaimes. Monroe, ME: Common Courage Press.

Churchill, Ward (1993). *Struggle for the Land: Indigenous Resistance to Genocide, Ecocide and Expropriation in Contemporary North America.* Monroe, ME: Common Courage Press.

Churchill, Ward (1994). *Indians Are Us? Culture and Genocide in Native North America.* Monroe, ME: Common Courage Press.

Churchill, Ward (1995). *Since Predator Came: Notes from the Struggle for American Indian Liberation.* Littleton, CO: Aigis Press.

Churchill, Ward (1996). *From a Native Son*: Selected Essays in Indigenism, 1985–1995. Boston, MA: South End Press.

Churchill, Ward (1997). *A Little Matter of Genocide: Holocaust and Denial in the Americas, 1492 to the Present*. San Francisco, CA: City Lights Books.

Churchill, Ward (2002). *Acts of Rebellion: A Ward Churchill Reader*. Danbury, CT: Rutledge (now Hudson House Publishing).

Churchill, Ward and J. J. Vander Wall (1991). *The COINTELPRO Papers: Documents from the FBI's Secret War against Domestic Dissent*. Boston, MA: South End Press.

Churchill, Ward and J. J. Vander Wall, eds. (1988). *Agents of Repression: The FBI's Secret Wars against the Black Panther Party and the American Indian Movement*. Boston, MA: South End Press.

Churchill, Ward and J. J. Vander Wall (1992). *Cages of Steel: the Politics of Imprisonment in the United States*. Washington, DC: Maisonneuve Press.

Clark, Blue (1994). *Lone Wolf v. Hitchcock: Treaty Rights and Indian Law at the End of the Nineteenth Century*. Lincoln: University of Nebraska Press.

Claassen, Cheryl (1997). *Women in Prehistory: North America and Mesoamerica*. Philadelphia: University of Pennsylvania Press.

Clinton, Robert N., Neil Jessup Newton, and Monroe E. Price, eds. (1991). *American Indian Law: Cases and Materials*. Charlottesville, VA: Michie.

Closs, Michael P., ed. (1986). *Native American Mathematics*. Austin: University of Texas Press.

Cohen, Felix S. (1942). *Handbook of Federal Indian Law*. Washington, DC: Government Printing Office.

Coltelli, Laura (1990). *Winged Words: American Indian Writers Speak*. Lincoln: University of Nebraska Press.

Cook, Noble David (1998). *Born to Die: Disease and New World Conquest, 1492–1650*. Cambridge, UK: Cambridge University Press.

Cook-Lynn, Elizabeth (1996). *Why I Can't Read Wallace Stegner and Other Essays: a Tribal Voice*. Madison: University of Wisconsin Press.

Cook-Lynn, Elizabeth (1998). *The Politics of Hallowed Ground: Wounded Knee and the Struggle for Indian Sovereignty*, with Mario Gonzalez. Urbana: University of Illinois Press.

Cook-Lynn, Elizabeth (2001). *Anti-Indianism in Modern America: A Voice from Tatekaya's Earth*. Urbana: University of Illinois Press.

Copway, George (1847). *The Life, History, and Travels of Kah-ge-ga-gah-bowh (George Copway): a Young Indian Chief of the Ojebwa Nation*. Albany, NY: Weed and Parsons.

Copway, George (1850a). *The Life, Letters and Speeches of Kah-ge-ga-gah-bowh, or G. Copway, Chief Ojibway Nation*. New York: S. W. Benedict.

Copway, George (1850b). *The Ojibway Conquest, a Tale of the Northwest by Kah-ge-ga-gah-bowh*. New York: Putman.

Copway, George (1850c). *Organization of a New Indian Territory, East of the Missouri River, Arguments and Reasons, Submitted to the Honorable Members of the Senate House of Representatives*. New York: S. W. Benedict.

Copway, George (1850d). *The Traditional History and Characteristic Sketches of the Ojibway Nation*. London: Charles Gilpin.

Copway, George (1851). *Running Sketches of Men and Places, in England, France, Germany, Belgium, and Scotland*. New York: Riker.

Cornell, Stephen and Joseph P. Kalt (1992). *What Can Tribes Do? Strategies and Institutions in American Indian Economic Development*. Los Angeles: UCLA American Indian Studies Center.

Cornplanter, Jesse (1963). *Legends of the Longhouse, Told to Sah-Nee-Wah, the White Sister*. Washington, NY: I. J. Friedman.

Courlander, Harold, ed. (1971). *The Fourth World of the Hopis: the Epic Story of the Hopi Indians as Preserved in Their Legends and Traditions*. Albuquerque: University of New Mexico Press.

Crandell, Samuel Benjamin (1916). *Treaties, Their Making and Enforcement*, 2nd edn. New York: Columbia University Press.

Cristecu, Aureliu (1981). *The Right to Self-determination: Historical and Current Developments on the Basis of United Nations Instruments* (UN DocE/CN.4/Sub.2/404 Rev. 1). New York: UN.

Cronon, William (1983). *Changes in the Land: Indians, Colonists, and the Ecology of New England*. New York: Hill and Wang.

Crosby, Alfred W. (1972). *The Columbian Exchange: Biological and Cultural Consequences of 1492*. Westport, CT: Greenwood Press.

Crow Dog, Mary (1990). *Lakota Woman*. New York: Grove Weidenfeld.

Crow Dog, Mary (1993). *Ohitika Woman*, 1st edn. New York: Grove Press.

Cruikshank, Julie (c. 1990). *Life Lived like a Story: Life Stories of Three Yukon Native Elders*. Lincoln: University of Nebraska Press.

Cutler, Charles L. (1994). *O Brave New Words! Native American Loanwords in Current English*. Norman: University of Oklahoma Press.

Davis, Mary B., ed. (1994). *Native America in the Twentieth Century: An Encyclopedia*. New York: Garland Publishing.

Debo, Angie (1943). *Tulsa: From Creek Town to Oil Capital*. Norman: University of Oklahoma Press.

Debo, Angie (1951). *The Five Civilized Tribes of Oklahoma: A Report on Social and Economic Conditions*. Philadelphia: Indian Rights Association.

Debo, Angie (1961). *The Rise and Fall of the Choctaw Republic*. Norman: University of Oklahoma Press. (Originally published 1934.)

Debo, Angie (1970). *A History of the Indians of the United States*. Norman: University of Oklahoma Press.

Debo, Angie (1973). *And Still the Waters Run*. Princeton, NJ: Princeton University Press. (Originally published in 1940.)

Debo, Angie (1976). *Geronimo: The Man, His Time, His Place*. Norman: University of Oklahoma Press.

Debo, Angie (1979). *The Road to Disappearance: A History of the Creek Indians*. Norman: University of Oklahoma Press. (Originally published 1941.)

Debo, Angie (1987). *Oklahoma: Foot-loose and Fancy-free*. Norman: University of Oklahoma Press. (Originally published 1949.)

Debo, Angie (1998). *Prairie City: The Story of an American Community*. Norman: University of Oklahoma Press. (Originally published 1944.)

Debo, Angie and J. Fred Rippy (1924). *The Historical Background of the American Policy of Isolation*. Northhampton, MA: Smith College Studies in History.

Deloria, Ella (1932). *Dakota Texts*. New York: G. E. Stechert and Co. (Reprinted AMS Press, 1974.)

Deloria, Ella (1944). *Speaking of Indians*. New York: Friendship Press.

Deloria, Ella Cara (1988). *Waterlily*. Lincoln: University of Nebraska Press.

Deloria, Philip (1998). *Playing Indian*. New Haven, CT: Yale University Press.

Deloria, Philip and Neal Salisbury, eds. (2001). *The Blackwell Companion to American History*. Oxford and Malden, MA: Blackwell.

Deloria, Vine, Jr. (1969). *Custer Died for your Sins: an Indian Manifesto*. New York: Macmillan.

Deloria, Vine, Jr. (1970). *We Talk, You Listen: New Tribes, New Turf*. New York: Macmillan.

Deloria, Vine, Jr. (1971a). *Of Utmost Good Faith*. San Francisco: Straight Arrow Books.

Deloria, Vine, Jr. (1971b). *The Red Man in the New World Drama: a Politico-legal Study with a Pageantry of American Indian History*. New York: Macmillan.

Deloria, Vine, Jr. (1972). *Reminiscences of Vine V. Deloria, Yankton Sioux Tribe of South Dakota 1970. New York Times* oral history program; American Indian oral history research project, Part II; no. 82.

Deloria, Vine, Jr. (1974a). *Behind the Trail of Broken Treaties: an Indian Declaration of Independence*. New York: Dell Publishing.

Deloria, Vine, Jr. (1974b). *The Indian Affair*. New York: Friendship Press.

Deloria, Vine, Jr. (1976). *A Better Day for Indians*. New York: Field Foundation.

Deloria, Vine, Jr. (1977). *Indians of the Pacific Northwest*. New York: Doubleday.

Deloria, Vine, Jr. (1978). *The Right to Know: a Paper*. Washington, DC: Office of Library and Information Services, US Department of the Interior.

Deloria, Vine, Jr. (1979a). *A Brief History of the Federal Responsibility to the American Indian*. Washington, DC: Department of Health, Education, and Welfare.

Deloria, Vine, Jr. (1979b). *The Metaphysics of Modern Existence*. San Francisco, CA: Harper and Row.

Deloria, Vine, Jr. (1983). *American Indians, American Justice*. Austin: University of Texas Press.

Deloria, Vine, Jr. (1984a). *Aggressions of Civilization: Federal Indian Policy since the 1880s*. Philadelphia: Temple University Press.

Deloria, Vine, Jr. (1984b). *The Nations Within: the Past and Future of American Indian Sovereignty*. New York: Pantheon Books.

Deloria, Vine, Jr. (1984c). *A Sender of Words: Essays in Memory of John G. Neihardt*. Salt Lake City, UT: Howe Brothers.

Deloria, Vine, Jr. (1985). *American Indian Policy in the Twentieth Century*. Norman: University of Oklahoma Press.

Deloria, Vine, Jr. (1993). *Frank Waters: Man and Mystic*. Athens, GA: Swallow Press; Akron: Ohio University Press.

Deloria, Vine, Jr. (1994). *God is Red: a Native View of Religion*. Golden, CO: North American Press.

Deloria, Vine, Jr. (1995). *Red Earth, White Lies: Native Americans and the Myth of Scientific Fact*. New York: Scribner.

Deloria, Vine, Jr. (1999a). *For This Land: Writings on Religion in America*. New York: Routledge.

Deloria, Vine, Jr. (1999b). *Singing for a Spirit: a Portrait of the Dakota Sioux*. Santa Fe, NM: Clear Light.

Deloria, Vine, Jr. (1999c). *Spirit and Reason: the Vine Deloria, Jr., Reader*, ed. Barbara Deloria, Kristen Foehner, and Sam Scinta. Golden, CO: Fulcrum.

Deloria, Vine, Jr. (2002). *Evolution, Creationism, and Other Modern Myths*. Golden, CO: Fulcrum.

Deloria, Vine, Jr., and Lee Irwin (1966). *The Dream Seekers: Native American Visionary Traditions of the Great Plains*. Norman: University of Oklahoma Press.

Deloria, Vine, Jr., and Clifford Lytle (1983). *American Indians, American Justice*. Austin: University of Texas Press.

Deloria, Vine, Jr., and Clifford Lytle (1984). *The Nations Within: The Past and Future of American Indian Sovereignty*. New York: Pantheon.

Deloria, Vine, Jr., and Daniel Wildcat (2001). *Indian Education in America*. Golden, CO: Fulcrum.

Deloria Vine, Jr., and David E. Wilkins (1999). *Tribes, Treaties, and Constitutional Tribulations*. Austin: University of Texas Press.

Devens, Carol (1992). *Countering Colonization: Native American Women and Great Lakes Missions, 1630–1900.* Berkeley, CA: University of California Press.

Drinnon, Richard (1977). *Facing West: The Metaphysics of Indian-hating and Empire-building.* Norman, OK: University of Oklahoma Press.

Drinnon, Richard (1987). *Keeper of Concentration Camps: Dillon S. Myer and American Racism.* Berkeley: University of California Press.

Durham, Jimmie (1978). *Les Sept points cardinaux: orientations écologiques.* Paris: Presses Universitaires de France.

Durham, Jimmie (1983). *Columbus Day.* Minneapolis: West End Press.

Durham, Jimmie (1987). *We the People: Pena Bonita, Jimmie Durham, Harry Fonseca.* New York: Artists Space.

Durham, Jimmie (1993a). *A Certain Lack of Coherence: Writings on Art and Cultural Politics.* London: Kala Press.

Durham, Jimmie (1993b). *My Book, The East London Coelacanth, sometimes called, Troubled Waters —the Story of British Sea-power.* London: ICA Book Works.

Eastman, Charles (1904). *Red Hunters and the Animal People.* New York: Harper and Brothers.

Eastman, Charles (1907). *Old Indian Days.* New York: McClure.

Eastman, Charles (1912). *Lorado Taft's Indian Statue "Black Hawk": an Account of the Unveiling Ceremonies. . . .* Chicago: Frank O. Lowden and Wallace Heckman.

Eastman, Charles (1913). *Indian Child Life.* New York: Little, Brown.

Eastman, Charles (1914). *Indian Scout Talks: A Guide for Scouts and Campfire Girls.* New York: Little, Brown. (Reprinted as *Indian Scout Craft and Lore,* 1974.)

Eastman, Charles (1915). *The Indian Today: The Past and Future of the First American.* Garden City, NY: Doubleday, Page & Co. (Series: The American books: a library of good citizenship.)

Eastman, Charles (1977). *From the Deep Woods to Civilization: Chapters in the Autobiography of an Indian.* Lincoln: University of Nebraska Press. (Originally Published in 1916.)

Eastman, Charles (1991a). *Indian Boyhood.* Lincoln: University of Nebraska Press.

Eastman, Charles (1991b). *Indian Heroes and Great Chieftains.* Lincoln: University of Nebraska Press.

Eastman, Charles (1993c). *The Soul of an Indian and Other Writings from Ohiyesa.* San Rafael, CA: New World Library.

Eastman, Charles, with Elaine Goddale Eastman (1909). *Wigwam Evenings: Sioux Folk Tales Retold, Legends.* New York: Little, Brown. (Republished as *Smoky Day's Wigwam Evenings: Indian Stories Retold,* 1910. Reprinted, Lincoln: University of Nebraska Press, 1990.)

Erdoes, Richard (1976). *The Rain Dance People: The Pueblo Indians, Their Past and Present.* New York: Knopf.

Erdrich, Louise (1984). *Love Medicine: a Novel.* New York: Holt, Rinehart, and Winston.

Erdrich, Louise (1988). *Tracks: a Novel.* New York: Holt, Rinehart, and Winston.

Ewen, Alexander, ed. (1994). *Voice of Indigenous Peoples: Native Peoples Address the United Nations.* Santa Fe, NM: Clear Light.

Falk, Richard (1981). *Human Rights and State Sovereignty.* New York: Holmes and Meyers.

Farella, John Robert (1984). *The Main Stalk: a Synthesis of Navajo Philosophy.* Tucson: University of Arizona Press.

Farrer, Claire Rafferty (1991). *Living Life's Circle: Mescalero Apache Cosmovision.* Albuquerque: University of New Mexico Press.

Fein, Judith and Judith Lynn (1993). *Indian Time: a Year of Discovery among the Native Americans of the Southwest.* New York: Simon and Schuster.

Fenton, William N. (1941). *Contacts between Iroquois Herbalism and Colonial Medicine*. Smithsonian Institution Report. Washington, DC: Government Printing Office.

Fire, John (Lame Deer) and Richard Erdoes (1972). *Lame Deer, Seeker of Visions: The Life of a Sioux Medicine Man*. New York: Simon and Schuster.

Fixico, Donald, ed. (1997). *Rethinking American Indian History*. Albuquerque: University of New Mexico Press.

Fixico, Donald (1986). *Termination and Relocation: Federal Indian Policy, 1945–1960*. Albuquerque: University of New Mexico Press.

Fixico, Donald (1998). *The Invasion of Indian Country in the Twentieth Century: American Capitalism and Tribal Natural Resources*. Boulder, CO: University of Colorado Press.

Forbes, Jack D. (1960). *Apache, Navaho, and Spaniard*. Norman: University of Oklahoma Press.

Forbes, Jack D., ed. (1964). *The Indian in America's Past*. Englewood Cliffs, NY: Prentice Hall.

Forbes, Jack D. (1965). *Warriors of the Colorado: The Quechuans and their Neighbors*. Norman: University of Oklahoma Press.

Forbes, Jack D. (1966). *Frontiers in American History and the Role of the Frontier Historian*. Reno, NV: Desert Research Institute.

Forbes, Jack D. (1967a). *Nevada Indians Speak*. Reno: University of Nevada Press.

Forbes, Jack D. (1967b). *Afro-Americans in the Far West*. Berkeley, CA: Far West Laboratory. (Reprinted US Government Printing Office, 1968.)

Forbes, Jack D. (1967c). *Mexican-Americans*. Berkeley, CA: Far West Laboratory.

Forbes, Jack D. (1969). *The Education of the Culturally Different: a Multi-cultural Approach*. Berkeley, CA: Far West Laboratory for Educational Research and Development.

Forbes, Jack D. (1972a). *The Establishment of D-Q University: an Example of Successful Indian–Chicano Community Development*. Davis, CA: D-Q University Press.

Forbes, Jack D. (1972b). *Wapanakamikok Language Relationships: an Introductory Study of Mutual Intelligibility among the Powhatan, Lanape, Natick, Nanticoke, and Otchipwe Languages*. Davis, CA: University of California, Davis.

Forbes, Jack D. (1973). *Aztecas del norte: the Chicanos of Aztlan*. Greenwich, CT: Fawcett Publications.

Forbes, Jack D. (1976a). *A Model of "Grass-roots" Community Development: the D-Q University Native American Language Education Project*. Davis, CA: University of California, Davis.

Forbes, Jack D. (1976b). *The Wapanakamikok Languages: A Comparative Study of Powhatan, Natick, Lenape, Nanticoke, and Ojibwe*. Davis, CA: University of California, Tecumseh Center.

Forbes, Jack D. (1977a). *Racism, Scholarship, and Cultural Pluralism in Higher Education*. Davis, CA: University of California, Davis.

Forbes, Jack D. (1977b). *Religious Freedom and the Protection of Native American Places of Worship and Cemeteries*. Davis, CA: University of California, Davis.

Forbes, Jack D. (1978a). *The Potential Role of Libraries and Information Services in Supporting Native American Cultures and the Quality of Life of Native People: a Paper*. Washington, DC: Office of Library and Information Services, US Department of the Interior.

Forbes, Jack D. (1978b). *Tribes and Masses: Explorations in Red, White, and Black*. Davis, CA: D-Q University Press.

Forbes, Jack D. (1979a). *American Words: an Introduction to Those Native Words Used in English in the United States and Canada*. Davis, CA: University of California, Davis.

Forbes, Jack D. (1979b). *Native American Languages: Preservation and Self-development*. Davis, CA: University of California, Davis.

Forbes, Jack D. (1979c). *The Papago–Apache Treaty of 1853: Property Rights and Religious Liberties of the 'O'odham, Maricopa, and Other Native Peoples.* Davis, CA: University of California, Davis.

Forbes, Jack D. (1979d). *A World Ruled by Cannibals: The Wetiko Disease of Aggression, Violence and Imperialism.* Davis, CA: D-Q University Press.

Forbes, Jack D., ed. (1980). *Colors from the Earth.* Davis, CA: University of California, Tecumseh Center.

Forbes, Jack D. (1981a). *Atlas of Native History.* Davis, CA: D-Q University Press.

Forbes, Jack D. (1981b). *Native Americans and Nixon: Presidential Politics and Minority Self-determination, 1969–1972.* Los Angeles: UCLA American Indian Studies Center.

Forbes, Jack D. (1982). *Native Americans of California and Nevada,* rev. edn. Happy Camp, CA: Naturegraph.

Forbes, Jack D. (1983). *Native American Philosophy: Social and Political Implications.* Medelingen van het Juridisch Instituut mo. 22, Juridische Faculteit, Erasmus Universiteit, Rotterdam.

Forbes, Jack D., ed. (1985). *Native American Higher Education: The Struggle for the Creation of D-Q University, 1960–1971.* Davis, CA: D-Q University Press.

Forbes, Jack D. (1988). *Black Africans and Native Americans: Race, Caste and Color in the Evolution of Red-Black Peoples.* Oxford: Blackwell.

Forbes, Jack D. (1990). *The Constitutional and Legal Background for a Non-racial Human Skeletal Remains Policy for the University of California and Other California Agencies.* California: J. D. Forbes.

Forbes, Jack D. (1992). *Columbus and Other Cannibals.* New York: Autonomedia.

Forbes, Jack D. (1993). *Africans and Native Americans: the Language of Race and the Evolution of Red-Black Peoples.* Urbana: University of Illinois Press.

Forbes, Jack D. (1995). *Only Approved Indians.* Norman: University of Oklahoma Press. (Series: American Indian literature and critical studies series, v. 12).

Forbes, Jack D. (1997a). *Red Blood.* Penticton, BC: Theytus Books.

Forbes, Jack D. (1997b). *Proposition 209: Radical Equalizer or Racist Trick? An Independent Analysis.* Bandon: Kahonkok Press. (Revised edn., 1998.)

Francis, Lee (1996). *Native Time: a Historical Time Line of Native America.* New York: St. Martin's Press.

Frank, L. (1999). *Acorn Soup.* Berkeley, CA: Hayday.

Freeman, Milton M. R., Lyudmila Bogoslovskaya, Richard A. Caulfield, Ingmar Egede, Igor I. Krupnik, and Marc G. Stevenson (1998). *Inuit, Whaling, and Sustainability.* Walnut Creek, CA: Alta Mira Press.

Frey, Rodney (1987). *The World of the Crow Indians: as Driftwood Lodges.* Norman, OK: University of Oklahoma Press.

Frisbie, Charlotte Johnson (1993). *Kinaalda: A Study of the Navaho Girl's Puberty Ceremony.* Salt Lake City: University of Utah Press. (Originally published 1967.)

Fritz, Henry E. (1963). *The Movement for Indian Assimilation, 1860–1890.* Philadelphia: University of Pennsylvania Press.

Gay, E. Jane (1981). *With the Nez Perces: Alice Fletcher in the Field, 1888–1892.* Lincoln: University of Nebraska Press.

Gayim, Eyassu (1994). *The UN Draft Declaration on Indigenous Peoples: Assessment of the Draft Prepared by the Working Group on Indigenous Populations.* Rovaniemi: Northern Institute for Environment and Minority Law, University of Lapland.

Geertz, Armin W. (1994). *The Invention of Prophecy: Continuity and Meaning in Hopi Indian Religion.* Berkeley: University of California Press.

277

Geiogamah, Hanay (1980). *New Native American Drama: Three Plays*, includes *Body Indian, Foghorn*, and *49*, ed. and introduced by Jeffrey Huntsman. Norman: University of Oklahoma Press.

Geiogamah, Hanay and Jaye T. Darby (1999). *Stories of Our Way: an Anthology of American Indian Plays*. Los Angeles: UCLA American Indian Studies.

Geiogamah, Hanay and Jaye T. Darby (2000). *American Indian Theater in Performance: A Reader*.

George-Kanentiio, Doug (2000). *Iroquois Culture and Commentary*. Santa Fe, NM: Clear Light.

Gerard-Landry, Chantal (1995). *Hopi: peuple de paix et d'harmonie*. Paris: A. Michel.

Getches, David H., Daniel M. Rosenfelt, and Charles F. Wilkinson (1979). *Cases and Materials on Federal Indian Law*. St. Paul, MN: West Publishing.

Givens, Douglas R. (1977). *An Analysis of Navajo Temporality*. Washington, DC: University Press of America.

Goldberg-Ambrose, Carole (1997). *Planting Tailfeathers: Tribal Survival and Public Law 280*. American Indian Studies Center, UCLA, Los Angeles.

Gray, Harold E. (1992). *Ni-kso-ko-wa: Blackfoot Spirituality, Traditions, Values, and Beliefs*. Browning, MT: Spirit Talk Press.

Green, Michael K., ed. (1995). *Issues in Native American Cultural Identity*. New York: Peter Lang.

Green, Rayna Diane (1983). *Native American Women: a Contextual Biography*. Bloomington: Indiana University Press.

Green, Rayna Diane (1984). *That's What She Said: Contemporary Poetry and Fiction by Native American Women*. Bloomington: Indiana University Press.

Green, Rayna Diane (1992). *Women in American Indian Society*. New York: Chelsea House.

Green, Rayna Diane (1999). *The British Museum Encyclopedia of Native North America* (with contributions by Melanie Fernandez). Bloomington: Indiana University Press.

Gridley, Marion Eleanor (1974). *American Indian Women*. New York: Hawthorn Books.

Griffin, Robert and Donald A. Grinde, Jr, eds. (1997). *Apocalypse of Chiokoyhikoy: Chief of the Iroquois*. Québec: Presses de L'Université Laval.

Grinde, Donald A., Jr. (1977). *The Iroquois and the Founding of the American Nation*. San Francisco, CA: Indian Historian Press.

Grinde, Donald A. Jr. and Carole M. Gentry (1992). *The Unheard Voices: American Indian Responses to the Columbian Quincentenary, 1492–1992*. Los Angeles: University of California Press and UCLA.

Grinde, Donald and Bruce E. Johansen (1991). *Exemplar of Liberty: Native America and the Evolution of Democracy*. Los Angeles: University of California Press and UCLA American Indian Studies.

Grinde, Donald A. and Bruce E. Johansen, eds. (1995). *Ecocide of Native America: Environmental Destruction of Indian Lands and Peoples*. Santa Fe, NM: Clear Light.

Grossman, Mark (1991). *The ABC-CLIO Companion to the Native American Rights Movement*. Santa Barbara, CA: ABC-CLIO.

Grumet, Robert S., ed. (1996). *Northeastern Indian Lives, 1632–1816*. Amherst: University of Massachusetts Press.

Hale, Janet Campbell (c. 1993). *Bloodlines: Odyssey of a Native Daughter*. New York: Random House.

Hanke, Lewis (1959). *Aristotle and the American Indians*. Bloomington: Indiana University Press.

Haring, Sidney (1994). *Crow Dog's Case: American Indian Sovereignty, Tribal Law, and United States Law in the Nineteenth Century*. Cambridge and New York: Cambridge University Press.

Harjo, Joy (1994). *The Woman who Fell through the Sky: Poems*. New York: Norton.

Harjo, Joy and Gloria Bird, eds. (1997). *Reinventing the Enemy's Language: Contemporary Native Women's Writing of North America.* New York: W. W. Norton.

Harris, Leonard, Scott Pratt, and Anne Waters (2001). *American Philosophies: An Anthology.* Oxford: Blackwell.

Hausman, Gerald (1987). *Meditations with the Navajo: Prayer-songs and Stories of Healing and Harmony.* Santa Fe, NM: Bear and Co.

Hill, Tom and Richard W. Hill, Sr (1994). *Creation's Journey: Native American Identity and Belief.* Washington, DC: Smithsonian Institution Press.

Hirschfelder, Arlene and Montaño, Martha Kreipe (1993). *The Native American Almanac: a Portrait of Native America Today.* New York: Prentice Hall General Reference.

Hirschfelder, Arlene B. and Paulette Molin (1992). *Encyclopedia of Native American Religion.* New York: Checkmark Books. (Updated 2000.)

Hirschfelder, Arlene B and Beverly R. Singer, eds. (1993). *Rising Voices: Writings of Young Native Americans.* New York: Ballatine Books.

Holler, Clyde (1995). *Black Elk's Religion: the Sun Dance and Lakota Catholicism,* 1st edn. Syracuse, NY: Syracuse University Press.

Horn, Gabriel (1996). *Contemplations of a Primal Mind.* Novato, CA (Emeryville, CA): New World Library.

Hotinonsionne (The Longhouse People, Iroquois, League of Six Nations) (1975). *Kaianerekowa – The Great Law of Peace.* Rooseveltown: Akwesasne Notes.

Hoxie, Frederick (1984). *A Final Promise: the Campaign to Assimilate the Indians, 1880–1920.* Lincoln: University of Nebraska Press.

Hoxie, Frederick, ed. (1988). *Indians in American History: An Introduction.* Arlington Heights, IL: Harlan Davidson.

Hoxie, Frederick (1989). *The Crow Indians.* New York: Chelsea House.

Hoxie, Frederick (1995). *Parading through History: the Making of the Crow Nation, 1805–1935.* New York: Cambridge University Press.

Hoxie, Frederick, ed. (1996). *The Encyclopedia of North American Indians.* Boston, MA: Houghton Mifflin.

Hungry Wolf, Beverly (1980). *The Ways of My Grandmothers.* New York: Morrow.

Jaimes-Guerrero, M. A., ed. (1992). *The State of Native America: Genocide, Colonization, and Resistance.* Boston, MA: South End Press.

Jennings, Francis (1976). *The Invasion of America.* New York: W. W. Norton.

Johansen, Bruce E. (1982). *Forgotten Founders: Benjamin Franklin, the Iroquois and the Rationale for the American Revolution.* Ipswich, MA: Gambit.

Johansen, Bruce E. (1996). *Native American Political Systems and the Evolution of Democracy: an Annotated Bibliography.* Westport, CT: Greenwood Press.

Johansen, Bruce E. and Donald A. Grinde, Jr. (1996). *The Encyclopedia of Native American Biography.* Cambridge, MA: Da Capo Press

Johansen, Bruce E. (1998a). *The Encyclopedia of Native American Legal Tradition.* Westport, CT: Greenwood Press.

Johansen, Bruce E. (1998b). *Debating Democracy: Native American Legacy of Freedom.* Santa Fe, NM: Clearlight.

Johansen, Bruce E., Donald A. Grinde, Jr., and Barbara Mann (1996). *Debating Democracy: The Iroquois Legacy of Freedom.* Santa Fe, NM: Clear Light.

Johansen, Bruce and Roberto Maestas (1979). *Wasi'shu: The Continuing Indian Wars.* New York: Monthly Review.

Johansen, Bruce E. and Barbara Alice Mann (2000). *Encyclopedia of the Haudenosaunee (Iroquois Confederacy)*. Westport, CT: Greenwood.

Johnson, Troy (1991). *The Indian Child Welfare Act: Indian Homes for Indian Children*. Los Angeles: American Indian Studies Center.

Johnson, Troy, ed. (1993). *Indian Child Welfare Act: Unto the Seventh Generations. Conference held at UCLA, January 15–17, 1992*, Los Angeles, CA: UCLA American Indian Studies Center.

Johnson, Troy (1994a). *Alcatraz: Indian Land Forever*. Los Angeles: UCLA American Indian Studies Center.

Johnson, Troy (1994b). *Chronology of Native North American History*. Detroit: Gale.

Johnson, Troy (1995). *You Are on Indian Land! Alcatraz Island 1969–1971*. Los Angeles, CA: American Indian Studies Center.

Johnson, Troy (1996). *The Indian Occupation of Alcatraz Island and the Rise of Indian Activism*. Champaign: University of Illinois Press.

Johnson, Troy (1997). *We Hold the Rock: the Indian Occupation of Alcatraz, 1969 to 1971*. San Francisco, CA: Golden Gate National Parks Association.

Johnson, Troy, ed. (1998). *Contemporary Native American Political Issues*. Walnut Creek, CA: Alta Mira Press.

Johnson, Troy (1999). *Contemporary Political Issues of the American Indian*. Walnut Creek, CA: Alta Mira Press.

Johnson, Troy (2002). *Distinguished Native American Spiritual Practitioners and Healers*. Salt Lake City, UT: Oryx Press.

Johnson, Troy (forthcoming). *Native American Nationalism: An Introduction to American Indian Studies*. New York: W. W. Norton.

Johnson, Troy, Joane Nagel, and Duane Champagne, eds. (1997). *American Indian Activism: Alcatraz to the Longest Walk*. Urbana: University of Illinois Press.

Johnson, Troy, Joane Nagel, and Alvin M. Josephy, Jr. (1999). *Red Power: The American Indians Fight for Freedom*. Lincoln: University of Nebraska Press.

Jorgenson, Joseph, ed. (1978). *American Indians and Energy Development*. Cambridge, MA: Anthropology Resource Center/Seventh Generation Fund.

Josephy, Alvin M., Jr. (1971). *Red Power: The American Indian's Fight for Freedom*. New York: McGraw-Hill.

Josephy, Alvin M., Jr. (1994). *500 Nations: An Illustrated History of North American Indians*. New York: Knopf.

Jumper, Betty Mae (1994). *Legends of the Seminoles*. Sarasota, FL: Pineapple Press.

Jumper, Betty Mae (2001). *A Seminole Legend: the Life of Betty Mae Tiger Jumper*. Gainesville: University Press of Florida.

Jumper, Moses (1990). *Echoes in the Wind: Seminole Indian Poetry of Moses Jumper, Jr*. Hollywood, FL: Seminole Tribe of Florida.

Jumper, Moses (1993). *Osceola, Patriot and Warrior*. Austin, TX: Raintree Steck-Vaugh.

Kappler, Charles J. (1973). *Indian Treaties, 1778–1883*. New York: Interland.

Katz, William Loren (1986). *Black Indians: a Hidden Heritage*. New York: Atheneum.

Kehoe, Alice B. (1981). *North American Indians: a Comprehensive Account*. Englewood Cliffs, NJ: Prentice Hall.

Kehoe, Alice B. (1989). *The Ghost Dancer: Ethnohistory and Revitalization*. New York: Holt, Rinehart, and Winston.

Kehoe, Alice B. (1998). *The Land of Prehistory: A Critical History of American Archaeology*. New York: Routledge.

Kehoe, Alice B. and Norman C. Sullivan (1996). *Cultural Anthropology*. Fort Worth, TX: Harcourt College Press.

Kelley, Jane Holden (1978). *Yaqui Women: Contemporary Life Histories*. Lincoln: University of Nebraska Press.

Kicking Bird, Kirk and Karen Ducheneaux (1973). *One Hundred Million Acres*. New York: Macmillan.

Klein, Laura F. and Lillian A. Ackerman, eds. (1995). *Women and Power in Native North America*. Norman: University of Oklahoma Press.

Kodjoe, W. Ofuatey (1972). *The Principle of Self-Determination in International Law*. Hamden, CT: Archon Books.

Krupat, Arnold (1985). *For Those Who Come After: a Study of Native American Autobiography*. Berkeley: University of California Press.

Krupat, Arnold (1989). *The Voice in the Margin: Native American Literature and the Canon*. Berkeley: University of California Press.

Krupat, Arnold (1992a). *Ethnocriticism: Ethnography, History, Literature*. Los Angeles: University of California Press.

Krupat, Arnold (1992b). *The Voice in the Margin: Native American Literature and the Canon*. Los Angeles: University of California Press.

Krupat, Arnold, ed. (1994a). *Native American Autobiography: An Anthology*. Madison: University of Wisconsin Press.

Krupat, Arnold, ed. (1994b). *New Voices in Native American Literary Criticism*. Upper Saddle, NJ: Prentice Hall and IBD.

Krupat, Arnold (1998). *The Turn to the Native: Studies in Criticism and Culture*. Lincoln: University of Nebraska Press.

Krupat, Arnold (2002). *Red Matters: Native American Studies* (Rethinking the Americas). Philadelphia: University of Pennsylvania Press.

Ladd, John (1957). *The Structure of a Moral Code: a Philosophical Analysis of Ethical Discourse Applied to the Ethics of the Navaho Indians*. Cambridge, MA: Harvard University Press.

Landes, Ruth (1971). *The Ojibwa Woman*. New York: Norton.

Landes, Ruth (1994). *The City of Women*, ed. with introduction Sally Cole. Albuquerque: University of New Mexico Press. (Originally published 1947.)

Langguth, A. J. (1978). *Hidden Terrors: the Truth about U.S. Police Operations in Latin America*. New York: Pantheon.

Las Casas, Bartolomé de (1971). History of the Indies, tr. and ed. Andree Collard. New York: Harper and Row.

Linderman, Frank Bird (1986). *Pretty-shield, Medicine Woman of the Crows*. New York: John Day Co.

Lummis, Charles (1968). *Bullying the Hopi*. Prescott, AZ: Prescott College Press.

Lyman, Stanley David (1993). *Wounded Knee 1973: A Personal Account*. Lincoln: University of Nebraska Press.

Lyons, Oren, John Mohawk, Vine Deloria Jr., Laurence Hauptman, Howard Berman, Donald Grinde, Jr., Curtis Berkey, and Robert Venable (1992). *Exiled in the Land of the Free: Democracy, Indian Nations, and the US Constitution*. Santa Fe, NM: Clear Light.

Mahaney, Joyce and Joy Hintz (1993). *Prairie Winds*. Tiffin, OH: Biology Museum, Heidelberg College.

Mankiller, Wilma Pearl (1993). *Mankiller: a Chief and her People*. New York: St. Martin's Press.

Martínez Cobo, José R. (1983). *Study of the Problem of Discrimination against Indigenous Populations* (U.S. Doc. E/CN.4/Sub 2/1983/21/Add.83, Sept. 1983). New York: United Nations Commission on Human Rights.

Mathews, John Joseph (1932). *Wah Kan-Tah: the Osage and the White Man's Road*. Norman, OK: University of Oklahoma Press.

Mathews, John Joseph (1945). *Talking to the Moon*. Chicago: University of Chicago Press.

Mathews, John Joseph (1961). *The Osages: Children of the Middle Waters*. Norman, OK: University of Oklahoma Press.

Mathews, John Joseph (1988). *Sundown*. Norman, OK: University of Oklahoma Press.

Matthiessen, Peter (1984). *Indian Country*. New York: Penguin Books.

Matthiessen, Peter (1991). *In the Spirit of Crazy Horse: the Story of Leonard Peltier*, 2nd edn. New York: Viking.

Maya Atlas (1997). *The Struggle to Preserve Maya Land in Southern Belize by Maya People of Southern Belize*. Toledo Maya Cultural Council. Berkeley, CA: North Atlantic Books.

McGaa, Ed (1990). *Mother Earth Spirituality: Native American Paths to Healing Ourselves and Our World*. San Francisco, CA: Harper and Row.

McGaa, Ed (Eagle Man) (1992). *Rainbow Tribe: Ordinary People Journeying on the Red Road*. San Francisco, CA: Harper.

McGaa, Ed (1995). *Native Wisdom: Perceptions of the Natural Way*. Edina, MN: Four Directions Publishing.

McGaa, Ed (Eagle Man) (1998). *Eagle Vision: Return of the Hoop*. Edina, MN: Four Directions Publishing.

McFadden, Steven S. H. (1991). *Profiles in Wisdom: Native Elders Speak about the Earth*. Santa Fe, NM: Bear and Co.

McNeley, James Kale (1981). *Holy Wind in Navajo Philosophy*. Tucson, AZ: University of Arizona Press.

Means, Russell, with Marvin J. Wolf (1995). *Where White Men Fear to Tread: the Autobiography of Russell Means*. New York: St. Martin's Press.

Medicine, Bea (1978). *The Native American Woman: A Perspective*. [Las Cruces, NM]: ERIC/CRESS: for sale by National Educational Laboratory Publishers, Austin, TX.

Meriam, Lewis, et al. (1928). *The Problem of Indian Administration*. Baltimore, MD: Johns Hopkins University Press.

Messerschmidt, Jim (1987). *The Trial of Leonard Peltier*, 2nd edn. Boston, MA: South End.

Mihesuah, Devon A. (1996). *American Indians: Stereotypes and Realities*. Atlanta, GA: Clarity.

Mihesuah, Devon A. (1993). *Cultivating the Rosebuds: the Education of Women at the Cherokee Female Seminary, 1851–1909*. Urbana: University of Illinois Press.

Mihesuah, Devon A. (1998). *Natives and Academics: Researching and Writing about American Indians*. Lincoln: University of Nebraska Press.

Mihesuah, Devon A., ed. (2000). *Repatriation: Social and Political Dialogues*. Lincoln: University of Nebraska Press.

Mihesuah, Devon A., ed. (2000a). *Repatriation Reader: Who Owns American Indian Remains?* Lincoln: University of Nebraska Press.

Mihesuah, Devon A. (2000b). *The Roads of My Relations*. Tucson: University of Arizona Press.

Mihesuah, Devon A. (forthcoming). *Indigenous North American Women: Decolonization, Empowerment, Activism*. Lincoln: University of Nebraska Press.

Mihesuah, Devon A. and Angela Cavender Wilson (forthcoming). *Indigenizing the Academy: Native Academics Sharpening the Edge* (sequel to *Natives and Academics: Researching and Writing About American Indians*). Lincoln: University of Nebraska Press.

Mihesuah, Henry (2002). *First to Fight*, ed. Devon Abbott Mihesuah. Lincoln: University of Nebraska Press.

Miner, H. Craig (1976). *The Corporation and the Indian: Tribal Sovereignty and Industrial Civilization in Indian Territory, 1865–1907*. Columbia: University of Missouri Press.

Minugh, Carol J., Glenn T. Morris, and Rudolph C. Ryser, eds. (1989). *Indian Self-governance: Perspectives on the Political Status of Indian Nations in the United States of America*. Kenmore, WA: World Center for Indigenous Studies.

Mohatt, Gerald and Joseph Eagle Elk (2000). *The Price of a Gift: a Lakota Healer's Story*. Lincoln: University of Nebraska Press.

Momaday, N. Scott (1968). *House Made of Dawn*. New York: Harper and Row.

Momaday, N. Scott (1976). *The Way to Rainy Mountain*, illus. Al Momaday. Albuquerque: University of New Mexico Press.

Monet, Don and Skanu'u (Ardythe Wilson) (1992). *Colonialism on Trial: Indigenous Land Rights and the Gitksan and Wet'suwet'en Sovereignty Case*. Philadelphia, PA: New Society Publishers.

Moore, Louis R. (1983). *Mineral Development on Indian Lands: Cooperation and Conflict*. Denver, CO: Rocky Mountain Mineral Law Foundation.

Moquin, Wayne and Charles Van Doren, eds. (1995). *Great Documents in American Indian History*. New York: Da Capo Press.

Moses, L. G. and Raymond Wilson, eds. (1993). *Indian Lives: Essays on Nineteenth- and Twentieth-century Native American Leaders*, rev. edn. Albuquerque: University of New Mexico Press.

Moses, L. G. and Raymond Wilson (1996). *Wild West Shows and the Images of American Indians, 1883–1933*. Albuquerque: University of New Mexico Press.

Moss, Maria (1993). *We've Been Here Before: Women in Creation Myths and Contemporary Literature of the Native American Southwest*. Hamburg, Germany: Munster.

Mullis, Angela and David Kamper, eds. (2000). *Indian Gaming: Who Wins?* Los Angeles, CA: UCLA American Indian Studies Center.

Nabokov, Peter (1981). *Indian Running: Native American History and Tradition*. Santa Fe, NM: Ancient City Press.

Nabokov, Peter (1986). *Architecture of Acoma Pueblo: The 1934 Historic American Buildings Survey Project*. Santa Fe, NM: Ancient City Press.

Nabokov, Peter (1987a). *Indian Running: Native American History and Tradition*. Santa Fe, NM: Ancient City Press.

Nabokov, Peter (1987b). *Tijerina and the Courthouse Raid*. Santa Fe, NM: Ancient City Press.

Nabokov, Peter, ed. (1988). *Native American Testimony: An Anthology of Indian and White Relations, First Encounter to Dispossession*. New York: Harper Torchbooks.

Nabokov, Peter, ed. (1991). *Native American Testimony: a Chronicle of Indian–White Relations from Prophecy to the Present, 1492–1992*, New York: Penguin.

Nabokov, Peter (2002). *A Forest of Time: American Indian Ways of History*. Cambridge, UK: Cambridge University Press.

Nabokov, Peter and Robert Easton (1989) *Native American Architecture*. New York: Viking Press, Oxford University Press.

Nagel, JoAnne (1996). *American Indian Ethnic Renewal: Red Power and the Resurgence of Identity and Culture*. New York: Oxford University Press.

Nannum Hurst (1990). *Autonomy, Sovereignty and Self-determination*. Philadelphia: University of Pennsylvania Press.

National Museum of the American Indian, Smithsonian Institution (1994a). *This Path We Travel: Celebrations of Contemporary Native American Creativity*. Golden, CO: Fulcrum Publishing.

National Museum of the American Indian, Smithsonian Institution (1994b). *All Roads Are Good: Native Voices on Life and Culture*. Washington, DC: Smithsonian Institution Press.

Neihart, John C. (1988). *Black Elk Speaks*. Lincoln: University of Nebraska Press.

Nerburn, Kent (1994). *Neither Wolf nor Dog: on Forgotten Roads with an Indian Elder*. San Rafael, CA: New World Library.

Nerburn, Kent, and L. Mengelkoch (1991). *Native American Wisdom*. San Rafael, CA: New World Library.

Newcomb, Franc Johnson (1964). *Hosteen Klah: Navaho Medicine Man and Sand Painter*. Norman: University of Oklahoma Press.

Niethammer, Carolyn (1977) *Daughters of the Earth: the Lives and Legends of American Indian Women*. New York: Macmillan Publishing.

Norgren, Jill (1996). *The Cherokee Cases: the Confrontation of Law and Politics*. New York: Macgraw-Hill.

Nunez, Bonita Wa Wa Calachaw (1980). *Spirit Woman: the Diaries and Paintings of Bonita Wa Wa Calachaw Nunez*, ed. Stan Steiner. New York: Harper and Row.

O'Brien, Sharon (1989). *American Indian Tribal Governments*. Norman: University of Oklahoma Press.

O'Meara, Sylvia and Douglas A. West (1996). *From Our Eyes: Learning from Indigenous Peoples*. Toronto: Garamond Press.

Ortiz, Alfonso (1969). *The Tewa World: Space, Time, Being and Becoming in a Pueblo Society*. Chicago: University of Chicago Press.

Ortiz, Alfonso (1972). *New Perspectives on the Pueblos*. Albuquerque: University of New Mexico Press.

Ortiz, Alfonso, ed. (1979, 1983). *Handbook of American Indians*, vol. 9 and vol. 10. Washington, DC: Smithsonian Institution Press.

Ortiz, Alfonso (1994). *The Pueblo*. New York: Chelsea House.

Ortiz, Alfonso (1994). *North American Indian Anthropology: Essays on Society and Culture*. Norman: University of Oklahoma Press.

Ortiz, Alfonso and Richard Erdoes (1984). *American Indian Myths and Legends*. New York: Pantheon Books.

Ortiz, Alfonso and Richard Erdoes (2002). *American Indian Trickster Tales*. Rear Collingdale, PA: Diane.

Ortiz, Roxanne Dunbar, ed. (1979a). *Economic Development in American Indian Reservations*. Albuquerque: University of New Mexico Development Series.

Ortiz, Roxanne Dunbar, ed. (1979b). *Economic Development in American Indian Reservations*. Albuquerque, NM: University of New Mexico Press.

Ortiz, Roxanne Dunbar (1980a). *Roots of Resistance: Land Tenure in New Mexico (1680–1980)*. Los Angeles: University of California American Studies Publications.

Ortiz, Roxanne Dunbar (1980b). *Roots of Resistance: Land Tenure in New Mexico, 1680–1980*. Los Angeles: University of California American Studies.

Ortiz, Roxanne Dunbar (1984a). *Indians of the Americas: Human Rights and Self-determination*. Westport, CT: Praeger.

Ortiz, Roxanne Dunbar (1984b). *Indians of the Americas: Human Rights and Self-Determination.* Westport, CT: Praeger.

Ortiz, Roxanne Dunbar (1997). *Red Dirt: Growing Up Okie.* London: Verso.

Ortiz, Roxanne Dunbar (2002). *Memoir of the War Years, 1960–1975.* Santa Fe, NM: City Lights.

Ortiz, Simon J. (1978a). *Howbah Indians.* Tucson, AZ: Blue Moon.

Ortiz, Simon J. (1978b). *Song, Poetry, Language.* Tsaile, AZ: Navajo Community College Press.

Ortiz, Simon J. (1978c). *Traditional and Hard-to-find Information Required by Members of American Indian Communities.* Albuquerque, NM: University of New Mexico Office of Library and Information Services.

Ortiz, Simon J. (1980). *Fight Back: For the Sake of the People, for the Sake of the Land.* Albuquerque, NM: Institute for Native American Development, University of New Mexico.

Ortiz, Simon J. (1981a). *A Ceremony of Brotherhood, 1680–1980.* Albuquerque, NM: Academia.

Ortiz, Simon J. (1981b). *From Sand Creek: Rising in this Heart which is our America.* New York: Thunder's Mouth Press.

Ortiz, Simon J. (1982a). *Blue and Red.* Acomita, NM: Pueblo of Acoma Press.

Ortiz, Simon J. (1982b). *The Importance of Childhood.* Acomita, NM: Pueblo of Acoma Press.

Ortiz, Simon J. (1984). *A Good Journey.* Tucson, AZ: University of Arizona Press.

Ortiz, Simon J. (1994). *After and Before the Lightning.* Tucson: University of Arizona Press.

Ortiz, Simon J. (1998). *Speaking for the Generation: Native Writers on Writing.* Tucson: University of Arizona Press.

Ortiz, Simon J. (2001). *Questions and Swords: Folktales of the Zapatista Revolution.* El Paso, TX: Cinco Puntos Press.

Otis, D. S. (1973). *The Dawes Act and the Allotment of American Indian Land.* Norman: University of Oklahoma Press.

Owens, Louis (1985). *John Steinbeck's Re-Vision of America.* Athens: University of Georgia Press.

Owens, Louis (1989a). *The Grapes of Wrath: Trouble in the Promised Land.* Boston, MA: Twayne.

Owens, Louis, ed. (1990a). *American Literary Scholarship: An Annual.* Durham, NC: Duke University Press.

Owens, Louis, ed. (1990b). *American Literary Scholarship: An Annual.* Durham, NC: Duke University Press.

Owens, Louis (1994). *Other Destinies: Understanding the American Indian Novel.* Norman: University of Oklahoma Press.

Owens, Louis (1998). *Mixedblood Messages: Literature, Film, Family, Place.* Norman: University of Oklahoma Press.

Owens, Louis (2001). *I Hear the Train: Reflections, Inventions, Refractions.* Norman: University of Oklahoma Press.

Owens, Louis and Tom Colonnese (1985). *American Indian Novelists: An Annotated Critical Bibliography.* New York: Garland Press.

Parker, Arthur (1907). *Excavations in an Erie Indian Village and Burial Site at Ripley, Chautauqua Co.* Albany: New York State Education Department.

Parker, Arthur (1910). *Iroquois Uses of Maize and Other Food Plants.* Albany: University of the State of New York.

Parker, Arthur (1919). *Life of General Ely S. Parker: Last Grand Sachem of the Iroquois and General Grant's Military Secretary.* Buffalo, NY: Buffalo Historical Society.

Parker, Arthur (1967). *The History of the Seneca Indians.* Port Washington, NY: I. J. Friedman.

Parker, Arthur (1989). *Seneca Myths and Folk Tales*. Lincoln: University of Nebraska Press. (Originally published in 1923.)

Parker, Arthur (1994). *Skunny Wundy: Seneca Indian Tales*. Syracuse, NY: Syracuse University Press.

Penn, W. S. (1995a). *The Absence of Angels*. Norman: University of Oklahoma Press.

Penn, W. S. (1995b). *All My Sins Are Relatives*. Lincoln: University of Nebraska Press.

Penn, W. S. (1996). *The Telling of the World: Native American Stories and Art*. New York: Stewart, Tabori, and Chang.

Penn, W. S. (2000a). *As We Are Now: Mixblood Essays on Race and Identity*. Berkeley: University of California Press.

Penn, W. S. (2000b). *Killing Time with Strangers*. Tucson: University of Arizona Press.

Penn, W. S. (2000c). *This is the World*. East Lansing: Michigan State University Press.

Penn, W. S. (2001). *Feathering Custer*. Lincoln: University of Nebraska Press.

Peroff, Nicholas (1982). *Menominee DRUMS: Tribal Termination and Restoration, 1954–1974*. Norman: University of Oklahoma Press.

Perrone, Bobette (1989). *Medicine Women, Curanderas, and Women Doctors*. Norman: University of Oklahoma Press.

Pertusati, Linda (1997). *In Defense of Mohawk Land: Ethnopolitical Conflict in Native North America*, Suny Series in Ethnicity and Race in American Life. Albany: State University of New York Press.

Philp, Kenneth (1983). *Assault on Assimilation: John Collier and the Origins of Indian Policy Reform*. Albuquerque: University of New Mexico Press.

Philp, Kenneth, ed. (1986). *Indian Self-rule: First-Hand Accounts of Indian/White Relations from Roosevelt to Reagan*. Salt Lake City: Howe Bros.

Pinxton, Rex, Ingrid van Dooren, and Frank Harvey (1983). *Anthropology of Space: Explorations into the Natural Philosophy and Semantics of the Navajo*. Philadelphia: University of Pennsylvania Press.

Pokagon, Simon (1893a). *Red Man's Greeting*. Hartford, MI: C. H. Engle.

Pokagon, Simon (1893b). *The Red Man's Rebuke*. Hartford, MI: C. H. Engle.

Pokagon, Simon (1899). *O-gi-maw-kwe mit-i-gwa-ki (Queen of the Woods). Also Brief Sketch of the Algaic Language by Chief Pokagon*. Hartford, MI: C. H. Engle.

Pokagon, Simon (1900). *Algonquin Legends of South Haven*. South Haven, MI: C. H. Engle.

Pokagon, Simon (1901). *Pottawattamie Book of Genesis: Legend of the Creation of Man*. Hartford, MI: C. H. Engle.

Pokagon, Simon (1897). *The Future of the Red Man* (etext). University of Virginia Electronic Text Archive. URL: <http://etext.lib.virginia.edu/cgibin/browse-mixed?id=PokFutu&tag=public&images=images/modeng&data=/lv1/Archive/eng-parsed>
See the following works by Pokagon at the same URL:
*An Indian on the Problems of His Race* (etext). University of Virginia Electronic Text Archive.
*Indian Superstitions and Legends* (etext). University of Virginia Electronic Text Archive.
*Naming the Indians* (etext). University of Virginia Electronic Text Archive.

Pomedli, Michael (1991). *Ethnophilosophical and Ethnolinguistic Perspectives on the Huron Indian Soul*. Lewiston: E. Mellen Press.

Pomerance, Michla (1982). *Self-determination in Law and Practice*. The Hague: Martinus Nijhoff.

Powers, Marla N. (1986). *Oglala Women: Myth, Ritual, and Reality*. Chicago: University of Chicago Press.

Prucha, Francis P. (1994). *American Indian Treaties: the History of a Political Anomaly.* Berkeley: University of California Press.

Rasmussen, Knud (1932). *Intellectual Culture of the Copper Eskimos.* Copenhagen: Gyldendal.

Rasmussen, Knud (1976). *Intellectual Culture of the Iglulik Eskimos,* reprint of 1929 edition. New York: AMS Press.

Reeser, Ralph (1992–1999). *Manual of Indian Gaming Law, Annotated.* Fairfax, VA: Falmouth Institute.

Rice, Julian (1991). *Black Elk's Story: Distinguishing its Lakota Purpose.* Albuquerque, NM: University of New Mexico Press.

Ridington, William Robin (1988). *Trail to Heaven: Knowledge and Narrative in a Northern Native Community.* Iowa City: University of Iowa Press.

Riley, Patricia, ed. (1993). *Growing Up Native American: An Anthology.* New York: William Morrow.

Roemer, Kenneth M., ed. (1997). *Native American Writers of the United States, Dictionary of Literary Biography,* vol. 5. Detroit, IL: Gale.

Roscoe, Will, ed. (1988). *Living the Spirit: a Gay American Indian Anthology.* New York: St. Martin's Press.

Ross, Allen Chuck (1997). *Mitakuye Oyasin: "We Are all Related,"* rev. edn. Denver, CO: Wisoni Waste.

Ross, Rupert (1992). *Dancing with a Ghost: Exploring Indian Reality.* Markham, ON: Octopus Books.

Royce, Charles C. (1899). *Indian Land Cessions in the United States,* 2 vols. Washington, DC: Smithsonian Institution Press.

Russell Tribunal (1980). *The Rights of the Indians of the Americas.* Rotterdam: Fourth Russell Tribunal.

Sandoz, Mari (1985). *These Were the Sioux.* Lincoln: University of Nebraska Press.

Sarris, Greg (1994). *Mabel McKay: Weaving the Dream.* Berkeley: University of California Press.

Schein, Anna M., ed. (2000). *Treaty of Canandaigua 1794. One Hundred Years of Treaty Relations Between the Iroquois Confederacy and the United States.* Santa Fe, NM: Clear Light.

Schuon, Frithjof (1990). *The Feathered Sun: Plains Indians in Art and Philosophy.* Bloomington, IN: World Wisdom Books.

Shattuck, Petra and Jill Norgren (1991). *Partial Justice: Federal Indian Law in a Lineal Constitutional System.* Oxford: Berg.

Shoemaker, Nancy, ed. (1995). *Negotiators of Change: Historical Perspectives on Native American Women.* New York: Routledge.

Silver, Shirley and Wick R. Miller (1997). *American Indian Language: Cultural and Social Contexts.* Tucson: University of Arizona Press.

Sinclair, Sir Ian (1984). *The Vienna Convention on the Law of Treaties,* 2nd edn. Manchester: Manchester University Press.

Sioui, Georges E. (1992). *For an Amerindian Autohistory: an Essay on the Foundations of a Social Ethic.* Montreal, Buffalo: McGill-Queen's University Press.

Slapin, Beverly and Doris Seale (1998). *Through Indian Eyes: the Native Experience in Books for Children, and How to Tell the Difference.* Philadelphia, PA: New Society. (Originally published 1993.)

Smith, Dean Howard (2000). *Modern Tribal Development: Paths to Self-sufficiency and Cultural Integrity in Indian Country.* Walnut Creek, CA: Alta Mira Press.

Smith, Paul Chaat and Robert Alan Warrior (1996). *Like a Hurricane: the American Indian Movement from Alcatraz to Wounded Knee*. New York: New Press.

Spaeth, Nicholas J. (1993). Chair of the editing committee, Conference of Western Attorneys General, *American Indian Law Deskbook*. Niwot: University Press of Colorado.

Spector, Janet D. (1993). *What Does Awl Mean? Feminist Archaeology at a Wahpeton Dakota Village*. St. Paul: Minnesota Historical Society Press.

Stannard, David E. (1992). *American Holocaust: Columbus and the Conquest of the New World*. New York and Oxford: Oxford University Press.

Stannard, David E. (2000). *Before the Horror: The Population of Hawaii on the Eve of Western Contact*. Honolulu: University of Hawaii Press.

Stedman, Raymond William (1982). *Shadows of the Indian: Stereotypes in American Culture*. Norman: University of Oklahoma Press.

Steiner, Stan (1968). *The New Indians*. New York: Harper and Row.

Steltenkamp, Michael F. (1993). *Black Elk: Holy Man of the Oglala*. Norman: University of Oklahoma Press.

Stockel, H. Henrietta (1991). *Women of the Apache Nation: Voices of Truth*. Reno: University of Nevada Press. 1991.

Sundquist, Asebrit (1987). *Pocahontas & Co.: the Fictional American Indian Woman in Nineteenth-century Literature: a Study of Method*. Atlantic Highlands, NJ: Humanities Press International; Oslo, Norway: Solum Forlag.

Swann, Brian and Arnold Krupat (1987). *I Tell You Now: Autobiographical Essays by Native American Writers*. Lincoln: University of Nebraska Press.

Swann, Brian and Arnold Krupat (2000). *Here First: Autobiographical Essays by Native American Writers*. New York: Modern Library.

Taiaiake, Al (1995). *Heeding the Voices of our Ancestors: Kahnawake Mohawk Politics and the Rise of Native Nationalism*. Toronto: Oxford University Press.

Taiaiake, Al (1999). *Peace, Power, Righteousness: an Indigenous Manifesto*. Toronto, ON: Oxford University Press.

Taylor, Graham D. (1980). *The New Deal and American Indian Tribalism: the Administration of the Indian Reorganization Act, 1934–45*. Lincoln: University of Nebraska Press.

Tedlock, Dennis, tr. (1985). *Popol Vuh: the Mayan Book of the Dawn of Life*. New York: Simon and Schuster.

Tedlock, Dennis and Barbara Tedlock (1975). *Teachings from the American Earth: Indian Religion and Philosophy*. New York: Liveright.

Terrell, John Upton (1974). *Indian Women of the Western Morning: Their Life in Early America*. New York: Dial Press.

Thomas, David Hurst (1983). *The Archaeology of Monitor Valley*. 1: *Epistemology*. New York: Coyote Press.

Thomas, David Hurst (2001). *Skull Wars: Kennewick Man, Archaeology, and the Battle for Native American Identity*. New York: Basic Books.

Thomas, David Hurst, Betty Ballantine, Ian Ballantine, and Philip Deloria, eds. (1993). *The Native Americans: An Illustrated History*. Atlanta, GA: Turner Publishing. (Book available on CD-ROM.)

Thornton, Russell (1987). *American Indian Holocaust and Survival: a Population History since 1492*. Norman: University of Oklahoma Press.

Thunder, Mary Elizabeth (1995). *Thunder's Grace: Walking the Road of Visions with my Lakota Grandmother*. Barrytown and New York: Station Hill Press.

Tierney, William G. (1992). *Official Encouragement, Institutional Discouragement: Minorities in Academe – The Native American Experience.* Norwood, NJ: Ablex Publishing.

Tilton, Robert S. (1994). *Pocahontas: The Evolution of an American Narrative.* Cambridge and New York: Cambridge University Press.

Todorov, Tzvetan (1987). *The Conquest of America.* New York: Harper and Row.

Trask, Haunani-Kay (1984). *Fighting the Battle of Double Colonization: the View of a Hawaiian Feminist.* East Lansing, MI: Office of Women in International Development.

Trask, Haunani-Kay (1986). *Eros and Power: the Promise of Feminist Theory.* Philadelphia: University of Pennsylvania Press.

Trask, Haunani-Kay (1993). *From a Native Daughter: Colonialism and Sovereignty in Hawai'i.* Monroe, ME: Common Courage Press.

Trask, Haunani-Kay (1994). *Light in the Crevice Never Seen.* Corvallis, OR: Calyx Books.

US Department of Interior, Bureau of Indian Affairs (1978). *Indian Lands Map: Oil, Gas and Minerals on Indian Reservations.* Washington, DC: US Government Printing Office.

US Department of the Interior (2000a). *From Mauka to Makai: The River of Justice Must Flow Freely. Report on the Reconciliation Process between the Federal Government and Native Hawaiians.* Washington, DC: Department of the Interior, Department of Justice.

US Department of the Interior (2000b). *Comments Received in Regard to the Draft Report on the Reconciliation Process between the Federal Government and Native Hawaiians.* Washington, DC: Department of the Interior.

Valencia, Heather (1991). *Queen of Dreams: the Story of a Yaqui Dreaming Woman.* New York: Simon and Schuster.

Vander, Judith (1988). *Songprints: the Musical Experience of Five Shoshone Women.* Urbana: University of Illinois Press.

Vanderworth, W. C. (1971). *Indian Oratory. Famous Speeches by Noted Indian Chieftains.* Norman: University of Oklahoma Press.

Vennum, Thomas, Jr. (1988). *Wild Rice and the Ojibway People.* St. Paul: Minnesota Historical Society Press.

Versluis, Arthur (1992). *Sacred Earth.* Rochester, NY: Inner Traditions International.

Vizenor, Gerald (1981). *Earthdivers: Tribal Narratives on Mixed Descent.* Minneapolis: University of Minnesota Press.

Vizenor, Gerald (1984). *The People Named the Chippewa: Narrative Histories.* Minneapolis: University of Minnesota Press.

Vizenor, Gerald (1987). *Touchwood: a Collection of Ojibway Prose.* St. Paul, MN: New Rivers Press.

Vizenor, Gerald (1989). *Narrative Chance: Postmodern Discourse on Native American Indian Literatures.* Albuquerque: University of New Mexico Press.

Vizenor, Gerald (1990a). *Bearheart: the Heirship Chronicles.* Minneapolis: University of Minnesota Press.

Vizenor, Gerald (1990b). *Crossbloods: Bone Courts, Bingo, and Other Reports.* Minneapolis: University of Minnesota Press.

Vizenor, Gerald (1990c). *Darkness in Saint Louis Bearheart.* Minneapolis: University of Minnesota Press.

Vizenor, Gerald (1990d). *Interior Landscapes: Autobiographical Myths and Metaphors.* Minneapolis: University of Minnesota Press.

Vizenor, Gerald (1991a). *The Heirs of Columbus.* Hanover, NH: Wesleyan University Press/ University Press of New England.

Vizenor, Gerald (1991b). *Landfill Meditation: Crossblood Stories*. Hanover, NH: Wesleyan University Press.

Vizenor, Gerald (1992). *Dead Voices: Natural Agonies in the New World*. Norman: University of Oklahoma Press.

Vizenor, Gerald (1994a). *Manifest Manners: Postindian Warriors of Survivance*. Hanover, NH: University Press of New England.

Vizenor, Gerald (1994b). *Shadow Distance: a Gerald Vizenor Reader*. Hanover, NH: Wesleyan University Press.

Vizenor, Gerald (1997). *Hotline Healers: an Almost Browne Novel*. Hanover, NH: Wesleyan University Press.

Vizenor, Gerald (1998). *Fugitive Poses: Native American Indian Scenes of Absence and Presence*. Lincoln: University of Nebraska Press.

Vizenor, Gerald (1999). *Postindian Conversations*. Lincoln: University of Nebraska Press.

Vizenor, Gerald (2000). *Chancers*. Norman: University of Oklahoma Press.

Vogel, Virgil J. (1972). *This Country Was Ours: a Documentary History of the American Indian*. New York: Harper and Row.

Wagner, Sally Roesch (1996). *The Untold Story of the Iroquois Influence on Early Feminists*. Aberdeen, SD: Carrier Press.

Wall, Steve and Harvey Arden (1990). *Wisdomkeepers. Meetings with Native American Spiritual Elders*. Hillsboro, OR: Beyond World Publishing.

Walters, Anna Lee (1981). *The Otoe-Missouria Tribe: Centennial Memoirs, 1881–1981*. Red Rock, OK: Otoe-Missouria Tribe.

Walters, Anna Lee (1985). *The Sun is not Merciful: Short Stories*. Ithaca, NY: Firebrand Books.

Walters, Anna Lee (1989). *The Spirit of Native America: Beauty and Mysticism in American Indian Art*. San Francisco, CA: Chronicle Books.

Walters, Anna Lee, Peggy V. Beck, Nia Francisco and Lee Walters (2000). *The Sacred Ways of Knowledge, Sources of Life*. Tsaile, AZ: Dineh Community College Press.

Warhus, Mark (1997). *Another America: Native American Maps and the History of Our Land*. New York: St. Martin's Griffin.

Warrior, Robert Allen, ed. (1995). *Tribal Secrets: Recovering American Indian Intellectual Traditions*. Minneapolis: University of Minnesota Press.

Warrior, Robert Allen and Paul Chaat Smith (1996). *Like a Hurricane: the Indian Movement from Alcatraz to Wounded Knee*. New York: New Press.

Waters, Anne et al., eds. (2003). *Hypatia: A Journal of Feminist Philosophy: Indigenist Women of the Americas*. Bloomington: Indiana University Press.

Weatherford, Jack (1989). *Indian Givers: How Indians Transformed the World*. New York: Crown Books. (Paperback edn: New York: Ballantine, 1989.)

Weatherford, Jack (1992). *Native Roots: How Indians Enriched America*. New York: Crown. (Paperback edn: New York: Ballantine, 1992.)

Weatherford, Jack (1995). *Savages and Civilization: Who Will Survive?* New York: Crown. (Paperback edn: New York: Ballantine, 1995.)

Weatherford, Jack (1998). *The History of Money*. New York: Crown Publishers; New York: Three Rivers Press.

Weaver, Jace, ed. (1997). *Defending Mother Earth: Native American Perspectives on Environmental Justice*. New York: Orbis Books.

Welch, James (1974). *Winter in the Blood*. New York: Penguin Books.

Weston, Burns H., Richard A. Falk and Anthony D'Amato, eds. (1990). *Basic Documents in International Law and World Order*, 2nd edn. St. Paul, MN: West Publishing, see esp. pp. 27–9.

Weyler, Rex (1992). *Blood of the Land: the Government and Corporate War against the American Indian Movement*, 2nd edn. Philadelphia, PA: New Society.

Wilkins, David E. (1997). *American Indian Sovereignty and the U.S. Supreme Court: the Making of Justice*. Austin: University of Texas Press.

Wilkinson, Charles F. (1987). *American Indians, Time and the Law: Native Societies in a Modern Constitutional Democracy*. New Haven, CT: Yale University Press.

Williams, Robert A., Jr. (1990). *The American Indian in Western Legal Thought: the Discourses of Conquest*. New York: Oxford University Press.

Williams, Robert A., Jr. (1993). *Cases and Materials on Federal Indian Law*. St Paul, MN: West Publishing.

Williams, Robert A., Jr. (1997). *Linking Arms Together: American Indian Treaty Visions of Law and Peace, 1600–1800*. New York: Oxford University Press.

Wilshire, Bruce (2000). *The Primal Roots of American Philosophy: Pragmatism, Phenomenology, and Native American Thought*. University Park: Pennsylvania State University Press.

Wilson, Terry P. (1978). *The Cart that Changed the World: the Career of Sylvan N. Goldman*. Norman: Published for the Oklahoma Heritage Association by the University of Oklahoma Press.

Wilson, Terry P. (1985). *The Underground Reservation: Osage Oil*. Lincoln: University of Nebraska Press.

Wilson, Terry P. (1988). *The Osage*. New York: Chelsea House.

Wilson, Terry P. (1993). *Teaching American Indian History*. Washington, DC: American Historical Association.

Womack, Craig (1999). *Red on Red: Native American Literary Separatism*. Minneapolis: University of Minnesota Press.

Worth, Sol and John Adair (1997). *Through Navajo Eyes: an Exploration in Film Communication and Anthropology*. Albuquerque: University of New Mexico Press.

Wright, Sam (1988). *Koviashuvik: a Time and Place of Joy*. San Francisco, CA: Sierra Club Books.

Wub E Ke Niew (1995). *We Have the Right to Exist: a Translation of Aboriginal Indigenous Thought. The First Book Ever Published from an Ahnishinahbaeotjibway Perspective*. New York: Black Thistle Press.

Wyler, Rex (1982). *Blood of the Land: the Government and Corporate War Against First Nations*. New York: Vintage Books.

Yazzie, Ethelou, ed. (1971). *Navajo History*, vol. 1. Many Farms, AZ: Navajo Community College Press.

Yazzie, Ethelou, ed. (1993). *Culture and Imperialism*. New York: A. A. Knopf; Random House.

Young Bear, Ray A. (1992). *Black Eagle Child*. Iowa City: University of Iowa Press.

Young-Bear, Severt and Theisz, R. D. (1994). *Standing in the Light: a Lakota Way of Seeing*. Lincoln: University of Nebraska Press.

# CHAPTERS AND ARTICLES

Albert, E. and Cazenueve, J. (1956). La philosophie des Indiens Zunis. *Revue de Psychologie des Peuples*, 11: 112–23.

Barsh, Russel (1983). Indigenous North American and Contemporary International Law. *Oregon Law Review*, 62.

Becker, D. M. (1954). The Comanches, their philosophy and religion. *Smoke Signals*, 6, 4: 4–5.

Benally, Herbert John (1994). Navajo philosophy of learning and pedagogy. *Journal of Navajo Education*, 12, 1: 23–31.

Benham, William J., Jr. (1975). A philosophy of Indian education. *Journal of American Indian Education*, 15, 1: 1–3.

Black, Mary B. (1977). Ojibwa power belief system. In *The Anthropology of Power*, ed. Raymond D. Fogelson and Richard N. Adams. New York: Academic Press.

Black Elk, Frank. (1984). Observations on Marxism and Lakota Tradition. In *Marxism and Native Americans*, ed. Ward Churchill. Boston, MA: South End Press.

Blanchard, Kendall Allan (1979). The Navajo and the idea of ultimate reality and meaning. *Ultimate Reality and Meaning*, 2, 2: 84–108.

Boice, L. Peter (1989). The Iroquois sense of place: legends as a source of environmental imagery. *New York Folklore*, 5, 3–4: 179–88.

Boldt, Menno (1981). Philosophy, politics and extralegal action: native Indian leaders in Canada. *Ethnic and Racial Studies*, 4: 5–22.

Booth, Annie L. and Harvey M. Jacobs (1990). Ties that bind: native American beliefs as a foundation for environmental conciousness. *Environmental Ethics*, 12: 87–93.

Broselow, Ellen I. (1978). West Greenlandic Eskimo: non-evidence for local ordering. *Minnesota Working Papers in Linguistics and Philosophy of Language*, 5: 1–6.

Churchill, Ward (1986). American Indian lands: the Native ethic and resource development. *Environment*, 28, 6.

Churchill, Ward (1996). I am Indigenist: Notes on the Ideology of the Fourth World. In *From a Native Son: Selected Essays on Indigenism, 1985–1995*. Boston, MA: South End Press.

Collier, John (1972). The genesis and philosophy of the Indian Reorganization Act. In *The Western American Indian*, ed. Richard N. Ellis. Lincoln, NE: University of Nebraska Press, p. 146–52.

Cook-Lynn, Elizabeth (1986). The rise of the academic "Chiefs" *Wicazo Sa Review*, 2, 38–40 (Spring).

Cook-Lynn, Elizabeth (1991). The radical conscience in Native American studies. *Wicazo Sa Review*, 7, 9–13 (Fall).

Cook-Lynn, Elizabeth (1993). Speech: who gets to tell the stories. *Wicazo Sa Review*, 9 (Spring).

Cook-Lynn, Elizabeth (1996). American Indian intellectualism and the new Indian story. *American Indian Quarterly*, 20, 1 (Winter) <http://www.uoknor.edu/aiq/aiq201.htm#lynn>

Cook-Lynn, Elizabeth (1997). Who stole Native American studies? *Wicazo Sa Review*, 12 (Spring).

Cook-Lynn, Elizabeth (2001). Anti-Indianism. In *Modern America: a Voice from Tatekeya's Earth*. Champaign: University of Illinois Press.

Couture, Joseph E. (1978). Philosophy and psychology of native education. In *One Century Later: Western Canadian Reserve Indians Since Treaty 7*, ed. Ian A. L. Getty and Donald Boyd Smith. Vancouver, BC: University of British Columbia Press, pp. 126–31.

Deloria, Vine, Jr. (1991). Perceptions and maturity: reflections on Paul Feyerabend's point of view. In *Beyond Reason: Essays on the Philosophy of Paul Feyerabend*, ed. Gonzalo Munevar. Dordrecht and Boston: Kluwer Academic, pp. 389–401.

Dunnigan, Timothy, Patrick O'Malley, and Linda Schwartz (1978). A functional analysis of the Algonquian obviative. *Minnesota Working Papers in Linguistics and Philosophy of Language*, 5: 7–21.

Elm, Lloyd Martin (1975). Needed: a philosophy of education for American Indians. *American Indian Journal*, 1, 2: 2–5.

Fenton, William N. (1985). Structure continuity and change in the process of Iroquois treaty making. In *The History and Culture of Iroquois Diplomacy*. New York: Syracuse University Press.

Flanagan, Thomas and Nicholas Griffin (1989). The agricultural argument and original appropriation: Indian lands and political philosophy. *Canadian Journal of Political Science*, 22, 3: 589–602.

Forbes, Jack D. (1990). Undercounting Native Americans: the 1980 Census and federal manipulation of racial identity in the United States. *Wicazo Sa Review*, 6, 1 (Spring).

Garrity, Michael (1980). The U.S. colonial empire is as near as the closest reservation. In *Trilateralism: The Trilateral Commission and Elite Planning for Global Management* ed. Holly Sklar. Boston: South End Press.

Geiogeemah, Hanay L. (1994). The new Native American theater. In *Dictionary of Native American Literature*, ed. Andrew Wiget. New York: Garland, pp. 377–81.

Griffin-Pierce, Trudy (1988). Cosmological order as a model for Navajo philosophy. *American Indian Culture and Research Journal*, 12, 4: 1–15.

Gross, Michael D. (1978). Indian self-determination and tribal sovereignty: an analysis of recent federal policy. *Texas Law Review*, 56.

Guilmet, George Michael (1985). The effects of traditional Eskimo patterns of cognition on the acceptance or rejection of technological innovation. *Research in Philosophy and Technology*, 8: 149–59.

Hallowell, A. Irving (1960). Ojibwa ontology, behavior, and worldview. In *Culture in History: Essays in Honor of Paul Radin*, ed. Stanley Diamond. New York: Columbia University Press.

Hammond, Michael (1985). Metrical structure in Lenakel and the directionality-dominance hypothesis. *Minnesota Papers in Linguistics and Philosophy of Language*, 10: 66–79.

Hornbuckle, Charles (1977). Cultural clash in our educational system: the need for a multicultural philosophy in higher education. *Indian Historian*, 10, 4: 33–9.

Iverson, Gregory K. (1981). On the government of phonological rules by laws. *Minnesota Working Papers in Linguistics and the Philosophy of Language*, 7: 8–28.

Jaimes, M. Annette (1995). Native American identity and survival: indigenism and environmental ethics. In *Issues in Native American Cultural Identity*, ed. Michael K. Green. New York: Peter Lang, pp. 223–72.

Jonaaitis, Aldona Claire (1981). Creations of mystics and philosophers: the white man's perceptions of Northwest Coast Indian art from the 1930s to the present. *American Indian Culture and Research Journal*, 5, 1: 1–45.

Jorns, Catherine J. (1992). Indigenous peoples and self-determination: challenging state sovereignty. *Case Western Reserve Journal of International Law*, 24.

Kaiser, Patricia L. (1984). The Lakota sacred pipe: its tribal use and religious philosophy. *American Indian Culture and Research Journal*, 8, 3: 1–26.

Kelly, Joseph B. (1973). National minorities in international law. *Denver Journal of International Law and Politics*, 3.

Kluckhohn, Clyde K. M. (1949). The philosophy of the Navaho Indians. In *Ideological Differences and World Order*, ed. F. S. C. Northrop. New Haven, CT, pp. 356–84.

Kunitz, Stephen Joshua (1971). The social philosophy of John Collier. *Ethnohistory*, 18: 213–29.

Linden, George (1977). Dakota philosophy. *American Studies*, 18.

McPherson, Dennis H. and J. Douglas Rabb (1993). Chapters 1–3 of *Indian from the Inside: a Study in Ethno-Metaphysics*. Thunder Bay: Center for Northern Studies, 1–83.

Mainone, Robert F. (1978). Philosophies. *Communicator*, 10, 1: 2–8.

Martin, Calvin (1981a). The American Indian as miscast ecologist. *History Teacher*, 14, 2: 243–51. (Also published in *Ecological Consciousness*, ed. Robert C. Schultz and J. Donald Hughes. Washington, DC: University Press of America, pp. 137–48.)

Maruyama, Magoroh (1967). The Navaho philosophy: an esthetic ethic of mutality. *Mental Hygiene*, 51: 242–9.

Means, Russell (1981). Identity of American Indian: uranium economy or Marxism. *Philosophy and Social Action*, 7, 3–4: 9–18.

Medicine Horse et al. (Otoe) (1991). *We Are not Children*. From US National Archives, Office of Indian Affairs. Letters Sent: Otoe Agency (1856–1876). Reprinted in *Native American Testimony*, ed. Peter Nabokov. New York: Penguin Books.

Merkur, Daniel (1985). Souls, spirits, and dwellers in nature: metaphysical dualism in Inuit religion. *Temenos*, 21: 91–126.

Mohawk, John (1992). The Indian way is a thinking tradition. In *Indian Roots of American Democracy*, ed. Jose Barreiro. Ithac, NY: Akwe:kon Press, Cornell University. (Originally published in 1988.)

Nanda, Ved (1981). Self-determination under international law: validity of claims to secede. *Case Western Reserve Journal of International Law*, 13.

Newcomb Steven T. (1993). The evidence of Christian nationalism in federal Indian law: the doctrine of discovery, *Johnson v. McIntosh*, and plenary power. *New York University Review of Law and Social Change*, 20, 2: 303–41.

Norton, Jack (1974). To walk the earth. *Indian Historian*, 7, 4: 28–30.

Ortiz, Alfonso (1970). American Indian philosophy: its relation to the modern world. In *Indian Voices: The First Convocation of American Indian Scholars*. San Francisco: Indian Historical Press, pp. 9–47.

Ortiz, Alfonso (1983a). Pima and Papago medicine and philosophy. In *Handbook of North American Indians*, vol. 10. *Southwest*, ed. Donald M. Bahr. Washington, DC: Smithsonian Institution, pp. 193–200.

Ortiz, Alfonso (1983b). A taxonomic view of the traditional Navajo universe. In *Handbook of North American Indians*, vol. 10. *Southwest*, volume ed. Oswald Werner, Kenneth Y. Begishe, and Allen Manning. Washington, DC: Smithsonian Institution, pp. 579–91.

Ortiz, Roxanne Dunbar (1985). Protection of American Indian territories in the United States: applicability of international law. In *Irredeemable America: The Indians' Estate and Land Claims*, ed. Imre Sutton. Albuquerque: University of New Mexico Press.

Ortiz, Roxanne Dunbar (2003). Introduction. In *Quiet Rumors: An Anarcho-Feminist Reader*, ed. Dark Star Collective. Oakland, CA: AK Press Distribution.

Parker, Arthur C. (1910). The Iroquois uses of maize and other food plants. *New York State Museum Bulletin*, 144: 5–113.

Parker, Arthur C. (1913). The code of Handsome Lake, the Seneca prophet. *New York State Museum Bulletin*, 163.

Parker, Arthur C. (1916). The Constitution of the Five Nations. *New York State Museum Bulletin*, 194: 7–158.

Parker, Arthur C. (1919). The life of General Ely S. Parker, last Grand Sachem of the Iroquois and General Grant's military secretary. *Publications of the Buffalo Historical Society*, 23.

Parker, Arthur C. (1922). The archaeological history of New York. *New York State Museum Bulletin*, issue number: 235–8.

Parker, Arthur C. (1970a). Philosophy of Indian education. *Indian Historian*, 3, 3: 42–5.

Parker, Arthur C. (1970b). Philosophy of Indian education. *Indian Historian*, 3, 2: 63–4.

Parsons, Elsie Clews (1919). Teshlatiwa at Zuni. *Journal of Philosophy, Psychology and Scientific Method*, 16: 272–3.

Pinxton, Rik (1979). Morality and knowledge: teachings from a Navajo experience. *Philosophica*, 23: 177–99.

Quintero, Gilbert A. (1995). Gender discord, and illness: Navajo philosophy and healing in the Native American Church. *Journal of Anthropological Research*, 51, 1: 69–89.

Roach, S. Fred (1984). Winter of discontent: the influence of Will Rogers' Indian heritage upon his life and philosophy. *Proceedings and Papers of the Georgia Association of Historians*, 5: 15–23.

Robbins, Rebecca L. (1983). John Dewey's philosophy and American Indians: a brief discussion of how it could work. *Journal of American Indian Education*, 22, 3: 1–9.

Robbins, Rebecca L. (1988). American Indian self-determination: comparative analysis and rhetorical criticism. *New Studies on the Left*, 13, 3–4 (Summer–Fall).

Sanders, Douglas (1983). The re-emergence of Indigenous questions in international law. *Canadian Human Rights Yearbook*, 3.

Sauders, Douglas (1989). The U.N. Working Group on Indigenous populations. *Human Rights Quarterly*, 11.

Savage, Mark (1991). Native Americans and the Constitution: the original understanding. *American Indian Law Review*, 16: 57–118.

Schulte-Tenckhoff, Isabelle (1995). The irresistible ascension of the UN Draft Declaration on the Rights of Indigenous Peoples: stopped dead in its tracks? *European Review of Native American Studies*, 9, 2.

Schwarz, Maureen Trudelle (1997). Snakes in the ladies room: Navajo views on personhood and effect. *American Ethnologist*, 24, 3: 602–27.

Scott, Craig (1996). Indigenous self-determination and decolonization of the international imagination: a plea. *Human Rights Quarterly*, 18: 814–20.

Sharp, Henry S. (1995). Asymmetric equals: women and men among the Chipewyan. In *Women and Power in Native North America*, ed. Laura F. Klein and Lillian A. Ackerman. Norman: University of Oklahoma Press.

Shelton, Anthony Allan (1987). Huichol natural philosophy. *Canadian Journal of Native Studies*, 7, 2: 339–54.

Simon, Wilma (1974). An introduction to aesthetics. *Tawow*, 4, 1: 5–9.

Sitting Bull (Hunkpapa Sioux) (1995). On freedom. A message for the President of the United States, 1881. From W. Fletcher Johnson, *Life of Sitting Bull* (1891), pp. 162–7. Reprinted in *Great Documents in American Indian History*, ed. Wayne Moquin with Charles Van Doren. New York: Da Capo Press.

Sobosan, Jeffrey C. (1974). The philosopher and the Indian: correlations between Plotinus and Black Elk. *Indian Historian*, 7, 2: 47–8.

Standing Bear, Luther (Sioux) (1995). What the Indian means to America (1933). From Chief Standing Bear, *Land of the Spotted Eagle* (Boston, 1933), chapter 9. Reprinted in *Great Documents in American Indian History*, ed. Wayne Moquin with Charles Van Doren. New York: Da Capo Press.

Steyaert, Marcia (1976). Verb reduplication in Dakota. *Minnesota Working Papers in Linguistics and Philosophy of Language*, 3: 127–43.

Sweezy, Carl (1972). The Indian concept of time: a cultural trait. Carl Sweezy, as told to Althea Bass, in *The Arapaho Way: A Memoir of an Indian Boyhood* (New York: Clarkson N. Potter,

1966: 5–6, 17–18). Reprinted in *This Country Was Ours: A Documentary History of the American Indian*, ed. Virgil J. Vogel. New York: Harper and Row: 263.

Thomas, Robert K. (1966–7). Colonialism: classic and internal. *New University Thought*, 1, 1 (Winter).

Tinker, George E. (1992). Spirituality, native American personhood, sovereignty, and solidarity. *Ecumenical Review*, 44: 312–24.

Venables, Robert W. (1980). Iroquois environments and "We The People of The United States". In *American Indian Environments: Ecological Issues in Native American History*, ed. Christopher Vecsey and Robert Venables. New York: Syracuse University Press.

Vernon, Irene S. (1999). The Claiming of Christ: Native American Postcolonial Discourses. *MELUS*, 24, Summer: 75–88.

Washburn, Wilcomb E. (1987). Distinguishing history from moral philosophy and public advocacy. In *The American Indian and the Problem of History*, ed. Calvin Martin. New York: Oxford University Press, pp. 91–7.

White, Raymond C. (1957). The Luiseno theory of "knowledge" *American Anthropologist*, 59: 1–19.

Whitt, Laurie Anne (1995). Indigenous peoples and the cultural politics of knowledge. In *Issues in Native American Cultural Identity*, ed. Michael K. Green. New York: Peter Lang, pp. 223–72.

Wilkinson, Charles F. and John M. Volman (1975). Judicial review of treaty abrogation: "As Long as the Water Flows, or the Grass Grows Upon the Earth"—How Long a Time is That? *California Law Review*, 62.

Williams, Robert A., Jr. (1990). Gendered checks and balances: Understanding the legacy of white patriarchy in an American Indian Cultural context. *Georgia Law Review*, 24: 1019.

Witherspoon, Gary (1971). Navajo categories of objects at rest. *American Anthropologist*, 73: 110–27.

Womack, Craig (1998). Fiction and politics: issues of activism in Native novels (etext). URL <http://nativeamericas.aip.cornell.edu/sum98/sum98r.html>

# WEB PAGES

American Indian Directories and Links   <http://cooday8.tripod.com/resource.htm>

*American Indian Quarterly*   <http://jan.ucc.nau.edu/~mihesuah/American_Indian_Quarterly.html>

American Indian Tribal Sovereignty Primer   <http://www.airpi.org/indinsov.html>

Center for World Indigenous Studies (CWIS) Home Page   <http://www.cwis.org/>

Culture: Native American Author: Native American Bibliography   <http://www.lib.cmich.edu/clarke/iculnaau.htm>

Electronic Text Center   <http://etext.lib.virginia.edu/subjects/Native-American.html>

First Nations E-Reference <http://www.library.ubc.ca/xwi7xwa/ref.htm>

First Nations—Maps   <http://www.library.ubc.ca/xwi7xwa/maps.htm>

First Nations Periodical Index   <http://www.lights.com/sifc/>

Hot Links for American Indian Tribal Libraries   <http://www.u.arizona.edu/~ecubbins/useful.html#prodev>

Index of Native American Electronic Text Resources on the Internet   <http://www.hanksville.org/NAresources/indices/NAetext.html>

Indigenous Peoples' Literature in English. <http://www.indigenouspeople.org/natlit/index1. htm>

Institute of American Indian Studies <http://www.usd.edu/iais/index.html>

Links to Aboriginal Resources <http://www.bloorstreet.com/300block/aborl.htm>

Native American Authors <http://www.ipl.org/ref/native/>

Native American Indian Resources <http://www.kstrom.net/isk/mainmenu.html>

Native American Internet Resources <http://www.saddleback.cc.ca.us/div/la/neh/sites. htm>

Native American Law <http://www.law.emory.edu/FOCAL/nativeam.html>

Native American Nations <http://www.nativeculture.com/lisamitten/nations.html>

Native American Organizations and Urban Indian Centers <http://www.nativeculture.com/ lisamitten/organizations.html>

Native American Political Systems and the Evolution of Democracy <http://www.ratical. com/many_worlds/6Nations/NAPSnEoD96.html>

Native American Print Media Resources <http://www.plumsite.com/shea/nativep.html>

Native American Stories: Books and Etexts <http://www.kstrom.net/isk/stories/ebooks. html>

Native American Women bibliography <http://www.radcliffe.edu/schles/libcolls/bksper/ bibs/native.html>

Native Americans in the Movies <http://www.lib.berkeley.edu/MRC/IndigenousBib.html>

Native Media – Film and Video, Journals and Newspapers, Radio and Television <http:// www.nativeculture.com/lisamitten/media.html>

Native Web: Resources and Reference Material <http://www.nativeweb.org/resources/ reference_materials/>

Sovereignty – in the Context of US "Indian Law" <http://www.umass.edu/legal/derrico/ sovereignty/html>

Strom, Karen. Author Index – Native American BOOKS <http://www.kstrom.net/isk/ books/auth_idx.html>

University of Arizona, American Indian Studies Reading List <http://w3.arizona.edu/~aisp/ reading_list.html>

# ON-LINE JOURNALS

*Aboriginal Voices, Journal* <http://www.aboriginal voices.com/>

*Alquimou News* <http://members.tripod.com/~alquimou/index.htm>

*American Indian Culture and Research Journal* <http://www.sscnet.ucla.edu/esp/aisc/main. html>

*AMMSA – Alberta Sweetgrass* <http://www.ammsa.com/sweetgrass/>

*AMMSA – SAGE* <http://www.ammsa.com/sage/>

*Ayaangwaamizin: The International Journal of Indigenous Philosophy* <http://www.lights.com/ sifc/ijip.html>

*Canadian Journal of Native Education* <http://www.lights.com/sifc/cjne.htm>

*Canadian Journal of Native Studies* <http://www.brandonu.ca/Library/CJNS/>

*Char-Koosta News Online* <http://www.ronan.net/~ckn/>

*First Nations Gazette* <http://www.usask.ca/nativelaw/fng.html>

*Journal of American Indian Education* <http://jaie.asu.edu/>

*Journal of Indigenous Studies*   <http://www.lights.com/sifc/jois.htm>
*Native American Times*   <http://www.okit.com/>
*Native Americas: Hemispheric Journal of Indigenous Issues*   <http://nativeamericas.aip.cornell.edu/>
*Native Peoples Magazine Online*   <http://www.nativepeoples.com/>
*Native Studies Review*   <http://www.usask.ca/native_studies/NSR/index.html>
*Native Youth News (Newspaper)*   <http://www.lights.com/sifc/nyouthn.htm>
*Nunatsiaq News.* Available at:   <http://www.nunatsiaq.com/>
*Ojibwe'Anishinaabe Biidaajimo*   <http://www.users.uswest.net/~rddez/index.html>
*Saskatchewan Indian*   <http://www.sicc.sk.ca/saskindian/saskpage.html>
*Tribal College Journal*   <http://www.tribalcollegejournal.org>
*Tudes Inuit Studies*   <http://www.lights.com/sifc/etudes.html>
*The Vision Maker*   <http://www.nativetelecom.org/news/index.html>
*Whispering Wind Magazine*   <http://www.whisperingwind.com/about.htm>

# INDEX